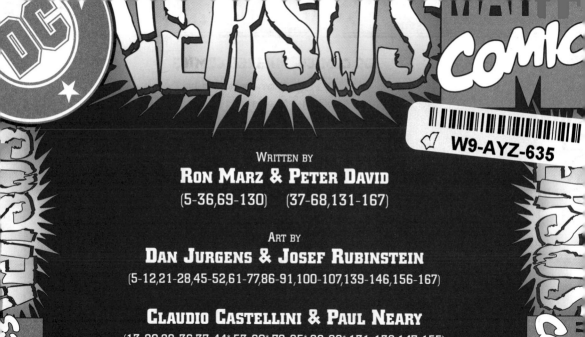

WRITTEN BY
RON MARZ & PETER DAVID
(5-36,69-130) (37-68,131-167)

ART BY
DAN JURGENS & JOSEF RUBINSTEIN
(5-12,21-28,45-52,61-77,86-91,100-107,139-146,156-167)

CLAUDIO CASTELLINI & PAUL NEARY
(13-20,29-36,37-44*,53-60*,78-85*,92-99*,131-138,147-155)
(*WITH THANKS TO SEAN HARDY)

JOSE LUIS GARCIA-LOPEZ & KEVIN NOWLAN
(109-130)

LETTERED BY
BILL OAKLEY
CHRIS ELIOPOULOS (109-130)

COLORED BY
GREGORY WRIGHT
MATT HOLLINGSWORTH (109-130)

SEPARATED BY
DIGITAL CHAMELEON
MATT HOLLINGSWORTH (109-130)

ASSISTANT EDITED BY
CHRIS DUFFY & JOE ANDREANI

EDITED BY
MIKE CARLIN & MARK GRUENWALD
DAN THORSLAND

COLLECTION EDITED BY
BOB KAHAN

DC Comics, 1700 Broadway, New York, NY 10019
A Warner Bros. Entertainment Company

Marvel Comics, 10 East 40th Street, New York, NY 10016

Printed in Canada. Fifth Printing.

ISBN: 1-56389-294-4
Cover illustration by Dan Jurgens and Josef Rubinstein
Cover color art by ColorWorks
Publication design by Eddie Ortiz

FOREWORD

When ultimate Armageddon rears its ugly head, the heroes' heroes join forces and cooperate! 'Least that's what I learned from reading comic books. Both DC comics and Marvel comics. Since 1938 the actions and examples set by the heroes of two universes have set down the guidelines for all mankind to follow.

When the high muckety-mucks (no offense intended, of course) said that it was time for Armageddon to rear its ugly head in 1995... the only course of action was to join forces and cooperate. Lucky for the readers here in the last vestiges of the twentieth century the creators of the comic-book battle of the century learned their lessons well.

Marvel and DC had cooperated before and they would cooperate again... but never before had the teamwork been attempted on a scale such as this. Starting with two low muckety-mucks (and in this case, offense *could* be intended), Mark Gruenwald, Executive Editor at Marvel Comics, and myself, Mike Carlin, Executive Editor at DC Comics, the project that would shape into DC VERSUS MARVEL began its explosive life! Joining forces, we rallied our editorial forces — for this awe-inspiring trek would involve not just one or two of each universe's mightiest, as crossovers between companies had in the past... no, this was going to be the team-up to end all team-ups. Batman was gonna meet Captain America. The Hulk was gonna meet Superman. Wonder Woman was gonna meet Storm. Spider-Man was gonna meet Superboy. And on and on and on and on. In short, everyone was gonna meet everyone. So that meant that everyone behind the scenes needed to be involved. All editors at the two largest comics companies in the United States would be overlooking this project at every stage. That's about thirty odd editors total. (No jokes, please).

We hired two writers, two pencillers and two inkers... one supplied by each company. Ron Marz and Peter David had each worked at both Marvel and DC at one time or another and they knew the two cosmos inside and out. They were two very brave writers because, as I mentioned earlier, they would be creating a scenario that would be overlooked by thirty or so editors — even before the general public would get their chance to judge!

Dan Jurgens has been a part of his share of big stories, but this would prove to be a pencil job that would need both Dan's experience as well as the surprise of discovering one of tomorrow's great talents! This is Claudio Castellini's first major pencil job for the states, an auspicious debut, no?

Josef Rubinstein is no stranger to inking legions of super-hero characters — he inked the whole Marvel Universe for their handbook. Guess the only surprise about Joe's work was that he was willing to do something like that again — and to double the headcount! Paul Neary is not only a renowned inker (having done most of his ink work with Alan Davis), he's pencilled AND headed Marvel's

by Mike Carlin

United Kingdom office as their editor-in-chief over the 20+ years he's been fraternizing with super-types.

Throw in the unparalleled coloring of Greg Wright and the masterful color separations of Lovern Kindzierski's Digital Chameleon (seems it took two of us in every department to get a project this big done!) and we had what would be the most sophisticated-looking crossover to date!

Hold it... I almost forgot: when MARVEL VERSUS DC was originally being published at the tail end of 1995 and the beginning of 1996 there was a team member more important than any other member of the awe-inspiring crew we'd already assembled — YOU! That's right, coordinating hundreds of characters, scores of creative types, AND making the legal guys at both companies mind their manners wasn't enough for us. Noooooooo, we had to go and make this an "inter-active" comic as well! Yup, there was a ballot included in every copy of the first issue, given out at thousands of comics stores, and featured on DC's America Online internet post. You, the general public, would decide who won each of the five main events between Marvel and DC's best of the best!

What is printed here contains the results of that historic voting: Does the Hulk beat Superman? Is Superboy cooler than Spider-Man? Is Batman better than Captain America? Can Storm best Wonder Woman in a thunderous battle? Would Lobo outfrag Wolverine? Find out here, in the collected DC VERSUS MARVEL!

And... find out what happens when those fights are fought! Probably the single coolest story-twist ever attempted in sixty years of American Super-Hero comics was pulled off when the "Amalgam Universe" was created. What's the Amalgam Universe? Can't tell you now, cause if you're the guy or gal who missed out on this story back then, I'd hate to ruin it for you. I'll let Mark G. cover it in his Afterword... Suffice it to say, everyone criticizes crossovers that boil down to "just fistfights"; well, we wouldn't dare try to foist something as traditional as "just a fistfight" on the followers of the two greatest fictional universes ever created, would we? Nope. And the Amalgam Universe raised the stakes and quite literally gave the world something it didn't expect! (We KNEW right from the start that this particular detour in "the Battle of the Century" would be the crowd pleaser — heck, it was the proof that we creators DID learn our lessons well!)

This was an intense project to be a part of, and I'm proud of everyone's contribution... now sit back and let the games begin!

Mike Carlin
Executive Editor - DC Universe

P.S. And what I said before about this being the team-up to end all team-ups... that was, um, just a manner of speakin', y'see, 'cause it's more likely the team-up to end all team-ups *for this century*. But y'know, it's still pretty cool to have been a part of something like that! Enjoy, folks...

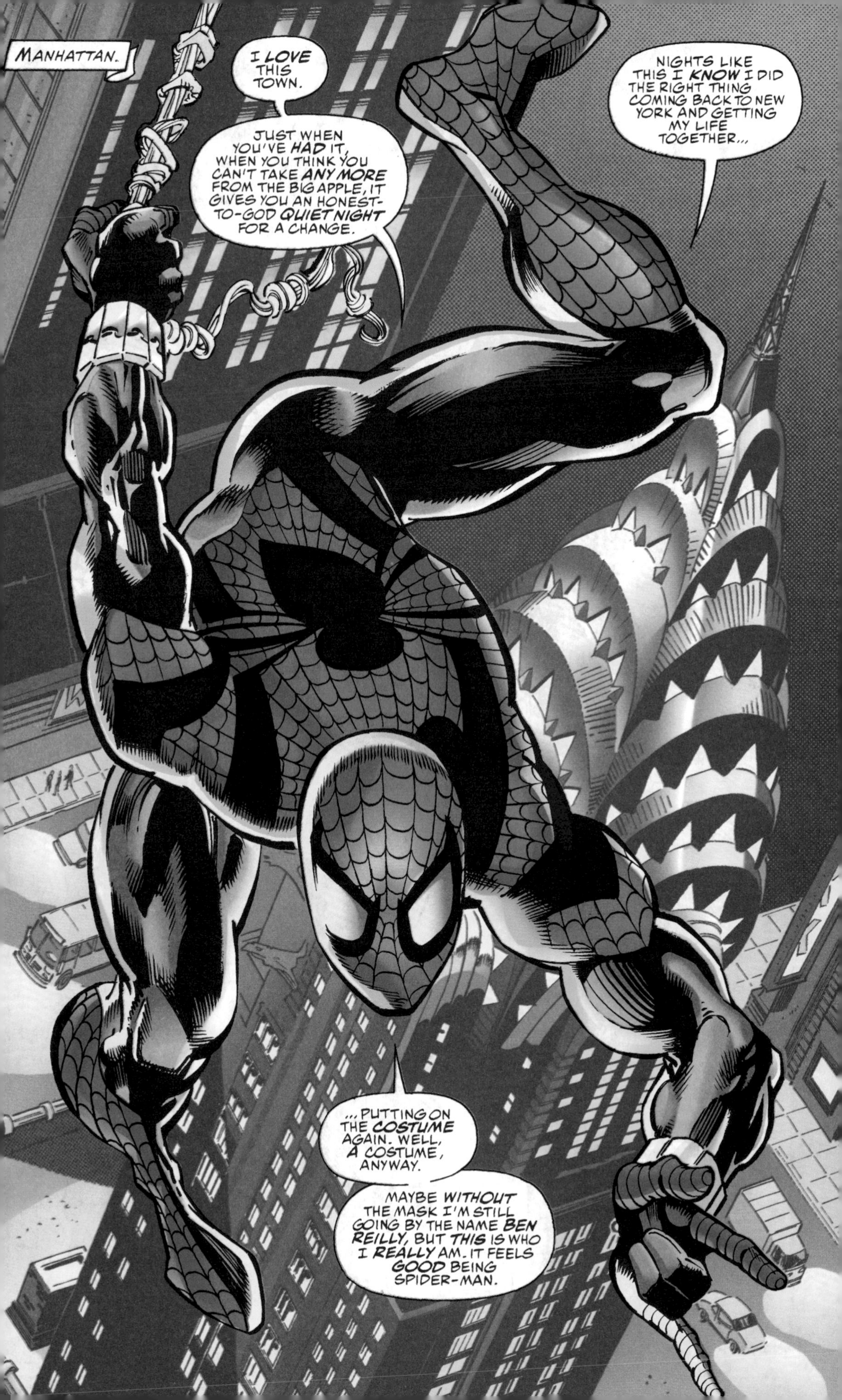
MANHATTAN.
I LOVE THIS TOWN.
JUST WHEN YOU'VE HAD IT, WHEN YOU THINK YOU CAN'T TAKE ANY MORE FROM THE BIG APPLE, IT GIVES YOU AN HONEST-TO-GOD QUIET NIGHT FOR A CHANGE.
NIGHTS LIKE THIS I KNOW I DID THE RIGHT THING COMING BACK TO NEW YORK AND GETTING MY LIFE TOGETHER...
...PUTTING ON THE COSTUME AGAIN. WELL, A COSTUME, ANYWAY.
MAYBE WITHOUT THE MASK I'M STILL GOING BY THE NAME BEN REILLY, BUT THIS IS WHO I REALLY AM. IT FEELS GOOD BEING SPIDER-MAN.

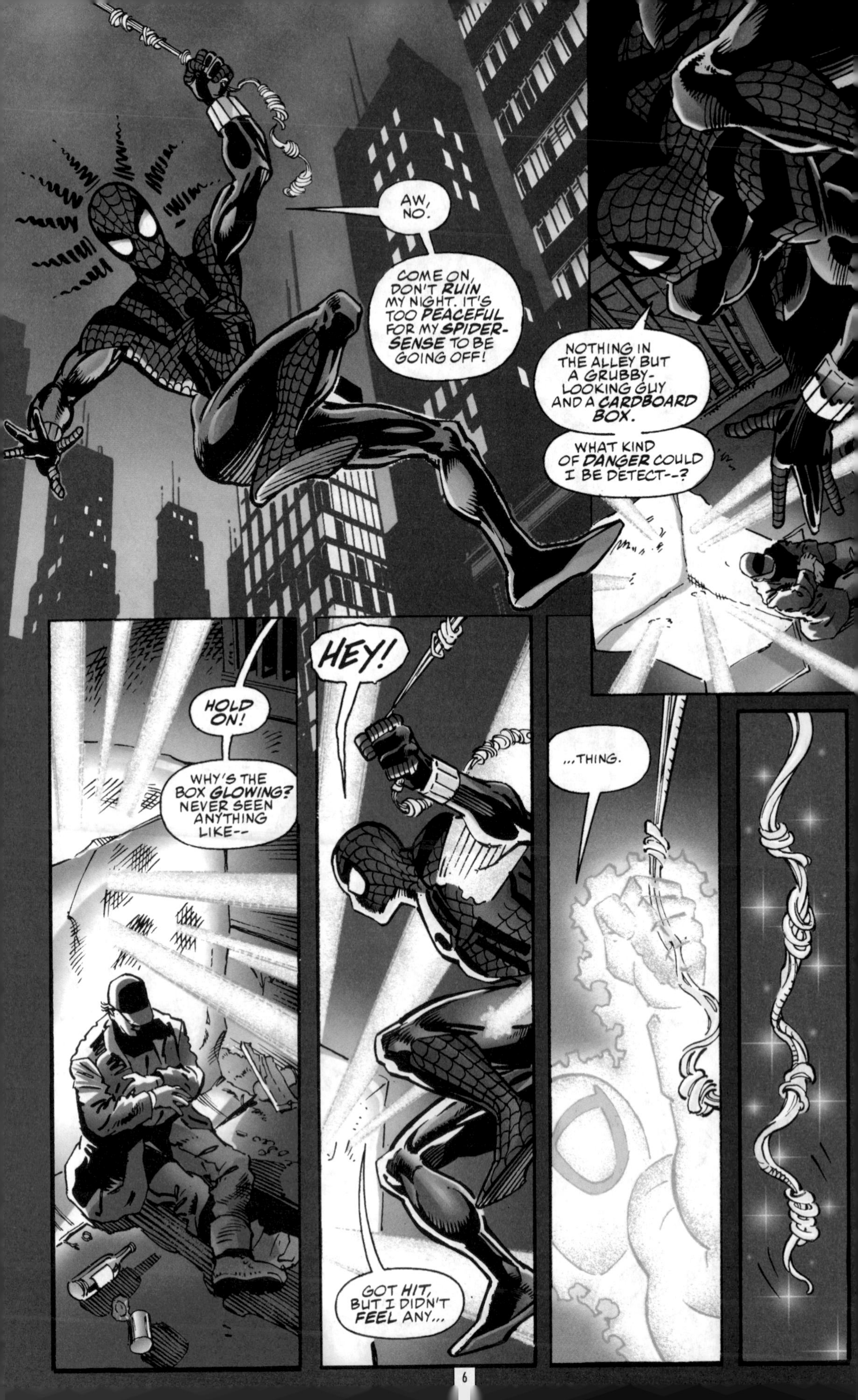
AW, NO.
COME ON, DON'T RUIN MY NIGHT. IT'S TOO PEACEFUL FOR MY SPIDER-SENSE TO BE GOING OFF!
NOTHING IN THE ALLEY BUT A GRUBBY-LOOKING GUY AND A CARDBOARD BOX.
WHAT KIND OF DANGER COULD I BE DETECT--?
HOLD ON!
WHY'S THE BOX GLOWING? NEVER SEEN ANYTHING LIKE--
HEY!
GOT HIT, BUT I DIDN'T FEEL ANY...
...THING.

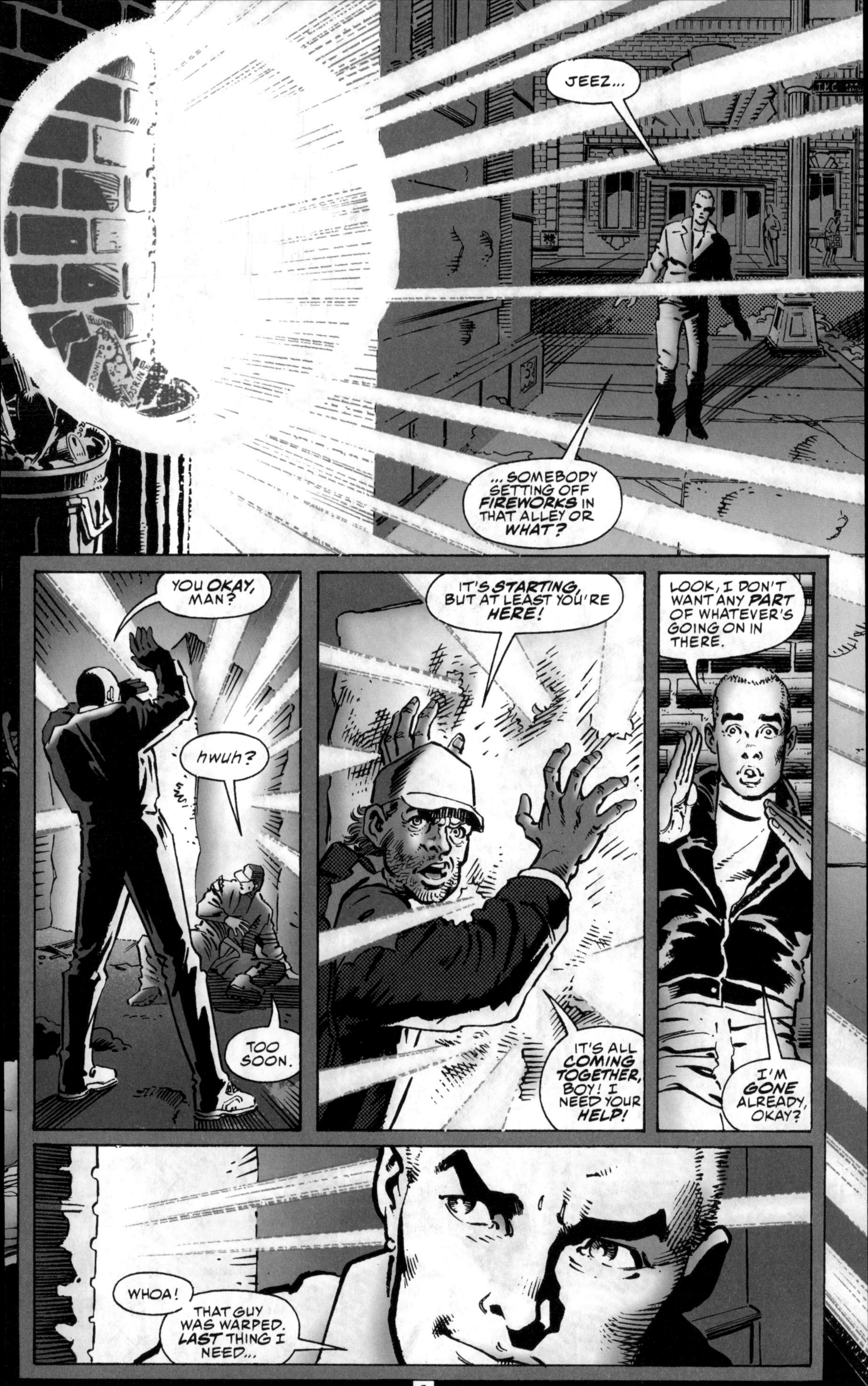
JEEZ...
...SOMEBODY SETTING OFF FIREWORKS IN THAT ALLEY OR WHAT?
YOU OKAY, MAN?
hwuh?
TOO SOON.
IT'S STARTING, BUT AT LEAST YOU'RE HERE!
IT'S ALL COMING TOGETHER, BOY! I NEED YOUR HELP!
LOOK, I DON'T WANT ANY PART OF WHATEVER'S GOING ON IN THERE.
I'M GONE ALREADY, OKAY?
WHOA!
THAT GUY WAS WARPED. LAST THING I NEED...

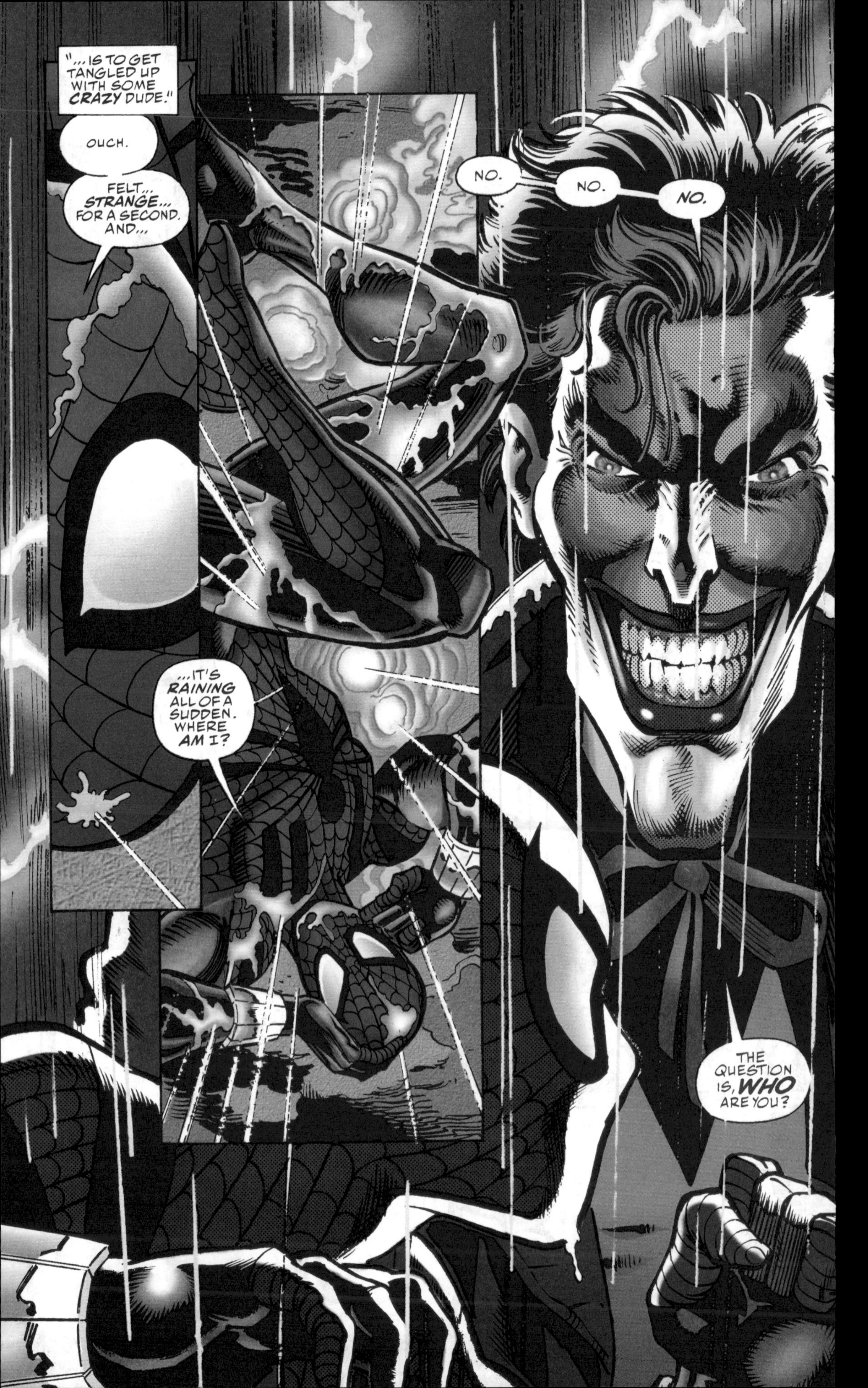
"...IS TO GET TANGLED UP WITH SOME CRAZY DUDE."
OUCH.
FELT... STRANGE... FOR A SECOND. AND...
NO.
NO.
NO.
...IT'S RAINING ALL OF A SUDDEN. WHERE AM I?
THE QUESTION IS, WHO ARE YOU?

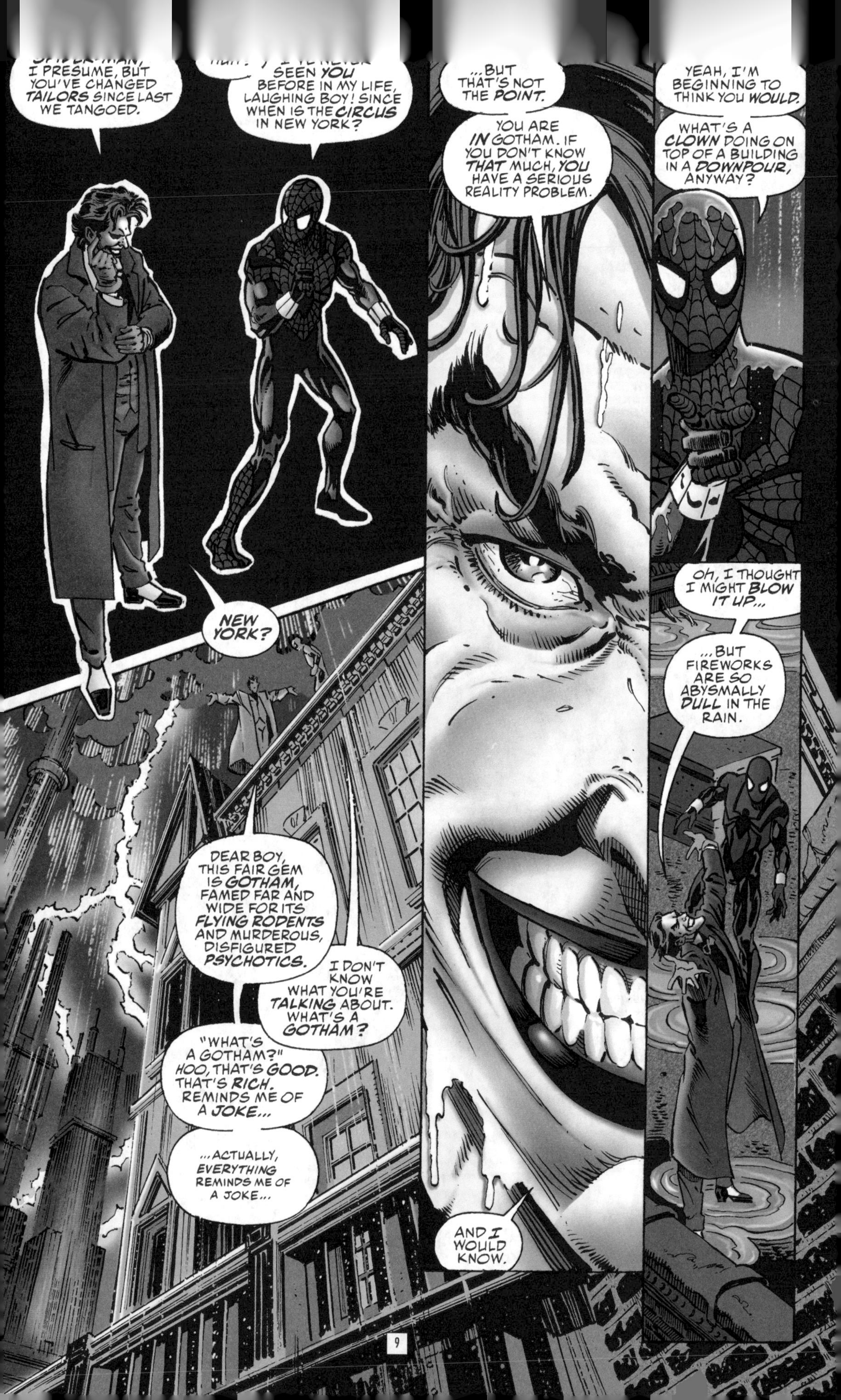
I PRESUME, BUT YOU'VE CHANGED TAILORS SINCE LAST WE TANGOED.
SEEN YOU BEFORE IN MY LIFE, LAUGHING BOY! SINCE WHEN IS THE CIRCUS IN NEW YORK?
NEW YORK?
DEAR BOY, THIS FAIR GEM IS GOTHAM, FAMED FAR AND WIDE FOR ITS FLYING RODENTS AND MURDEROUS, DISFIGURED PSYCHOTICS.
I DON'T KNOW WHAT YOU'RE TALKING ABOUT. WHAT'S A GOTHAM?
"WHAT'S A GOTHAM?" HOO, THAT'S GOOD. THAT'S RICH. REMINDS ME OF A JOKE...
...ACTUALLY, EVERYTHING REMINDS ME OF A JOKE...
...BUT THAT'S NOT THE POINT.
YOU ARE IN GOTHAM. IF YOU DON'T KNOW THAT MUCH, YOU HAVE A SERIOUS REALITY PROBLEM.
AND I WOULD KNOW.
YEAH, I'M BEGINNING TO THINK YOU WOULD.
WHAT'S A CLOWN DOING ON TOP OF A BUILDING IN A DOWNPOUR, ANYWAY?
OH, I THOUGHT I MIGHT BLOW IT UP...
...BUT FIREWORKS ARE SO ABYSMALLY DULL IN THE RAIN.

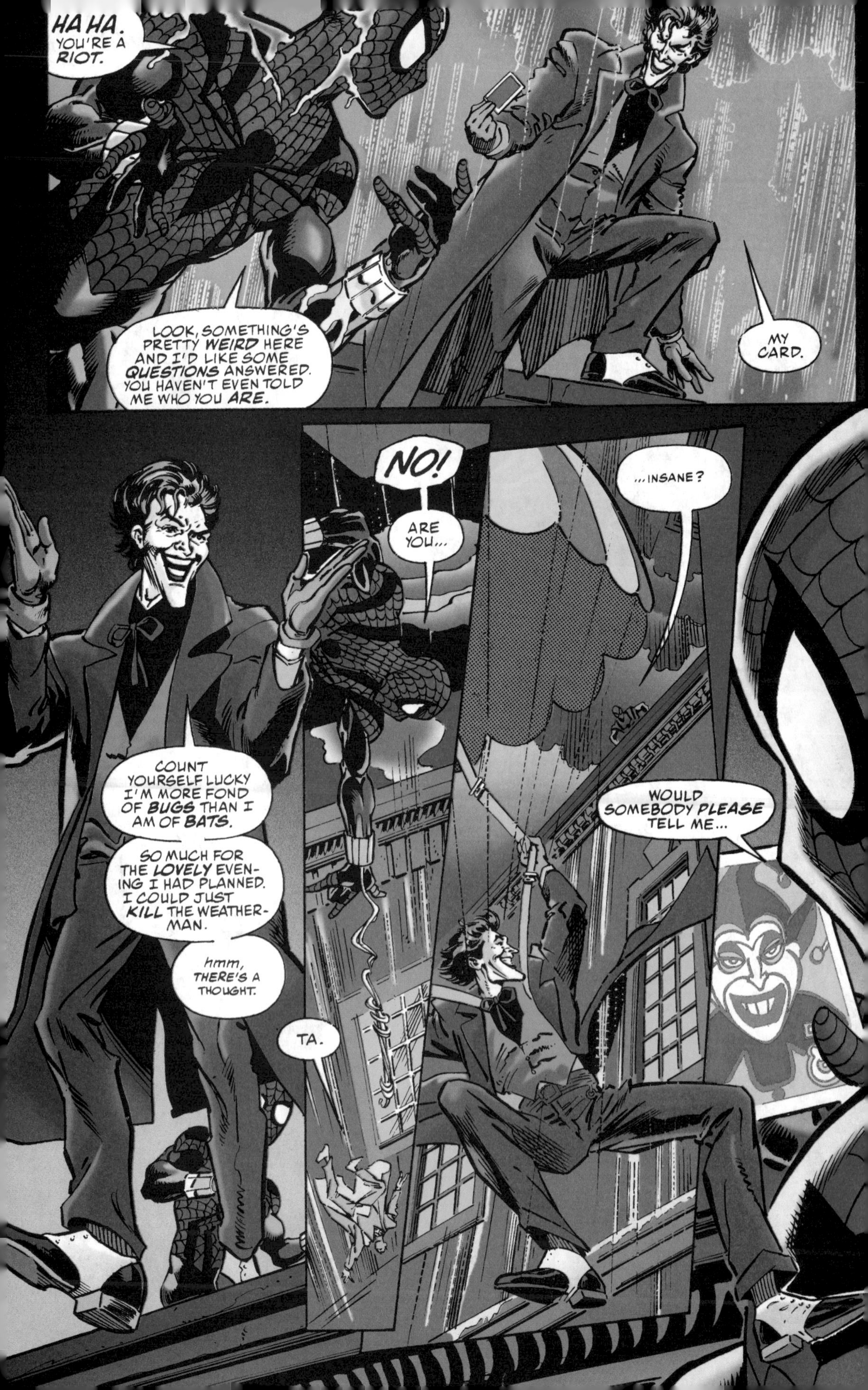
HA HA. YOU'RE A RIOT.
LOOK, SOMETHING'S PRETTY WEIRD HERE AND I'D LIKE SOME QUESTIONS ANSWERED. YOU HAVEN'T EVEN TOLD ME WHO YOU ARE.
MY CARD.
COUNT YOURSELF LUCKY I'M MORE FOND OF BUGS THAN I AM OF BATS.
SO MUCH FOR THE LOVELY EVENING I HAD PLANNED. I COULD JUST KILL THE WEATHERMAN.
hmm, THERE'S A THOUGHT.
TA.
NO!
ARE YOU...
...INSANE?
WOULD SOMEBODY PLEASE TELL ME...

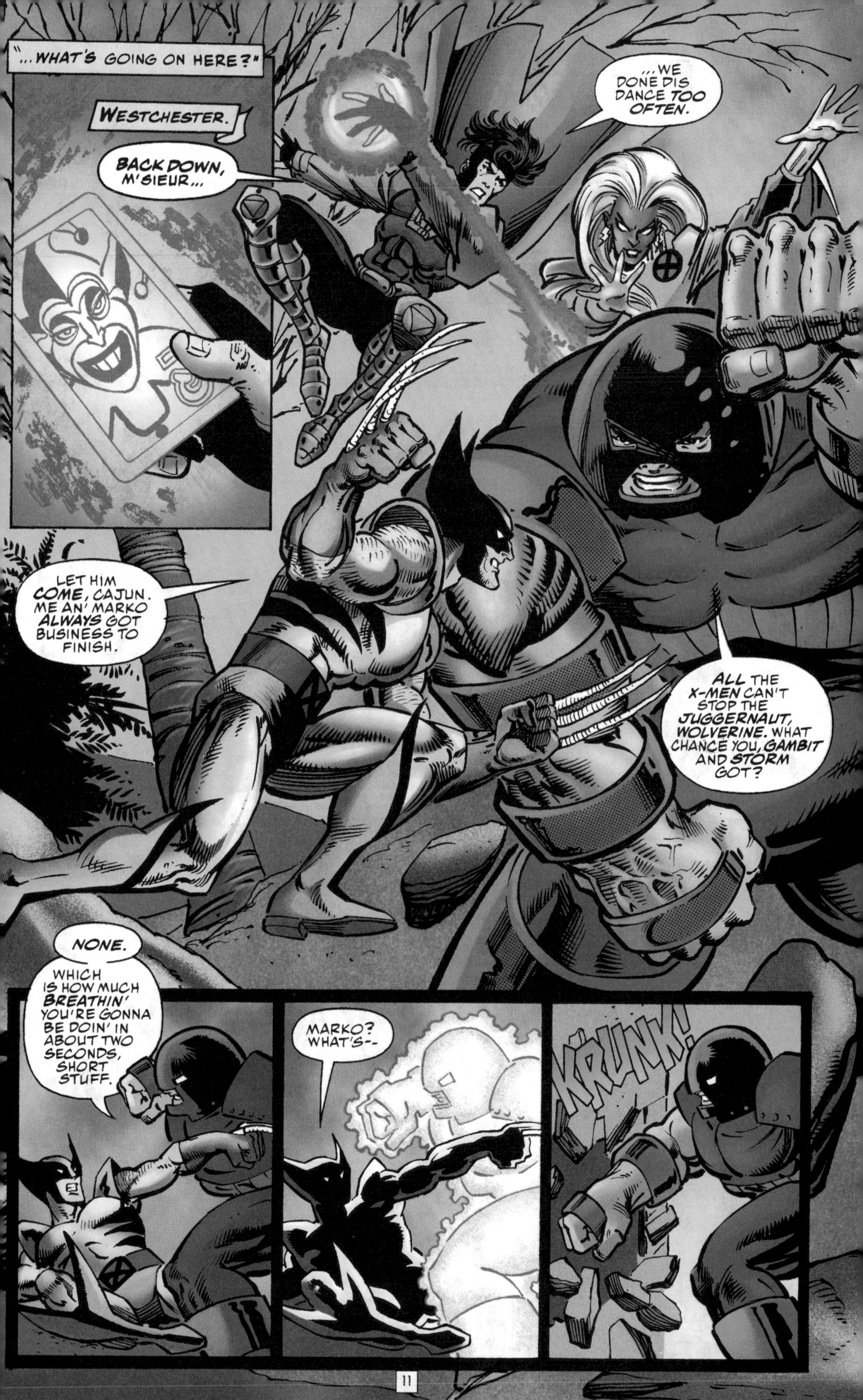
"...WHAT'S GOING ON HERE?"
WESTCHESTER.
BACK DOWN, M'SIEUR...
...WE DONE DIS DANCE TOO OFTEN.
LET HIM COME, CAJUN. ME AN' MARKO ALWAYS GOT BUSINESS TO FINISH.
ALL THE X-MEN CAN'T STOP THE JUGGERNAUT, WOLVERINE. WHAT CHANCE YOU, GAMBIT AND STORM GOT?
NONE.
WHICH IS HOW MUCH BREATHIN' YOU'RE GONNA BE DOIN' IN ABOUT TWO SECONDS, SHORT STUFF.
MARKO? WHAT'S--
KRUNK!

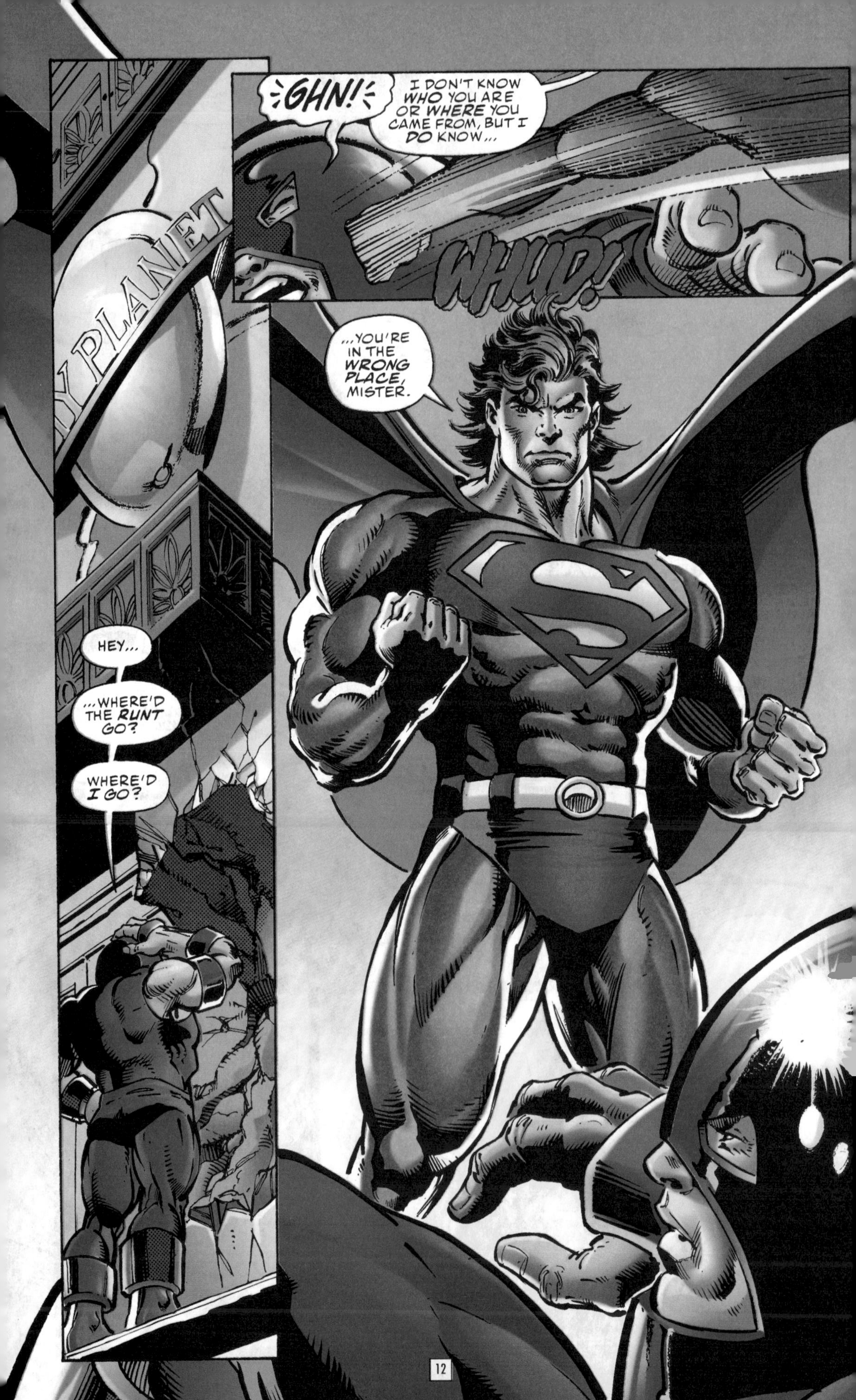

GHN!
I DON'T KNOW WHO YOU ARE OR WHERE YOU CAME FROM, BUT I DO KNOW...
WHUD!
...YOU'RE IN THE WRONG PLACE, MISTER.
HEY...
...WHERE'D THE RUNT GO?
WHERE'D I GO?

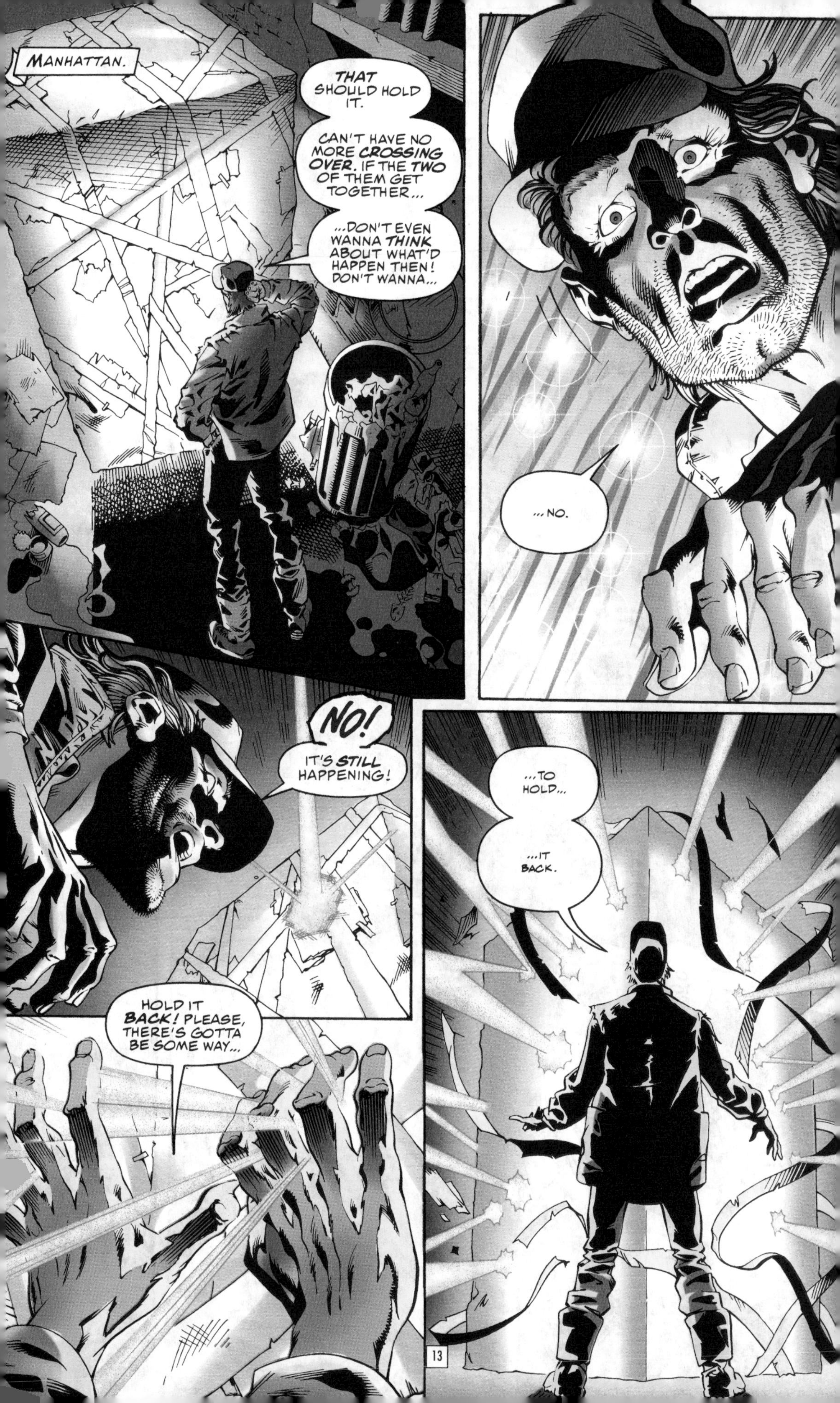
MANHATTAN.
THAT SHOULD HOLD IT.
CAN'T HAVE NO MORE CROSSING OVER. IF THE TWO OF THEM GET TOGETHER...
...DON'T EVEN WANNA THINK ABOUT WHAT'D HAPPEN THEN! DON'T WANNA...
...NO.
NO!
IT'S STILL HAPPENING!
HOLD IT BACK! PLEASE, THERE'S GOTTA BE SOME WAY...
...TO HOLD...
...IT BACK.

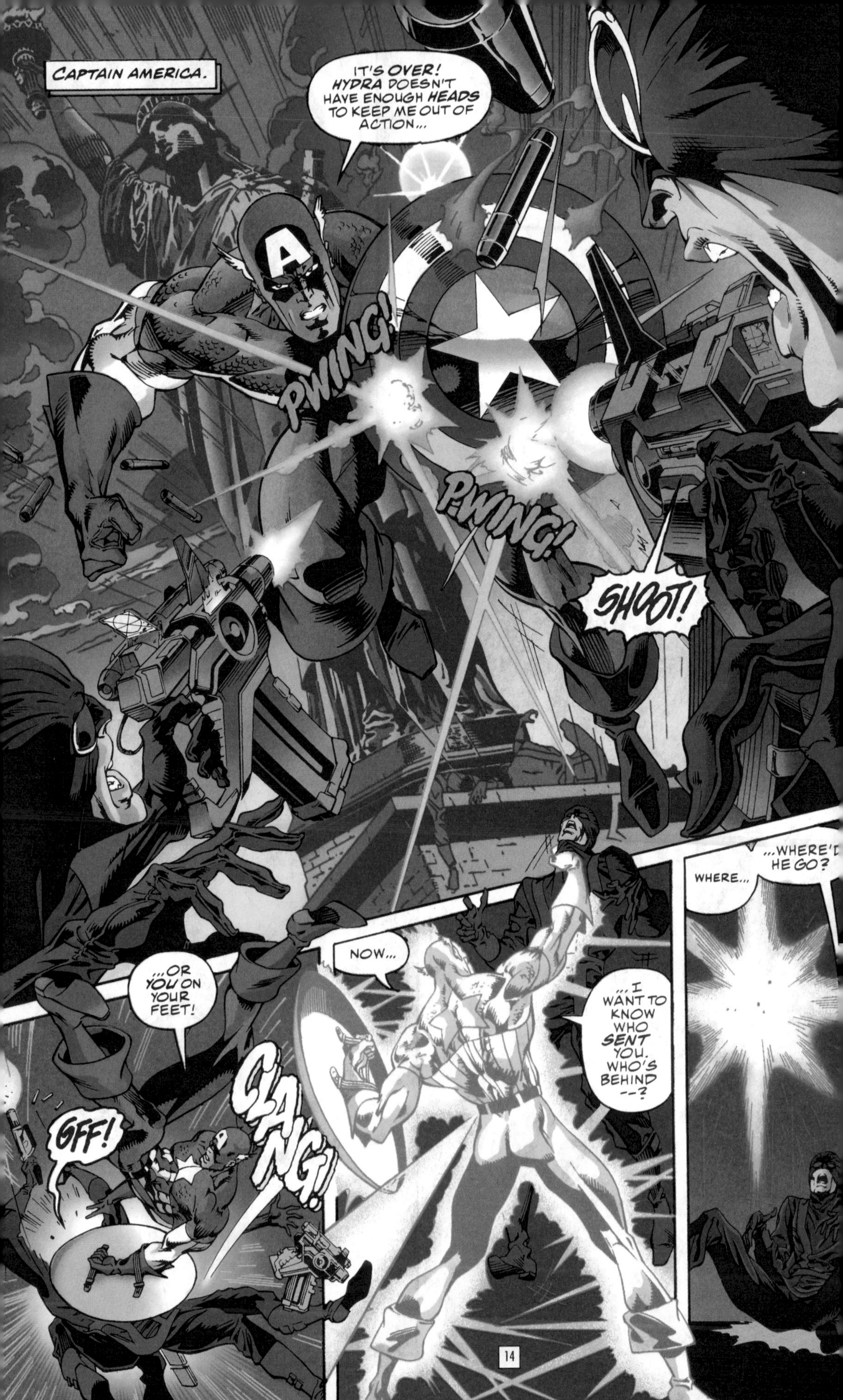

CAPTAIN AMERICA.
IT'S OVER! HYDRA DOESN'T HAVE ENOUGH HEADS TO KEEP ME OUT OF ACTION...
PWING!
PWING!
SHOOT!
...OR YOU ON YOUR FEET!
GFF!
CLANG!
NOW...
...I WANT TO KNOW WHO SENT YOU. WHO'S BEHIND --?
WHERE...
...WHERE'D HE GO?

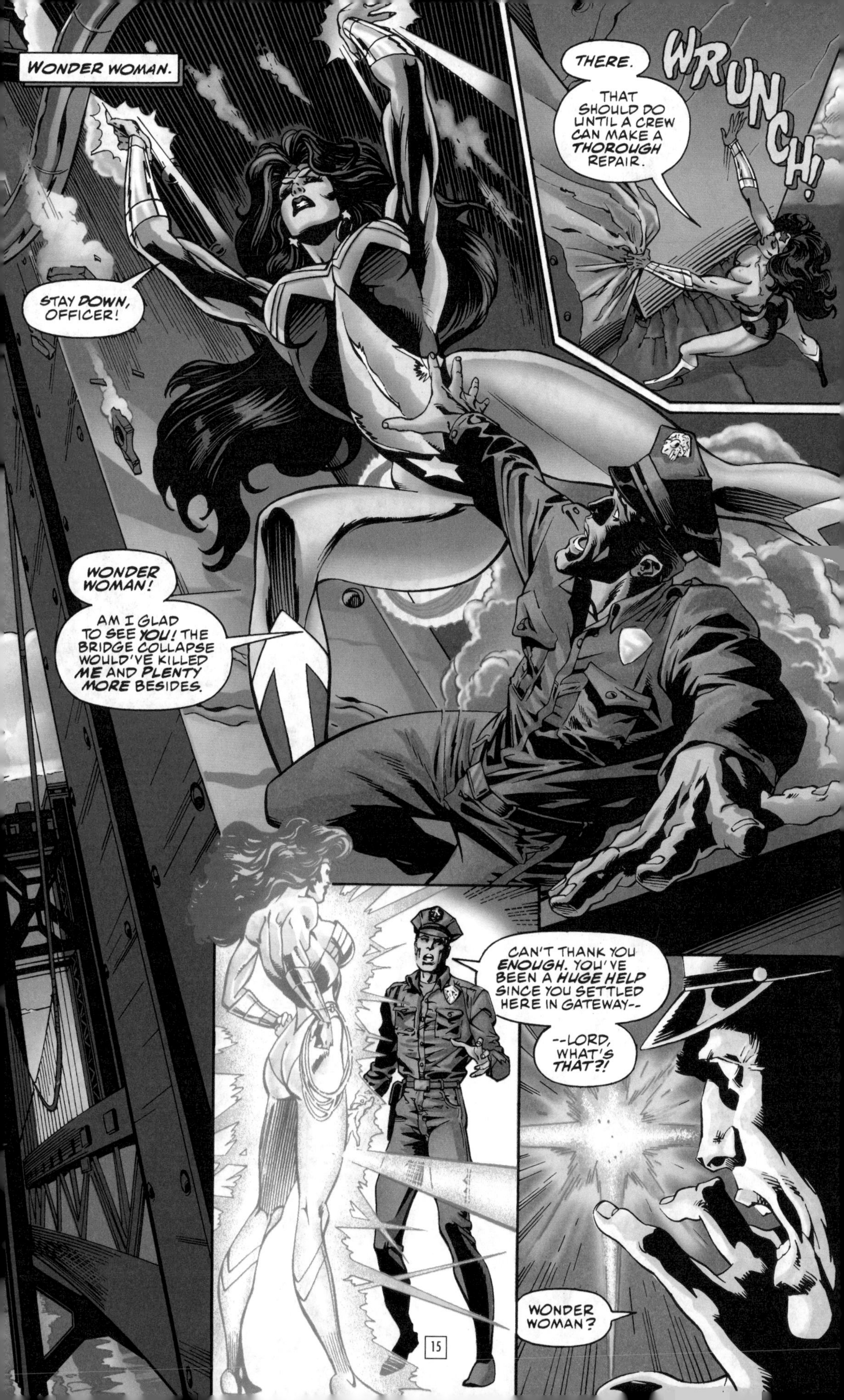
WONDER WOMAN.
STAY DOWN, OFFICER!
THERE.
THAT SHOULD DO UNTIL A CREW CAN MAKE A THOROUGH REPAIR.
WRUNCH!
WONDER WOMAN!
AM I GLAD TO SEE YOU! THE BRIDGE COLLAPSE WOULD'VE KILLED ME AND PLENTY MORE BESIDES.
CAN'T THANK YOU ENOUGH. YOU'VE BEEN A HUGE HELP SINCE YOU SETTLED HERE IN GATEWAY--
--LORD, WHAT'S THAT?!
WONDER WOMAN?

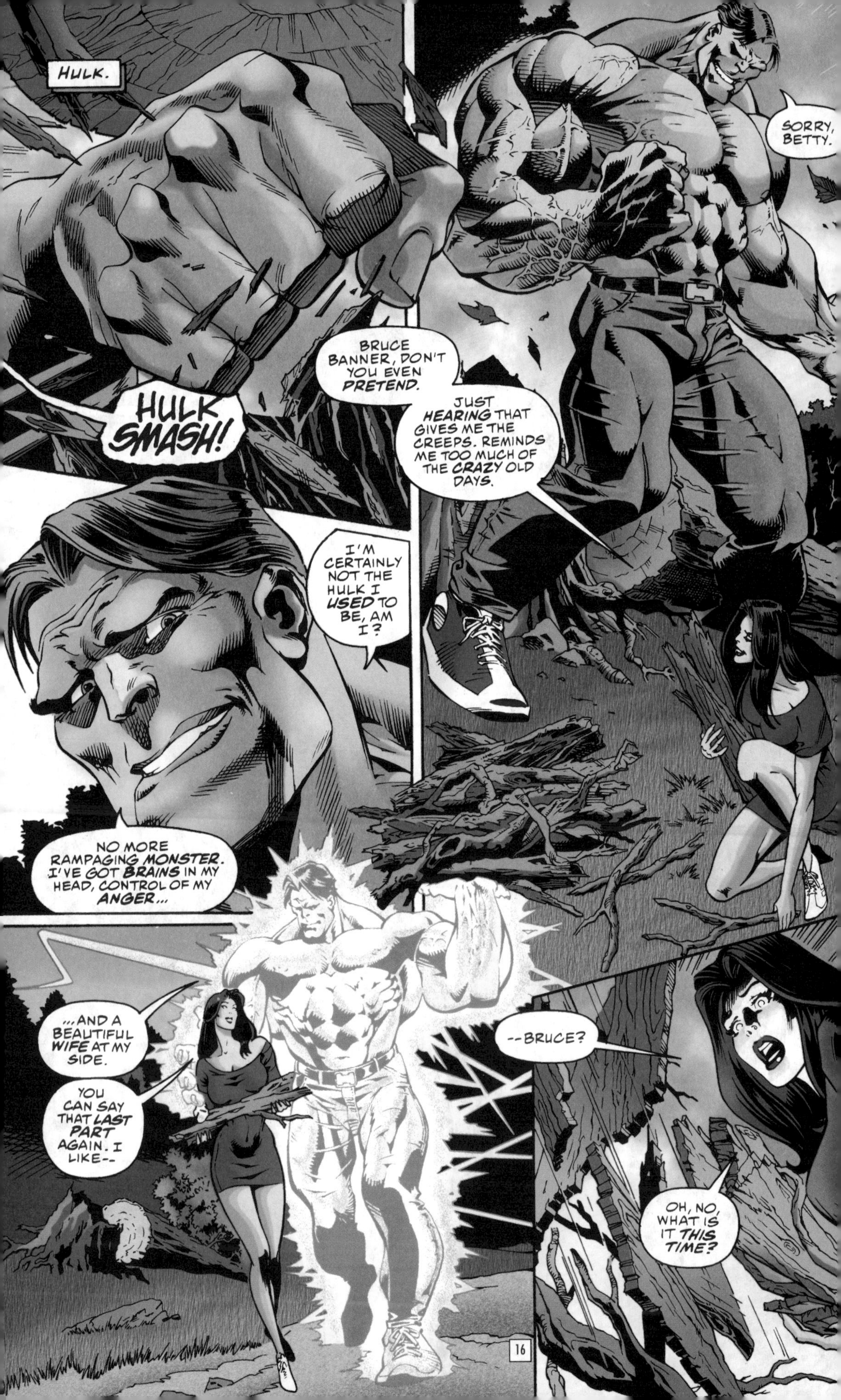
HULK.
HULK SMASH!
BRUCE BANNER, DON'T YOU EVEN PRETEND.
JUST HEARING THAT GIVES ME THE CREEPS. REMINDS ME TOO MUCH OF THE CRAZY OLD DAYS.
SORRY, BETTY.
I'M CERTAINLY NOT THE HULK I USED TO BE, AM I?
NO MORE RAMPAGING MONSTER. I'VE GOT BRAINS IN MY HEAD, CONTROL OF MY ANGER...
...AND A BEAUTIFUL WIFE AT MY SIDE.
YOU CAN SAY THAT LAST PART AGAIN. I LIKE--
--BRUCE?
OH, NO, WHAT IS IT THIS TIME?

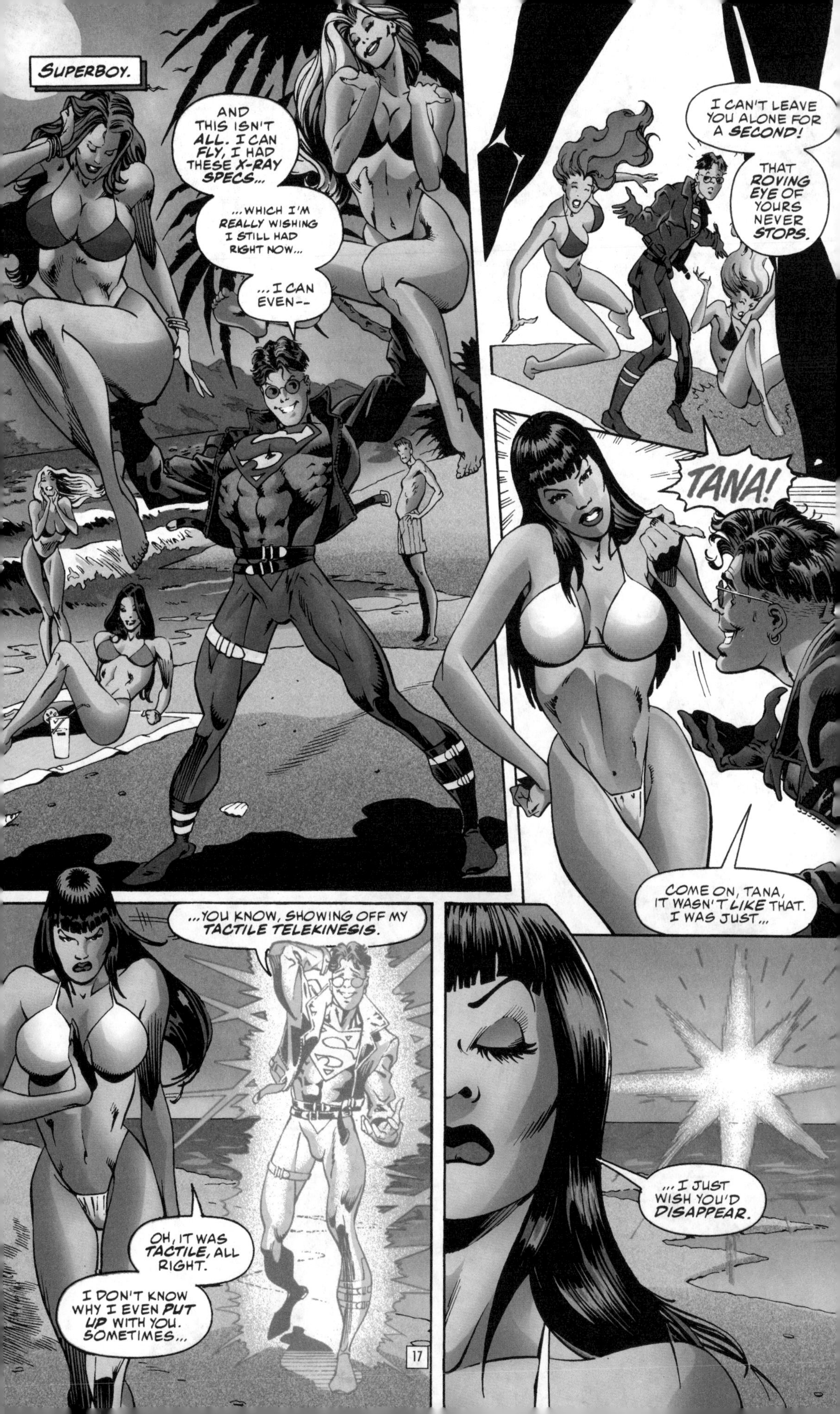
SUPERBOY.
AND THIS ISN'T ALL. I CAN FLY, I HAD THESE X-RAY SPECS...
...WHICH I'M REALLY WISHING I STILL HAD RIGHT NOW...
...I CAN EVEN--
I CAN'T LEAVE YOU ALONE FOR A SECOND!
THAT ROVING EYE OF YOURS NEVER STOPS.
TANA!
COME ON, TANA, IT WASN'T LIKE THAT. I WAS JUST...
...YOU KNOW, SHOWING OFF MY TACTILE TELEKINESIS.
OH, IT WAS TACTILE, ALL RIGHT.
I DON'T KNOW WHY I EVEN PUT UP WITH YOU. SOMETIMES...
...I JUST WISH YOU'D DISAPPEAR.

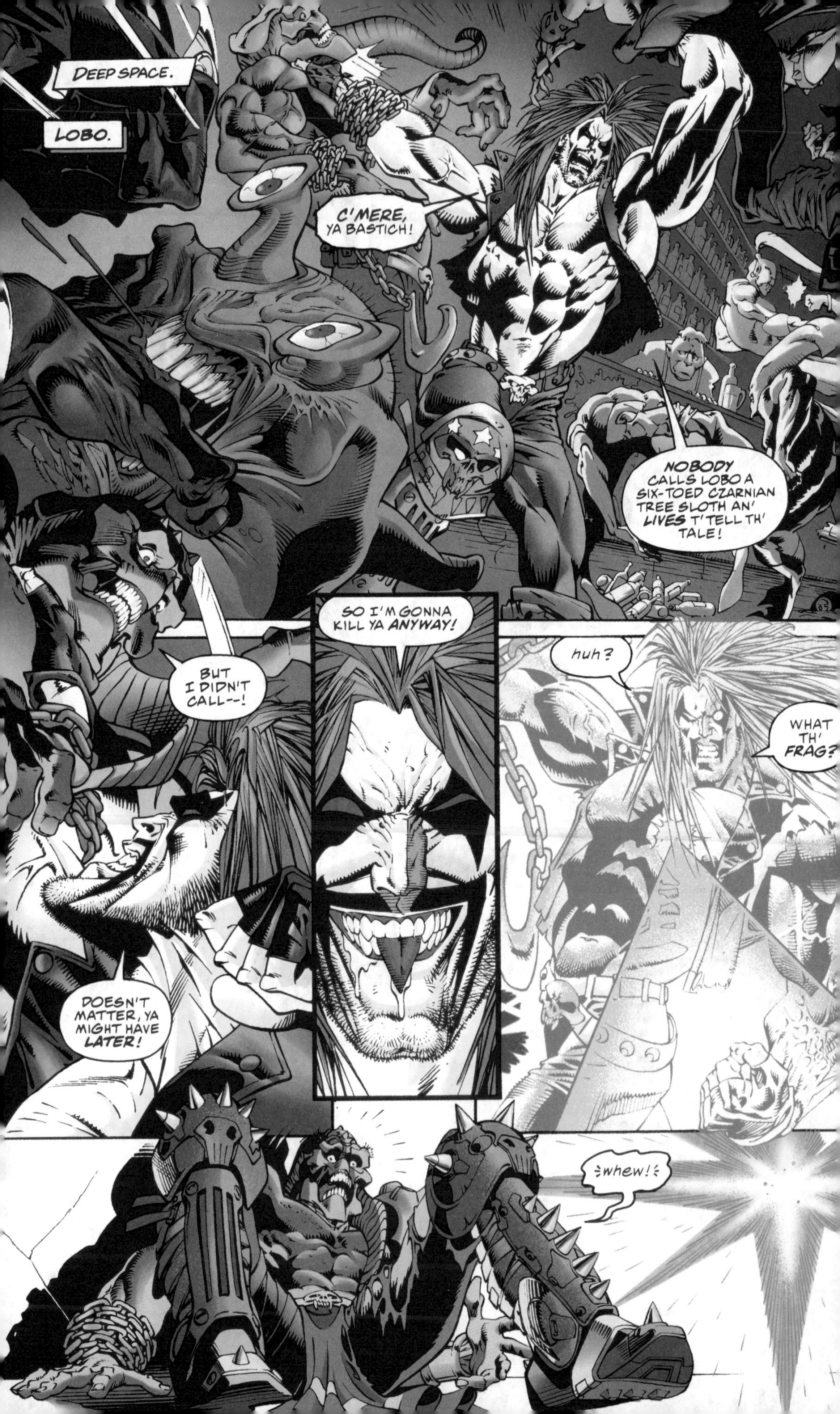
DEEP SPACE.
LOBO.
C'MERE, YA BASTICH!
NOBODY CALLS LOBO A SIX-TOED CZARNIAN TREE SLOTH AN' LIVES T'TELL TH' TALE!
BUT I DIDN'T CALL--!
DOESN'T MATTER, YA MIGHT HAVE LATER!
SO I'M GONNA KILL YA ANYWAY!
huh?
WHAT TH' FRAG?
whew!

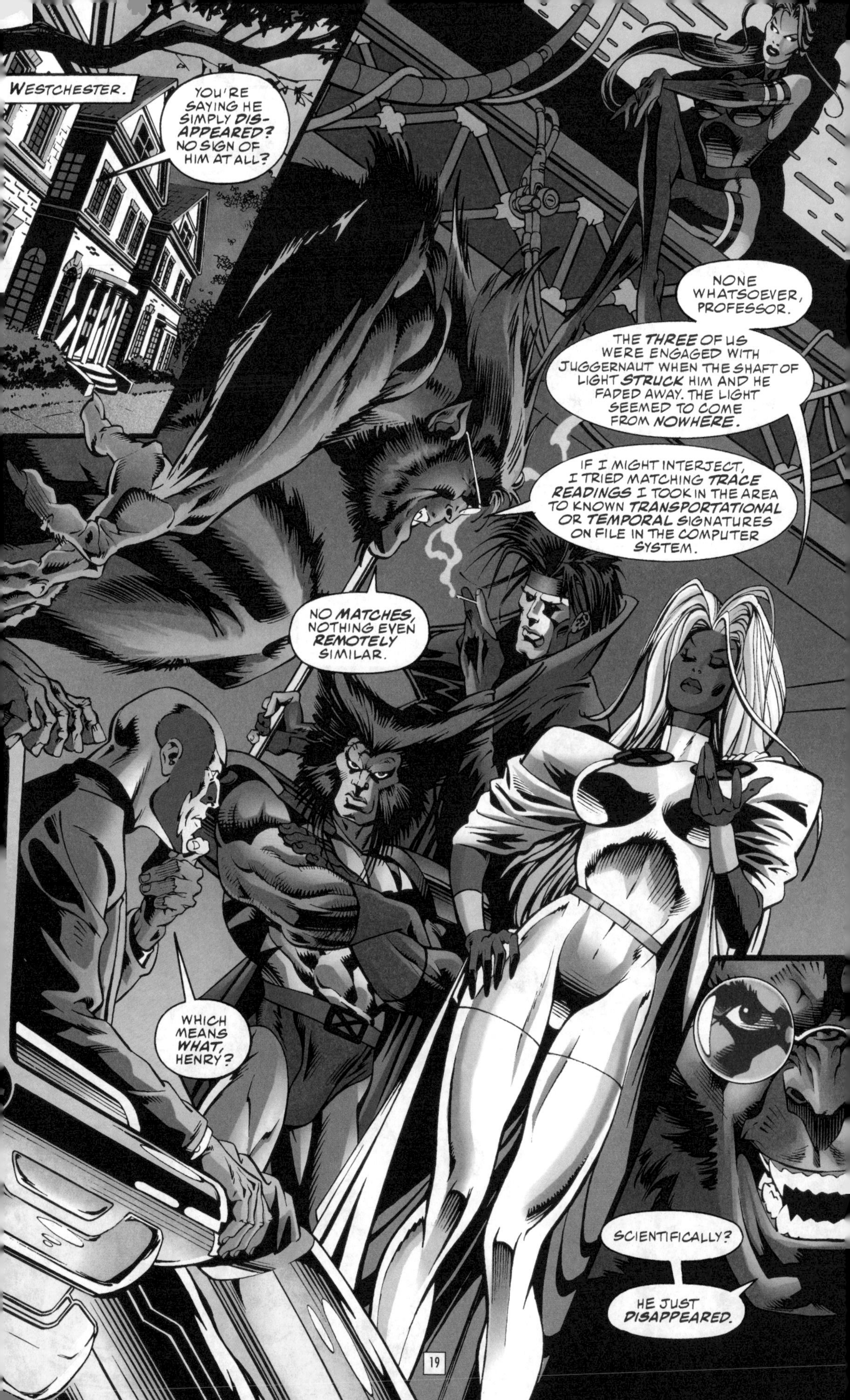
WESTCHESTER.
YOU'RE SAYING HE SIMPLY DIS-APPEARED? NO SIGN OF HIM AT ALL?
NONE WHATSOEVER, PROFESSOR.
THE THREE OF US WERE ENGAGED WITH JUGGERNAUT WHEN THE SHAFT OF LIGHT STRUCK HIM AND HE FADED AWAY. THE LIGHT SEEMED TO COME FROM NOWHERE.
IF I MIGHT INTERJECT, I TRIED MATCHING TRACE READINGS I TOOK IN THE AREA TO KNOWN TRANSPORTATIONAL OR TEMPORAL SIGNATURES ON FILE IN THE COMPUTER SYSTEM.
NO MATCHES, NOTHING EVEN REMOTELY SIMILAR.
WHICH MEANS WHAT, HENRY?
SCIENTIFICALLY?
HE JUST DISAPPEARED.

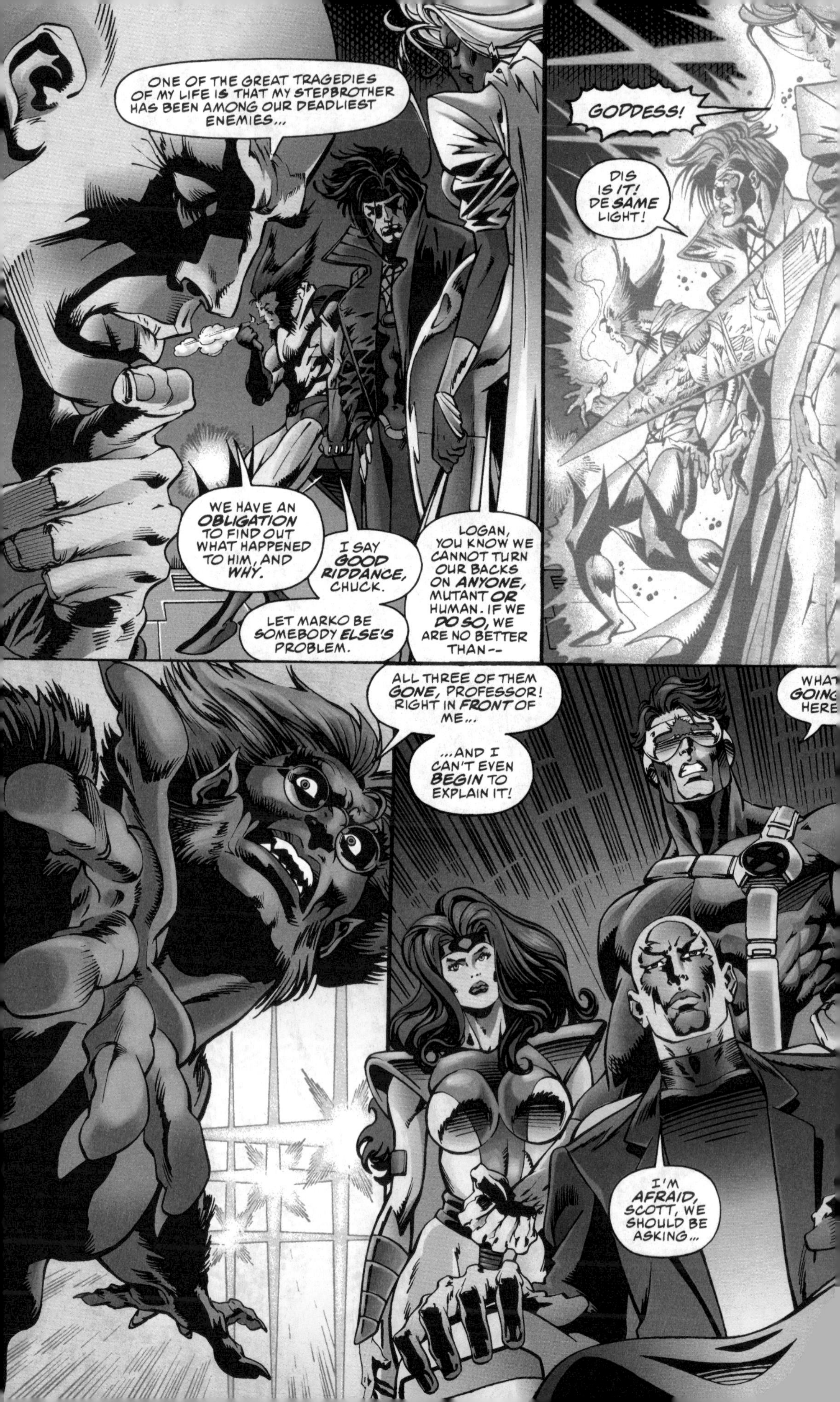
ONE OF THE GREAT TRAGEDIES OF MY LIFE IS THAT MY STEPBROTHER HAS BEEN AMONG OUR DEADLIEST ENEMIES...
WE HAVE AN OBLIGATION TO FIND OUT WHAT HAPPENED TO HIM, AND WHY.
I SAY GOOD RIDDANCE, CHUCK.
LET MARKO BE SOMEBODY ELSE'S PROBLEM.
LOGAN, YOU KNOW WE CANNOT TURN OUR BACKS ON ANYONE, MUTANT OR HUMAN. IF WE DO SO, WE ARE NO BETTER THAN--
GODDESS!
DIS IS IT! DE SAME LIGHT!
ALL THREE OF THEM GONE, PROFESSOR! RIGHT IN FRONT OF ME...
...AND I CAN'T EVEN BEGIN TO EXPLAIN IT!
I'M AFRAID, SCOTT, WE SHOULD BE ASKING...

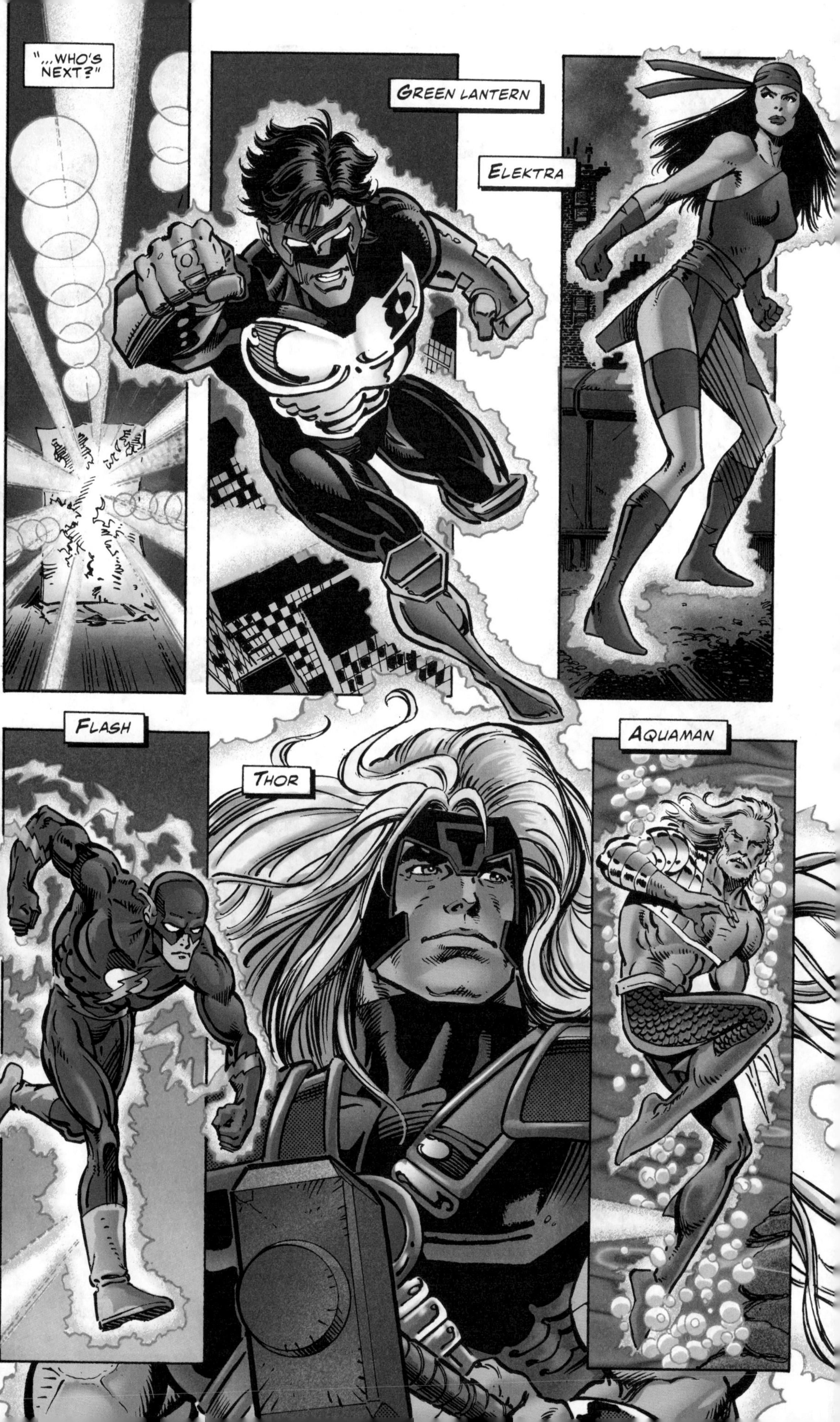
"...WHO'S NEXT?"
GREEN LANTERN
ELEKTRA
FLASH
THOR
AQUAMAN

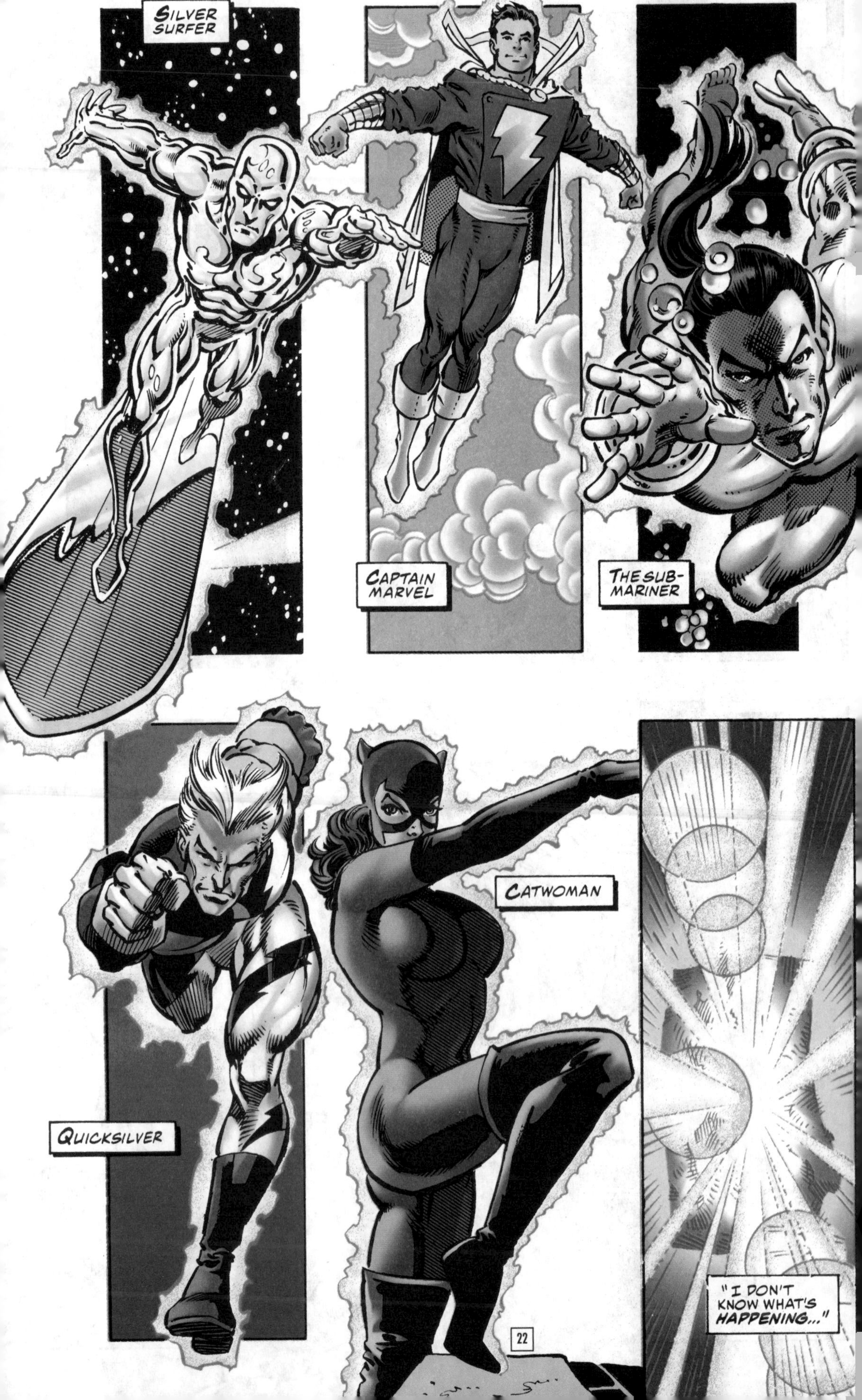
SILVER SURFER
CAPTAIN MARVEL
THE SUB-MARINER
QUICKSILVER
CATWOMAN
"I DON'T KNOW WHAT'S HAPPENING..."

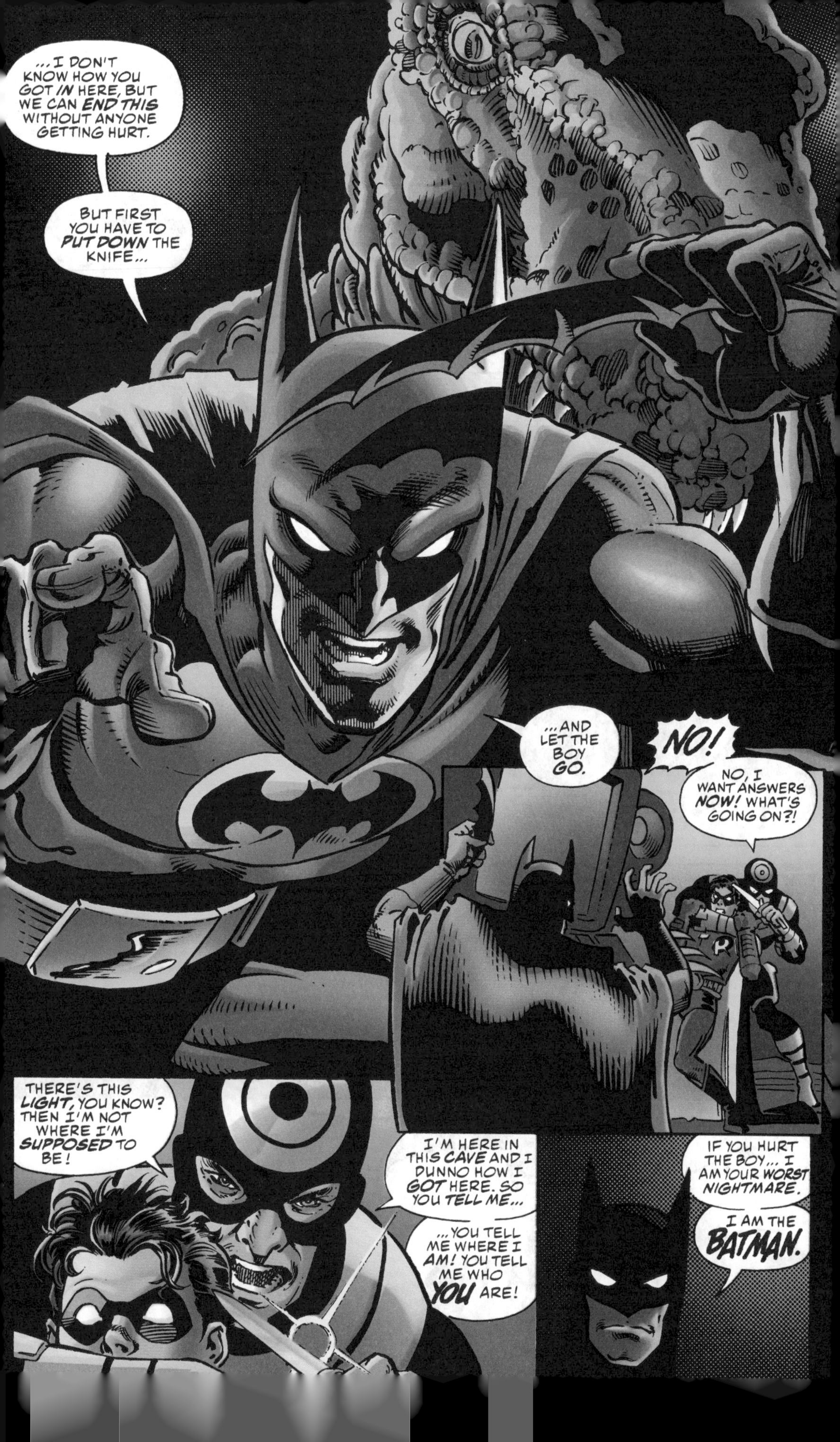
...I DON'T KNOW HOW YOU GOT IN HERE, BUT WE CAN END THIS WITHOUT ANYONE GETTING HURT.
BUT FIRST YOU HAVE TO PUT DOWN THE KNIFE...
...AND LET THE BOY GO.
NO!
NO, I WANT ANSWERS NOW! WHAT'S GOING ON?!
THERE'S THIS LIGHT, YOU KNOW? THEN I'M NOT WHERE I'M SUPPOSED TO BE!
I'M HERE IN THIS CAVE AND I DUNNO HOW I GOT HERE. SO YOU TELL ME...
...YOU TELL ME WHERE I AM! YOU TELL ME WHO YOU ARE!
IF YOU HURT THE BOY... I AM YOUR WORST NIGHTMARE.
I AM THE BATMAN.

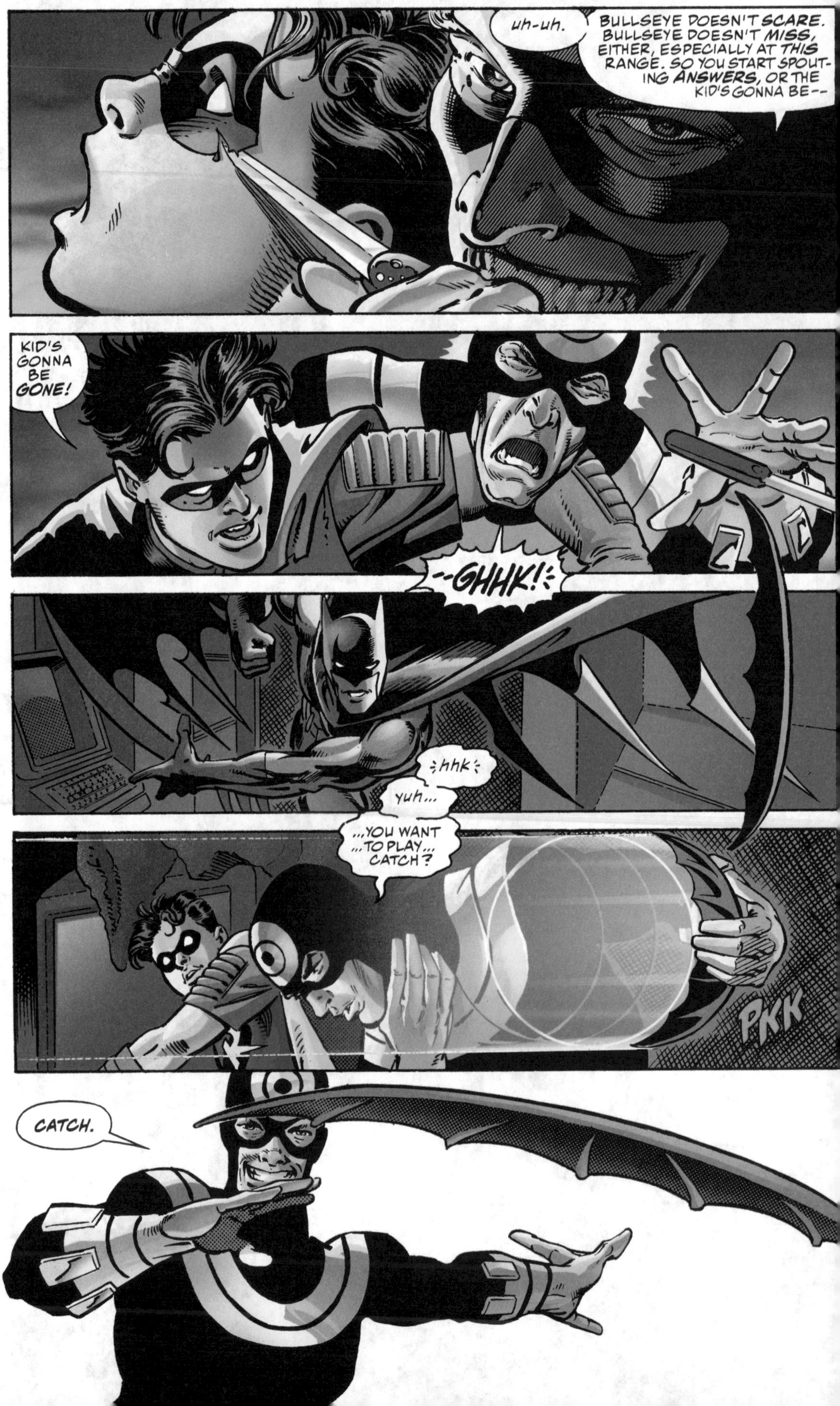
uh-uh.
BULLSEYE DOESN'T SCARE. BULLSEYE DOESN'T MISS, EITHER, ESPECIALLY AT THIS RANGE. SO YOU START SPOUTING ANSWERS, OR THE KID'S GONNA BE--
KID'S GONNA BE GONE!
--GHHK!
hhk
yuh...
...YOU WANT ...TO PLAY... CATCH?
PKK
CATCH.

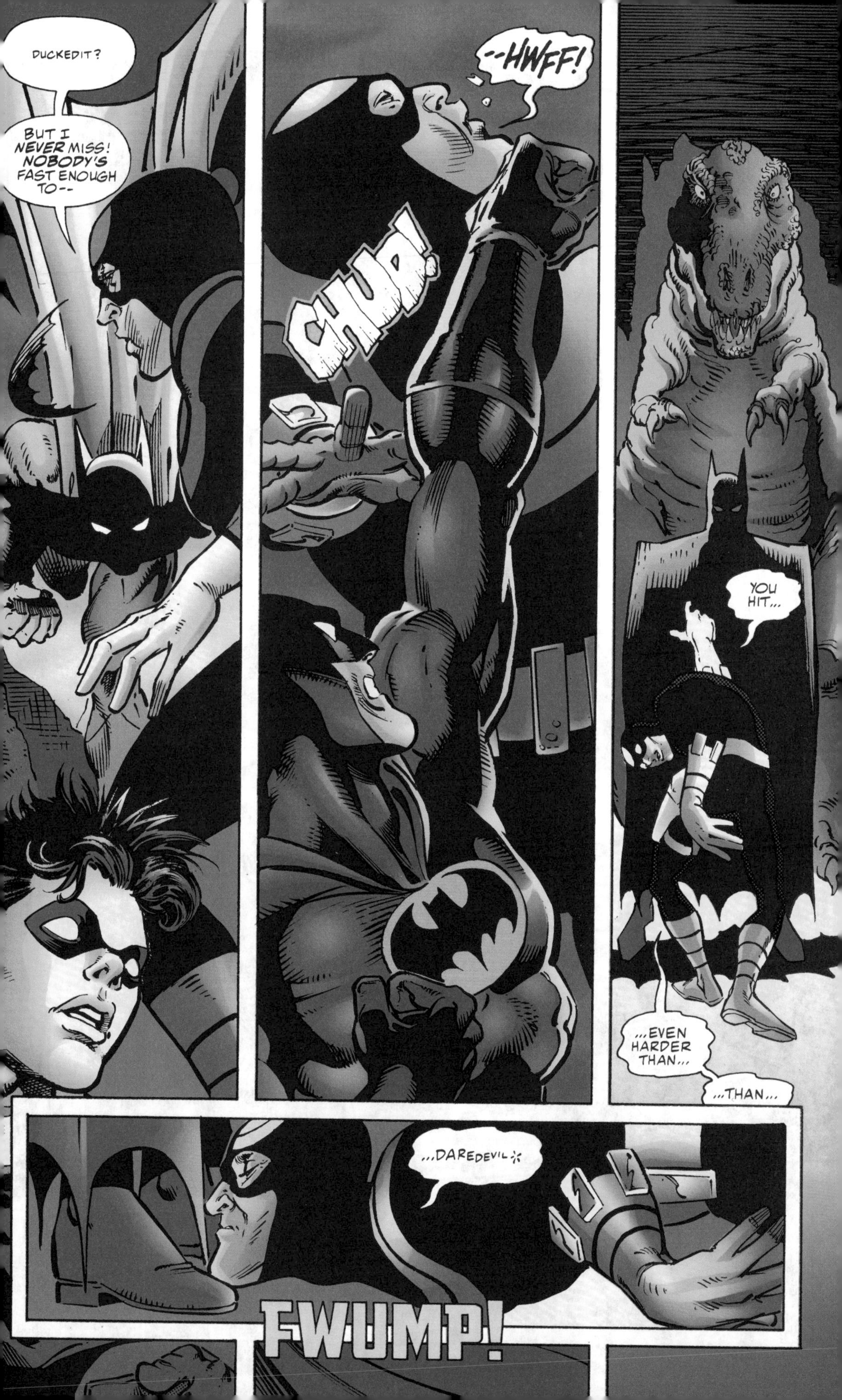
DUCKEDIT?
BUT I NEVER MISS! NOBODY'S FAST ENOUGH TO--
--HWFF!
CHUD!
YOU HIT...
...EVEN HARDER THAN...
...THAN...
...DAREDEVIL
FWUMP!

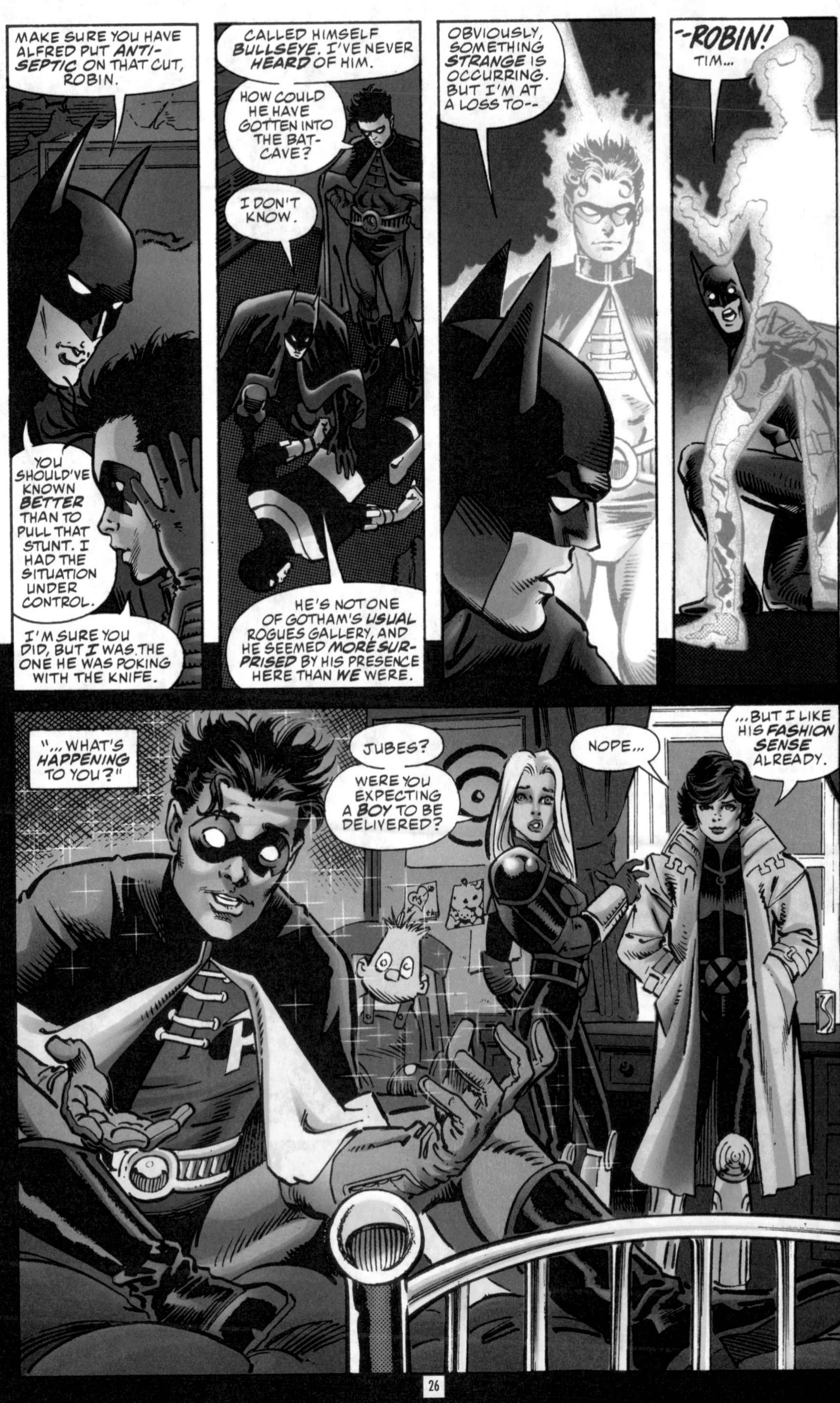

MAKE SURE YOU HAVE ALFRED PUT ANTI-SEPTIC ON THAT CUT, ROBIN.
YOU SHOULD'VE KNOWN BETTER THAN TO PULL THAT STUNT. I HAD THE SITUATION UNDER CONTROL.
I'M SURE YOU DID, BUT I WAS THE ONE HE WAS POKING WITH THE KNIFE.
CALLED HIMSELF BULLSEYE. I'VE NEVER HEARD OF HIM.
HOW COULD HE HAVE GOTTEN INTO THE BAT-CAVE?
I DON'T KNOW.
HE'S NOT ONE OF GOTHAM'S USUAL ROGUES GALLERY, AND HE SEEMED MORE SUR-PRISED BY HIS PRESENCE HERE THAN WE WERE.
OBVIOUSLY, SOMETHING STRANGE IS OCCURRING. BUT I'M AT A LOSS TO--
--ROBIN! TIM...
"...WHAT'S HAPPENING TO YOU?"
JUBES?
WERE YOU EXPECTING A BOY TO BE DELIVERED?
NOPE...
...BUT I LIKE HIS FASHION SENSE ALREADY.

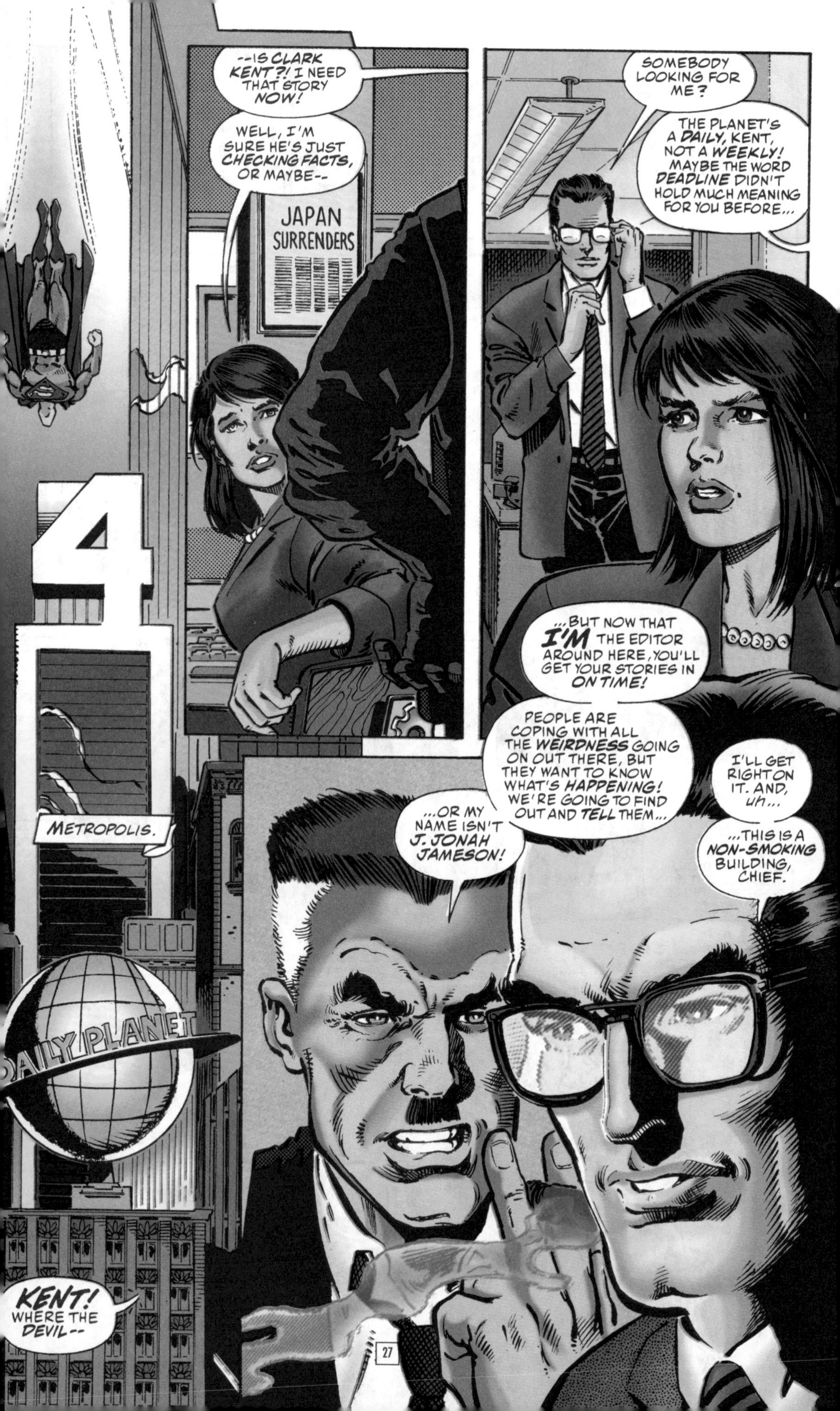

4
METROPOLIS.
DAILY PLANET
KENT! WHERE THE DEVIL--
--IS CLARK KENT?! I NEED THAT STORY NOW!
WELL, I'M SURE HE'S JUST CHECKING FACTS, OR MAYBE--
JAPAN SURRENDERS
SOMEBODY LOOKING FOR ME?
THE PLANET'S A DAILY, KENT, NOT A WEEKLY! MAYBE THE WORD DEADLINE DIDN'T HOLD MUCH MEANING FOR YOU BEFORE...
...BUT NOW THAT I'M THE EDITOR AROUND HERE, YOU'LL GET YOUR STORIES IN ON TIME!
PEOPLE ARE COPING WITH ALL THE WEIRDNESS GOING ON OUT THERE, BUT THEY WANT TO KNOW WHAT'S HAPPENING! WE'RE GOING TO FIND OUT AND TELL THEM...
...OR MY NAME ISN'T J. JONAH JAMESON!
I'LL GET RIGHT ON IT. AND, uh...
...THIS IS A NON-SMOKING BUILDING, CHIEF.

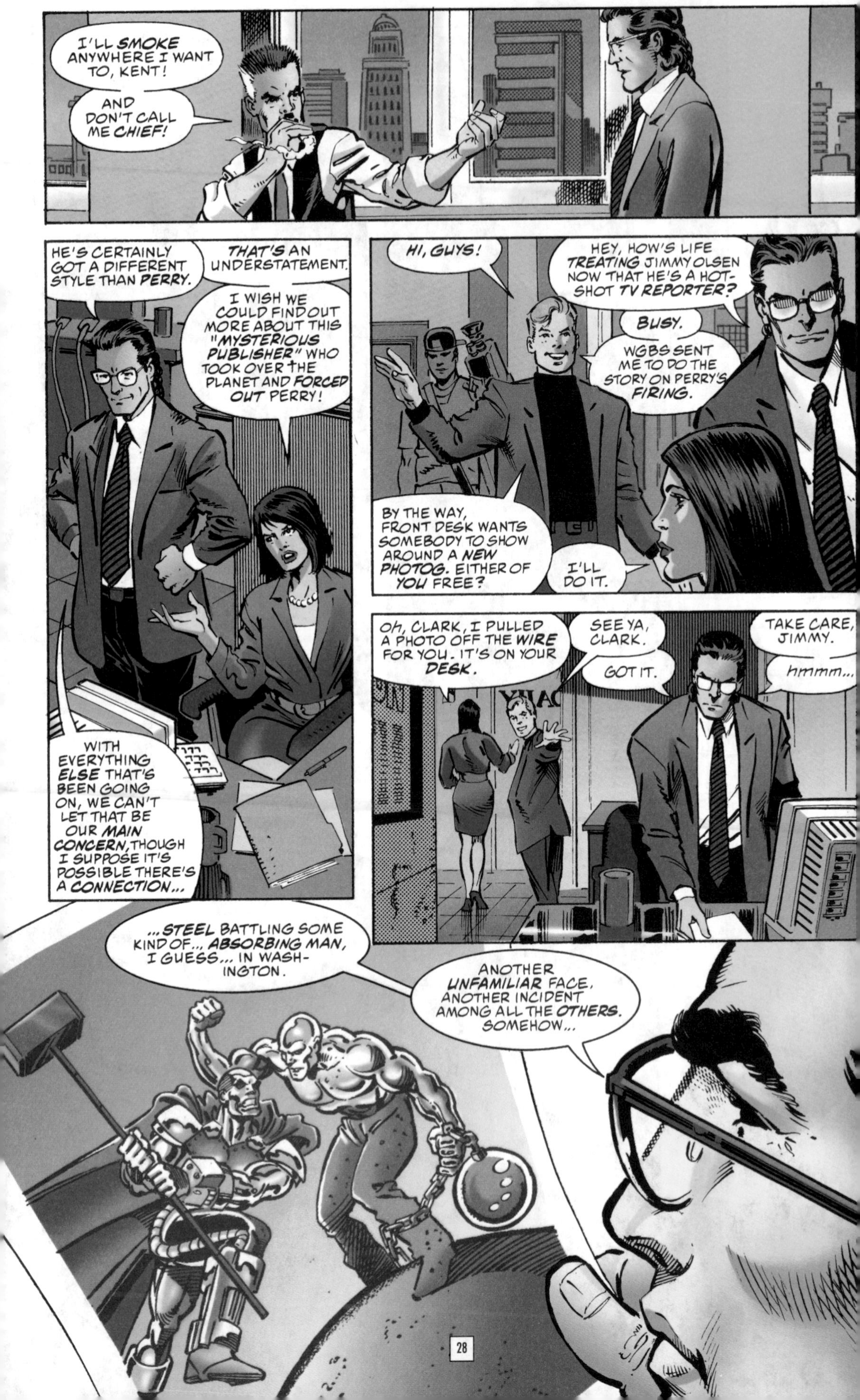

I'LL SMOKE ANYWHERE I WANT TO, KENT!
AND DON'T CALL ME CHIEF!
HE'S CERTAINLY GOT A DIFFERENT STYLE THAN PERRY.
THAT'S AN UNDERSTATEMENT.
I WISH WE COULD FIND OUT MORE ABOUT THIS "MYSTERIOUS PUBLISHER" WHO TOOK OVER THE PLANET AND FORCED OUT PERRY!
WITH EVERYTHING ELSE THAT'S BEEN GOING ON, WE CAN'T LET THAT BE OUR MAIN CONCERN, THOUGH I SUPPOSE IT'S POSSIBLE THERE'S A CONNECTION...
HI, GUYS!
HEY, HOW'S LIFE TREATING JIMMY OLSEN NOW THAT HE'S A HOT-SHOT TV REPORTER?
BUSY.
WGBS SENT ME TO DO THE STORY ON PERRY'S FIRING.
BY THE WAY, FRONT DESK WANTS SOMEBODY TO SHOW AROUND A NEW PHOTOG. EITHER OF YOU FREE?
I'LL DO IT.
OH, CLARK, I PULLED A PHOTO OFF THE WIRE FOR YOU. IT'S ON YOUR DESK.
SEE YA, CLARK.
GOT IT.
TAKE CARE, JIMMY.
hmmm...
...STEEL BATTLING SOME KIND OF... ABSORBING MAN, I GUESS... IN WASHINGTON.
ANOTHER UNFAMILIAR FACE, ANOTHER INCIDENT AMONG ALL THE OTHERS. SOMEHOW...

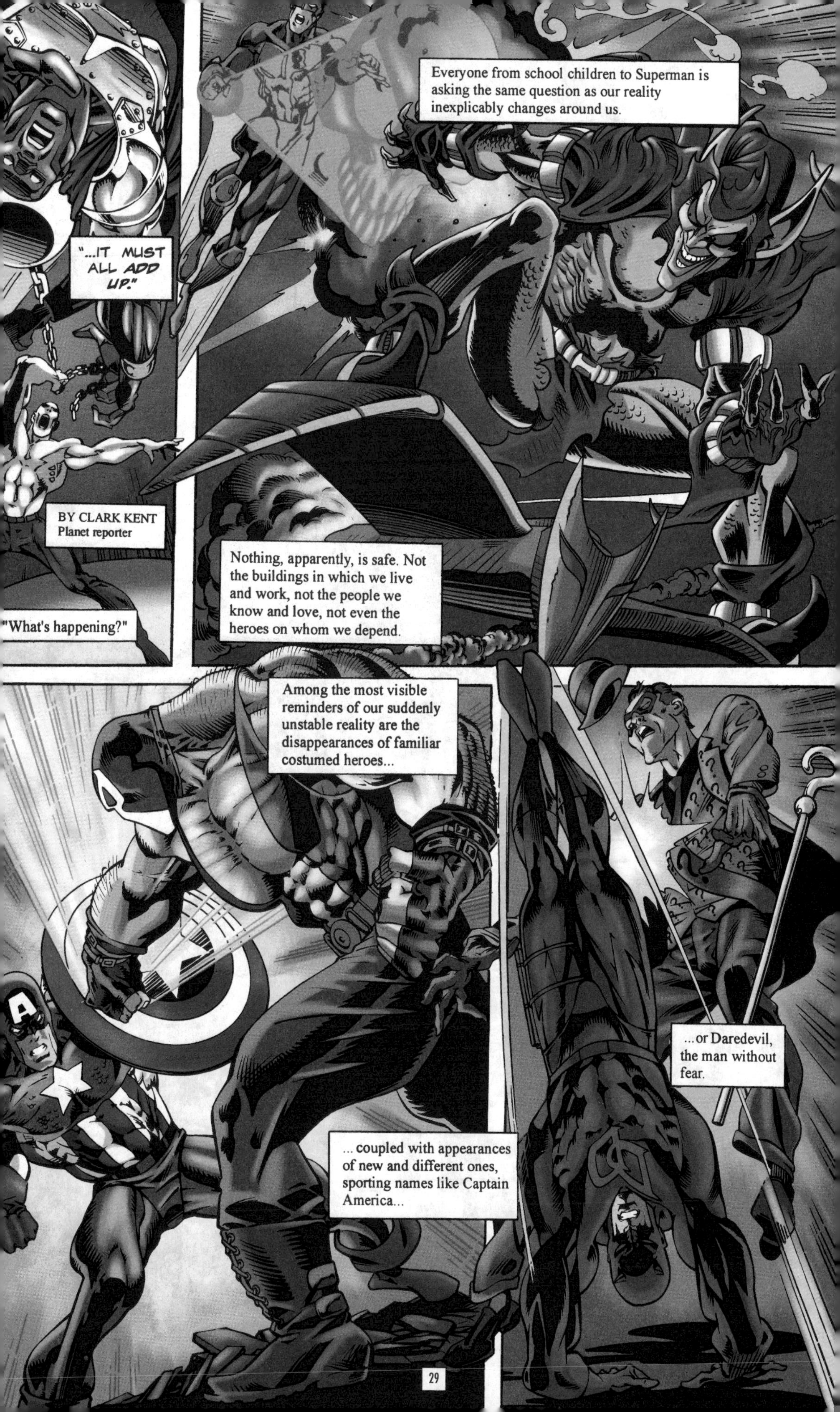

"...IT MUST ALL ADD UP."
BY CLARK KENT
Planet reporter
"What's happening?"
Everyone from school children to Superman is asking the same question as our reality inexplicably changes around us.
Nothing, apparently, is safe. Not the buildings in which we live and work, not the people we know and love, not even the heroes on whom we depend.
Among the most visible reminders of our suddenly unstable reality are the disappearances of familiar costumed heroes...
... coupled with appearances of new and different ones, sporting names like Captain America...
...or Daredevil, the man without fear.

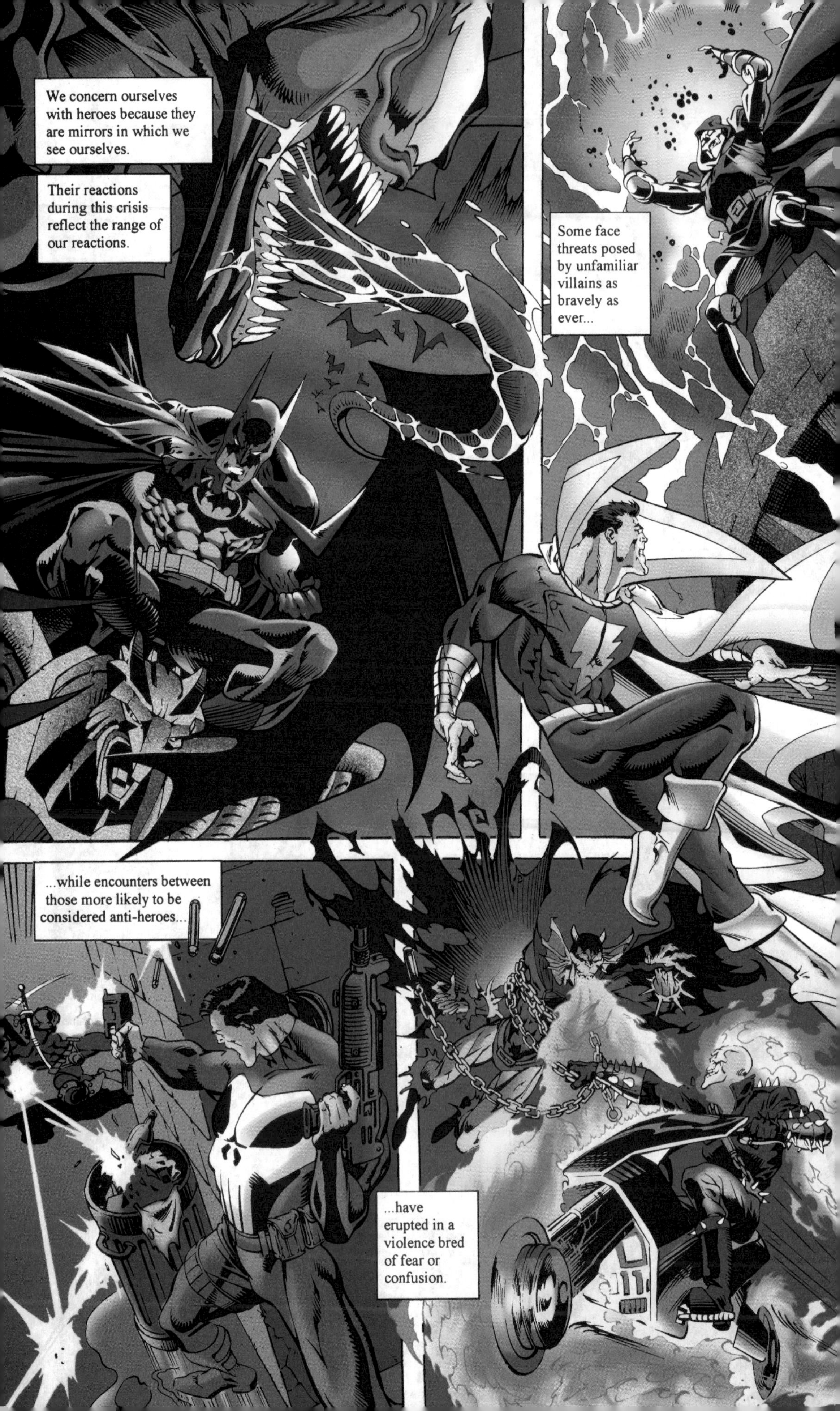
We concern ourselves with heroes because they are mirrors in which we see ourselves.
Their reactions during this crisis reflect the range of our reactions.
Some face threats posed by unfamiliar villains as bravely as ever...
...while encounters between those more likely to be considered anti-heroes...
...have erupted in a violence bred of fear or confusion.

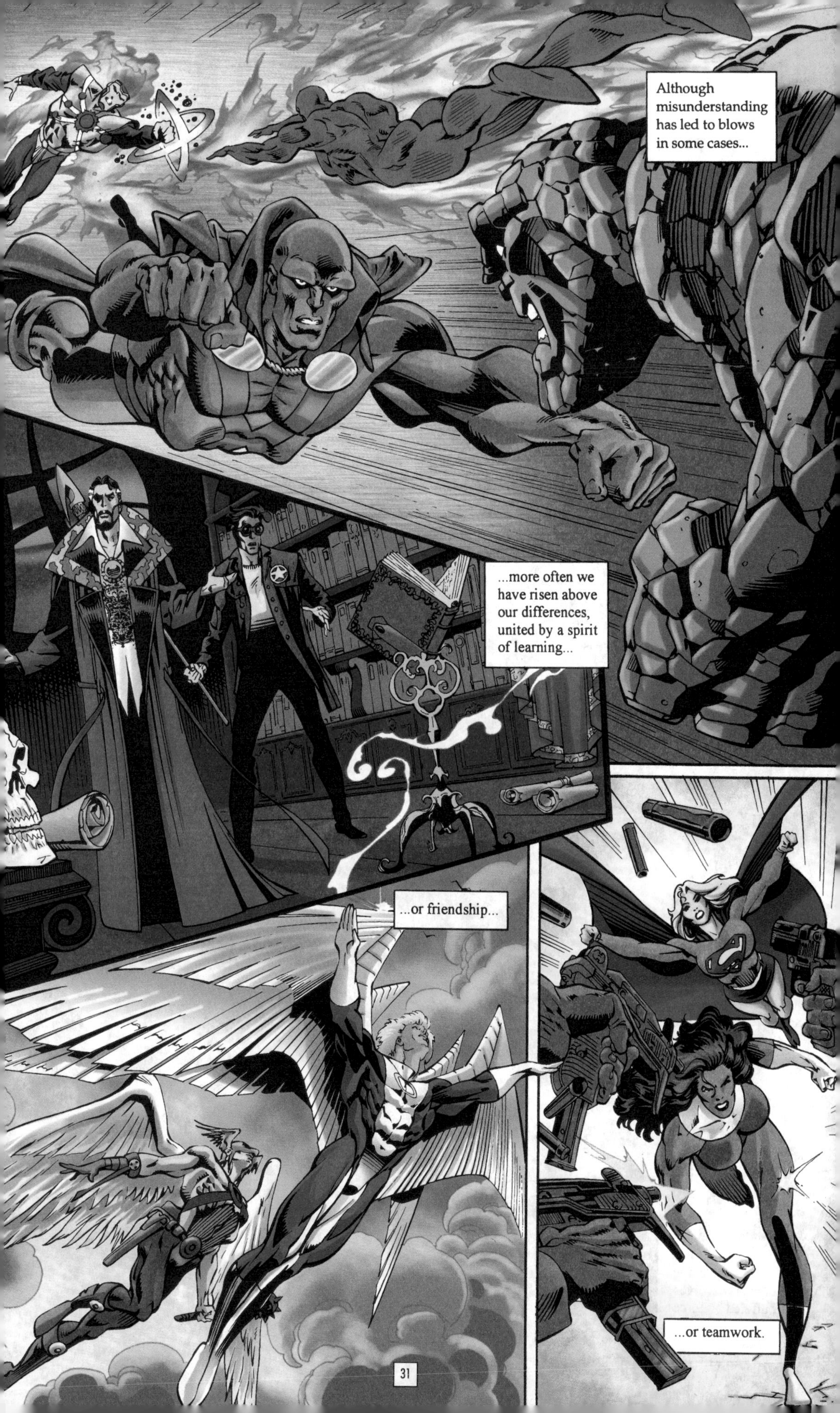

Although misunderstanding has led to blows in some cases...
...more often we have risen above our differences, united by a spirit of learning...
...or friendship...
...or teamwork.

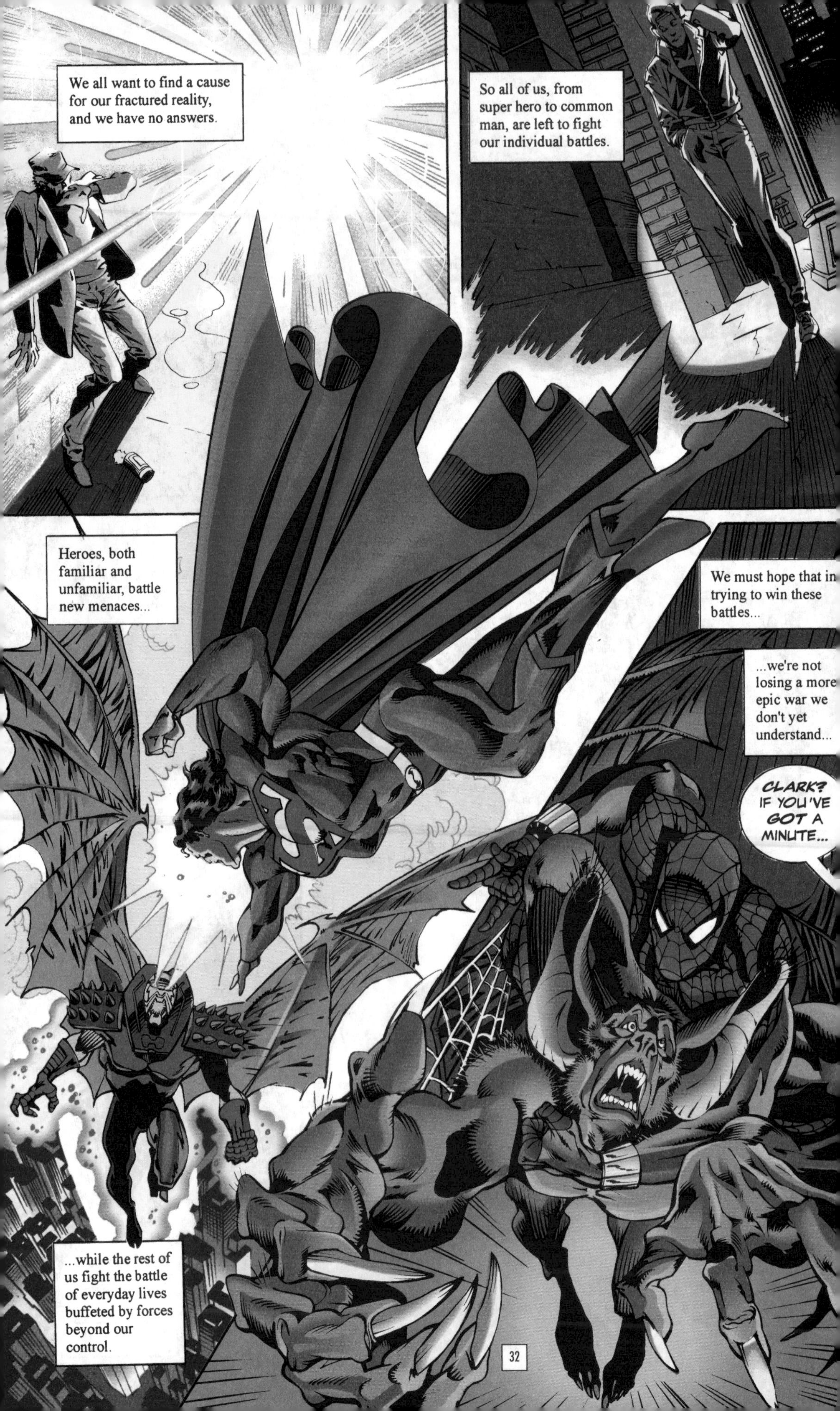
We all want to find a cause for our fractured reality, and we have no answers.
So all of us, from super hero to common man, are left to fight our individual battles.
Heroes, both familiar and unfamiliar, battle new menaces...
We must hope that in trying to win these battles...
...we're not losing a more epic war we don't yet understand...
CLARK? IF YOU'VE GOT A MINUTE...
...while the rest of us fight the battle of everyday lives buffeted by forces beyond our control.

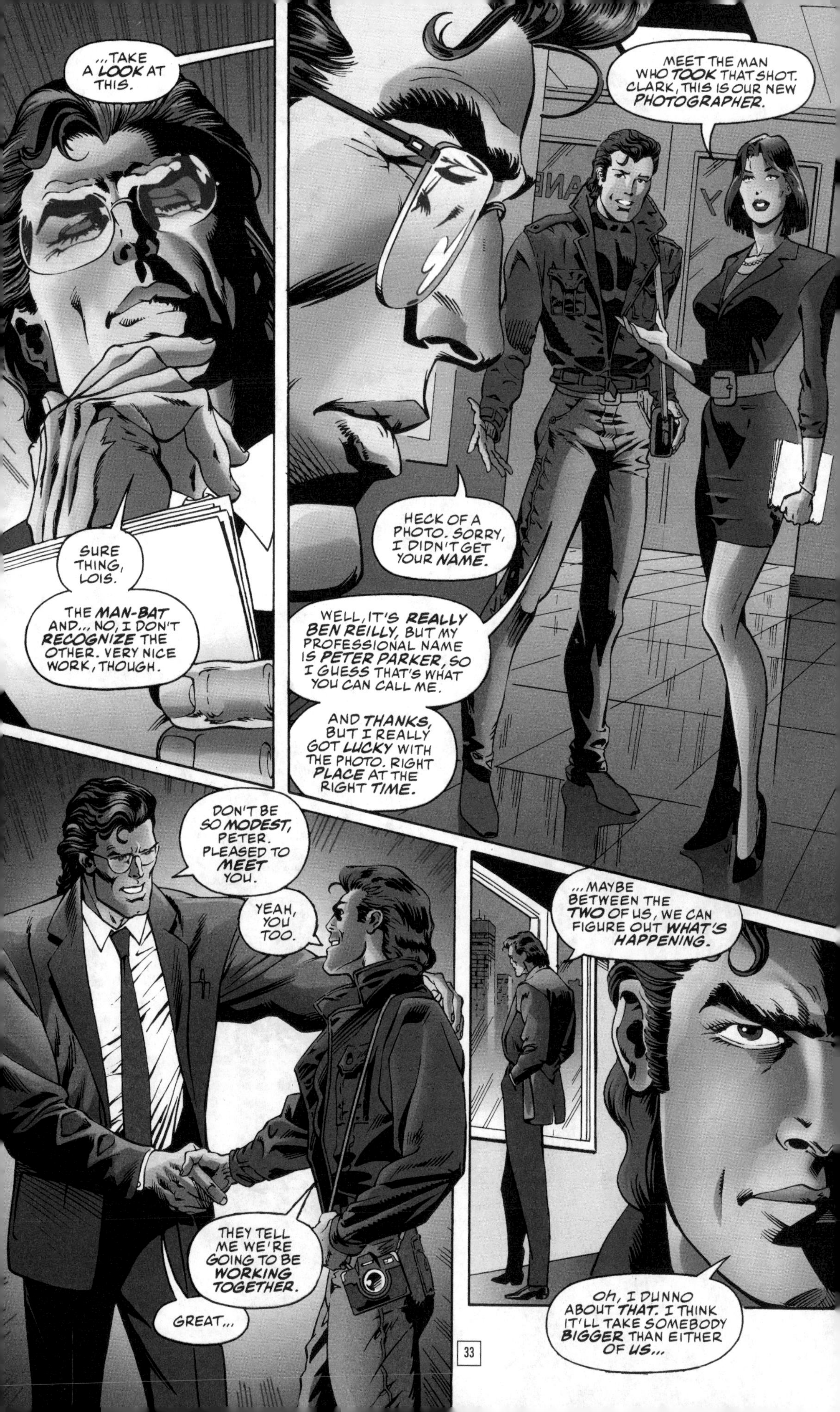
...TAKE A LOOK AT THIS.
MEET THE MAN WHO TOOK THAT SHOT. CLARK, THIS IS OUR NEW PHOTOGRAPHER.
SURE THING, LOIS.
THE MAN-BAT AND... NO, I DON'T RECOGNIZE THE OTHER. VERY NICE WORK, THOUGH.
HECK OF A PHOTO. SORRY, I DIDN'T GET YOUR NAME.
WELL, IT'S REALLY BEN REILLY, BUT MY PROFESSIONAL NAME IS PETER PARKER, SO I GUESS THAT'S WHAT YOU CAN CALL ME.
AND THANKS, BUT I REALLY GOT LUCKY WITH THE PHOTO. RIGHT PLACE AT THE RIGHT TIME.
DON'T BE SO MODEST, PETER. PLEASED TO MEET YOU.
YEAH, YOU TOO.
THEY TELL ME WE'RE GOING TO BE WORKING TOGETHER.
GREAT...
...MAYBE BETWEEN THE TWO OF US, WE CAN FIGURE OUT WHAT'S HAPPENING.
OH, I DUNNO ABOUT THAT. I THINK IT'LL TAKE SOMEBODY BIGGER THAN EITHER OF US...

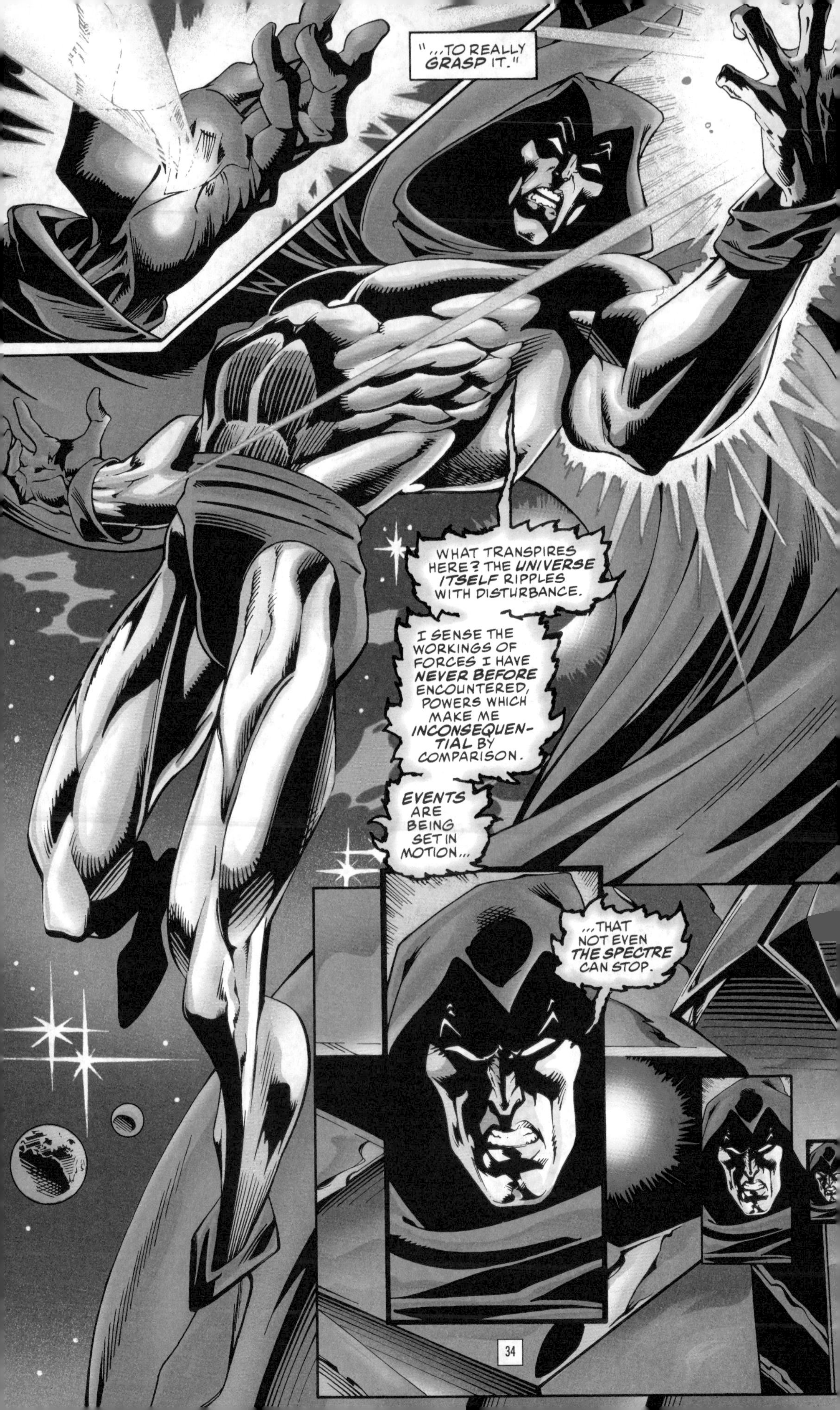
"...TO REALLY GRASP IT."
WHAT TRANSPIRES HERE? THE UNIVERSE ITSELF RIPPLES WITH DISTURBANCE.
I SENSE THE WORKINGS OF FORCES I HAVE NEVER BEFORE ENCOUNTERED, POWERS WHICH MAKE ME INCONSEQUENTIAL BY COMPARISON.
EVENTS ARE BEING SET IN MOTION...
...THAT NOT EVEN THE SPECTRE CAN STOP.

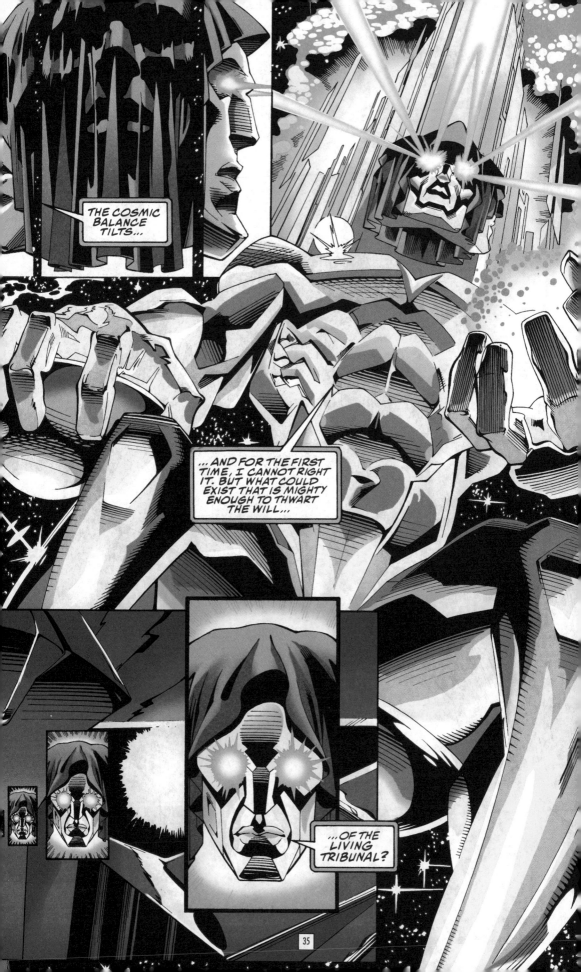

THE COSMIC BALANCE TILTS...

...AND FOR THE FIRST TIME, I CANNOT RIGHT IT. BUT WHAT COULD EXIST THAT IS MIGHTY ENOUGH TO THWART THE WILL...

...OF THE LIVING TRIBUNAL?

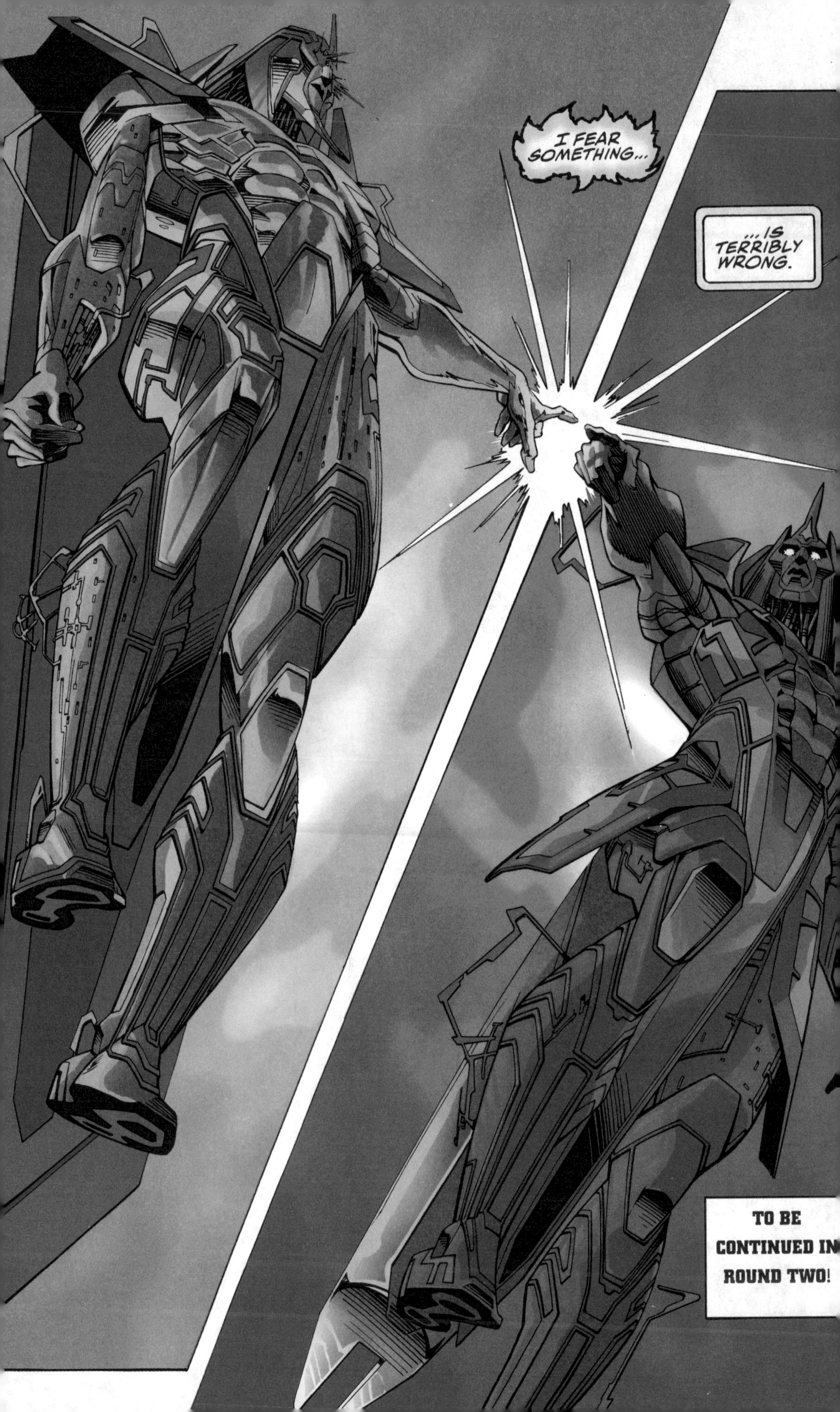
I FEAR SOMETHING...
...IS TERRIBLY WRONG.
TO BE CONTINUED IN ROUND TWO!

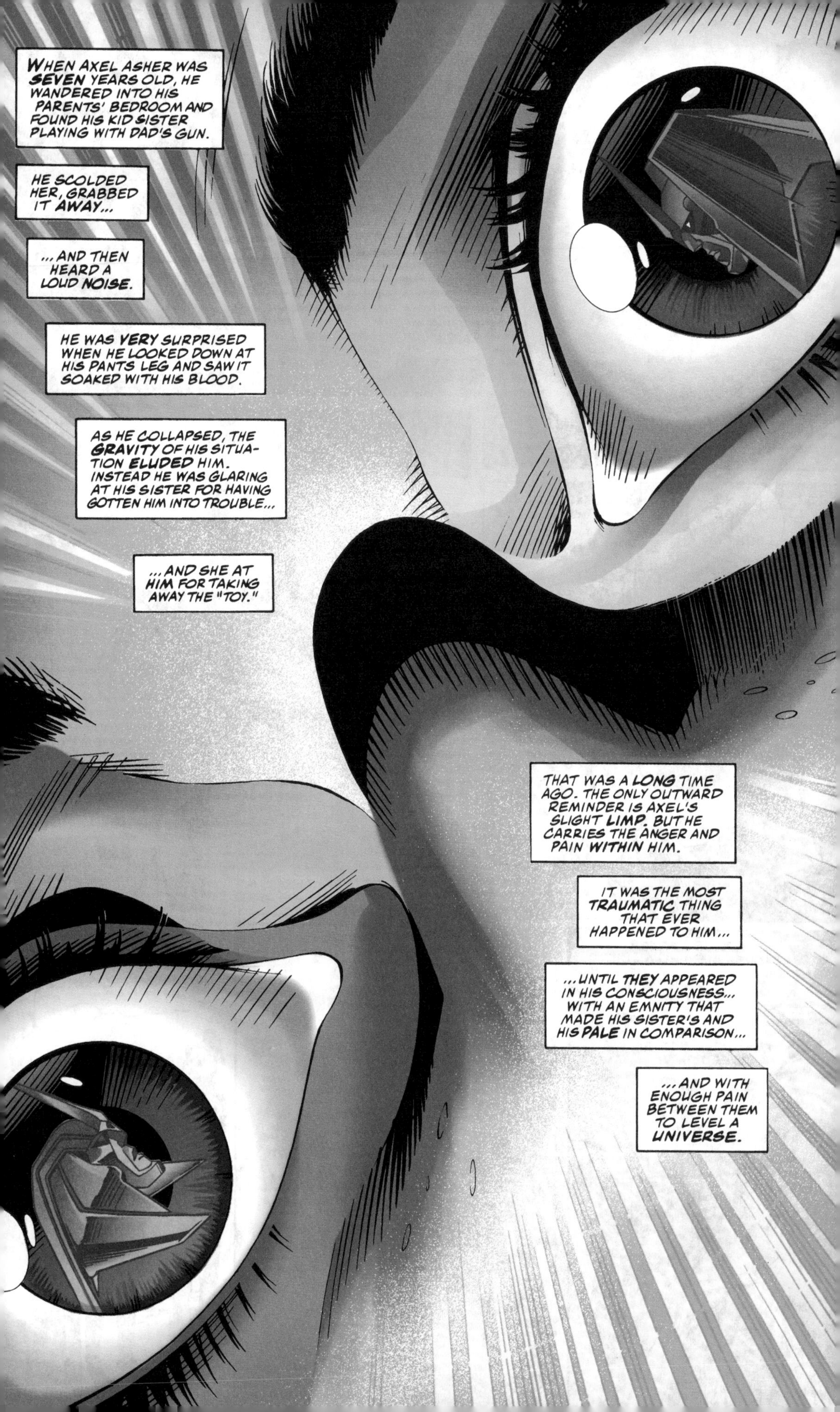
WHEN AXEL ASHER WAS SEVEN YEARS OLD, HE WANDERED INTO HIS PARENTS' BEDROOM AND FOUND HIS KID SISTER PLAYING WITH DAD'S GUN.
HE SCOLDED HER, GRABBED IT AWAY...
...AND THEN HEARD A LOUD NOISE.
HE WAS VERY SURPRISED WHEN HE LOOKED DOWN AT HIS PANTS LEG AND SAW IT SOAKED WITH HIS BLOOD.
AS HE COLLAPSED, THE GRAVITY OF HIS SITUATION ELUDED HIM. INSTEAD HE WAS GLARING AT HIS SISTER FOR HAVING GOTTEN HIM INTO TROUBLE...
...AND SHE AT HIM FOR TAKING AWAY THE "TOY."
THAT WAS A LONG TIME AGO. THE ONLY OUTWARD REMINDER IS AXEL'S SLIGHT LIMP. BUT HE CARRIES THE ANGER AND PAIN WITHIN HIM.
IT WAS THE MOST TRAUMATIC THING THAT EVER HAPPENED TO HIM...
...UNTIL THEY APPEARED IN HIS CONSCIOUSNESS... WITH AN EMNITY THAT MADE HIS SISTER'S AND HIS PALE IN COMPARISON...
...AND WITH ENOUGH PAIN BETWEEN THEM TO LEVEL A UNIVERSE.

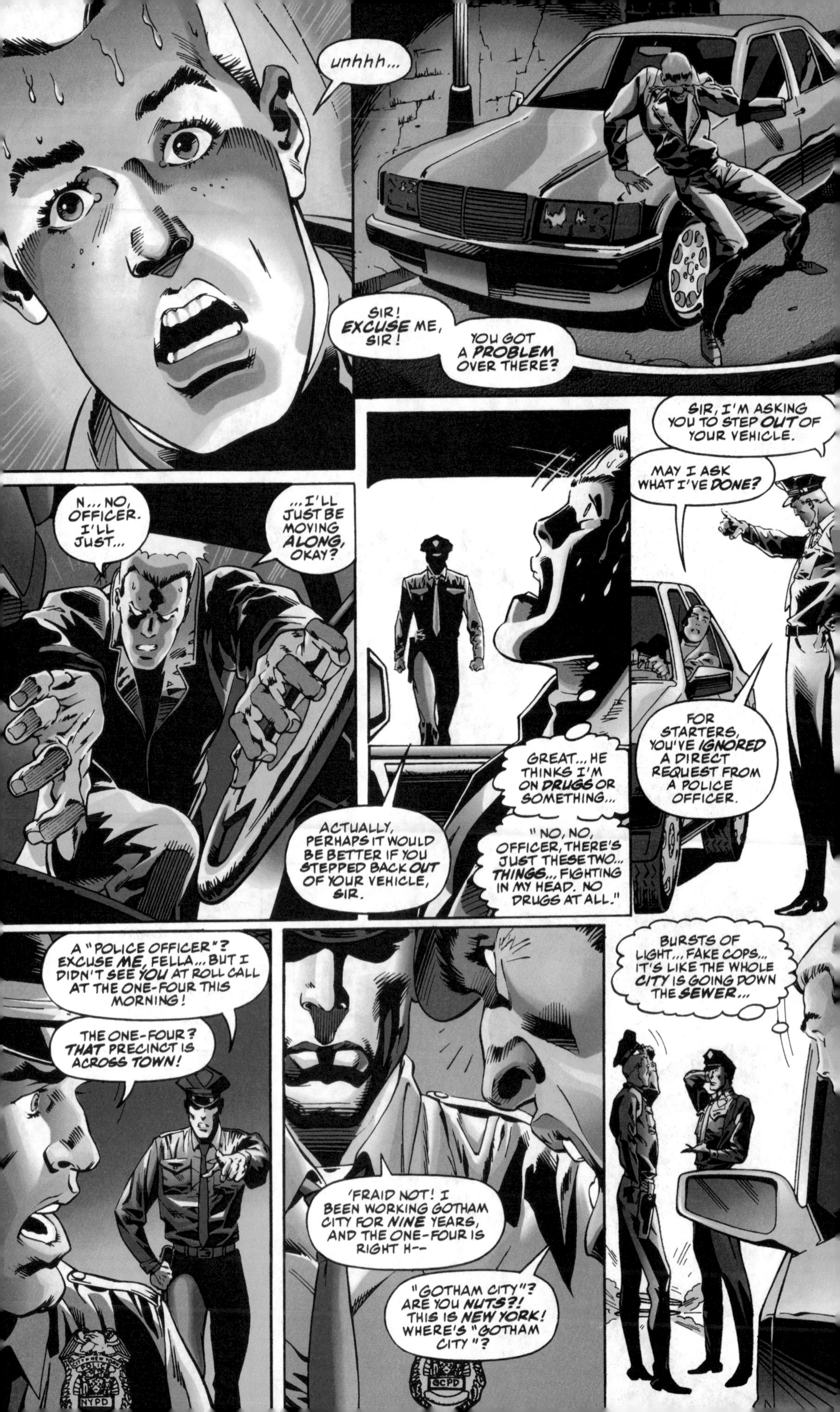
unhhh...
SIR! EXCUSE ME, SIR!
YOU GOT A PROBLEM OVER THERE?
N... NO, OFFICER. I'LL JUST...
...I'LL JUST BE MOVING ALONG, OKAY?
ACTUALLY, PERHAPS IT WOULD BE BETTER IF YOU STEPPED BACK OUT OF YOUR VEHICLE, SIR.
GREAT... HE THINKS I'M ON DRUGS OR SOMETHING...
"NO, NO, OFFICER, THERE'S JUST THESE TWO... THINGS... FIGHTING IN MY HEAD. NO DRUGS AT ALL."
SIR, I'M ASKING YOU TO STEP OUT OF YOUR VEHICLE.
MAY I ASK WHAT I'VE DONE?
FOR STARTERS, YOU'VE IGNORED A DIRECT REQUEST FROM A POLICE OFFICER.
A "POLICE OFFICER"? EXCUSE ME, FELLA... BUT I DIDN'T SEE YOU AT ROLL CALL AT THE ONE-FOUR THIS MORNING!
THE ONE-FOUR? THAT PRECINCT IS ACROSS TOWN!
NYPD
'FRAID NOT! I BEEN WORKING GOTHAM CITY FOR NINE YEARS, AND THE ONE-FOUR IS RIGHT H--
"GOTHAM CITY"? ARE YOU NUTS?! THIS IS NEW YORK! WHERE'S "GOTHAM CITY"?
GCPD
BURSTS OF LIGHT... FAKE COPS... IT'S LIKE THE WHOLE CITY IS GOING DOWN THE SEWER...

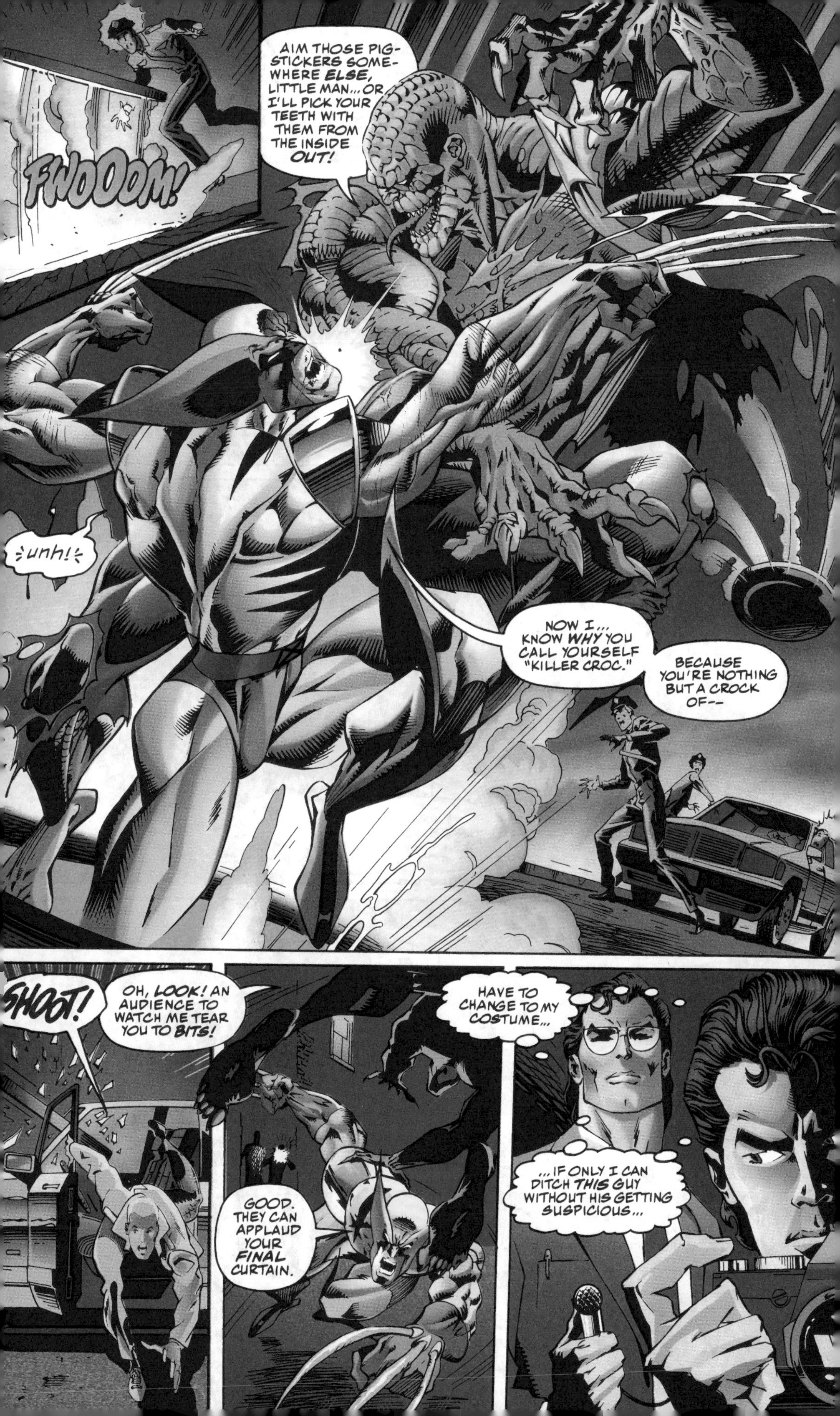
FWOOOM!
AIM THOSE PIG-STICKERS SOMEWHERE ELSE, LITTLE MAN... OR I'LL PICK YOUR TEETH WITH THEM FROM THE INSIDE OUT!
unh!
NOW I... KNOW WHY YOU CALL YOURSELF "KILLER CROC."
BECAUSE YOU'RE NOTHING BUT A CROCK OF--
SHOOT!
OH, LOOK! AN AUDIENCE TO WATCH ME TEAR YOU TO BITS!
GOOD. THEY CAN APPLAUD YOUR FINAL CURTAIN.
HAVE TO CHANGE TO MY COSTUME...
...IF ONLY I CAN DITCH THIS GUY WITHOUT HIS GETTING SUSPICIOUS...

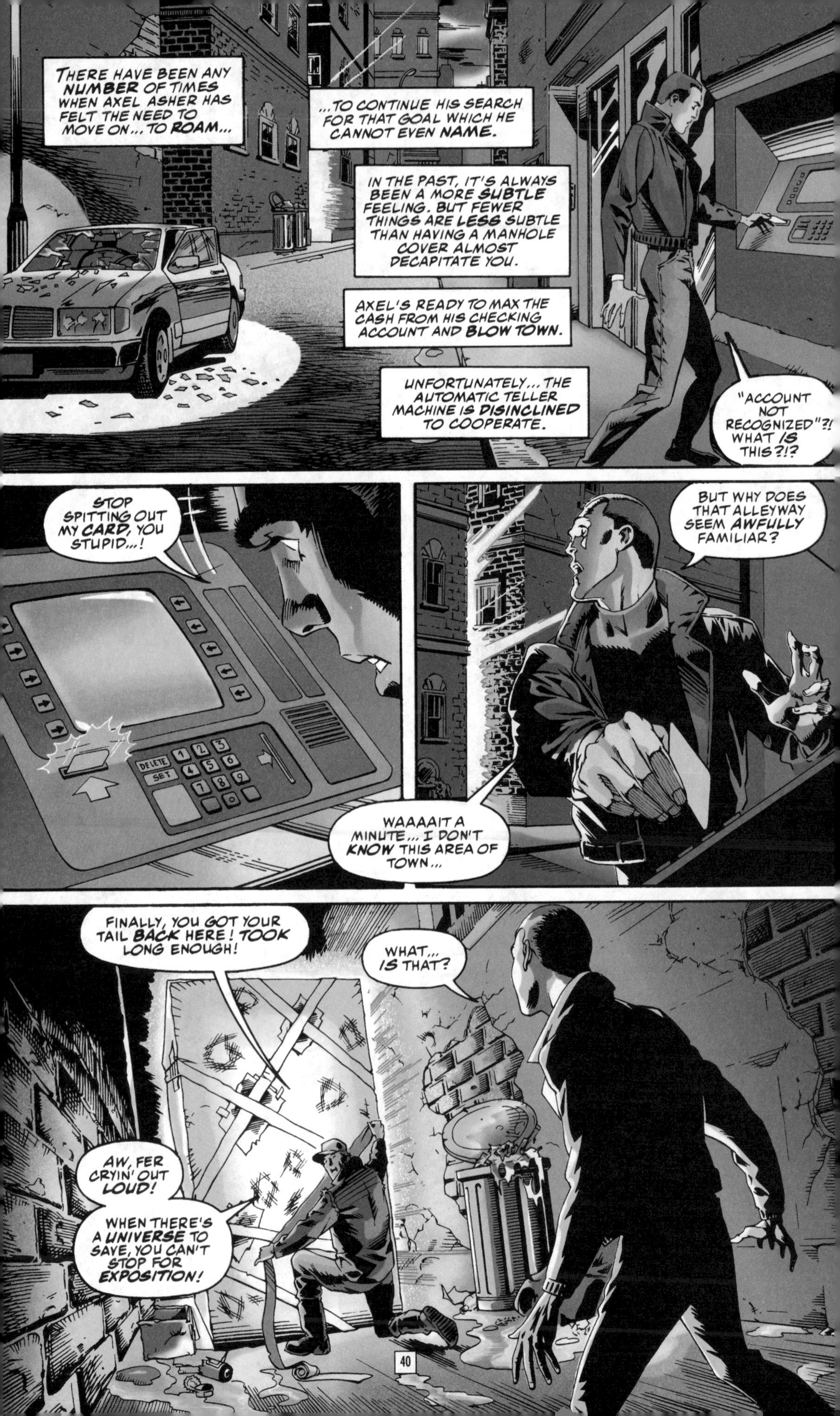

THERE HAVE BEEN ANY NUMBER OF TIMES WHEN AXEL ASHER HAS FELT THE NEED TO MOVE ON... TO ROAM...
...TO CONTINUE HIS SEARCH FOR THAT GOAL WHICH HE CANNOT EVEN NAME.
IN THE PAST, IT'S ALWAYS BEEN A MORE SUBTLE FEELING. BUT FEWER THINGS ARE LESS SUBTLE THAN HAVING A MANHOLE COVER ALMOST DECAPITATE YOU.
AXEL'S READY TO MAX THE CASH FROM HIS CHECKING ACCOUNT AND BLOW TOWN.
UNFORTUNATELY... THE AUTOMATIC TELLER MACHINE IS DISINCLINED TO COOPERATE.
"ACCOUNT NOT RECOGNIZED"?! WHAT IS THIS?!?
STOP SPITTING OUT MY CARD, YOU STUPID...!
DELETE
SET
BUT WHY DOES THAT ALLEYWAY SEEM AWFULLY FAMILIAR?
WAAAAIT A MINUTE... I DON'T KNOW THIS AREA OF TOWN...
FINALLY, YOU GOT YOUR TAIL BACK HERE! TOOK LONG ENOUGH!
WHAT... IS THAT?
AW, FER CRYIN' OUT LOUD!
WHEN THERE'S A UNIVERSE TO SAVE, YOU CAN'T STOP FOR EXPOSITION!

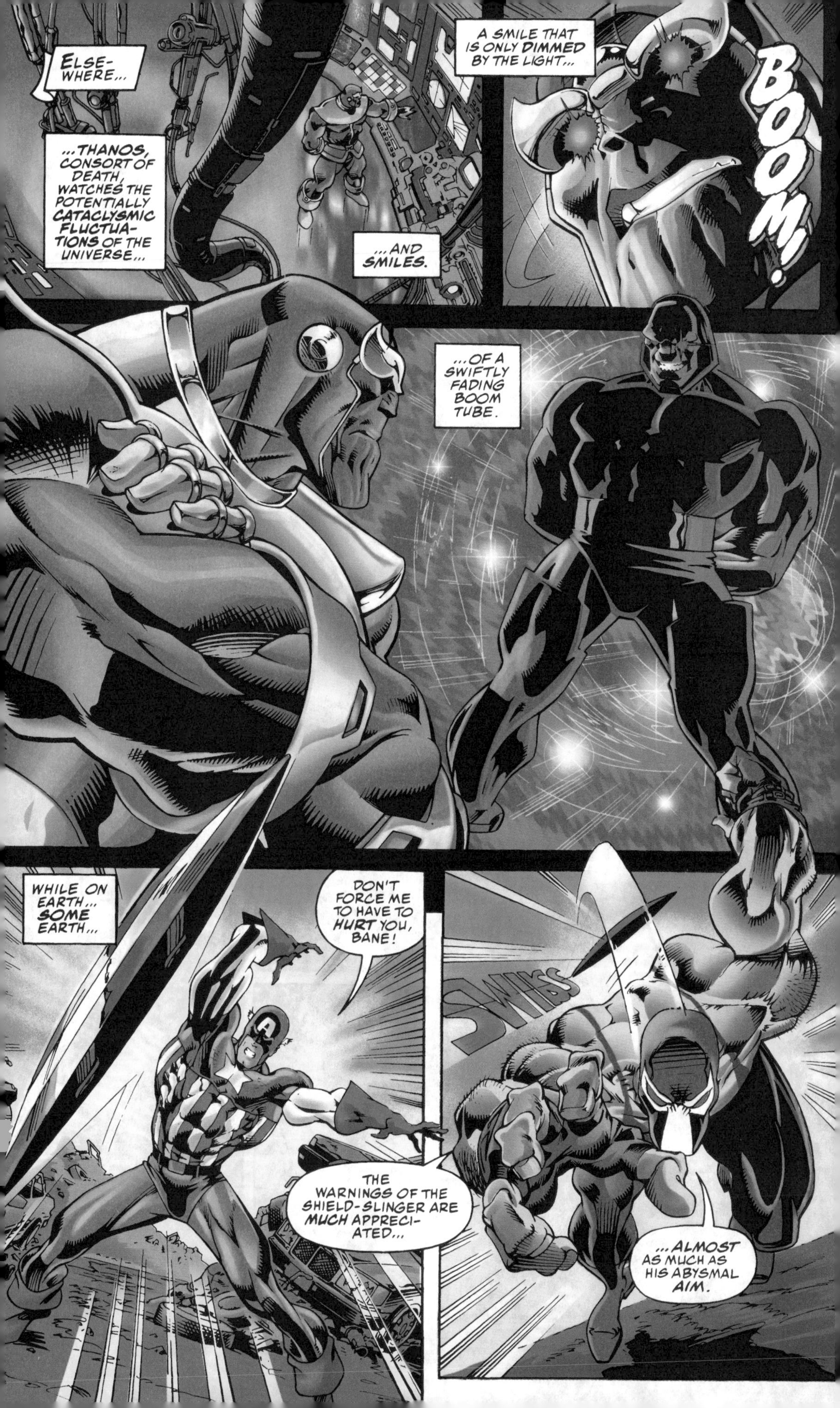
ELSE-WHERE...
...THANOS, CONSORT OF DEATH, WATCHES THE POTENTIALLY CATACLYSMIC FLUCTUATIONS OF THE UNIVERSE...
...AND SMILES.
A SMILE THAT IS ONLY DIMMED BY THE LIGHT...
BOOOM!
...OF A SWIFTLY FADING BOOM TUBE.
WHILE ON EARTH... SOME EARTH...
DON'T FORCE ME TO HAVE TO HURT YOU, BANE!
THE WARNINGS OF THE SHIELD-SLINGER ARE MUCH APPRECIATED...
SWISS
...ALMOST AS MUCH AS HIS ABYSMAL AIM.

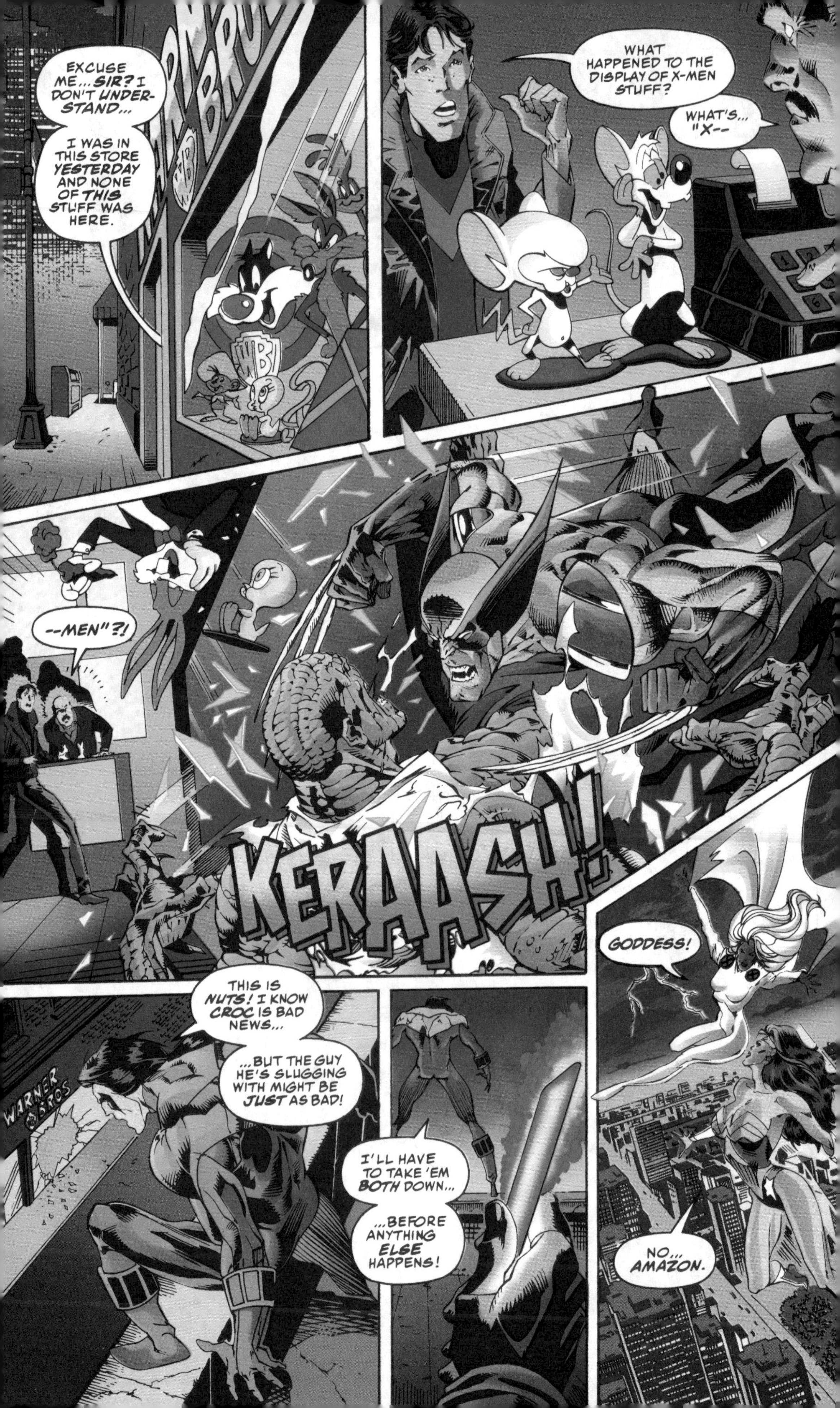

EXCUSE ME... SIR? I DON'T UNDERSTAND...
I WAS IN THIS STORE YESTERDAY AND NONE OF THIS STUFF WAS HERE.
WHAT HAPPENED TO THE DISPLAY OF X-MEN STUFF?
WHAT'S... "X--
--MEN"?!
KERAASH!
THIS IS NUTS! I KNOW CROC IS BAD NEWS...
...BUT THE GUY HE'S SLUGGING WITH MIGHT BE JUST AS BAD!
I'LL HAVE TO TAKE 'EM BOTH DOWN...
...BEFORE ANYTHING ELSE HAPPENS!
GODDESS!
NO... AMAZON.

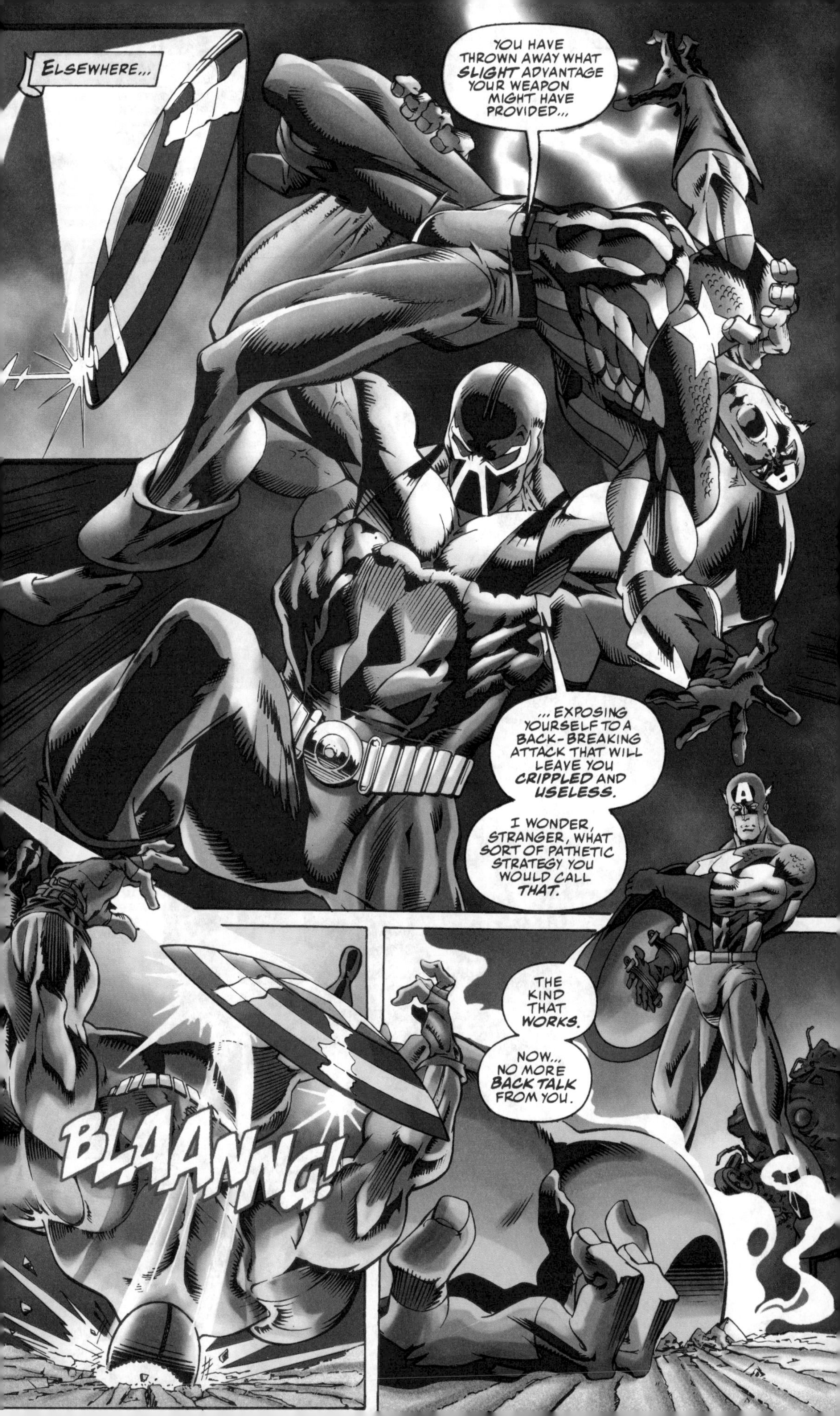

ELSEWHERE...
YOU HAVE THROWN AWAY WHAT SLIGHT ADVANTAGE YOUR WEAPON MIGHT HAVE PROVIDED...
...EXPOSING YOURSELF TO A BACK-BREAKING ATTACK THAT WILL LEAVE YOU CRIPPLED AND USELESS.
I WONDER, STRANGER, WHAT SORT OF PATHETIC STRATEGY YOU WOULD CALL THAT.
THE KIND THAT WORKS.
NOW... NO MORE BACK TALK FROM YOU.
BLAANNG!

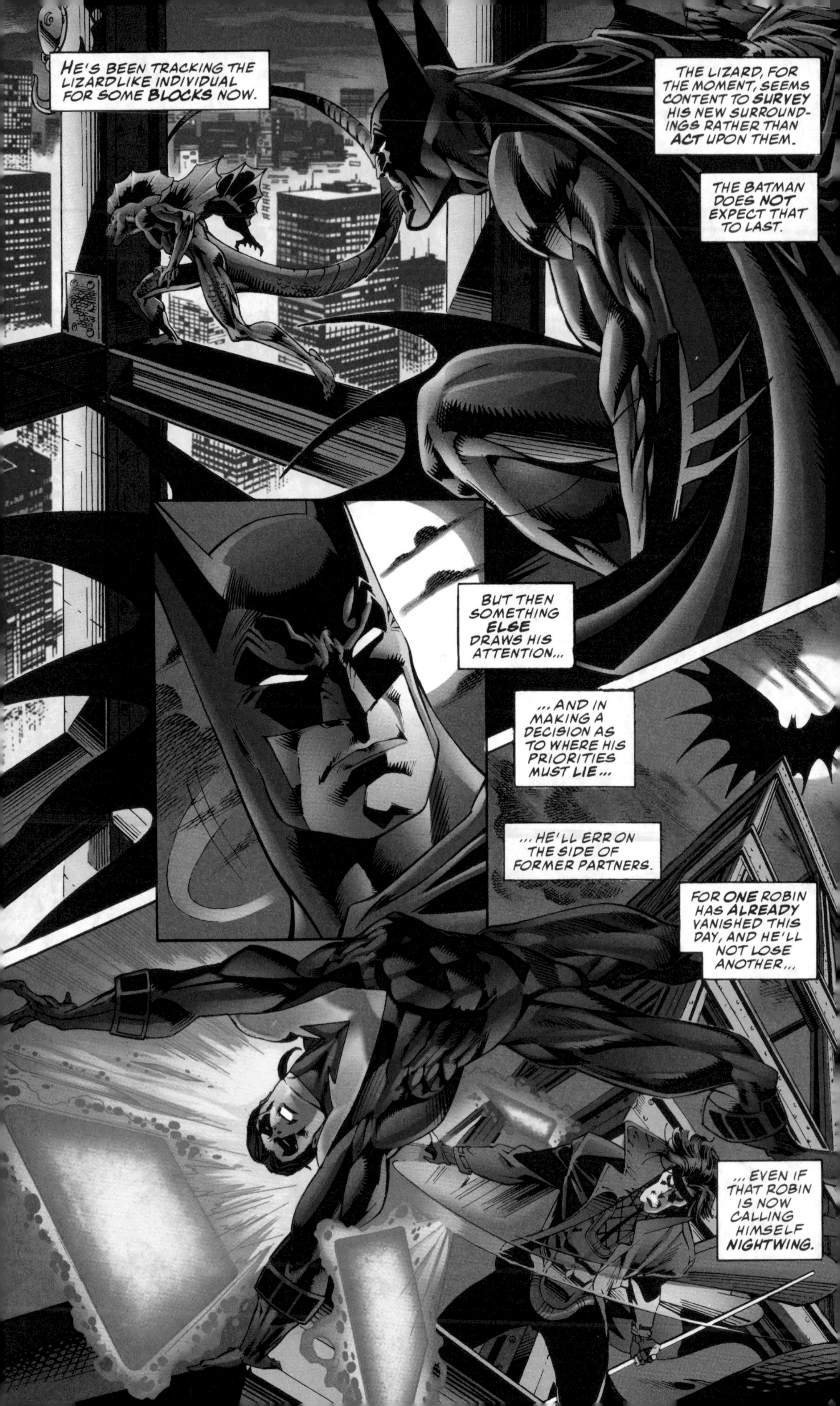
HE'S BEEN TRACKING THE LIZARDLIKE INDIVIDUAL FOR SOME BLOCKS NOW.
THE LIZARD, FOR THE MOMENT, SEEMS CONTENT TO SURVEY HIS NEW SURROUNDINGS RATHER THAN ACT UPON THEM.
THE BATMAN DOES NOT EXPECT THAT TO LAST.
BUT THEN SOMETHING ELSE DRAWS HIS ATTENTION...
...AND IN MAKING A DECISION AS TO WHERE HIS PRIORITIES MUST LIE...
...HE'LL ERR ON THE SIDE OF FORMER PARTNERS.
FOR ONE ROBIN HAS ALREADY VANISHED THIS DAY, AND HE'LL NOT LOSE ANOTHER...
...EVEN IF THAT ROBIN IS NOW CALLING HIMSELF NIGHTWING.

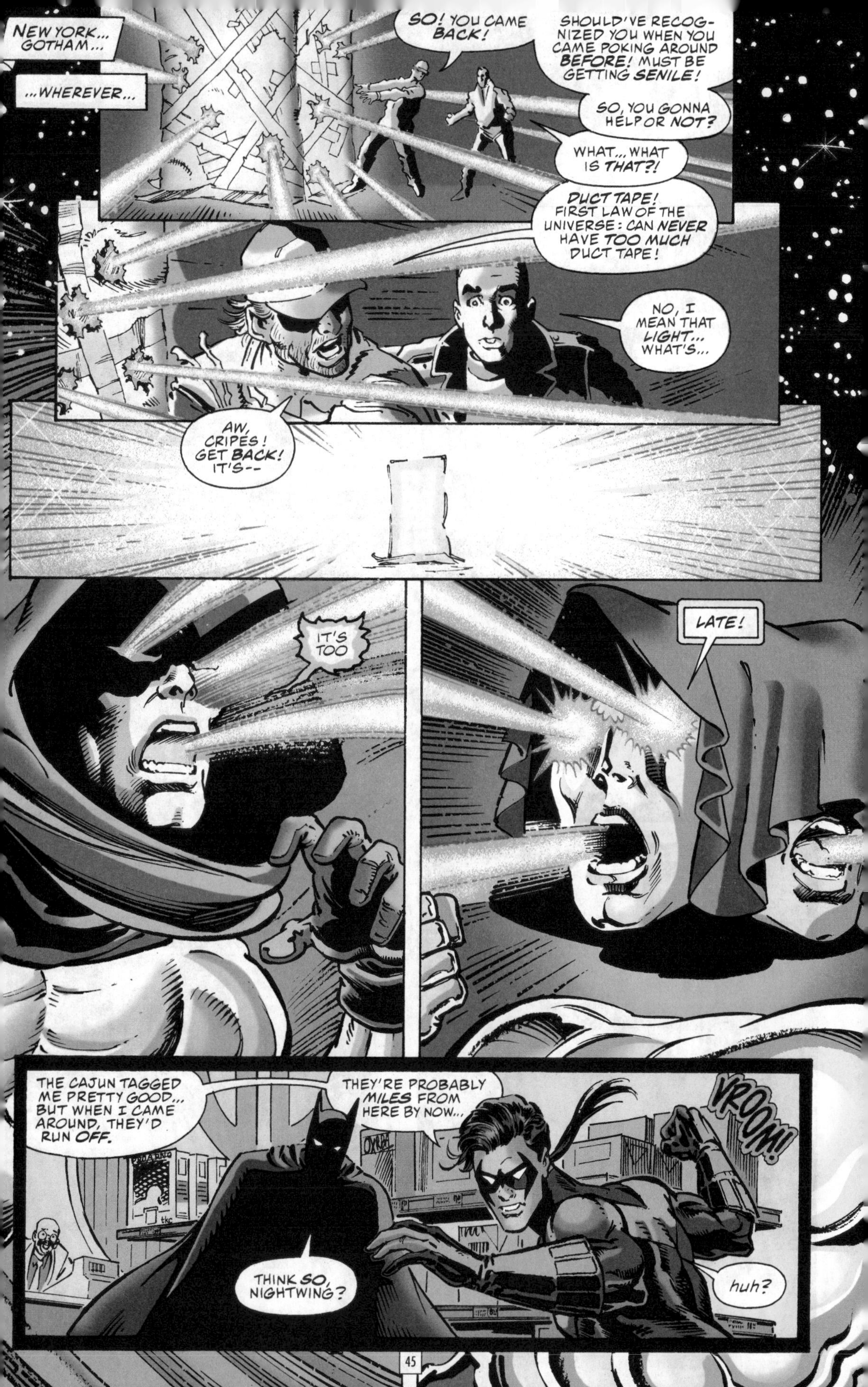

NEW YORK... GOTHAM...
...WHEREVER...
SO! YOU CAME BACK!
SHOULD'VE RECOGNIZED YOU WHEN YOU CAME POKING AROUND BEFORE! MUST BE GETTING SENILE!
SO, YOU GONNA HELP OR NOT?
WHAT... WHAT IS THAT?!
DUCT TAPE! FIRST LAW OF THE UNIVERSE: CAN NEVER HAVE TOO MUCH DUCT TAPE!
NO, I MEAN THAT LIGHT... WHAT'S...
AW, CRIPES! GET BACK! IT'S--
IT'S TOO
LATE!
THE CAJUN TAGGED ME PRETTY GOOD... BUT WHEN I CAME AROUND, THEY'D RUN OFF.
THEY'RE PROBABLY MILES FROM HERE BY NOW...
VROOM!
THINK SO, NIGHTWING?
huh?

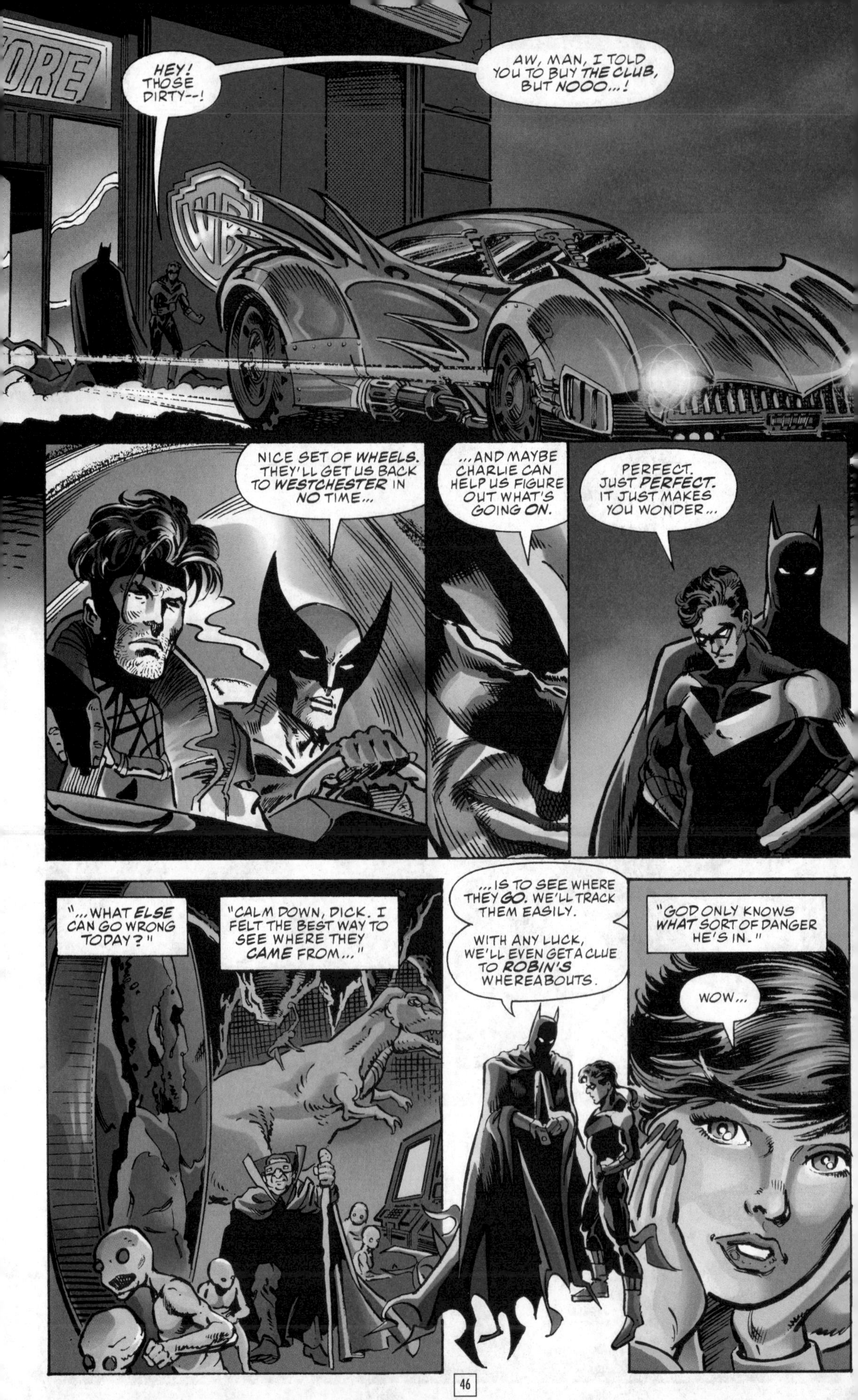

ORE
HEY! THOSE DIRTY--!
AW, MAN, I TOLD YOU TO BUY THE CLUB, BUT NOOO...!
NICE SET OF WHEELS. THEY'LL GET US BACK TO WESTCHESTER IN NO TIME...
...AND MAYBE CHARLIE CAN HELP US FIGURE OUT WHAT'S GOING ON.
PERFECT. JUST PERFECT. IT JUST MAKES YOU WONDER...
"...WHAT ELSE CAN GO WRONG TODAY?"
"CALM DOWN, DICK. I FELT THE BEST WAY TO SEE WHERE THEY CAME FROM..."
...IS TO SEE WHERE THEY GO. WE'LL TRACK THEM EASILY.
WITH ANY LUCK, WE'LL EVEN GET A CLUE TO ROBIN'S WHEREABOUTS.
"GOD ONLY KNOWS WHAT SORT OF DANGER HE'S IN."
WOW...

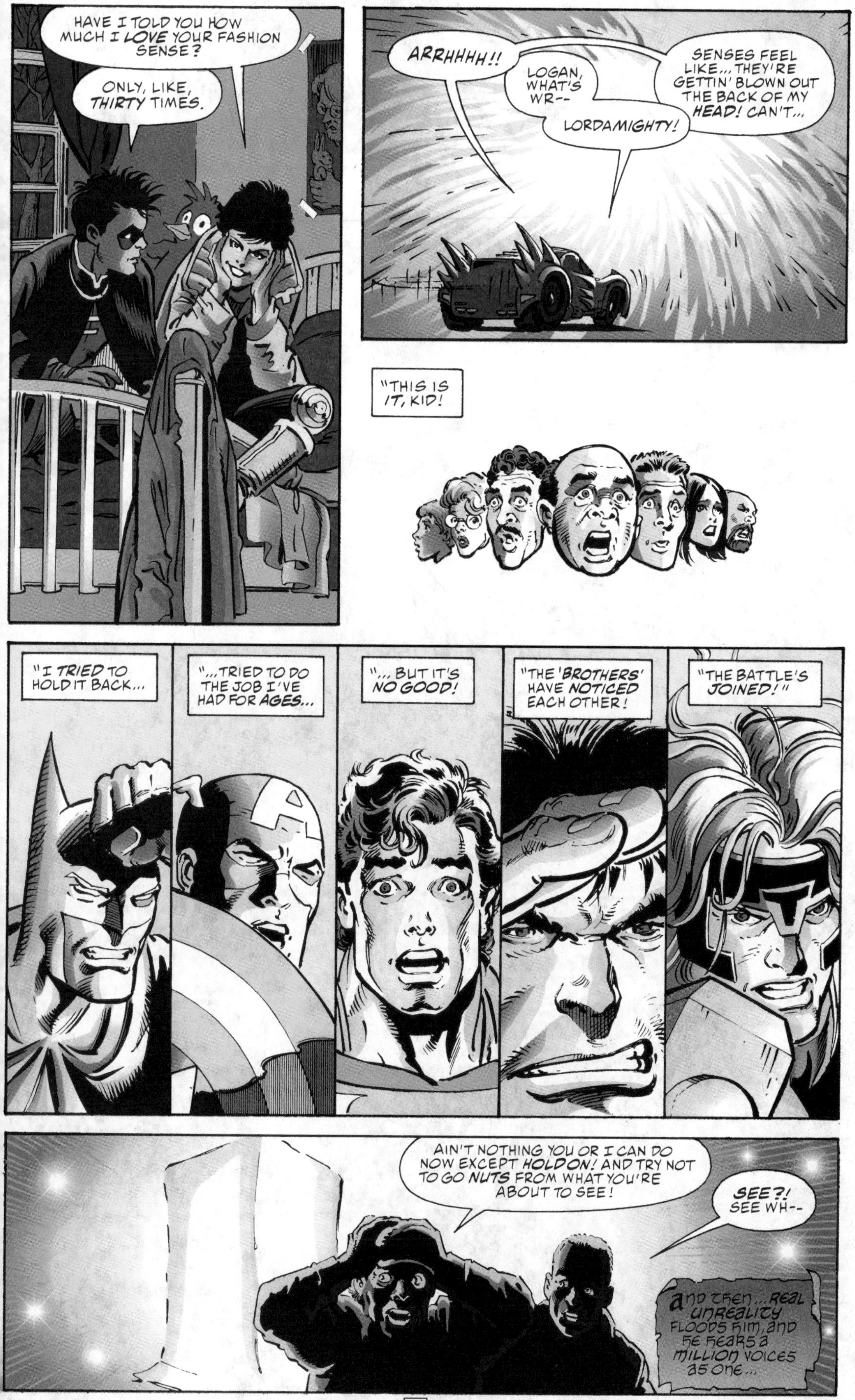
HAVE I TOLD YOU HOW MUCH I LOVE YOUR FASHION SENSE?
ONLY, LIKE, THIRTY TIMES.
ARRHHHH!!
LOGAN, WHAT'S WR--
SENSES FEEL LIKE... THEY'RE GETTIN' BLOWN OUT THE BACK OF MY HEAD! CAN'T...
LORDAMIGHTY!
"THIS IS IT, KID!
"I TRIED TO HOLD IT BACK...
"...TRIED TO DO THE JOB I'VE HAD FOR AGES...
"...BUT IT'S NO GOOD!
"THE 'BROTHERS' HAVE NOTICED EACH OTHER!
"THE BATTLE'S JOINED!"
AIN'T NOTHING YOU OR I CAN DO NOW EXCEPT HOLD ON! AND TRY NOT TO GO NUTS FROM WHAT YOU'RE ABOUT TO SEE!
SEE?! SEE WH--
And then... real unreality floods him, and he hears a million voices as one...

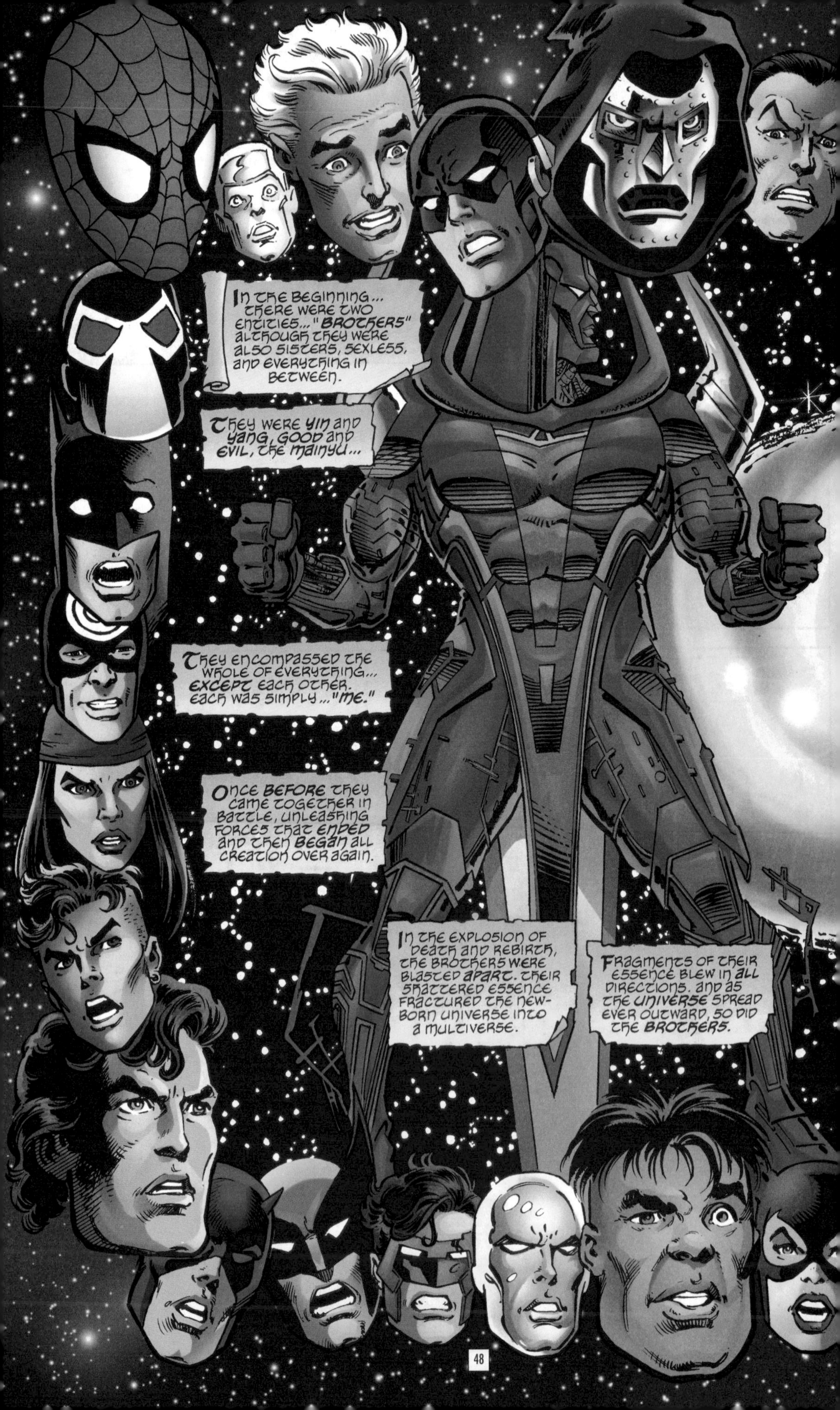

IN THE BEGINNING... THERE WERE TWO ENTITIES... "BROTHERS" ALTHOUGH THEY WERE ALSO SISTERS, SEXLESS, AND EVERYTHING IN BETWEEN.
THEY WERE YIN AND YANG, GOOD AND EVIL, THE MAINYU...
THEY ENCOMPASSED THE WHOLE OF EVERYTHING... EXCEPT EACH OTHER. EACH WAS SIMPLY..."ME."
ONCE BEFORE THEY CAME TOGETHER IN BATTLE, UNLEASHING FORCES THAT ENDED AND THEN BEGAN ALL CREATION OVER AGAIN.
IN THE EXPLOSION OF DEATH AND REBIRTH, THE BROTHERS WERE BLASTED APART. THEIR SHATTERED ESSENCE FRACTURED THE NEW-BORN UNIVERSE INTO A MULTIVERSE.
FRAGMENTS OF THEIR ESSENCE BLEW IN ALL DIRECTIONS. AND AS THE UNIVERSE SPREAD EVER OUTWARD, SO DID THE BROTHERS.

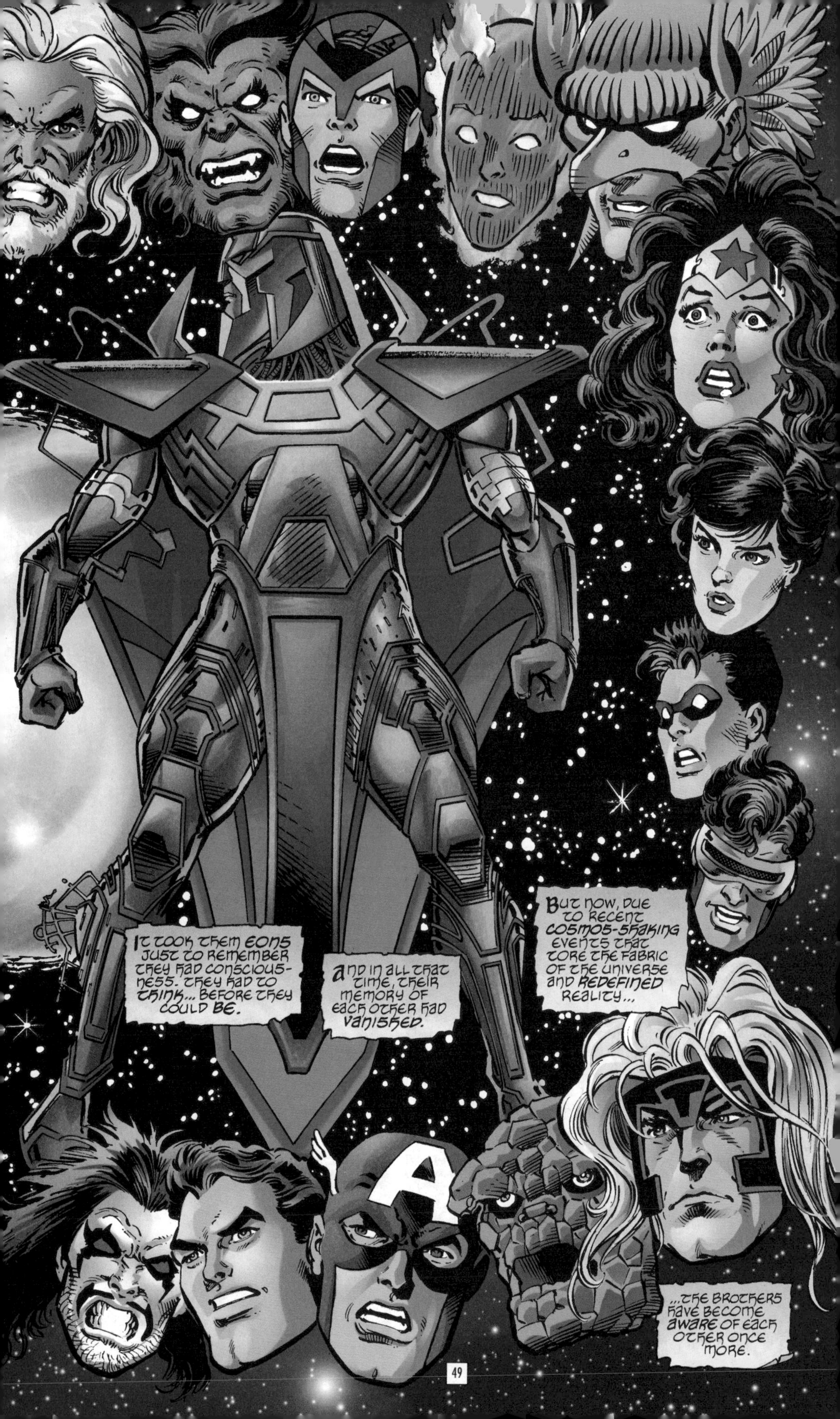
IT TOOK THEM EONS JUST TO REMEMBER THEY HAD CONSCIOUS-NESS. THEY HAD TO THINK... BEFORE THEY COULD BE.
AND IN ALL THAT TIME, THEIR MEMORY OF EACH OTHER HAD VANISHED.
BUT NOW, DUE TO RECENT COSMOS-SHAKING EVENTS THAT TORE THE FABRIC OF THE UNIVERSE AND REDEFINED REALITY...
...THE BROTHERS HAVE BECOME AWARE OF EACH OTHER ONCE MORE.

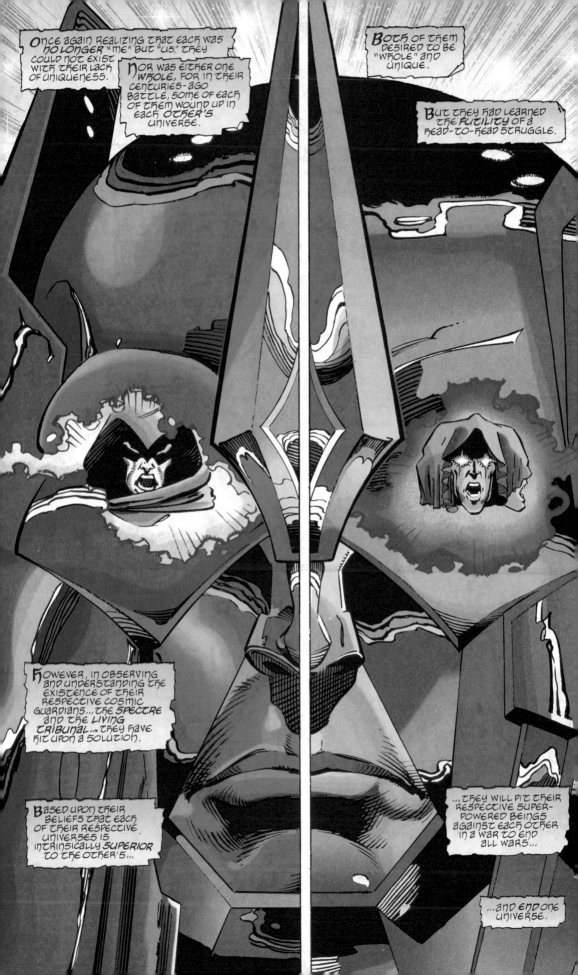

ONCE AGAIN REALIZING THAT EACH WAS NO LONGER "ME" BUT "US," THEY COULD NOT EXIST WITH THEIR LACK OF UNIQUENESS.

NOR WAS EITHER ONE WHOLE, FOR IN THEIR CENTURIES-AGO BATTLE, SOME OF EACH OF THEM WOUND UP IN EACH OTHER'S UNIVERSE.

BOTH OF THEM DESIRED TO BE "WHOLE" AND UNIQUE.

BUT THEY HAD LEARNED THE FUTILITY OF A HEAD-TO-HEAD STRUGGLE.

HOWEVER, IN OBSERVING AND UNDERSTANDING THE EXISTENCE OF THEIR RESPECTIVE COSMIC GUARDIANS... THE SPECTRE AND THE LIVING TRIBUNAL... THEY HAVE HIT UPON A SOLUTION.

BASED UPON THEIR BELIEFS THAT EACH OF THEIR RESPECTIVE UNIVERSES IS INTRINSICALLY SUPERIOR TO THE OTHER'S...

...THEY WILL PIT THEIR RESPECTIVE SUPER-POWERED BEINGS AGAINST EACH OTHER IN A WAR TO END ALL WARS...

...AND END ONE UNIVERSE.

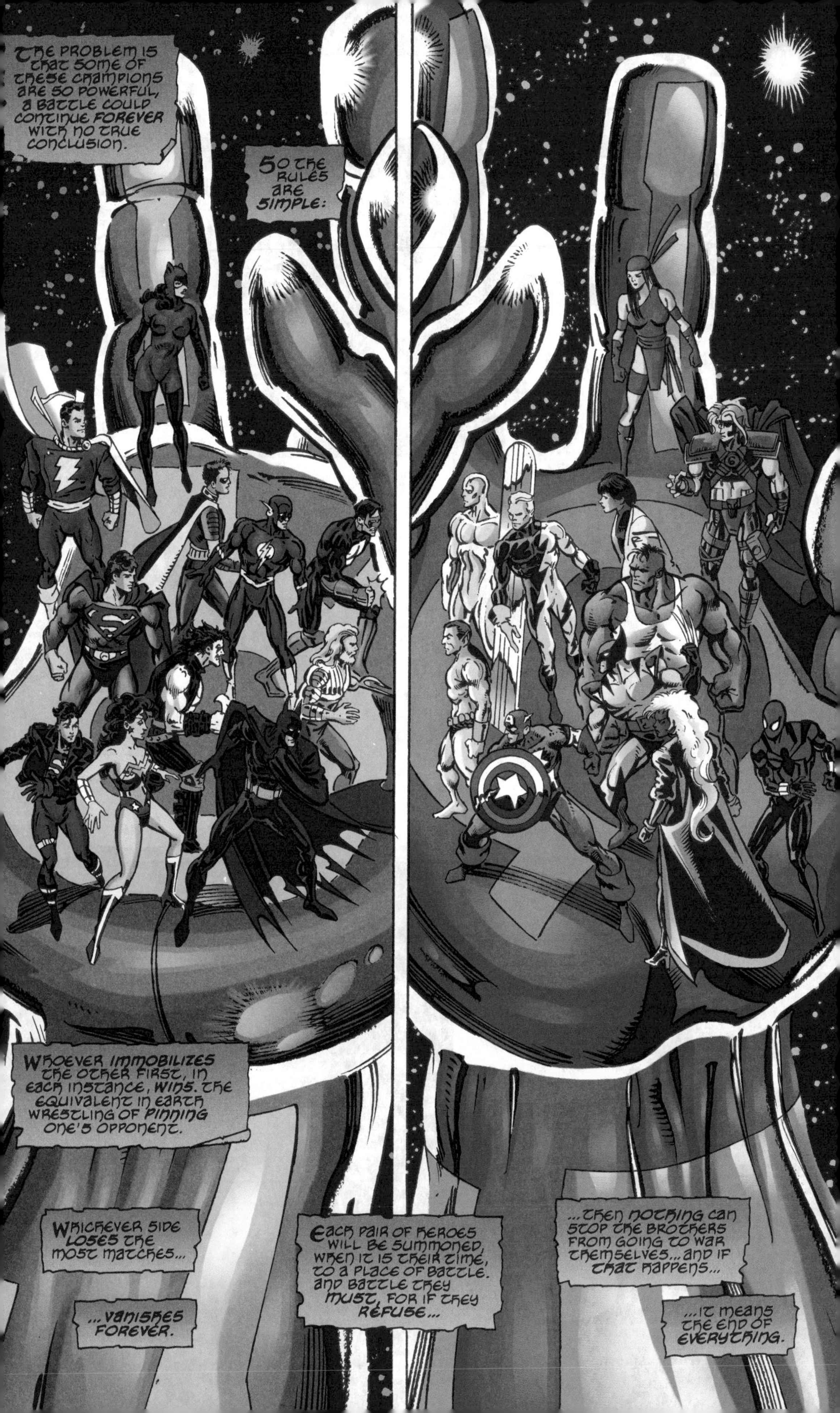

THE PROBLEM IS THAT SOME OF THESE CHAMPIONS ARE SO POWERFUL, A BATTLE COULD CONTINUE FOREVER WITH NO TRUE CONCLUSION.
SO THE RULES ARE SIMPLE:
WHOEVER IMMOBILIZES THE OTHER FIRST, IN EACH INSTANCE, WINS. THE EQUIVALENT IN EARTH WRESTLING OF PINNING ONE'S OPPONENT.
WHICHEVER SIDE LOSES THE MOST MATCHES...
...VANISHES FOREVER.
EACH PAIR OF HEROES WILL BE SUMMONED, WHEN IT IS THEIR TIME, TO A PLACE OF BATTLE. AND BATTLE THEY MUST, FOR IF THEY REFUSE...
...THEN NOTHING CAN STOP THE BROTHERS FROM GOING TO WAR THEMSELVES... AND IF THAT HAPPENS...
...IT MEANS THE END OF EVERYTHING.

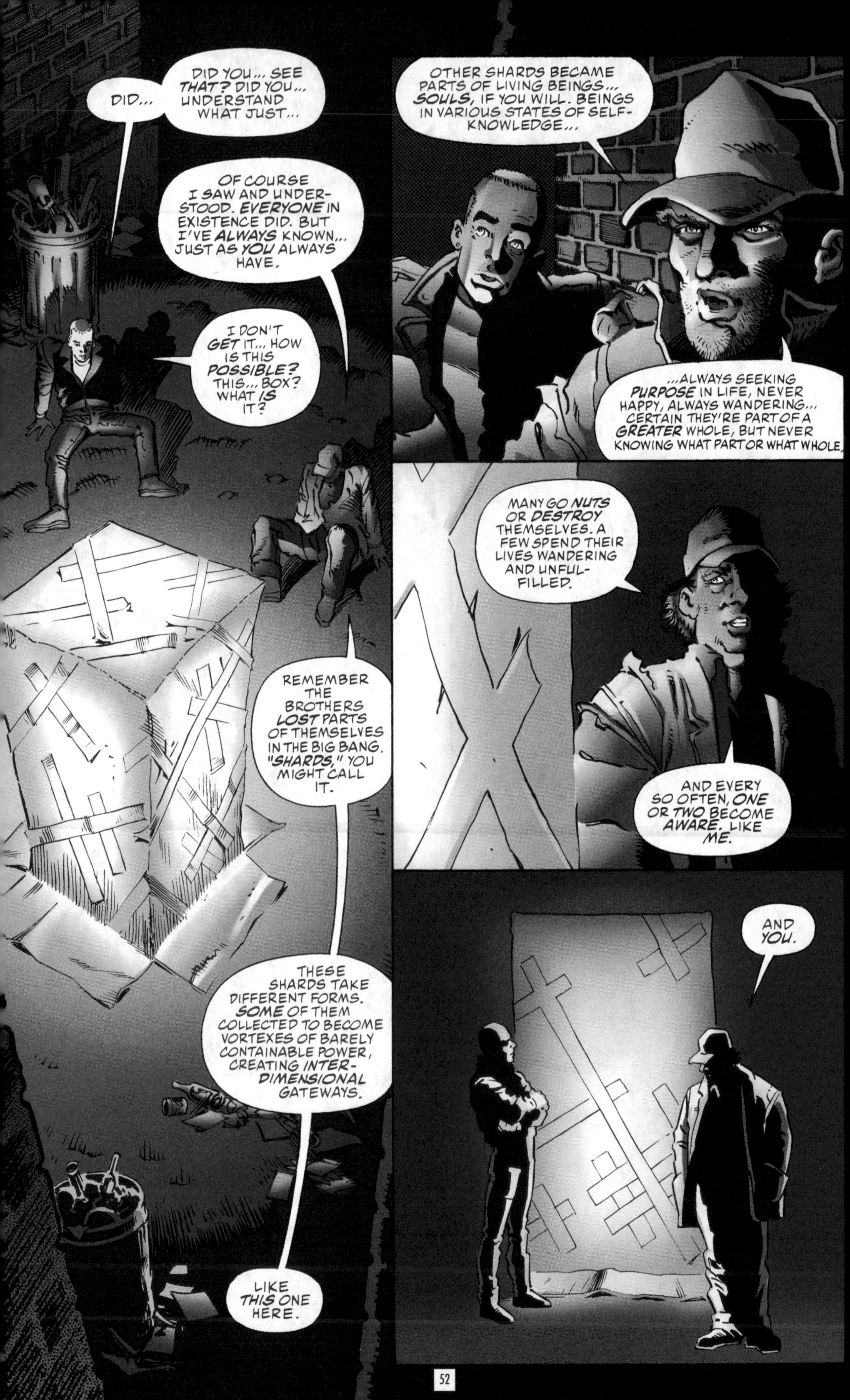
DID...
DID YOU... SEE THAT? DID YOU... UNDERSTAND WHAT JUST...
OF COURSE I SAW AND UNDERSTOOD. EVERYONE IN EXISTENCE DID. BUT I'VE ALWAYS KNOWN... JUST AS YOU ALWAYS HAVE.
I DON'T GET IT... HOW IS THIS POSSIBLE? THIS... BOX? WHAT IS IT?
REMEMBER THE BROTHERS LOST PARTS OF THEMSELVES IN THE BIG BANG. "SHARDS," YOU MIGHT CALL IT.
THESE SHARDS TAKE DIFFERENT FORMS. SOME OF THEM COLLECTED TO BECOME VORTEXES OF BARELY CONTAINABLE POWER, CREATING INTER-DIMENSIONAL GATEWAYS.
LIKE THIS ONE HERE.
OTHER SHARDS BECAME PARTS OF LIVING BEINGS... SOULS, IF YOU WILL. BEINGS IN VARIOUS STATES OF SELF-KNOWLEDGE...
...ALWAYS SEEKING PURPOSE IN LIFE, NEVER HAPPY, ALWAYS WANDERING... CERTAIN THEY'RE PART OF A GREATER WHOLE, BUT NEVER KNOWING WHAT PART OR WHAT WHOLE.
MANY GO NUTS OR DESTROY THEMSELVES. A FEW SPEND THEIR LIVES WANDERING AND UNFULFILLED.
AND EVERY SO OFTEN, ONE OR TWO BECOME AWARE. LIKE ME.
AND YOU.

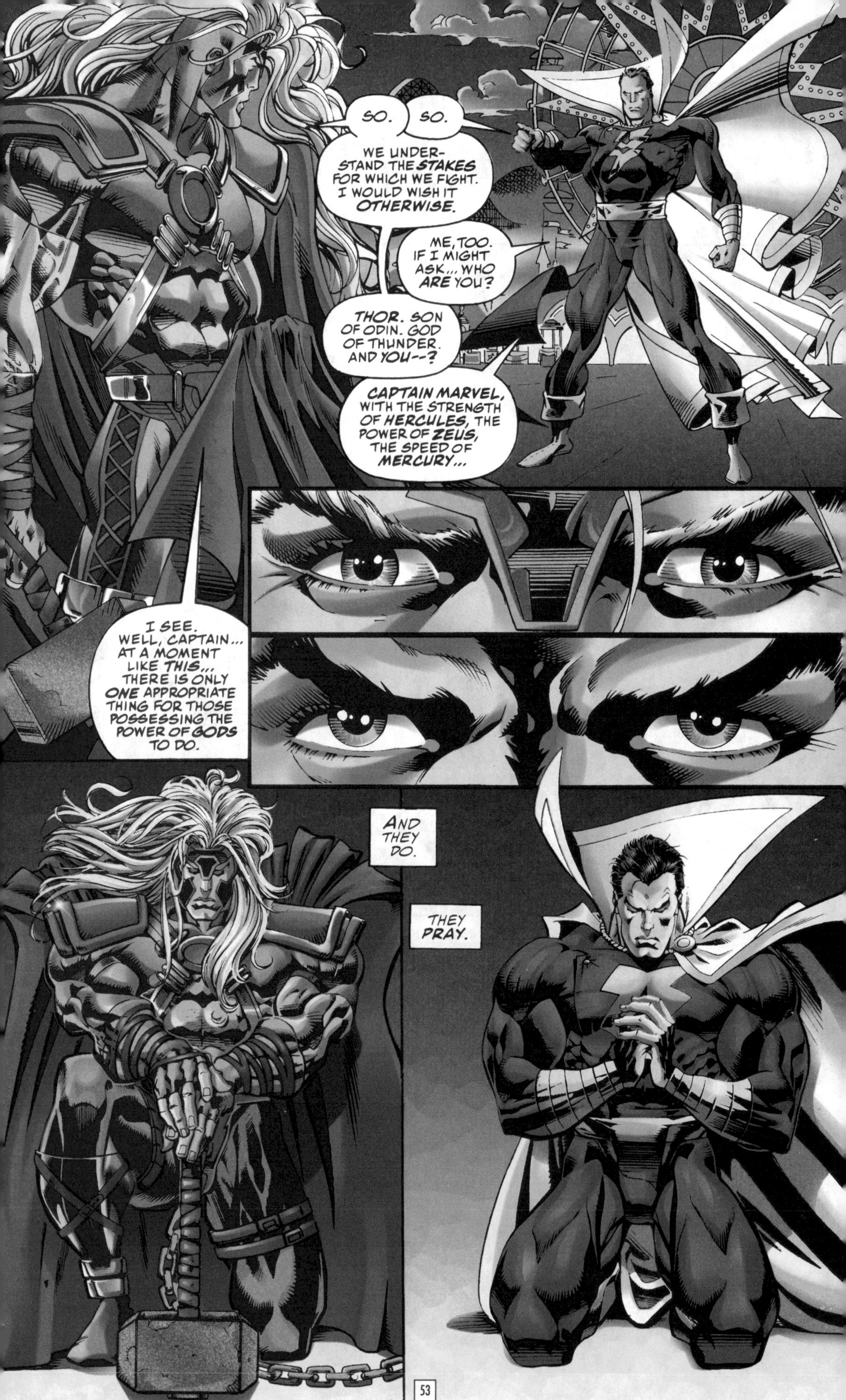
SO.
SO.
WE UNDERSTAND THE STAKES FOR WHICH WE FIGHT. I WOULD WISH IT OTHERWISE.
ME, TOO. IF I MIGHT ASK... WHO ARE YOU?
THOR. SON OF ODIN. GOD OF THUNDER. AND YOU--?
CAPTAIN MARVEL, WITH THE STRENGTH OF HERCULES, THE POWER OF ZEUS, THE SPEED OF MERCURY...
I SEE. WELL, CAPTAIN... AT A MOMENT LIKE THIS... THERE IS ONLY ONE APPROPRIATE THING FOR THOSE POSSESSING THE POWER OF GODS TO DO.
AND THEY DO.
THEY PRAY.

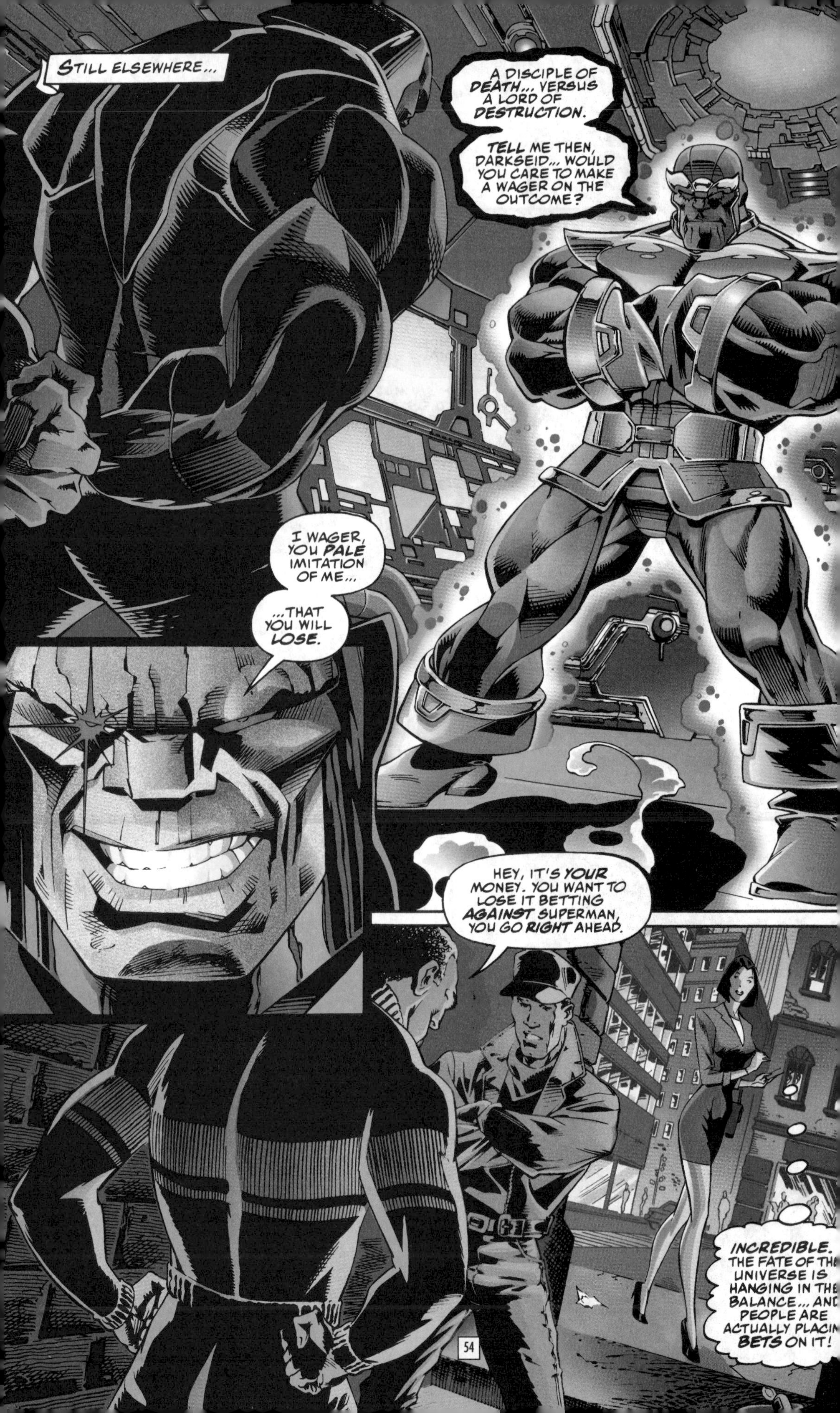
STILL ELSEWHERE...
A DISCIPLE OF DEATH... VERSUS A LORD OF DESTRUCTION.
TELL ME THEN, DARKSEID... WOULD YOU CARE TO MAKE A WAGER ON THE OUTCOME?
I WAGER, YOU PALE IMITATION OF ME...
...THAT YOU WILL LOSE.
HEY, IT'S YOUR MONEY. YOU WANT TO LOSE IT BETTING AGAINST SUPERMAN, YOU GO RIGHT AHEAD.
INCREDIBLE. THE FATE OF THE UNIVERSE IS HANGING IN THE BALANCE... AND PEOPLE ARE ACTUALLY PLACING BETS ON IT!

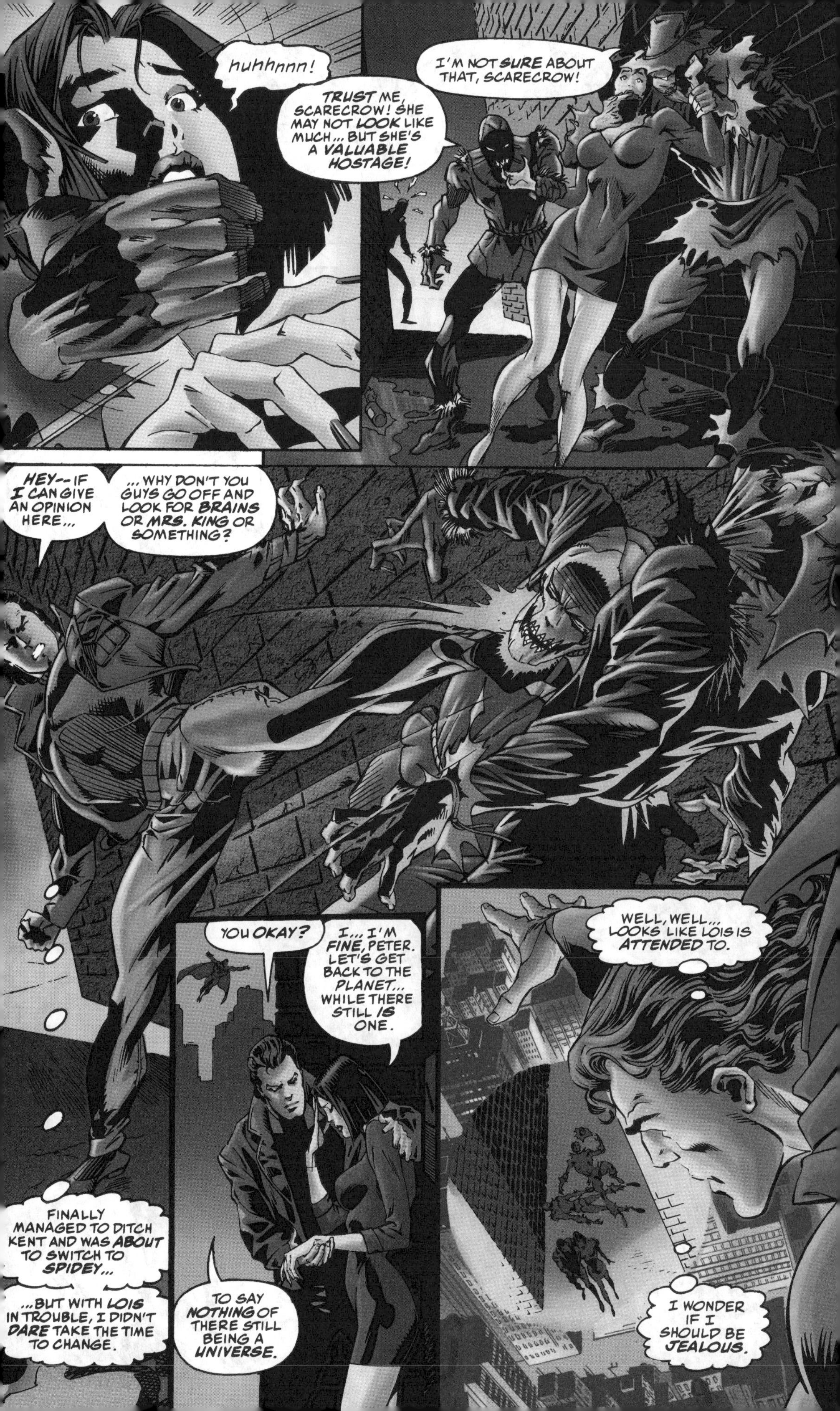
huhhnnn!
TRUST ME, SCARECROW! SHE MAY NOT LOOK LIKE MUCH... BUT SHE'S A VALUABLE HOSTAGE!
I'M NOT SURE ABOUT THAT, SCARECROW!
HEY--IF I CAN GIVE AN OPINION HERE...
...WHY DON'T YOU GUYS GO OFF AND LOOK FOR BRAINS OR MRS. KING OR SOMETHING?
FINALLY MANAGED TO DITCH KENT AND WAS ABOUT TO SWITCH TO SPIDEY...
...BUT WITH LOIS IN TROUBLE, I DIDN'T DARE TAKE THE TIME TO CHANGE.
YOU OKAY?
I... I'M FINE, PETER. LET'S GET BACK TO THE PLANET... WHILE THERE STILL IS ONE.
TO SAY NOTHING OF THERE STILL BEING A UNIVERSE.
WELL, WELL... LOOKS LIKE LOIS IS ATTENDED TO.
I WONDER IF I SHOULD BE JEALOUS.

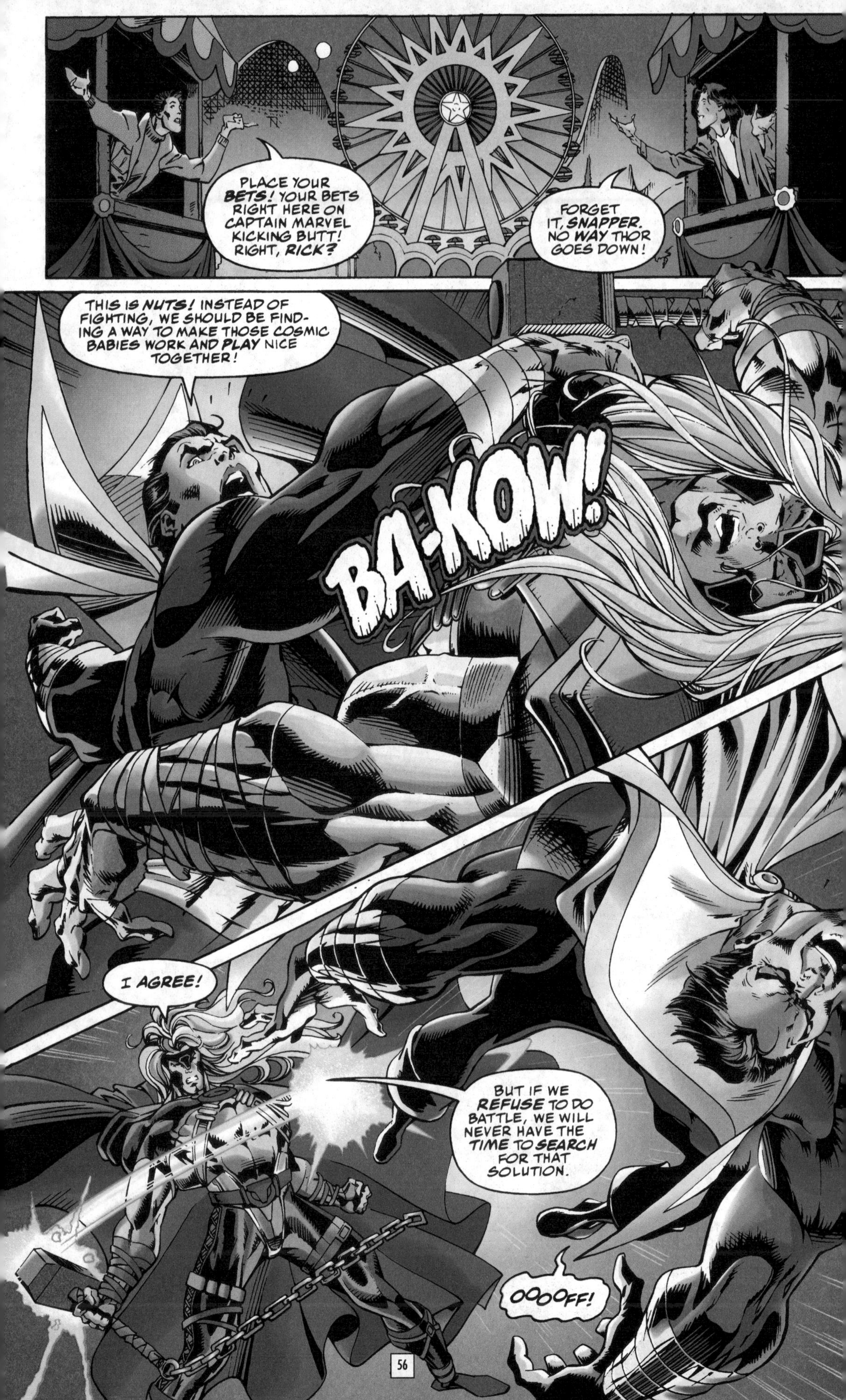
PLACE YOUR BETS! YOUR BETS RIGHT HERE ON CAPTAIN MARVEL KICKING BUTT! RIGHT, RICK?
FORGET IT, SNAPPER. NO WAY THOR GOES DOWN!
THIS IS NUTS! INSTEAD OF FIGHTING, WE SHOULD BE FINDING A WAY TO MAKE THOSE COSMIC BABIES WORK AND PLAY NICE TOGETHER!
BA-KOW!
I AGREE!
BUT IF WE REFUSE TO DO BATTLE, WE WILL NEVER HAVE THE TIME TO SEARCH FOR THAT SOLUTION.
OOOOFF!

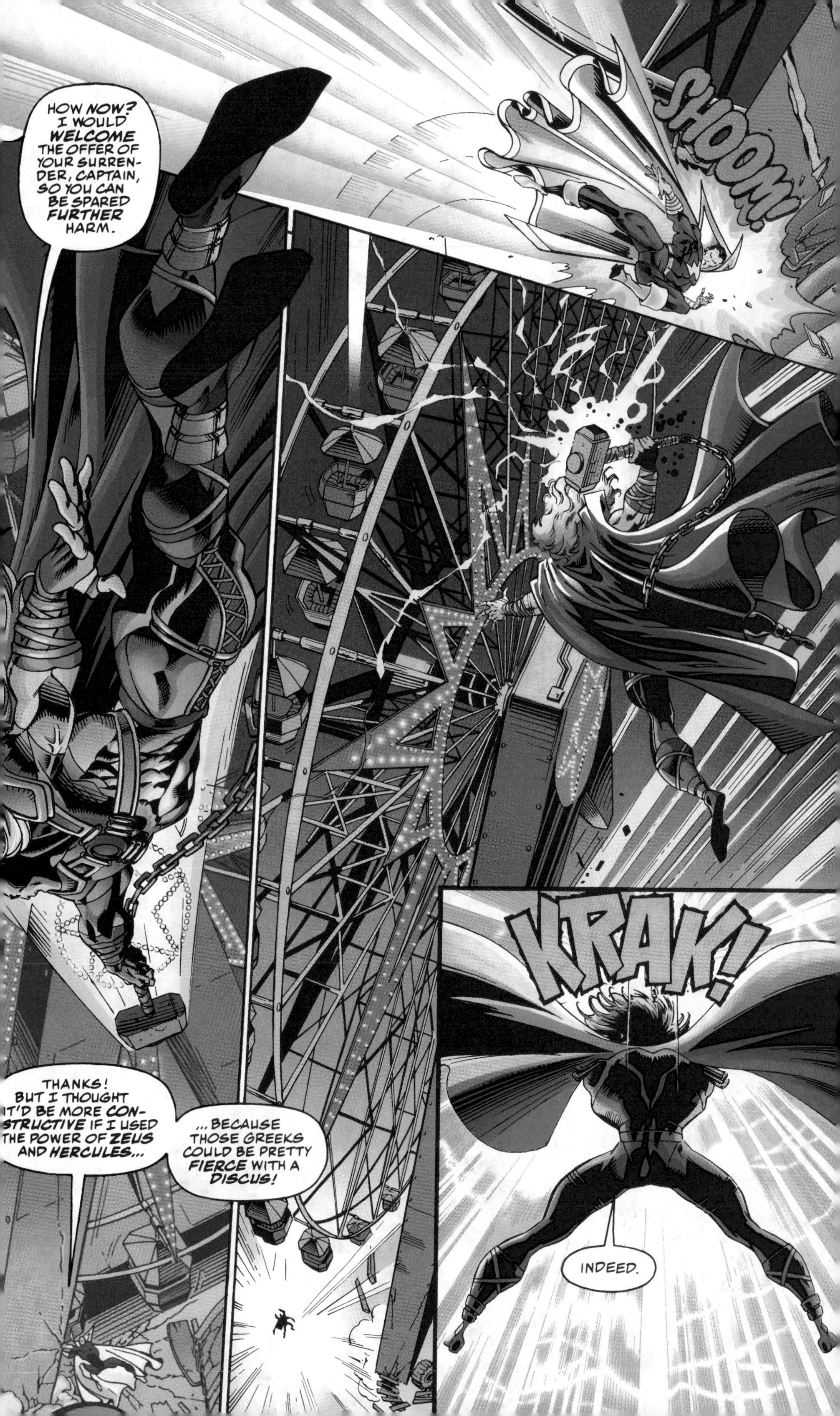
HOW NOW? I WOULD WELCOME THE OFFER OF YOUR SURRENDER, CAPTAIN, SO YOU CAN BE SPARED FURTHER HARM.
SHOOOM!
THANKS! BUT I THOUGHT IT'D BE MORE CONSTRUCTIVE IF I USED THE POWER OF ZEUS AND HERCULES...
...BECAUSE THOSE GREEKS COULD BE PRETTY FIERCE WITH A DISCUS!
KRAK!
INDEED.

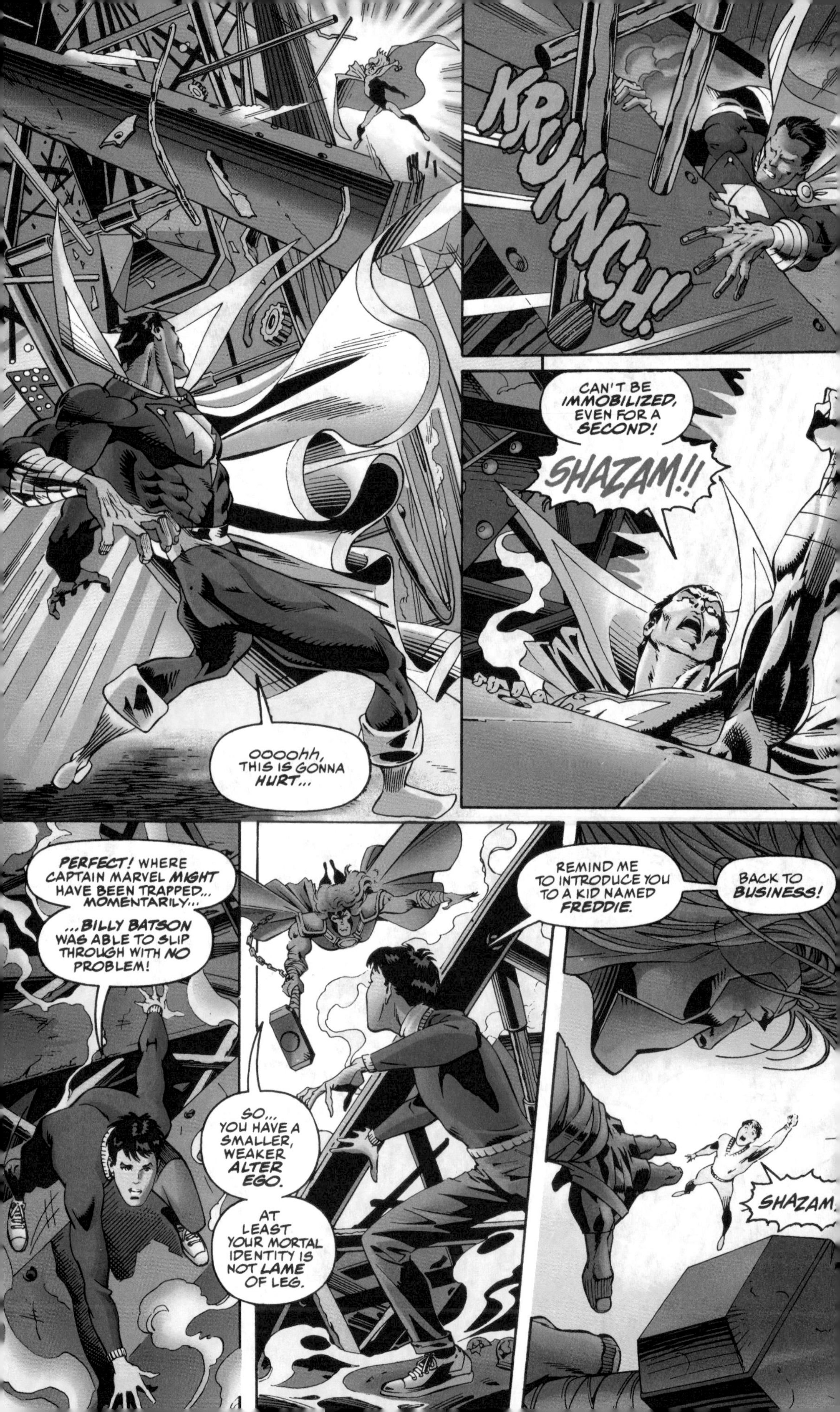
KRUNNCH!
OOOOHH, THIS IS GONNA HURT...
CAN'T BE IMMOBILIZED, EVEN FOR A SECOND!
SHAZAM!!
PERFECT! WHERE CAPTAIN MARVEL MIGHT HAVE BEEN TRAPPED... MOMENTARILY...
...BILLY BATSON WAS ABLE TO SLIP THROUGH WITH NO PROBLEM!
SO... YOU HAVE A SMALLER, WEAKER ALTER EGO.
AT LEAST YOUR MORTAL IDENTITY IS NOT LAME OF LEG.
REMIND ME TO INTRODUCE YOU TO A KID NAMED FREDDIE.
BACK TO BUSINESS!
SHAZAM

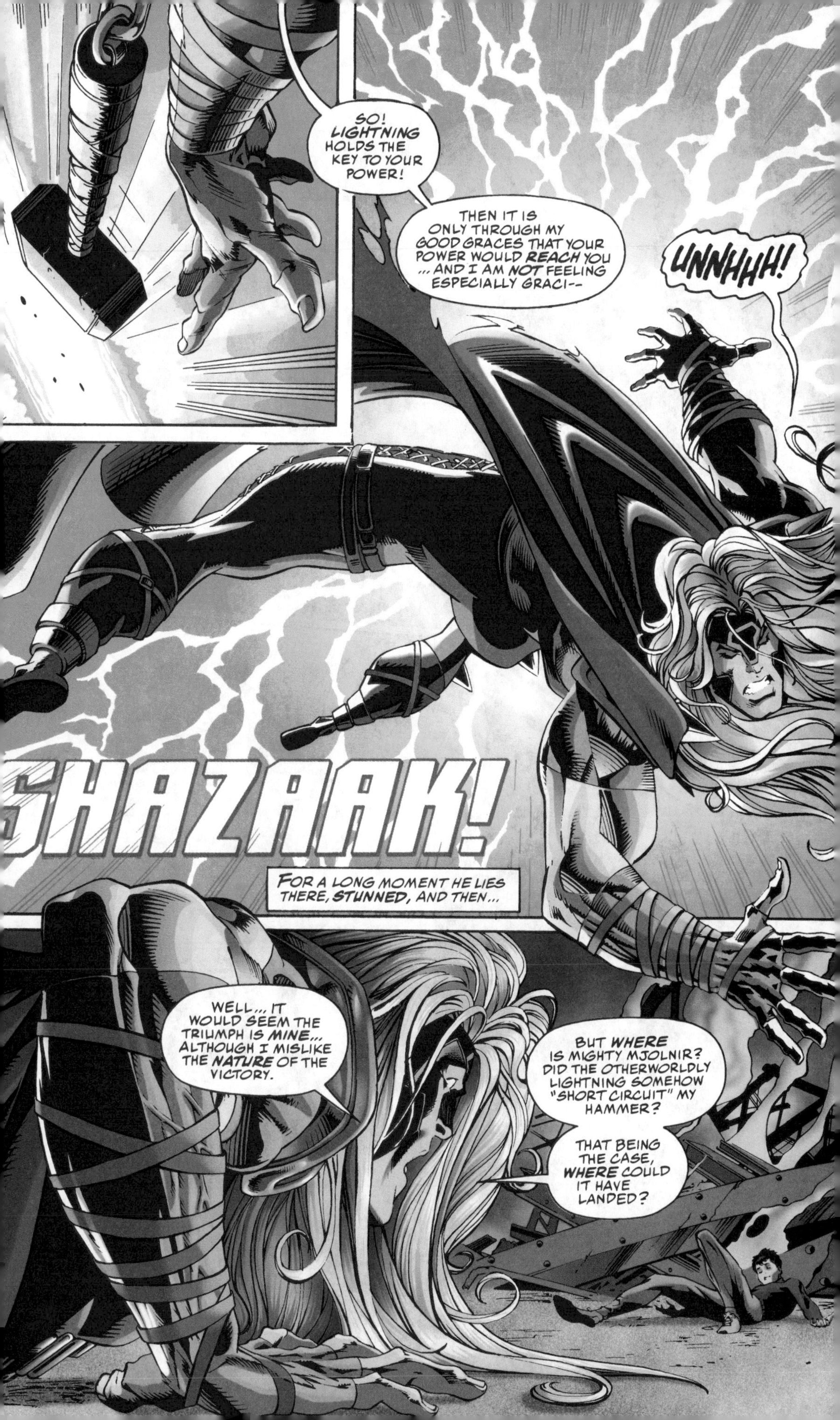
SO! LIGHTNING HOLDS THE KEY TO YOUR POWER!
THEN IT IS ONLY THROUGH MY GOOD GRACES THAT YOUR POWER WOULD REACH YOU ... AND I AM NOT FEELING ESPECIALLY GRACI--
UNNHHH!
SHAZAAK!
FOR A LONG MOMENT HE LIES THERE, STUNNED, AND THEN...
WELL... IT WOULD SEEM THE TRIUMPH IS MINE... ALTHOUGH I MISLIKE THE NATURE OF THE VICTORY.
BUT WHERE IS MIGHTY MJOLNIR? DID THE OTHERWORLDLY LIGHTNING SOMEHOW "SHORT CIRCUIT" MY HAMMER?
THAT BEING THE CASE, WHERE COULD IT HAVE LANDED?

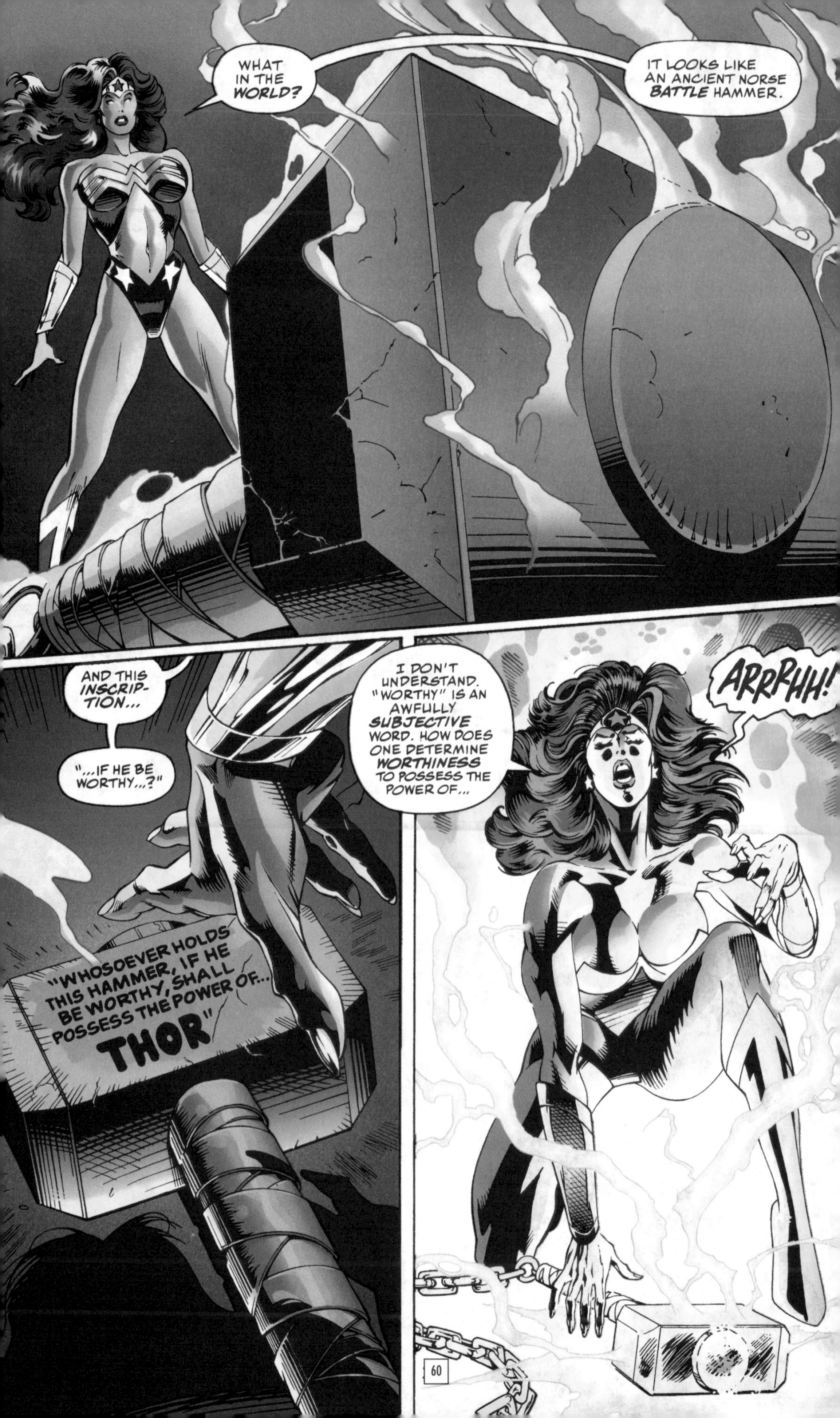

WHAT IN THE WORLD?
IT LOOKS LIKE AN ANCIENT NORSE BATTLE HAMMER.
AND THIS INSCRIPTION...
"...IF HE BE WORTHY...?"
"WHOSOEVER HOLDS THIS HAMMER, IF HE BE WORTHY, SHALL POSSESS THE POWER OF... THOR"
I DON'T UNDERSTAND. "WORTHY" IS AN AWFULLY SUBJECTIVE WORD. HOW DOES ONE DETERMINE WORTHINESS TO POSSESS THE POWER OF...
ARRRHH!

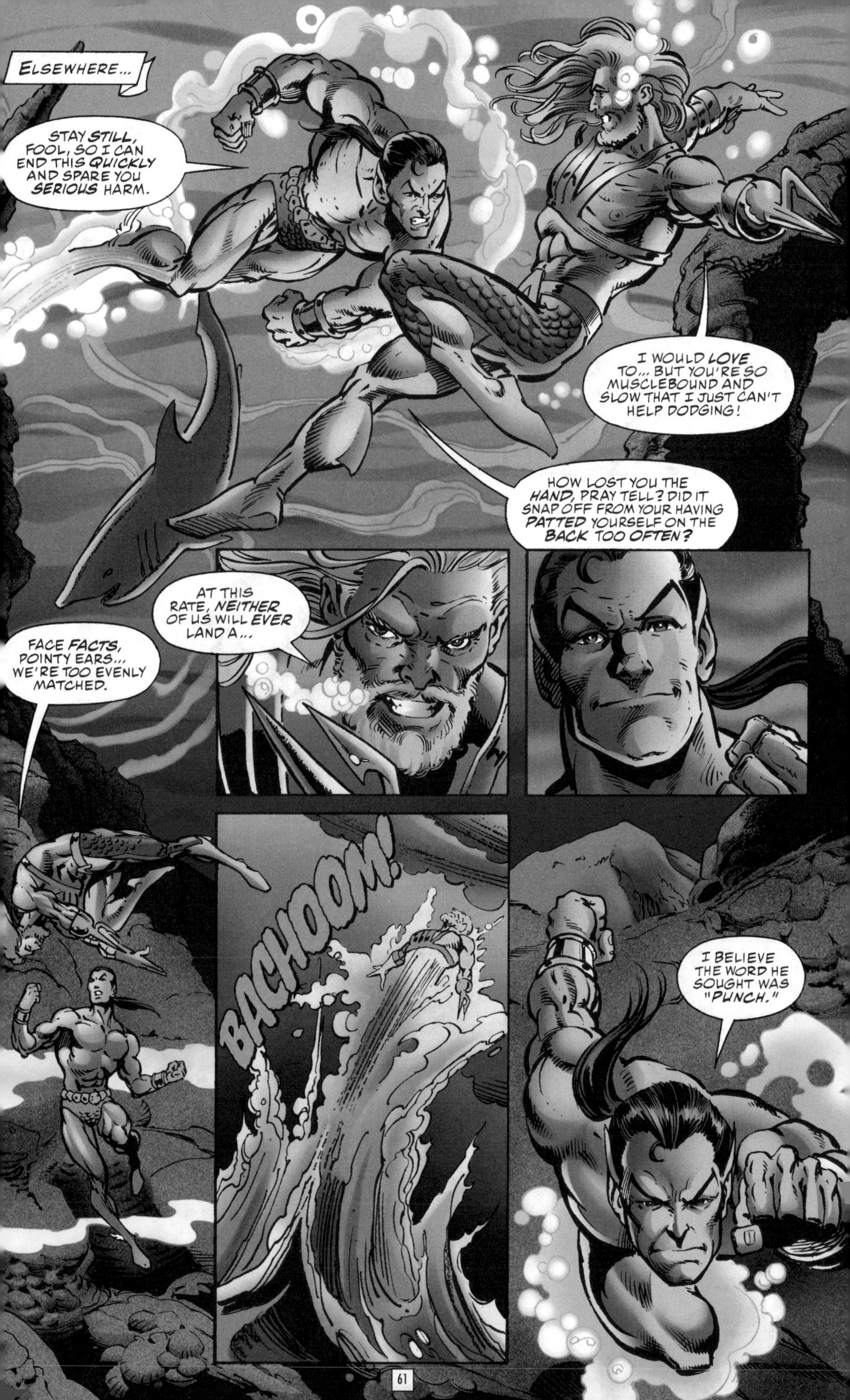

ELSEWHERE...
STAY STILL, FOOL, SO I CAN END THIS QUICKLY AND SPARE YOU SERIOUS HARM.
I WOULD LOVE TO... BUT YOU'RE SO MUSCLEBOUND AND SLOW THAT I JUST CAN'T HELP DODGING!
HOW LOST YOU THE HAND, PRAY TELL? DID IT SNAP OFF FROM YOUR HAVING PATTED YOURSELF ON THE BACK TOO OFTEN?
FACE FACTS, POINTY EARS... WE'RE TOO EVENLY MATCHED.
AT THIS RATE, NEITHER OF US WILL EVER LAND A...
BACHOOM!
I BELIEVE THE WORD HE SOUGHT WAS "PUNCH."

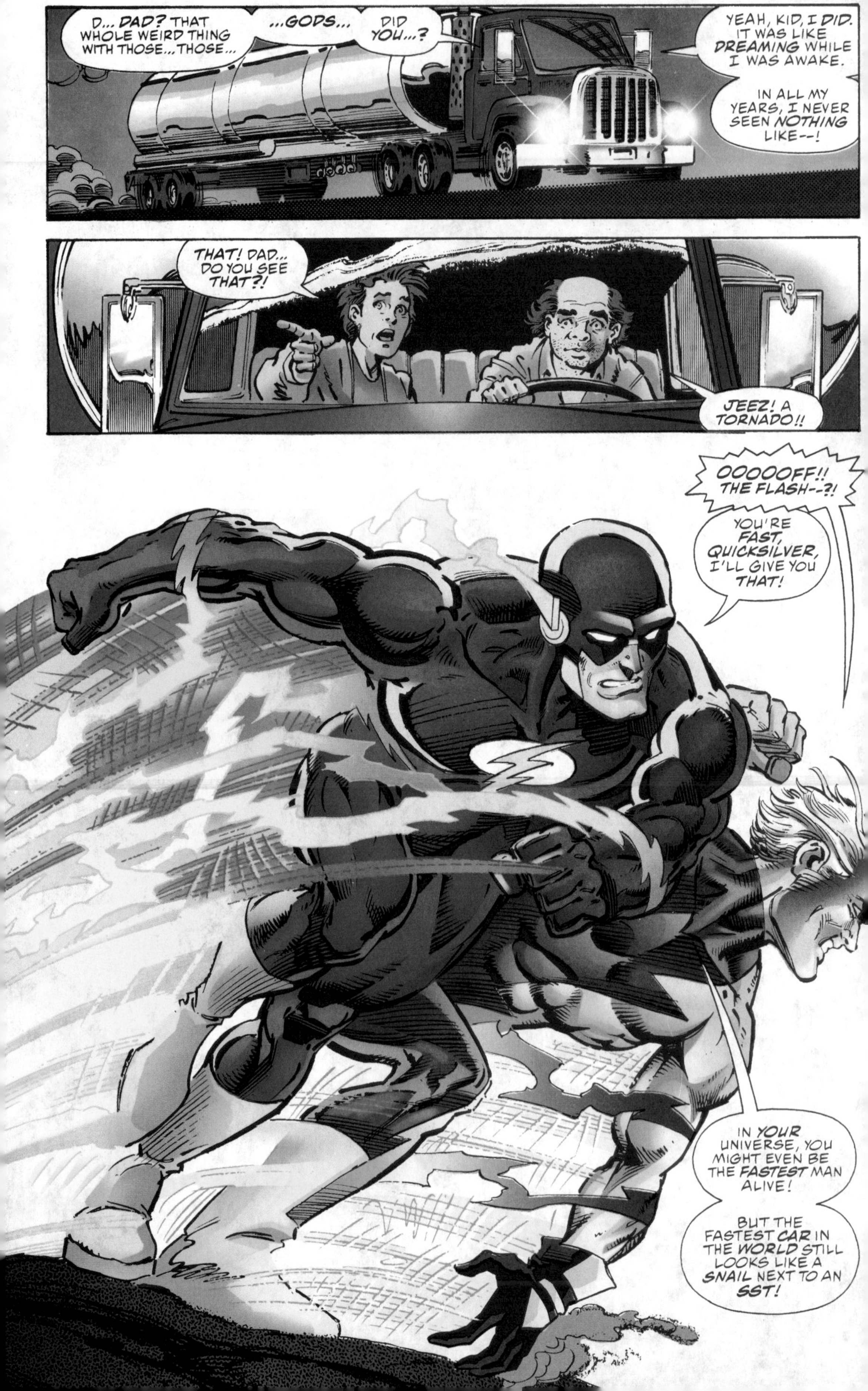

D... DAD? THAT WHOLE WEIRD THING WITH THOSE... THOSE...
...GODS...
DID YOU...?
YEAH, KID, I DID. IT WAS LIKE DREAMING WHILE I WAS AWAKE.
IN ALL MY YEARS, I NEVER SEEN NOTHING LIKE--!
THAT! DAD... DO YOU SEE THAT?!
JEEZ! A TORNADO!!
OOOOOFF!! THE FLASH--?!
YOU'RE FAST, QUICKSILVER, I'LL GIVE YOU THAT!
IN YOUR UNIVERSE, YOU MIGHT EVEN BE THE FASTEST MAN ALIVE!
BUT THE FASTEST CAR IN THE WORLD STILL LOOKS LIKE A SNAIL NEXT TO AN SST!

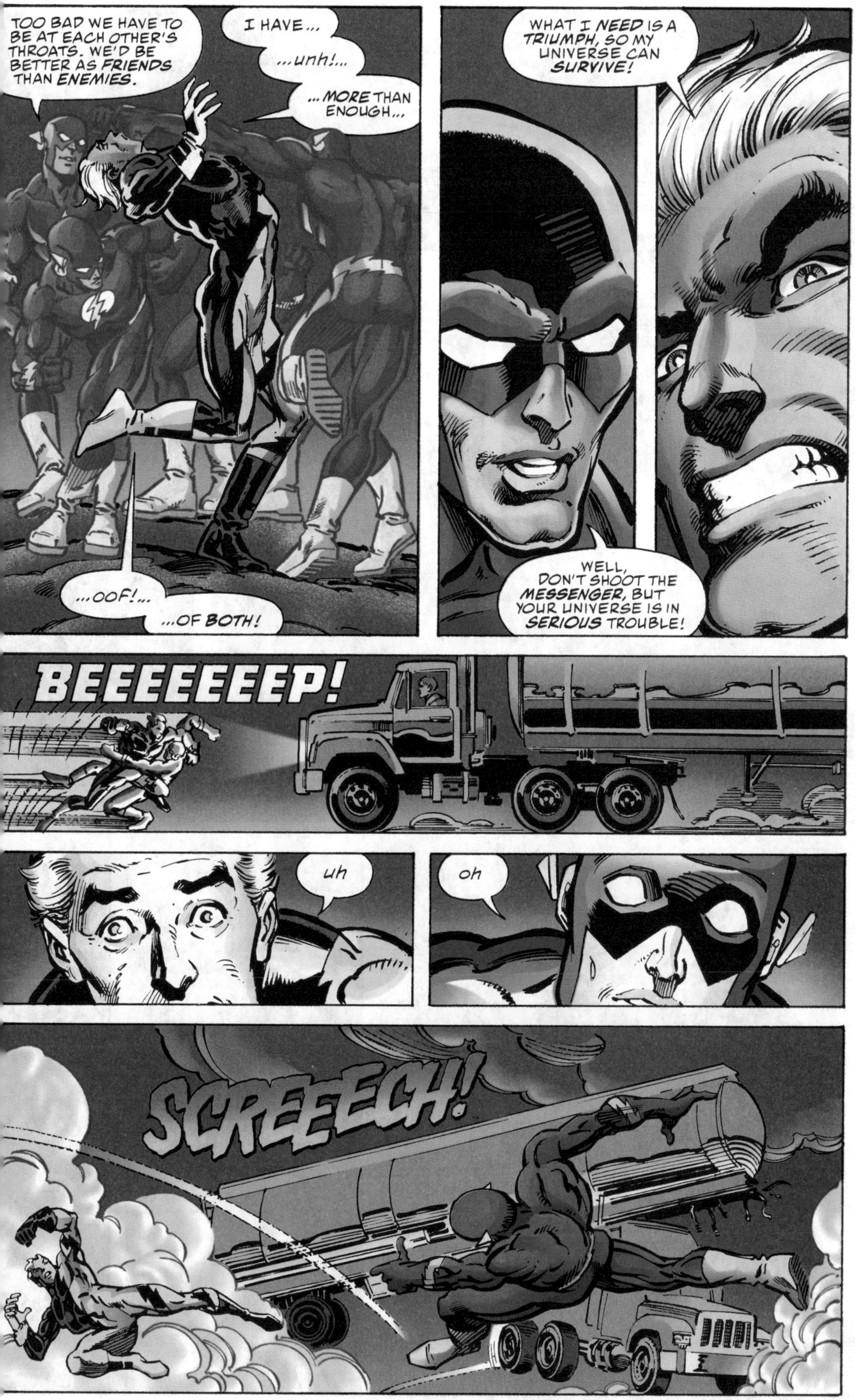
TOO BAD WE HAVE TO BE AT EACH OTHER'S THROATS. WE'D BE BETTER AS FRIENDS THAN ENEMIES.
I HAVE...
...unh!...
...MORE THAN ENOUGH...
...OOF!...
...OF BOTH!
WHAT I NEED IS A TRIUMPH, SO MY UNIVERSE CAN SURVIVE!
WELL, DON'T SHOOT THE MESSENGER, BUT YOUR UNIVERSE IS IN SERIOUS TROUBLE!
BEEEEEEEP!
uh
oh
SCREEECH!

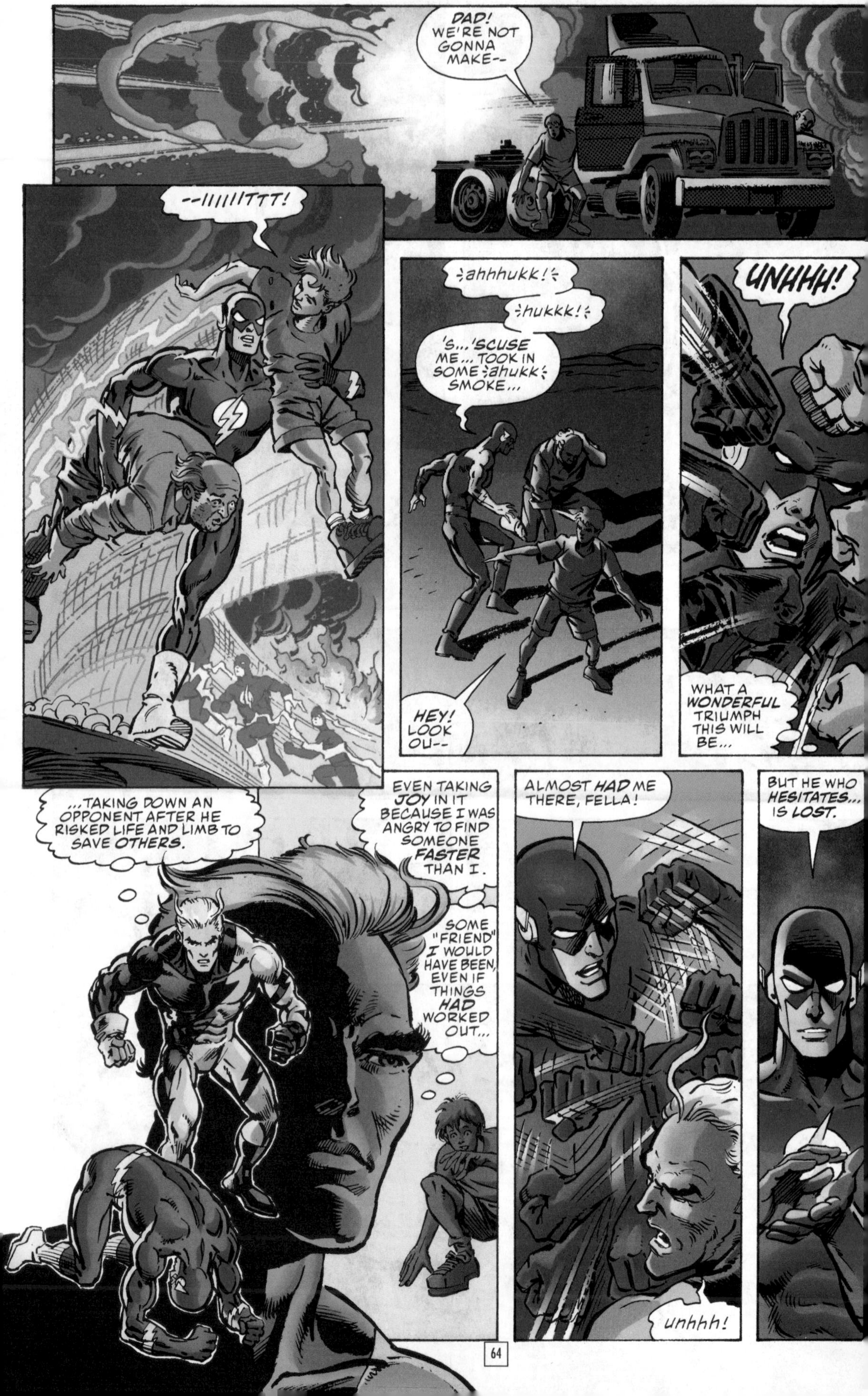
DAD! WE'RE NOT GONNA MAKE--
--IIIIIITTT!
ahhhukk!
hukkk!
'S...'SCUSE ME...TOOK IN SOME ahukk SMOKE...
HEY! LOOK OU--
UNHHH!
WHAT A WONDERFUL TRIUMPH THIS WILL BE...
...TAKING DOWN AN OPPONENT AFTER HE RISKED LIFE AND LIMB TO SAVE OTHERS.
EVEN TAKING JOY IN IT BECAUSE I WAS ANGRY TO FIND SOMEONE FASTER THAN I.
SOME "FRIEND" I WOULD HAVE BEEN, EVEN IF THINGS HAD WORKED OUT...
ALMOST HAD ME THERE, FELLA!
unhhh!
BUT HE WHO HESITATES... IS LOST.

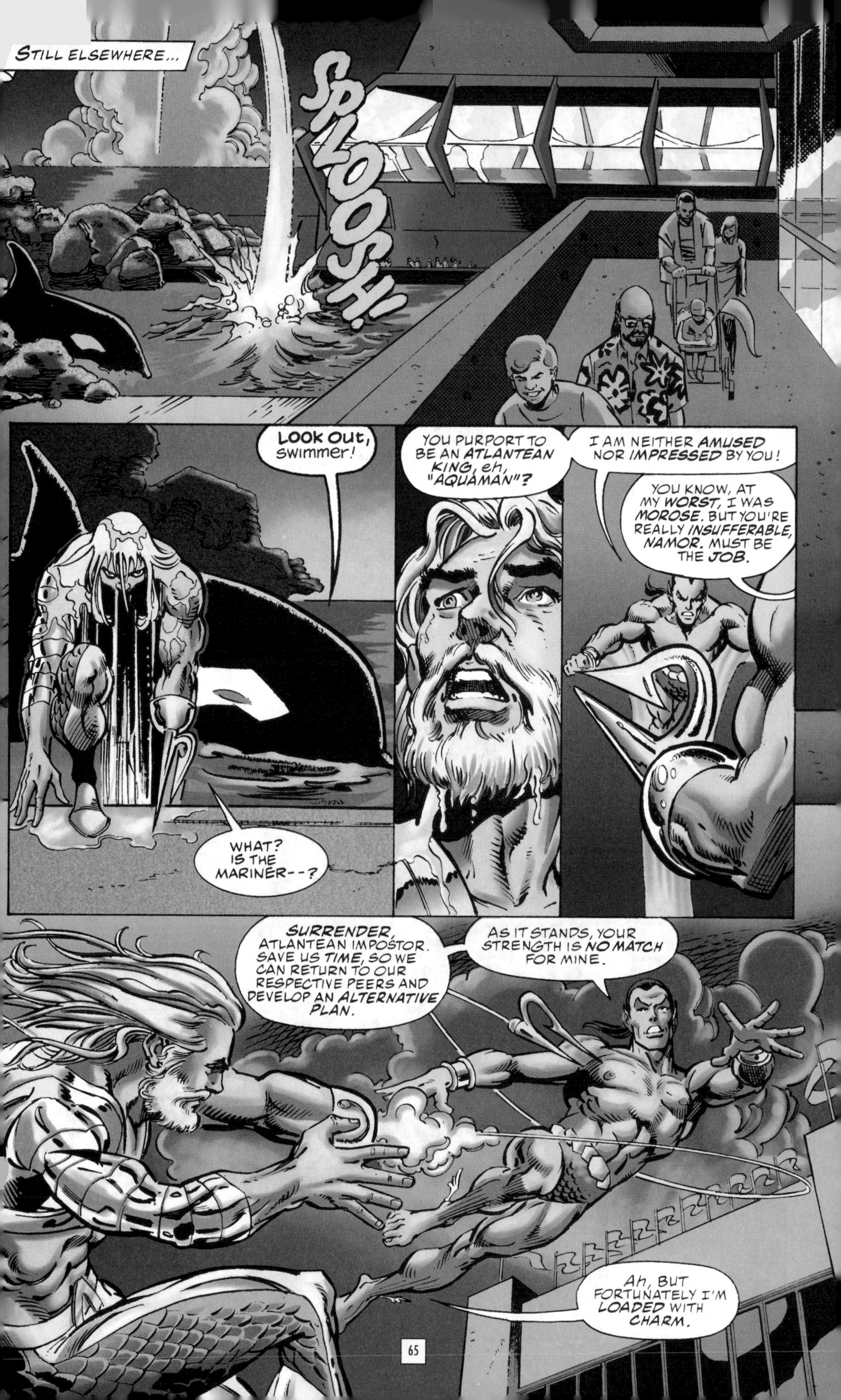

STILL ELSEWHERE...
SPLOOSH!
LOOK OUT, swimmer!
WHAT? IS THE MARINER--?
YOU PURPORT TO BE AN ATLANTEAN KING, eh, "AQUAMAN"?
I AM NEITHER AMUSED NOR IMPRESSED BY YOU!
YOU KNOW, AT MY WORST, I WAS MOROSE. BUT YOU'RE REALLY INSUFFERABLE, NAMOR. MUST BE THE JOB.
SURRENDER, ATLANTEAN IMPOSTOR. SAVE US TIME, SO WE CAN RETURN TO OUR RESPECTIVE PEERS AND DEVELOP AN ALTERNATIVE PLAN.
AS IT STANDS, YOUR STRENGTH IS NO MATCH FOR MINE.
Ah, BUT FORTUNATELY I'M LOADED WITH CHARM.

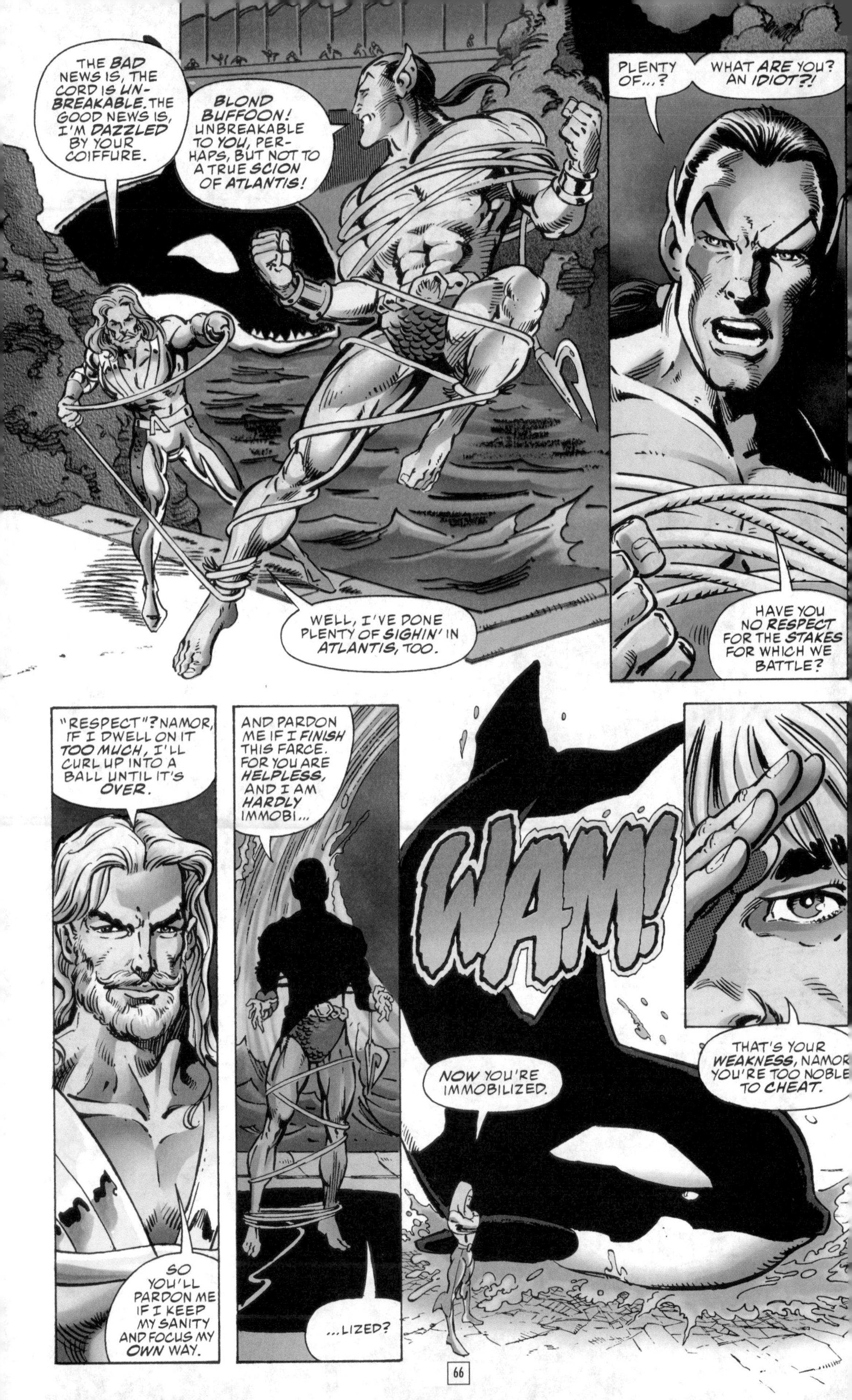
THE BAD NEWS IS, THE CORD IS UNBREAKABLE. THE GOOD NEWS IS, I'M DAZZLED BY YOUR COIFFURE.
BLOND BUFFOON! UNBREAKABLE TO YOU, PERHAPS, BUT NOT TO A TRUE SCION OF ATLANTIS!
WELL, I'VE DONE PLENTY OF SIGHIN' IN ATLANTIS, TOO.
PLENTY OF...?
WHAT ARE YOU? AN IDIOT?!
HAVE YOU NO RESPECT FOR THE STAKES FOR WHICH WE BATTLE?
"RESPECT"? NAMOR, IF I DWELL ON IT TOO MUCH, I'LL CURL UP INTO A BALL UNTIL IT'S OVER.
SO YOU'LL PARDON ME IF I KEEP MY SANITY AND FOCUS MY OWN WAY.
AND PARDON ME IF I FINISH THIS FARCE. FOR YOU ARE HELPLESS, AND I AM HARDLY IMMOBI...
...LIZED?
WAM!
NOW YOU'RE IMMOBILIZED.
THAT'S YOUR WEAKNESS, NAMOR. YOU'RE TOO NOBLE TO CHEAT.

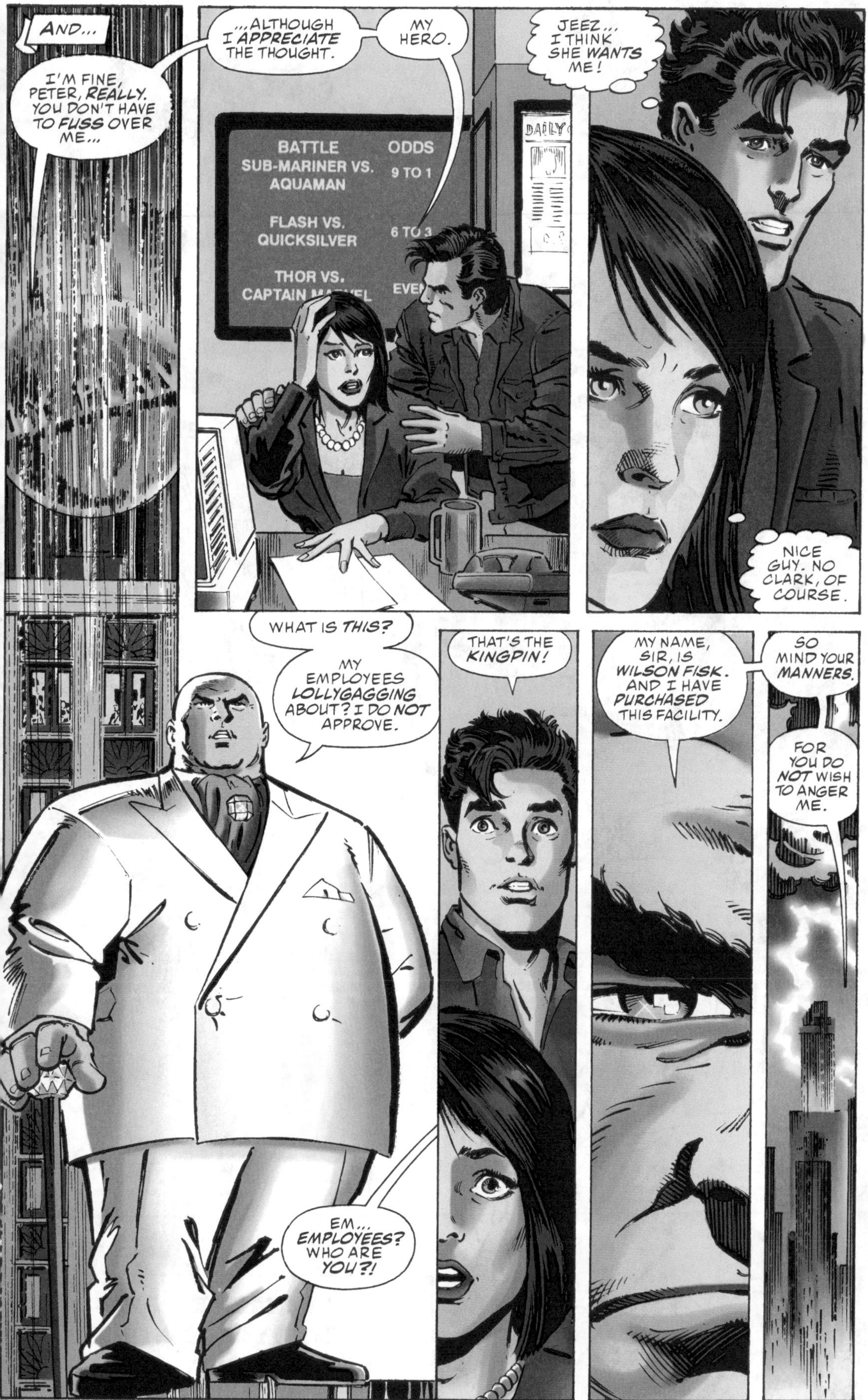

AND...
I'M FINE, PETER, REALLY. YOU DON'T HAVE TO FUSS OVER ME...
...ALTHOUGH I APPRECIATE THE THOUGHT.
MY HERO.
BATTLE ODDS
SUB-MARINER VS. AQUAMAN 9 TO 1
FLASH VS. QUICKSILVER 6 TO 3
THOR VS. CAPTAIN MARVEL EVEN
JEEZ... I THINK SHE WANTS ME!
NICE GUY. NO CLARK, OF COURSE.
WHAT IS THIS?
MY EMPLOYEES LOLLYGAGGING ABOUT? I DO NOT APPROVE.
EM... EMPLOYEES? WHO ARE YOU?!
THAT'S THE KINGPIN!
MY NAME, SIR, IS WILSON FISK. AND I HAVE PURCHASED THIS FACILITY.
SO MIND YOUR MANNERS.
FOR YOU DO NOT WISH TO ANGER ME.

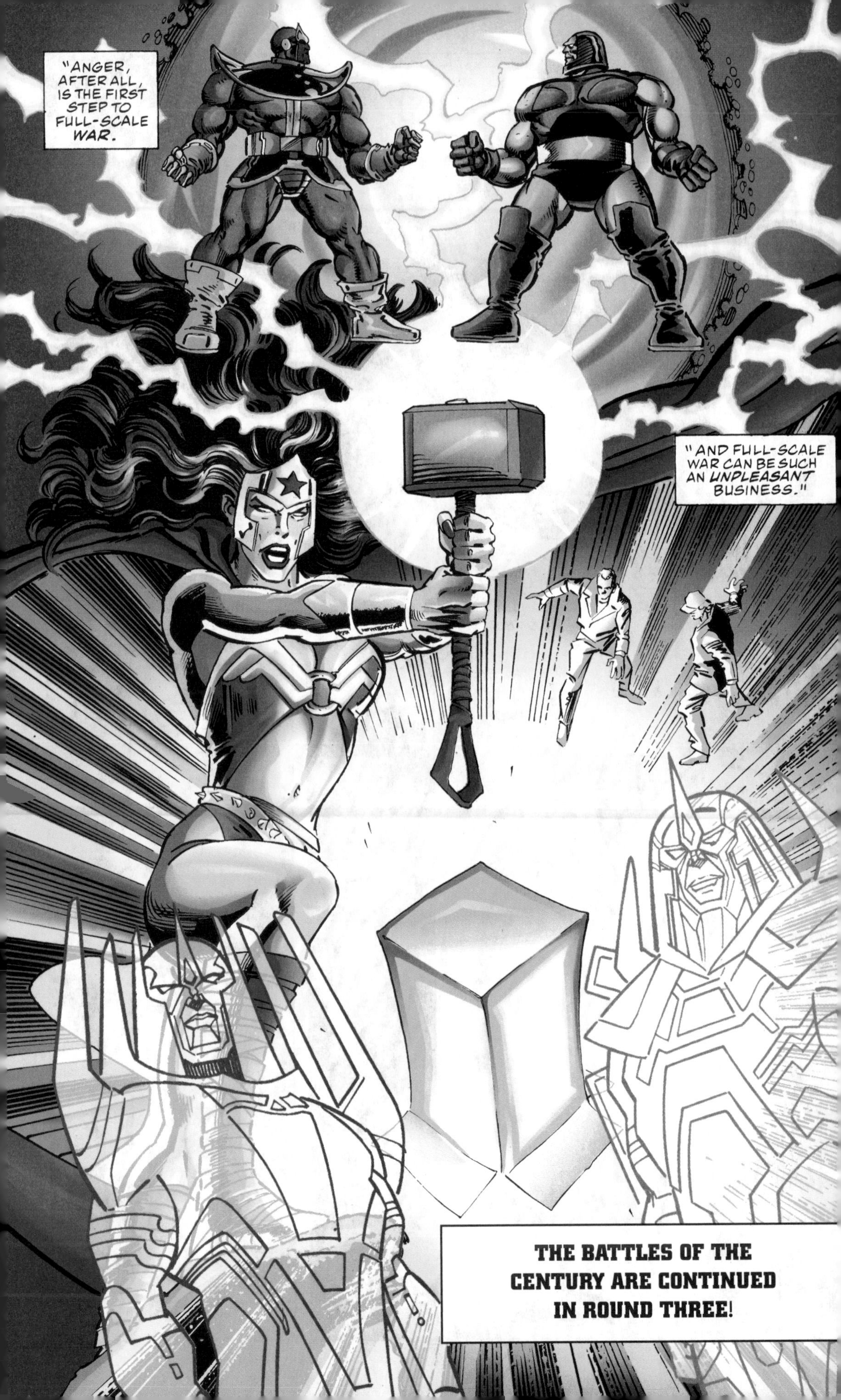
"ANGER, AFTER ALL, IS THE FIRST STEP TO FULL-SCALE WAR.
"AND FULL-SCALE WAR CAN BE SUCH AN UNPLEASANT BUSINESS."
THE BATTLES OF THE CENTURY ARE CONTINUED IN ROUND THREE!

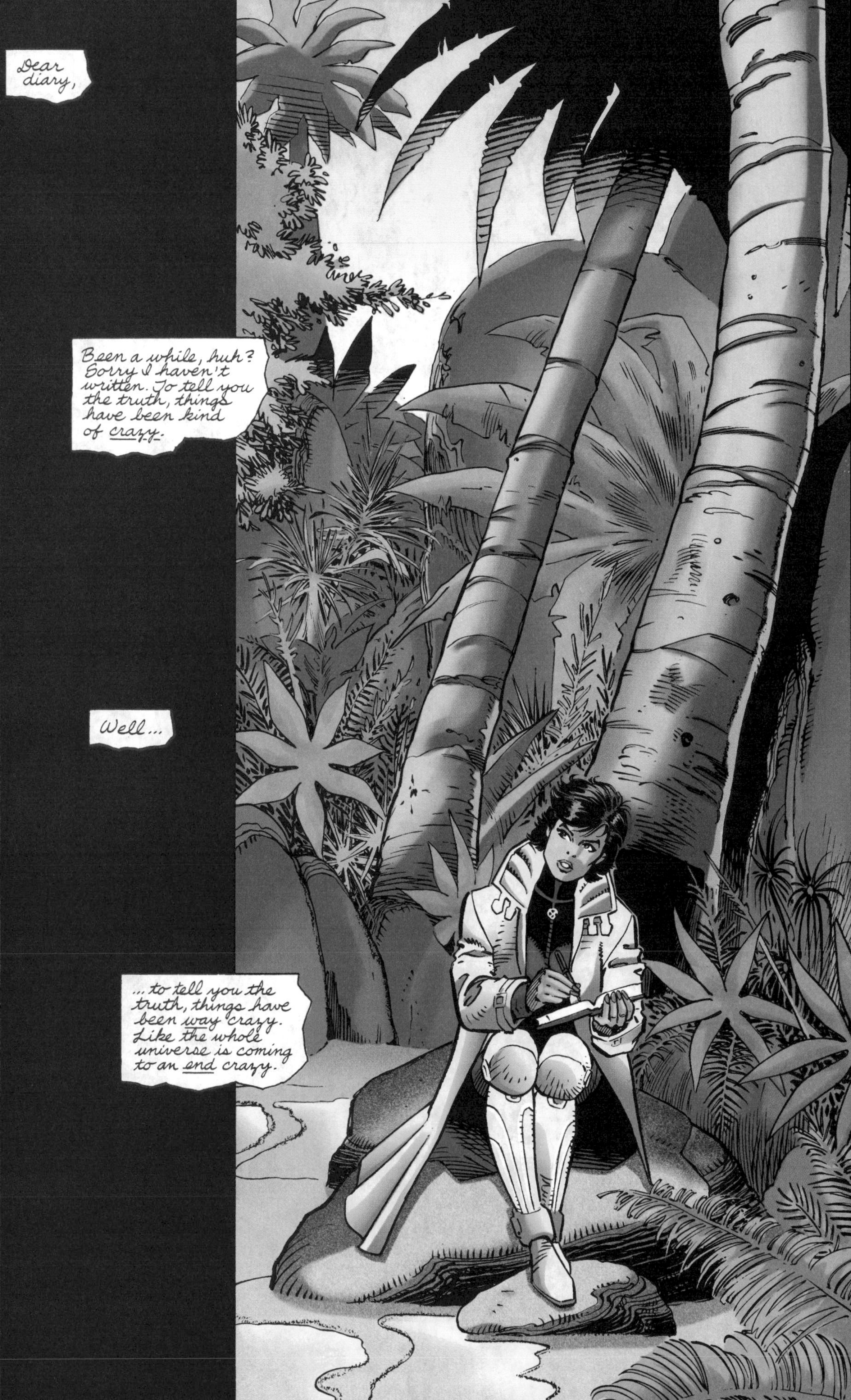
Dear diary,
Been a while, huh? Sorry I haven't written. To tell you the truth, things have been kind of crazy.
Well...
...to tell you the truth, things have been way crazy. Like the whole universe is coming to an end crazy.

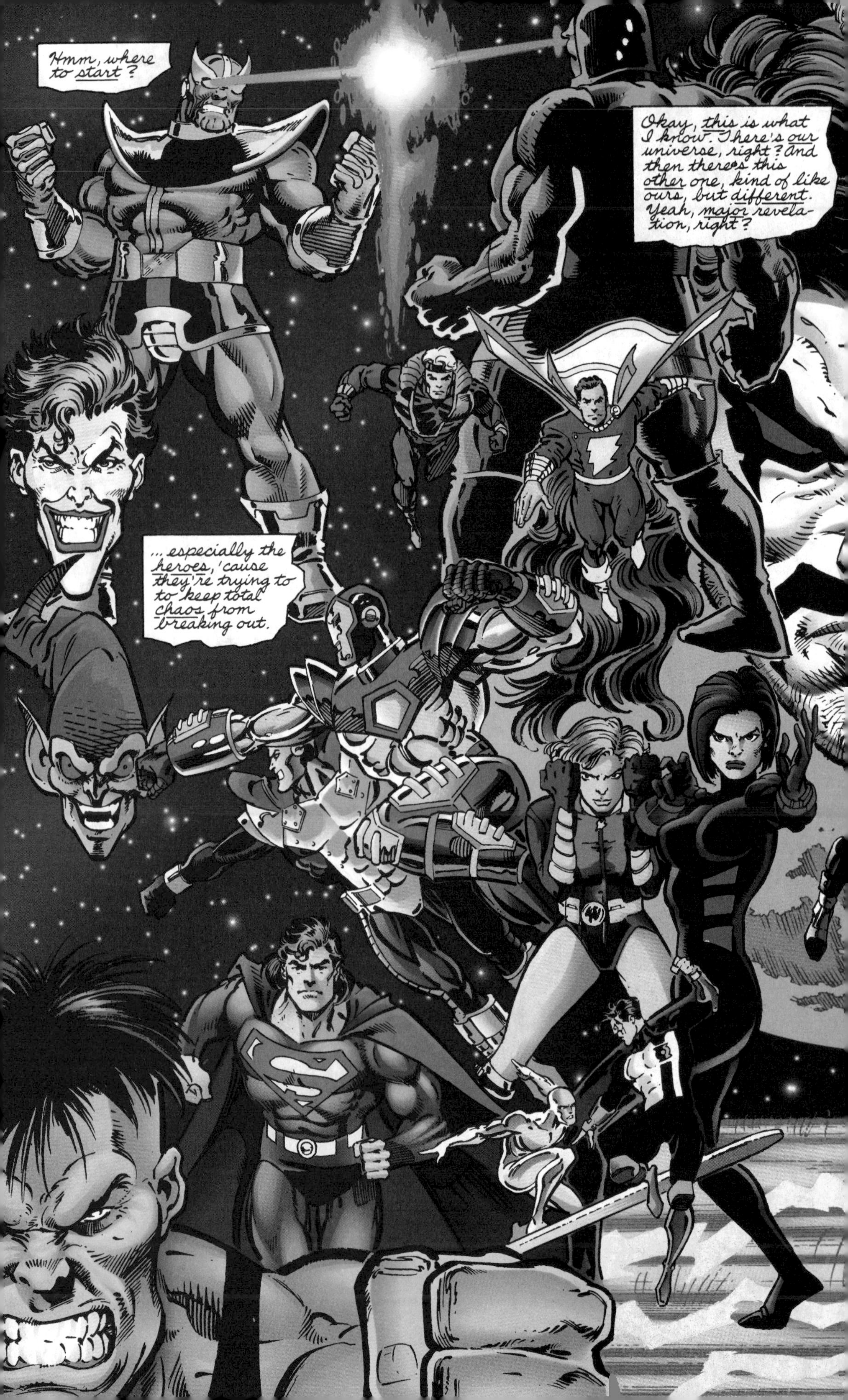
Hmm, where to start?
Okay, this is what I know. There's our universe, right? And then there's this other one, kind of like ours, but different. Yeah, major revelation, right?
...especially the heroes, 'cause they're trying to to keep total chaos from breaking out.

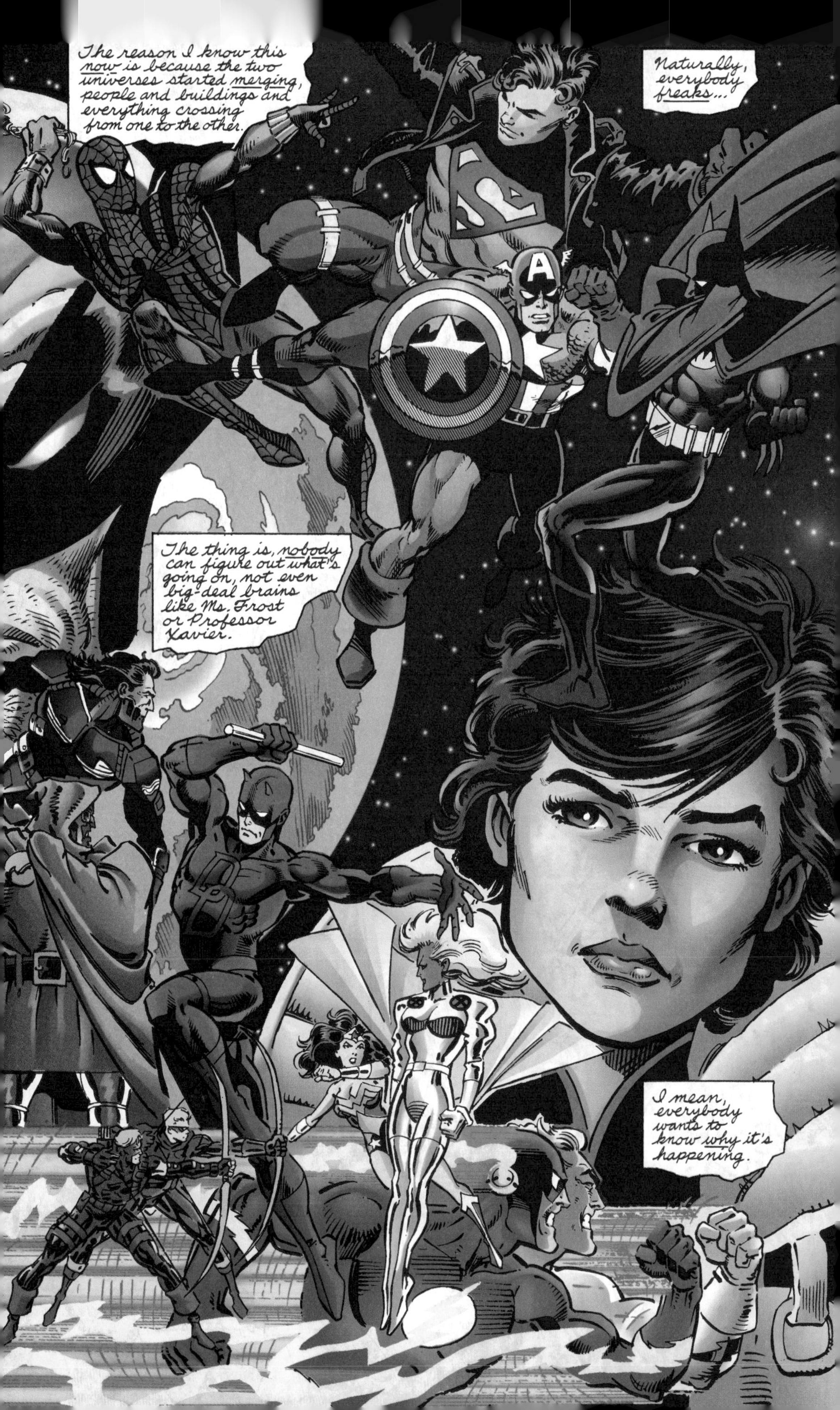
The reason I know this now is because the two universes started merging, people and buildings and everything crossing from one to the other.
Naturally, everybody freaks...
The thing is, nobody can figure out what's going on, not even big-deal brains like Ms. Frost or Professor Xavier.
I mean, everybody wants to know why it's happening.

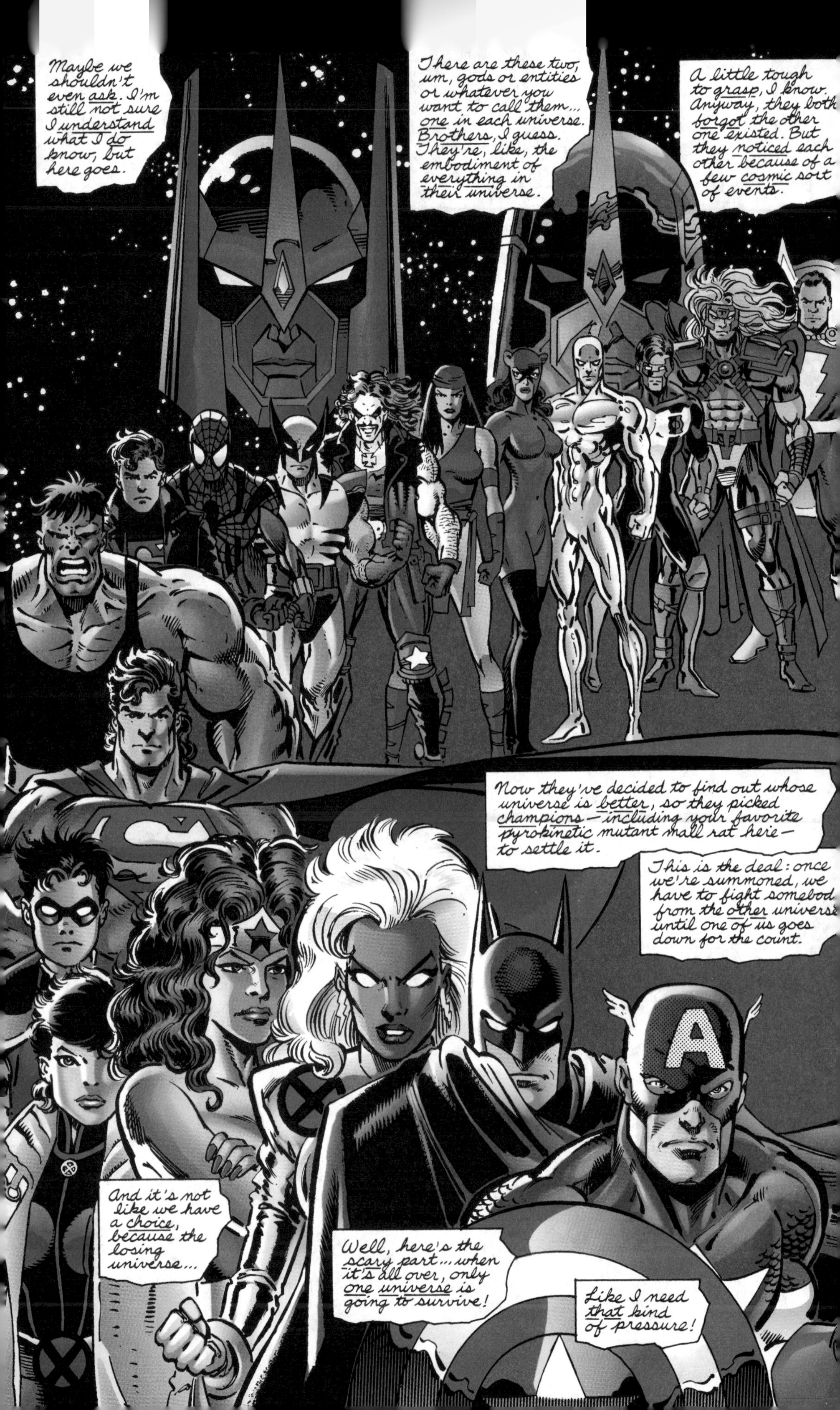
Maybe we shouldn't even ask. I'm still not sure I understand what I do know, but here goes.
There are these two, um, gods or entities or whatever you want to call them... one in each universe. Brothers, I guess. They're, like, the embodiment of everything in their universe.
A little tough to grasp, I know. Anyway, they both forgot the other one existed. But they noticed each other because of a few cosmic sort of events.
Now they've decided to find out whose universe is better, so they picked champions — including your favorite pyrokinetic mutant mall rat here — to settle it.
This is the deal: once we're summoned, we have to fight somebod from the other universe until one of us goes down for the count.
And it's not like we have a choice, because the losing universe...
Well, here's the scary part... when it's all over, only one universe is going to survive!
Like I need that kind of pressure!

It's already started. Thor defeated this guy called Captain Marvel...

...but Namor lost to Aquaman...

...and Quicksilver couldn't outrun the Flash. So right now we're losing two-to-one.

It's weird— creepy weird, I mean— how people are reacting, treating this like it's the Super Bowl or something.

BIBBO'S TOTE BOARD

THOR DEF. CAPTAIN MARVEL
AQ— DEF. NAMOR
FLA— QUICKSILVER
SUP— 3-5 OVER HUL—
BAT— TAIN A—— LA
— RBOY.
— RN
— EVEN

...and I've gotta fight him for the fate of two universes. Does that stink or what?

Maybe it's easier to do that than really think about the consequences. Sort of whistling in the dark.

But you want to know the worst thing? I finally find the right guy...I mean Mr. Right...

73

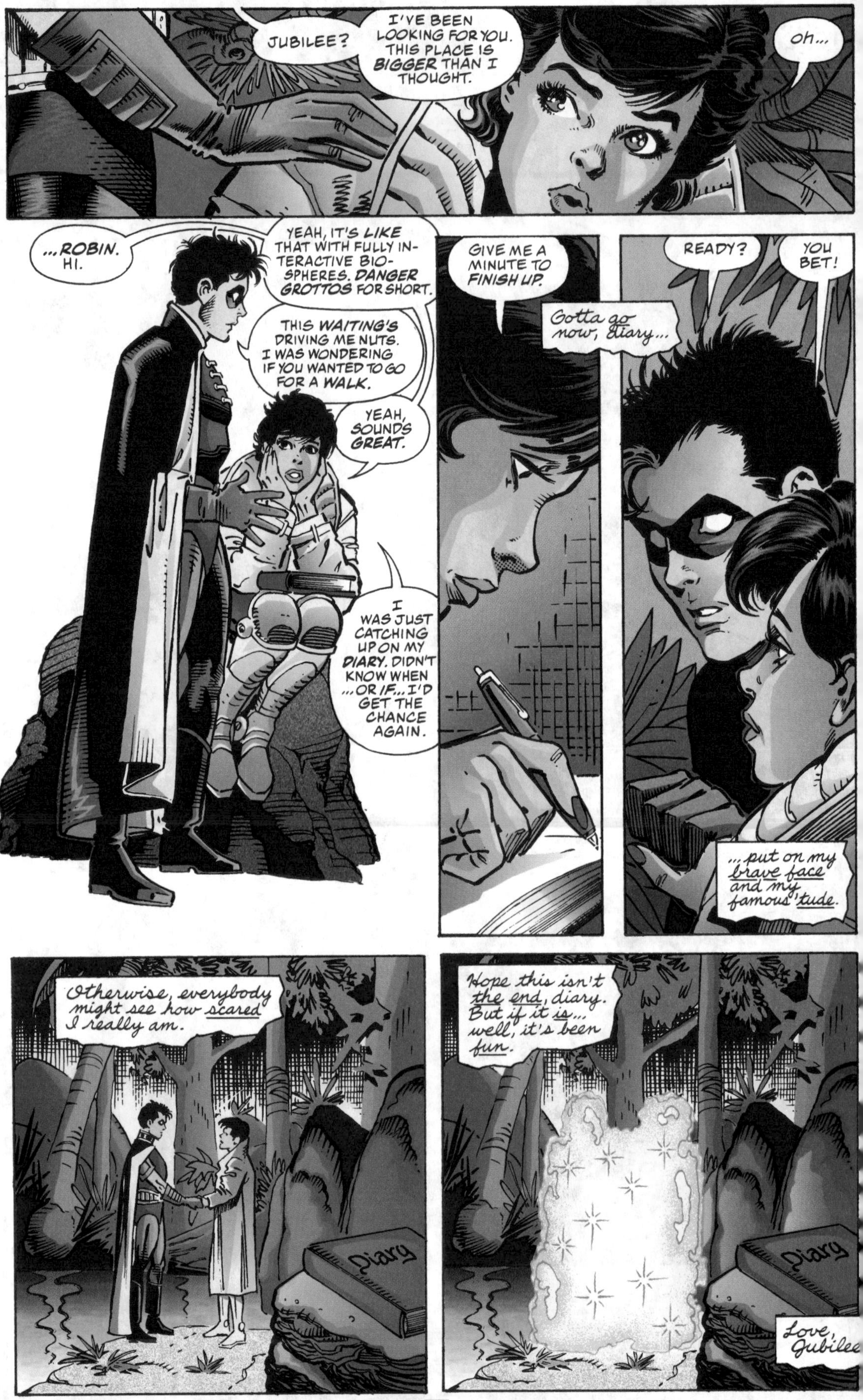
JUBILEE?
I'VE BEEN LOOKING FOR YOU. THIS PLACE IS BIGGER THAN I THOUGHT.
oh...
...ROBIN. HI.
YEAH, IT'S LIKE THAT WITH FULLY INTERACTIVE BIO-SPHERES. DANGER GROTTOS FOR SHORT.
THIS WAITING'S DRIVING ME NUTS. I WAS WONDERING IF YOU WANTED TO GO FOR A WALK.
YEAH, SOUNDS GREAT.
I WAS JUST CATCHING UP ON MY DIARY. DIDN'T KNOW WHEN ...OR IF... I'D GET THE CHANCE AGAIN.
GIVE ME A MINUTE TO FINISH UP.
Gotta go now, diary...
READY?
YOU BET!
...put on my brave face and my famous 'tude.
Otherwise, everybody might see how scared I really am.
Diary
Hope this isn't the end, diary. But if it is... well, it's been fun.
Diary
Love, Jubilee

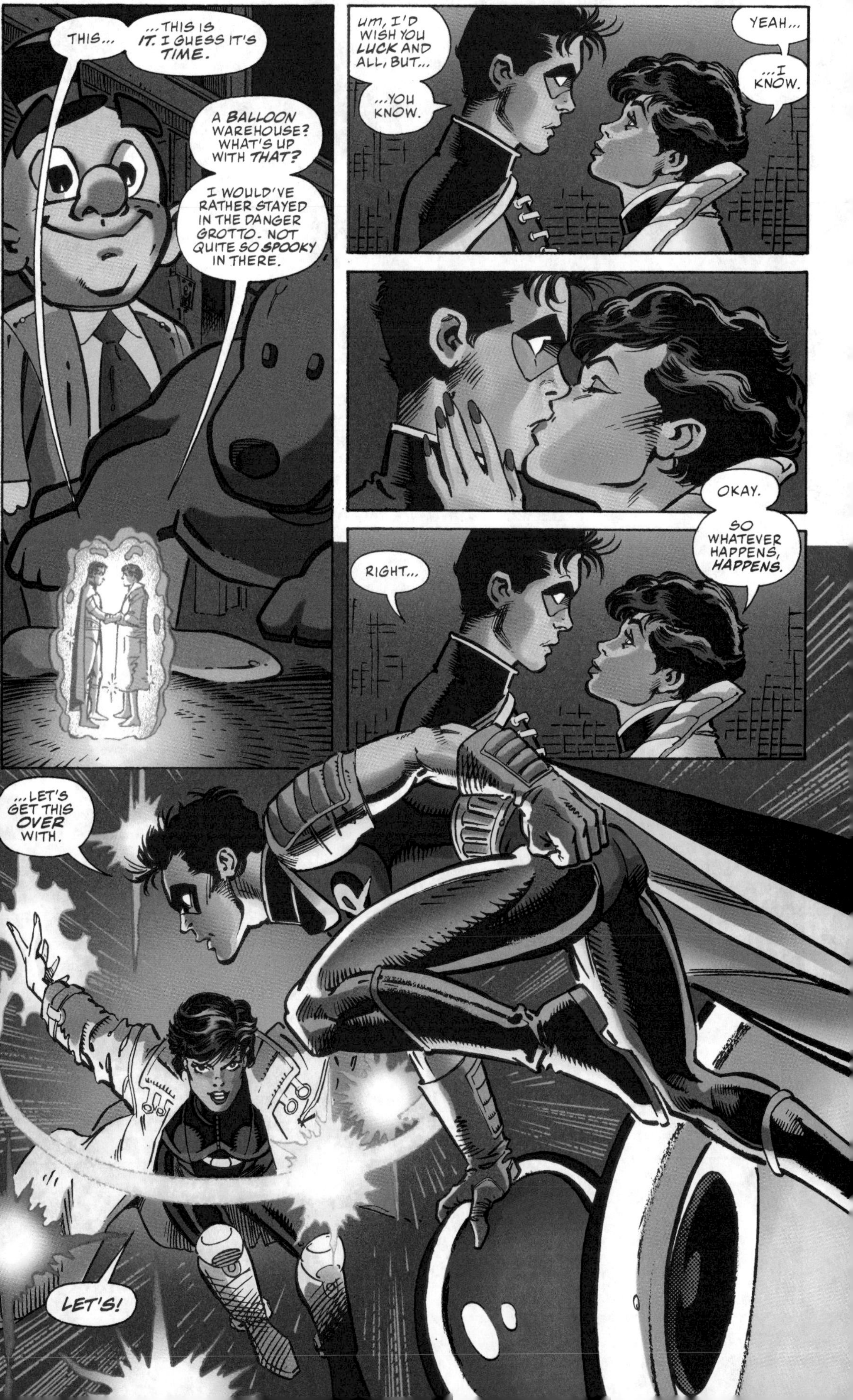
THIS...
...THIS IS IT. I GUESS IT'S TIME.
A BALLOON WAREHOUSE? WHAT'S UP WITH THAT?
I WOULD'VE RATHER STAYED IN THE DANGER GROTTO. NOT QUITE SO SPOOKY IN THERE.
UM, I'D WISH YOU LUCK AND ALL, BUT...
...YOU KNOW.
YEAH...
...I KNOW.
RIGHT...
OKAY.
SO WHATEVER HAPPENS, HAPPENS.
...LET'S GET THIS OVER WITH.
LET'S!

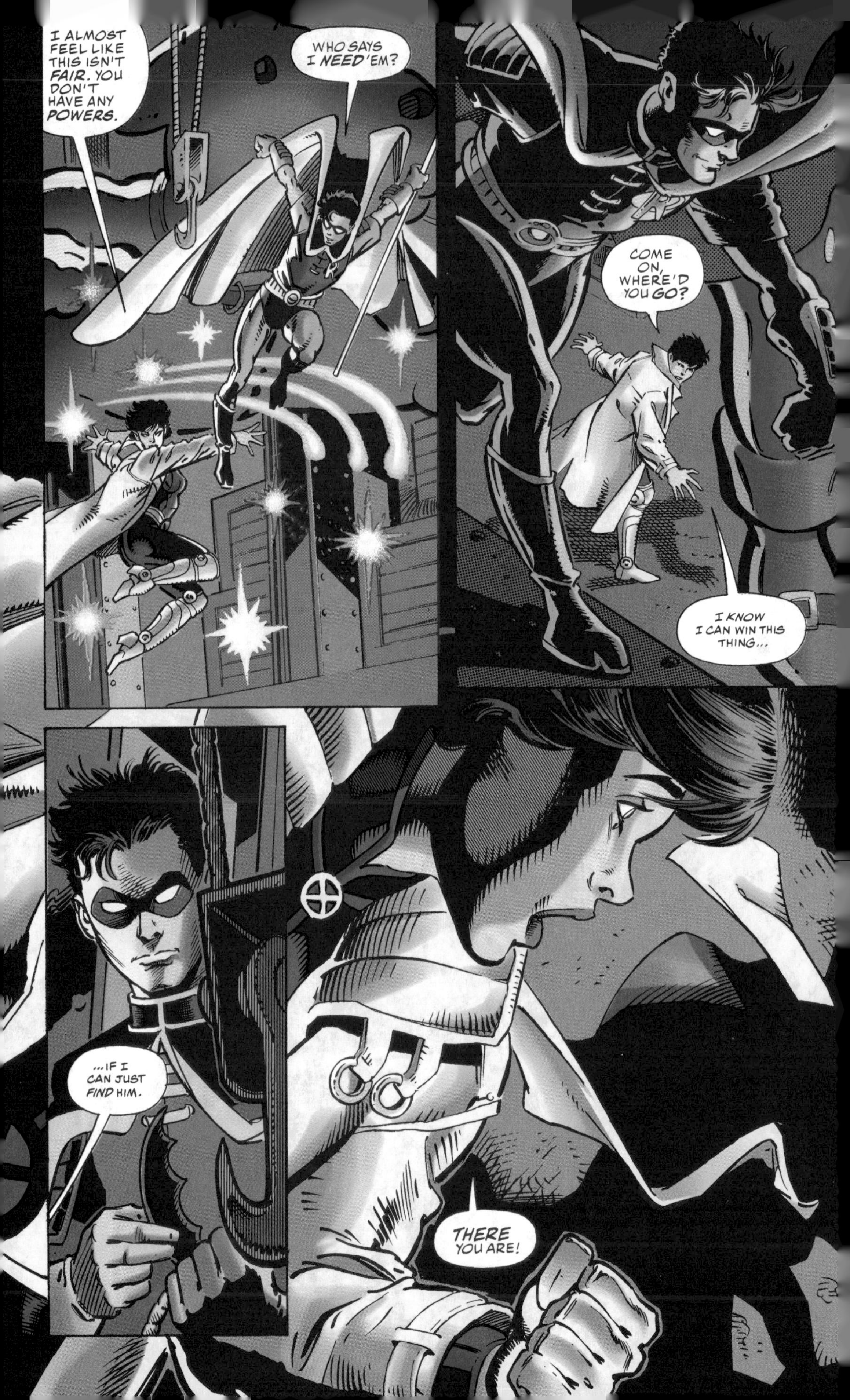
I ALMOST FEEL LIKE THIS ISN'T FAIR. YOU DON'T HAVE ANY POWERS.
WHO SAYS I NEED 'EM?
COME ON, WHERE'D YOU GO?
I KNOW I CAN WIN THIS THING...
...IF I CAN JUST FIND HIM.
THERE YOU ARE!

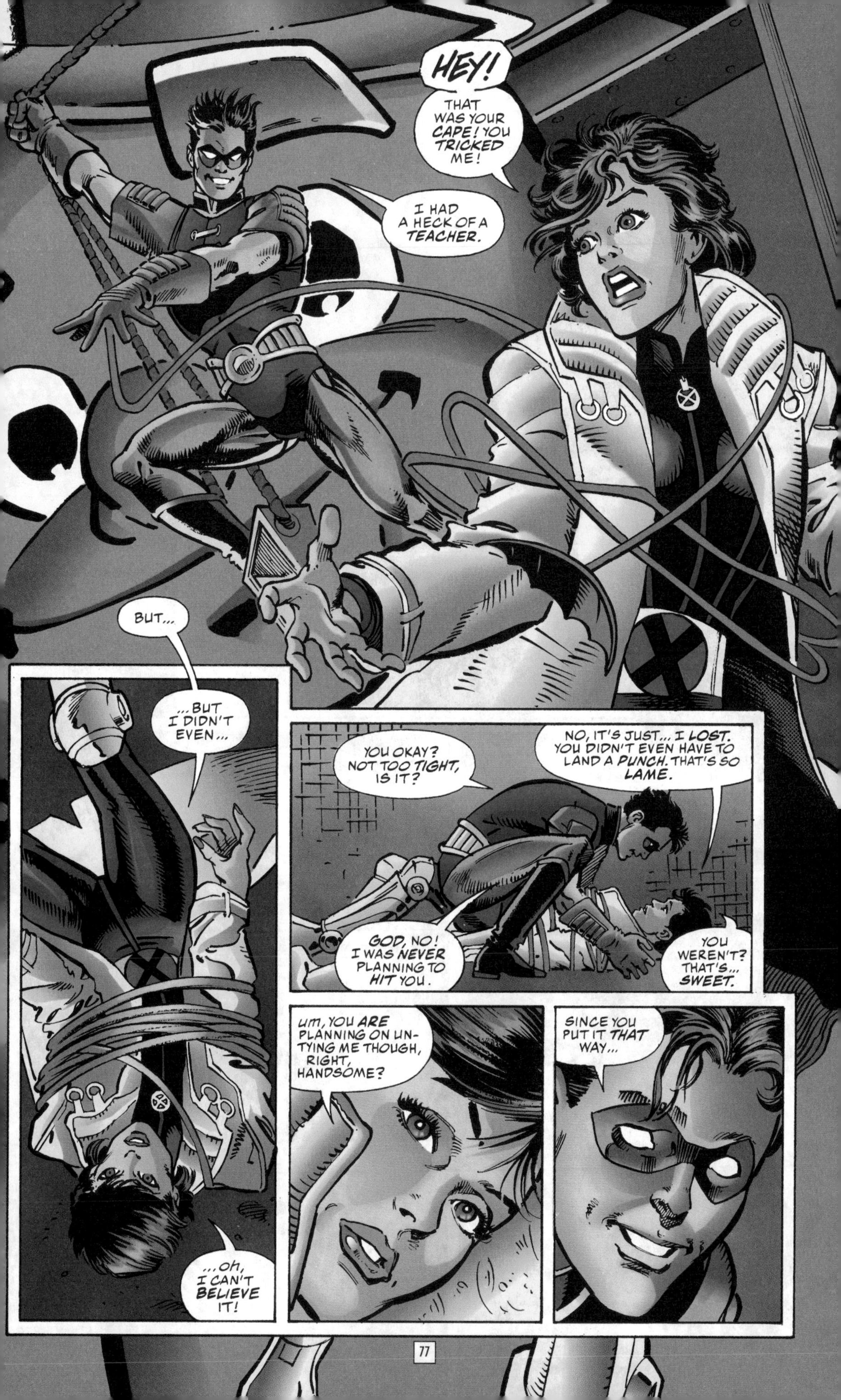
HEY!
THAT WAS YOUR CAPE! YOU TRICKED ME!
I HAD A HECK OF A TEACHER.
BUT...
...BUT I DIDN'T EVEN...
...OH, I CAN'T BELIEVE IT!
YOU OKAY? NOT TOO TIGHT, IS IT?
NO, IT'S JUST... I LOST. YOU DIDN'T EVEN HAVE TO LAND A PUNCH. THAT'S SO LAME.
GOD, NO! I WAS NEVER PLANNING TO HIT YOU.
YOU WEREN'T? THAT'S... SWEET.
UM, YOU ARE PLANNING ON UN-TYING ME THOUGH, RIGHT, HANDSOME?
SINCE YOU PUT IT THAT WAY...

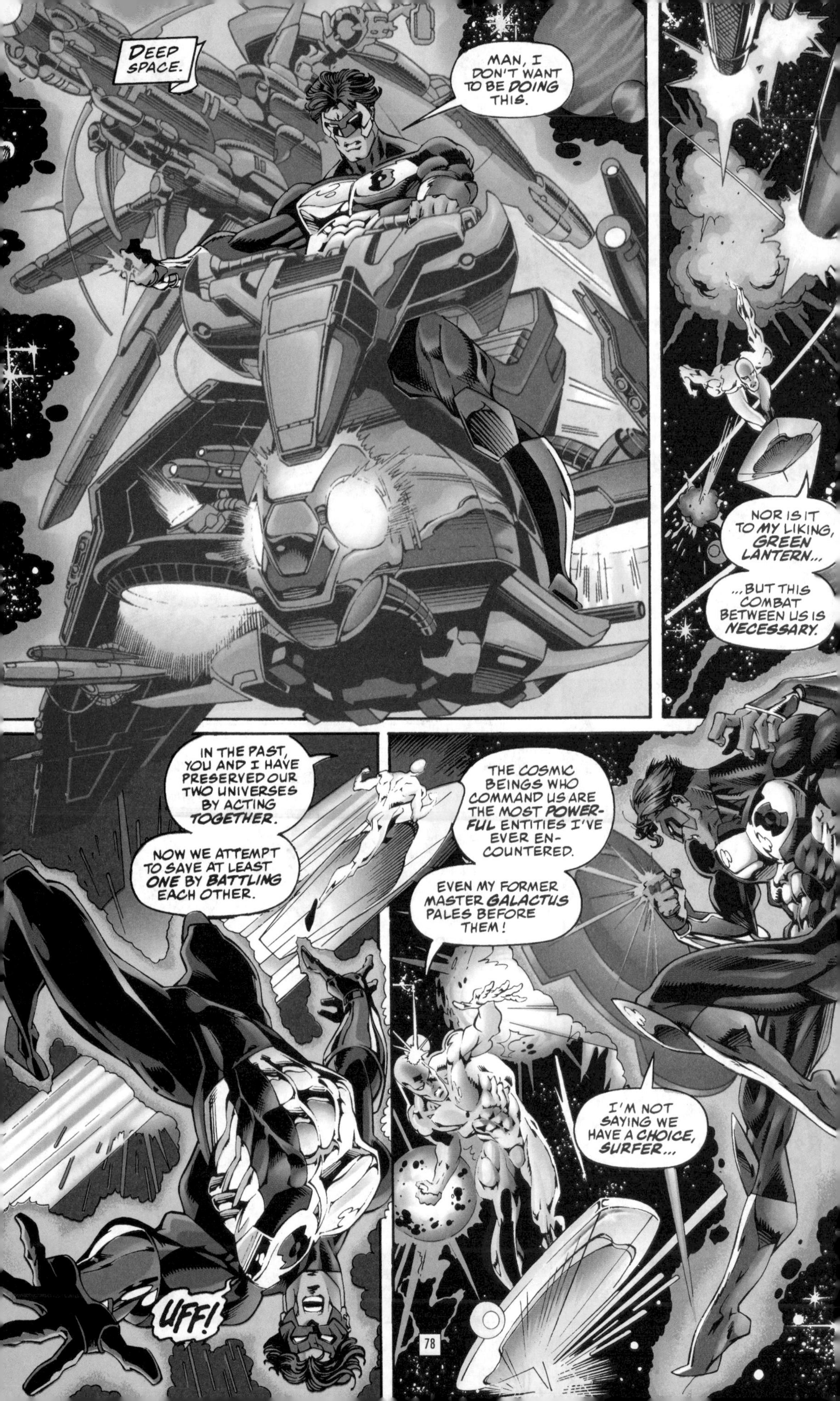
DEEP SPACE.
MAN, I DON'T WANT TO BE DOING THIS.
NOR IS IT TO MY LIKING, GREEN LANTERN...
...BUT THIS COMBAT BETWEEN US IS NECESSARY.
IN THE PAST, YOU AND I HAVE PRESERVED OUR TWO UNIVERSES BY ACTING TOGETHER.
NOW WE ATTEMPT TO SAVE AT LEAST ONE BY BATTLING EACH OTHER.
UFF!
THE COSMIC BEINGS WHO COMMAND US ARE THE MOST POWERFUL ENTITIES I'VE EVER ENCOUNTERED.
EVEN MY FORMER MASTER GALACTUS PALES BEFORE THEM!
I'M NOT SAYING WE HAVE A CHOICE, SURFER...

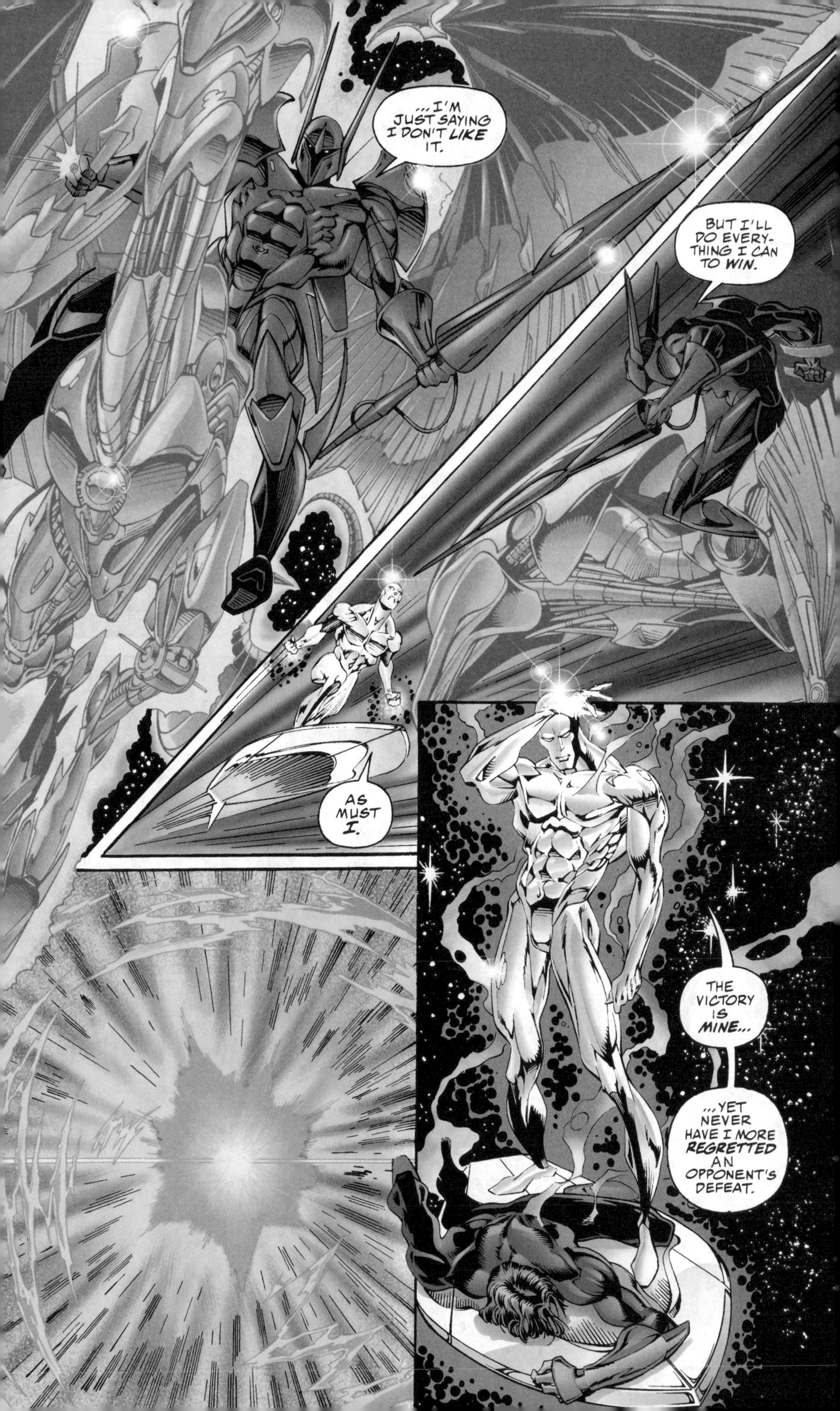
...I'M JUST SAYING I DON'T LIKE IT.
BUT I'LL DO EVERY-THING I CAN TO WIN.
AS MUST I.
THE VICTORY IS MINE...
...YET NEVER HAVE I MORE REGRETTED AN OPPONENT'S DEFEAT.

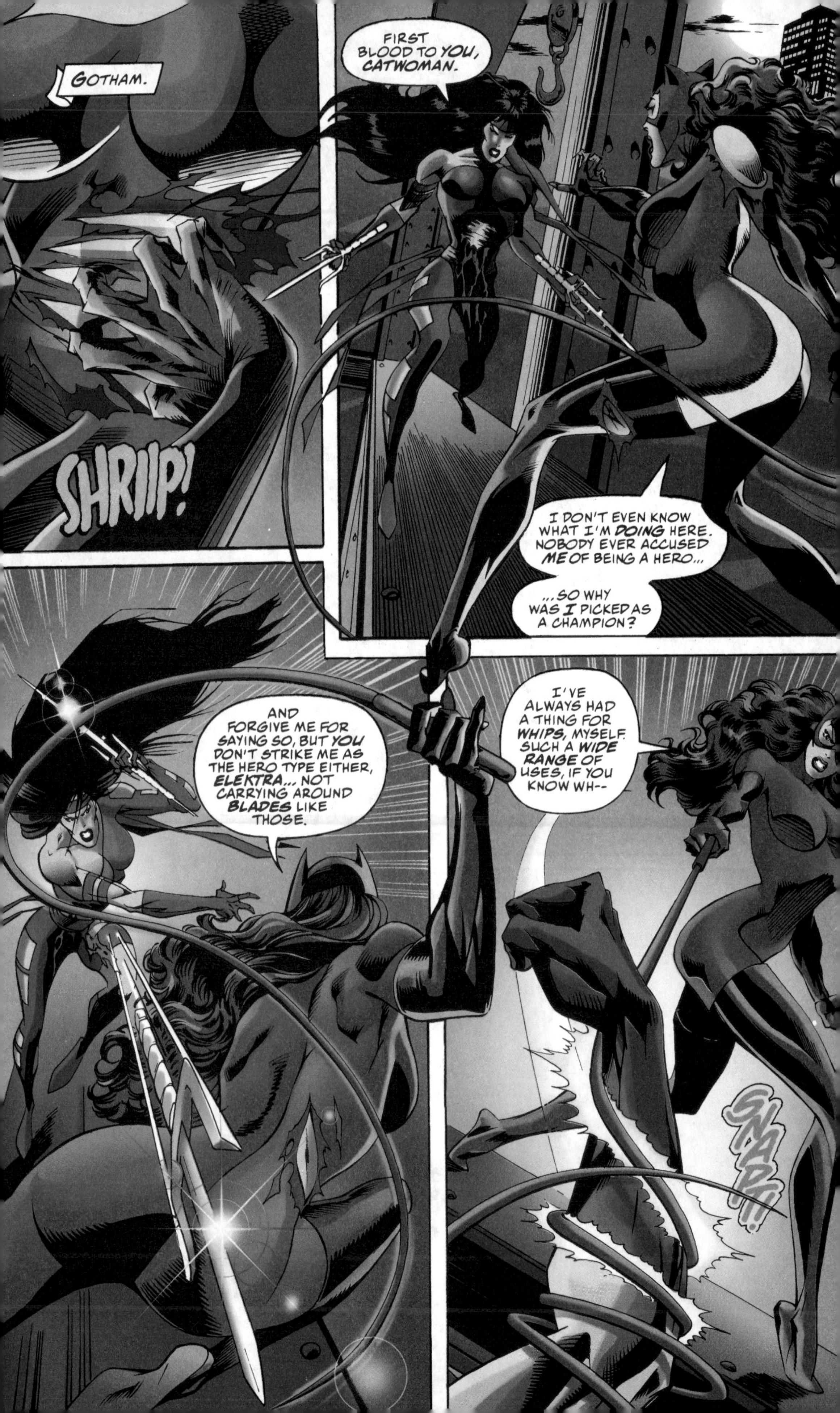
GOTHAM.
SHRIIP!
FIRST BLOOD TO YOU, CATWOMAN.
I DON'T EVEN KNOW WHAT I'M DOING HERE. NOBODY EVER ACCUSED ME OF BEING A HERO...
...SO WHY WAS I PICKED AS A CHAMPION?
AND FORGIVE ME FOR SAYING SO, BUT YOU DON'T STRIKE ME AS THE HERO TYPE EITHER, ELEKTRA... NOT CARRYING AROUND BLADES LIKE THOSE.
I'VE ALWAYS HAD A THING FOR WHIPS, MYSELF. SUCH A WIDE RANGE OF USES, IF YOU KNOW WH--
SNAP!!

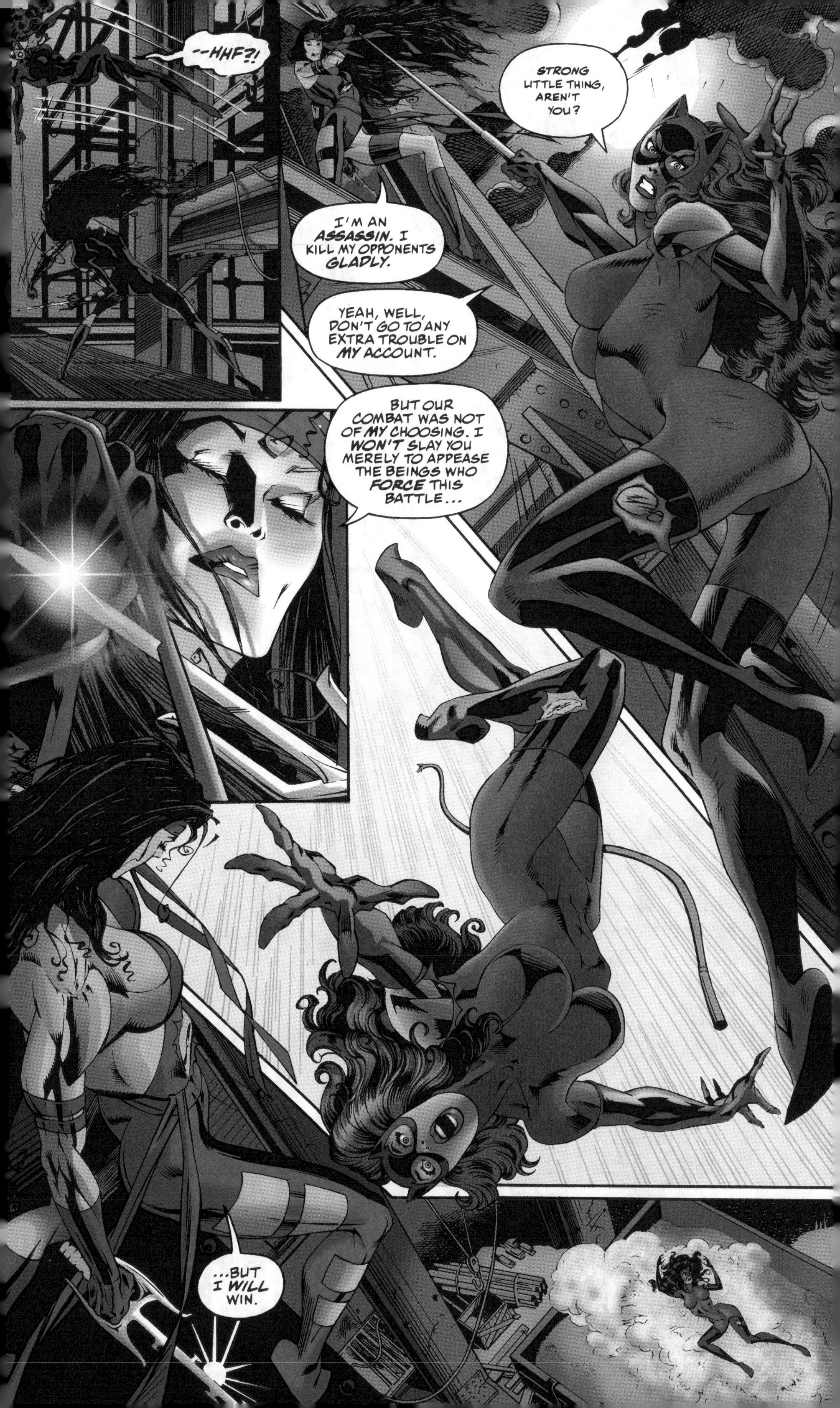
--HHF?!
STRONG LITTLE THING, AREN'T YOU?
I'M AN ASSASSIN. I KILL MY OPPONENTS GLADLY.
YEAH, WELL, DON'T GO TO ANY EXTRA TROUBLE ON MY ACCOUNT.
BUT OUR COMBAT WAS NOT OF MY CHOOSING. I WON'T SLAY YOU MERELY TO APPEASE THE BEINGS WHO FORCE THIS BATTLE...
...BUT I WILL WIN.

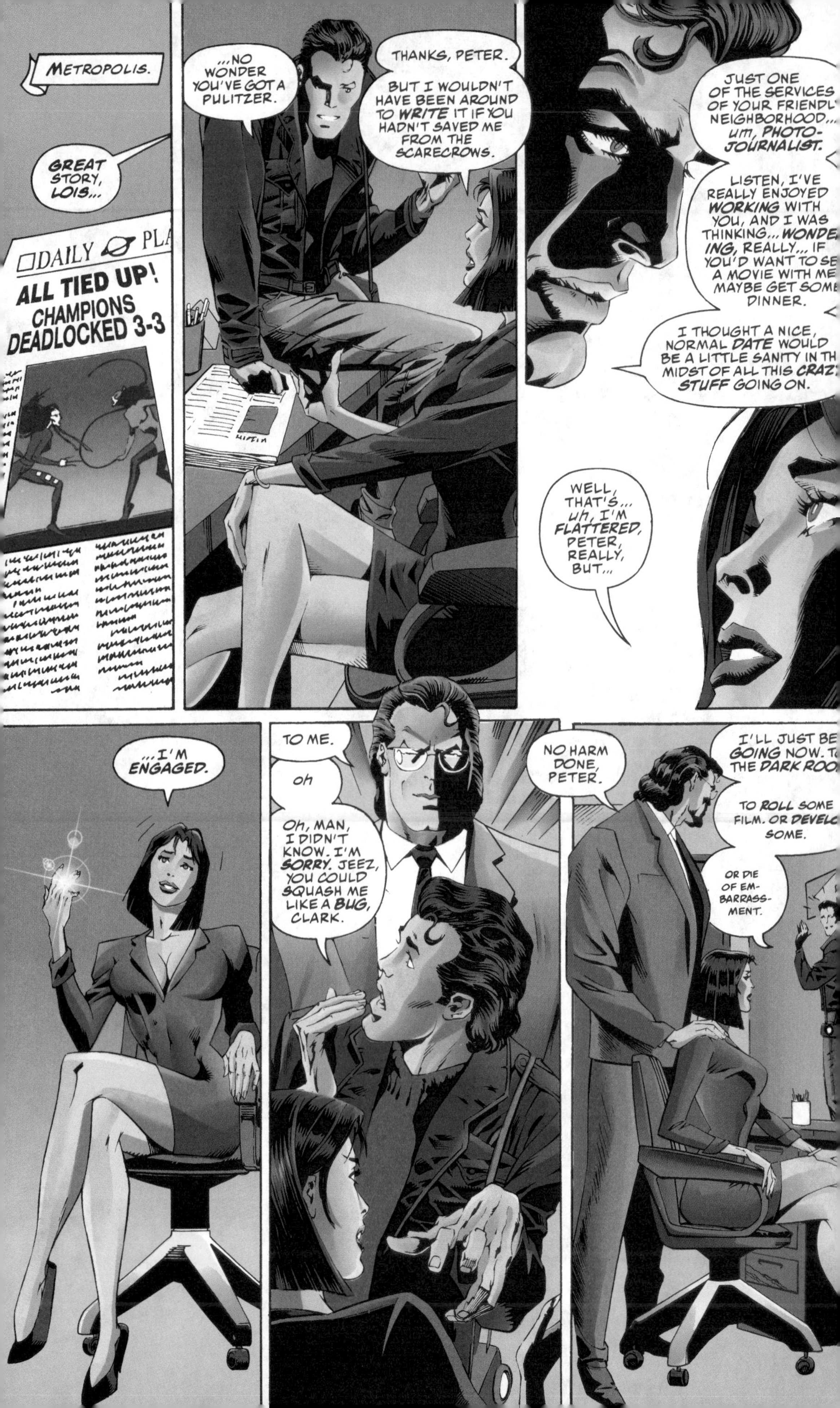

METROPOLIS.
GREAT STORY, LOIS...
DAILY PLA
ALL TIED UP!
CHAMPIONS DEADLOCKED 3-3
...NO WONDER YOU'VE GOT A PULITZER.
THANKS, PETER.
BUT I WOULDN'T HAVE BEEN AROUND TO WRITE IT IF YOU HADN'T SAVED ME FROM THE SCARECROWS.
JUST ONE OF THE SERVICES OF YOUR FRIENDL NEIGHBORHOOD... um, PHOTO-JOURNALIST.
LISTEN, I'VE REALLY ENJOYED WORKING WITH YOU, AND I WAS THINKING... WONDE ING, REALLY... IF YOU'D WANT TO SE A MOVIE WITH ME MAYBE GET SOME DINNER.
I THOUGHT A NICE, NORMAL DATE WOULD BE A LITTLE SANITY IN TH MIDST OF ALL THIS CRAZ STUFF GOING ON.
WELL, THAT'S... uh, I'M FLATTERED, PETER, REALLY, BUT...
...I'M ENGAGED.
TO ME.
oh
OH, MAN, I DIDN'T KNOW. I'M SORRY. JEEZ, YOU COULD SQUASH ME LIKE A BUG, CLARK.
NO HARM DONE, PETER.
I'LL JUST BE GOING NOW. T THE DARK ROO
TO ROLL SOME FILM. OR DEVEL SOME.
OR DIE OF EM-BARRASS-MENT.

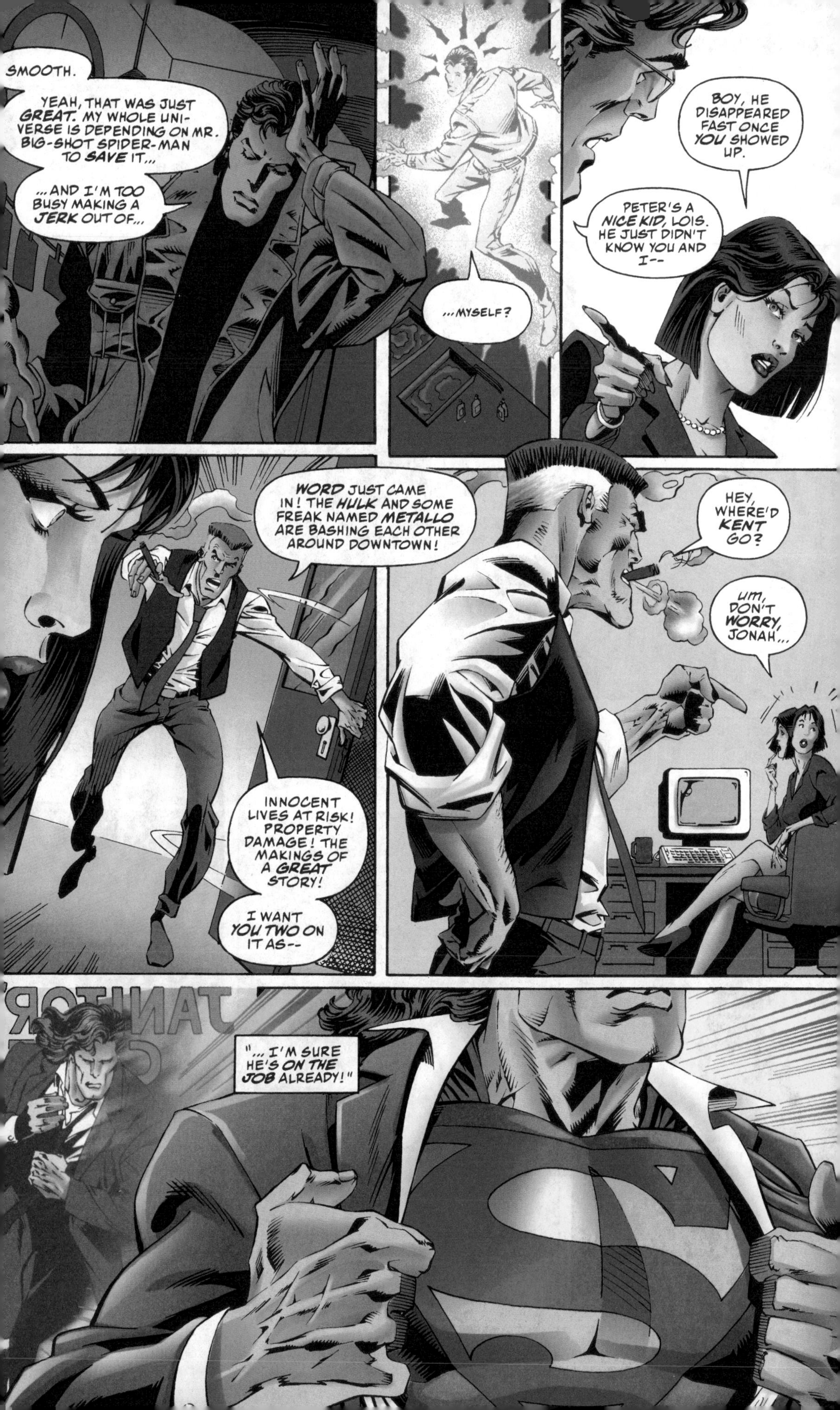
SMOOTH.
YEAH, THAT WAS JUST GREAT. MY WHOLE UNIVERSE IS DEPENDING ON MR. BIG-SHOT SPIDER-MAN TO SAVE IT...
...AND I'M TOO BUSY MAKING A JERK OUT OF...
...MYSELF?
BOY, HE DISAPPEARED FAST ONCE YOU SHOWED UP.
PETER'S A NICE KID, LOIS. HE JUST DIDN'T KNOW YOU AND I--
WORD JUST CAME IN! THE HULK AND SOME FREAK NAMED METALLO ARE BASHING EACH OTHER AROUND DOWNTOWN!
INNOCENT LIVES AT RISK! PROPERTY DAMAGE! THE MAKINGS OF A GREAT STORY!
I WANT YOU TWO ON IT AS--
HEY, WHERE'D KENT GO?
UM, DON'T WORRY, JONAH...
JANITOR
"...I'M SURE HE'S ON THE JOB ALREADY!"

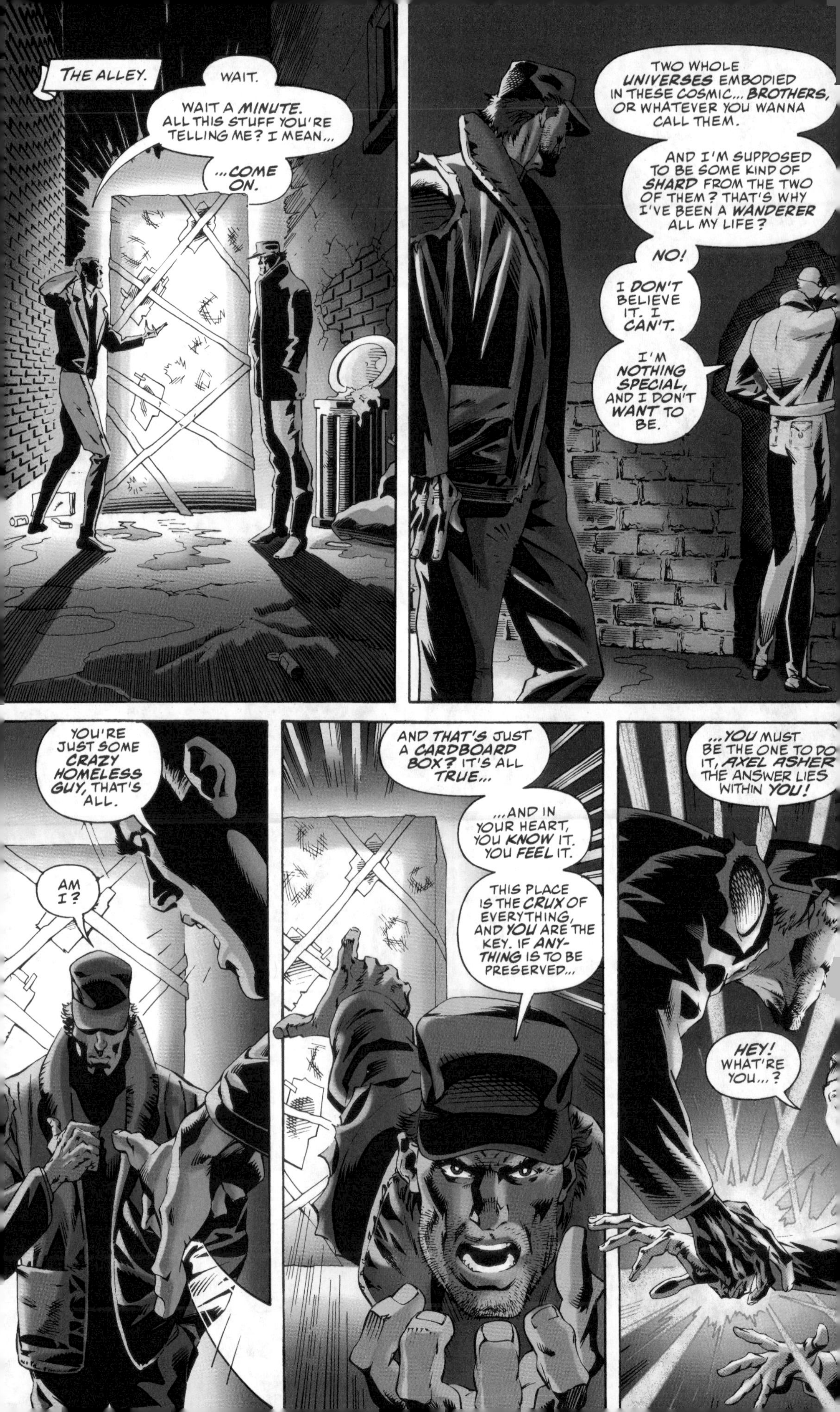
THE ALLEY.
WAIT.
WAIT A MINUTE. ALL THIS STUFF YOU'RE TELLING ME? I MEAN...
...COME ON.
TWO WHOLE UNIVERSES EMBODIED IN THESE COSMIC... BROTHERS, OR WHATEVER YOU WANNA CALL THEM.
AND I'M SUPPOSED TO BE SOME KIND OF SHARD FROM THE TWO OF THEM? THAT'S WHY I'VE BEEN A WANDERER ALL MY LIFE?
NO!
I DON'T BELIEVE IT. I CAN'T.
I'M NOTHING SPECIAL, AND I DON'T WANT TO BE.
YOU'RE JUST SOME CRAZY HOMELESS GUY, THAT'S ALL.
AM I?
AND THAT'S JUST A CARDBOARD BOX? IT'S ALL TRUE...
...AND IN YOUR HEART, YOU KNOW IT. YOU FEEL IT.
THIS PLACE IS THE CRUX OF EVERYTHING, AND YOU ARE THE KEY. IF ANY-THING IS TO BE PRESERVED...
...YOU MUST BE THE ONE TO DO IT, AXEL ASHER. THE ANSWER LIES WITHIN YOU!
HEY! WHAT'RE YOU...?

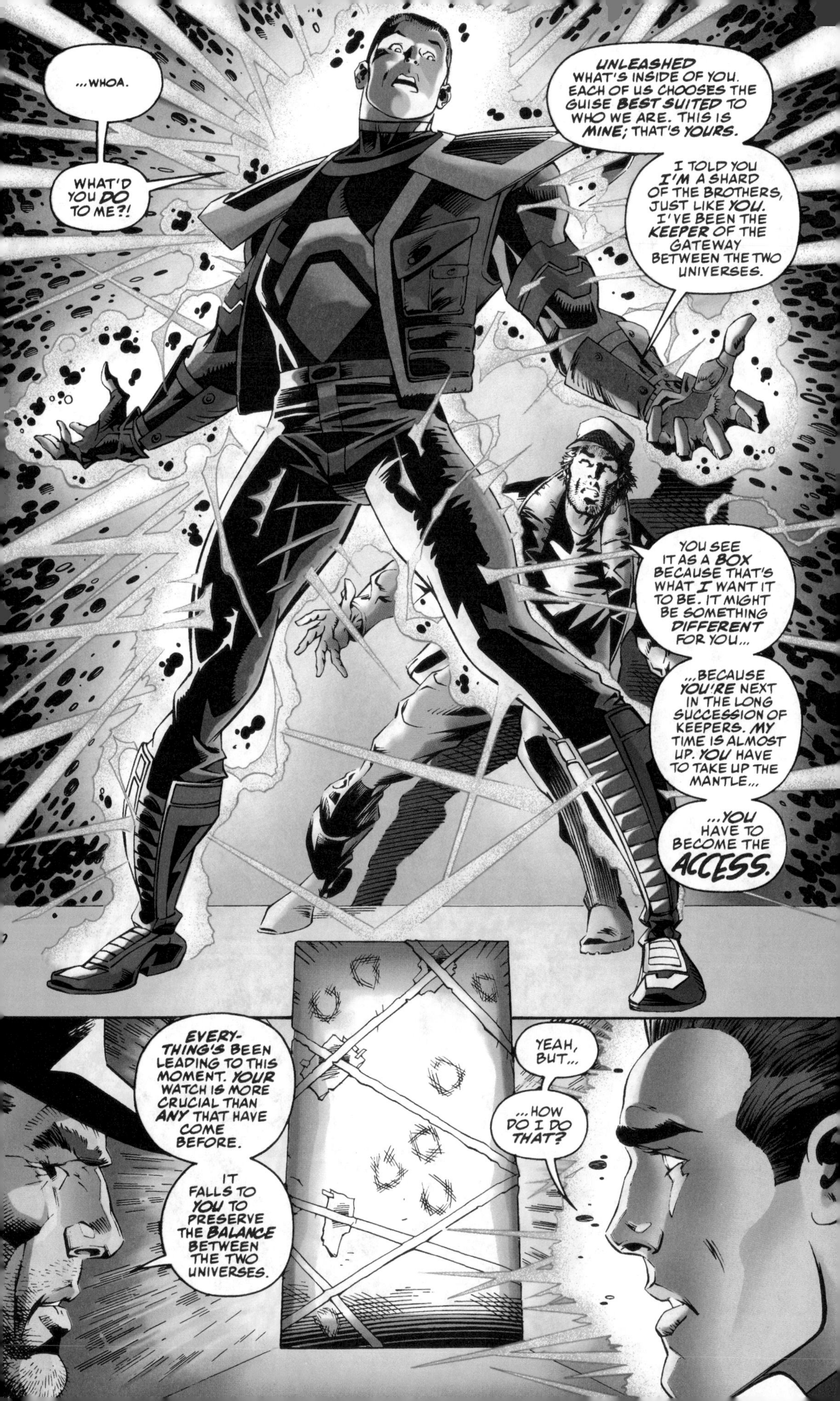
...WHOA.
WHAT'D YOU DO TO ME?!
UNLEASHED WHAT'S INSIDE OF YOU. EACH OF US CHOOSES THE GUISE BEST SUITED TO WHO WE ARE. THIS IS MINE; THAT'S YOURS.
I TOLD YOU I'M A SHARD OF THE BROTHERS, JUST LIKE YOU. I'VE BEEN THE KEEPER OF THE GATEWAY BETWEEN THE TWO UNIVERSES.
YOU SEE IT AS A BOX BECAUSE THAT'S WHAT I WANT IT TO BE. IT MIGHT BE SOMETHING DIFFERENT FOR YOU...
...BECAUSE YOU'RE NEXT IN THE LONG SUCCESSION OF KEEPERS. MY TIME IS ALMOST UP. YOU HAVE TO TAKE UP THE MANTLE...
...YOU HAVE TO BECOME THE ACCESS.
EVERYTHING'S BEEN LEADING TO THIS MOMENT. YOUR WATCH IS MORE CRUCIAL THAN ANY THAT HAVE COME BEFORE.
IT FALLS TO YOU TO PRESERVE THE BALANCE BETWEEN THE TWO UNIVERSES.
YEAH, BUT...
...HOW DO I DO THAT?

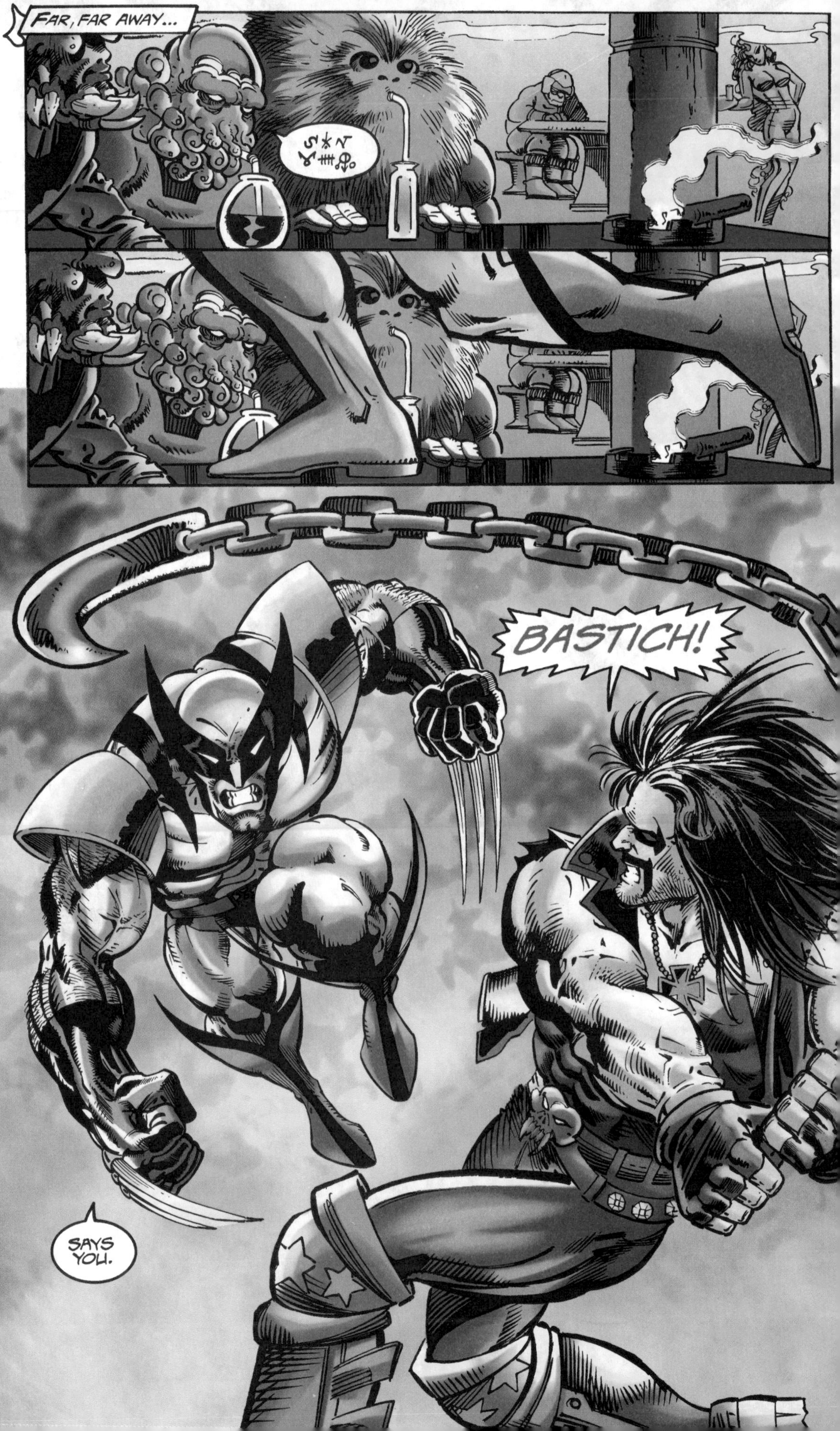
FAR, FAR AWAY...
BASTICH!
SAYS YOU.

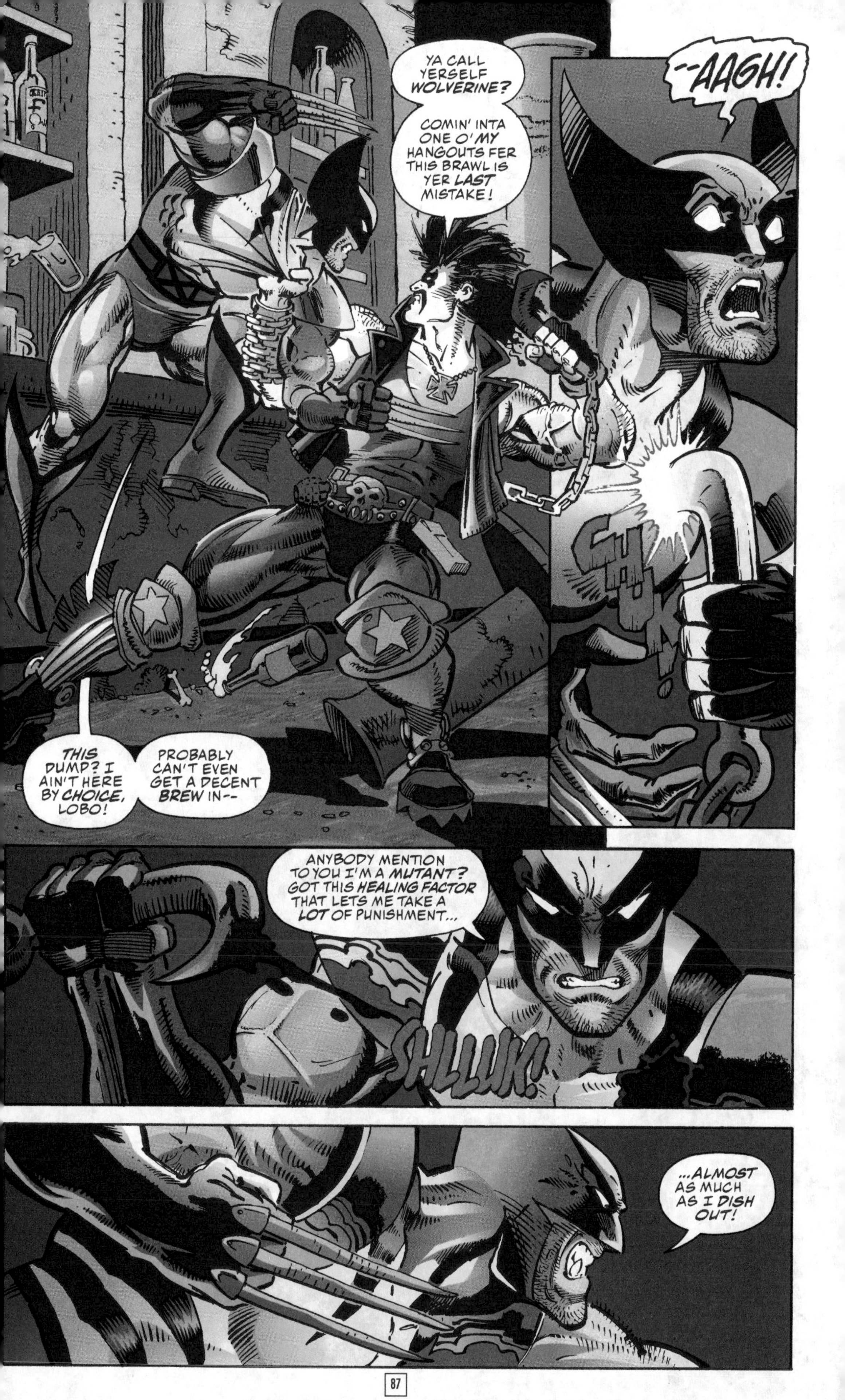
YA CALL YERSELF WOLVERINE?
COMIN' INTA ONE O' MY HANGOUTS FER THIS BRAWL IS YER LAST MISTAKE!
--AAGH!
THIS DUMP? I AIN'T HERE BY CHOICE, LOBO!
PROBABLY CAN'T EVEN GET A DECENT BREW IN--
CHUK!
ANYBODY MENTION TO YOU I'M A MUTANT? GOT THIS HEALING FACTOR THAT LETS ME TAKE A LOT OF PUNISHMENT...
SHLLUK!
...ALMOST AS MUCH AS I DISH OUT!

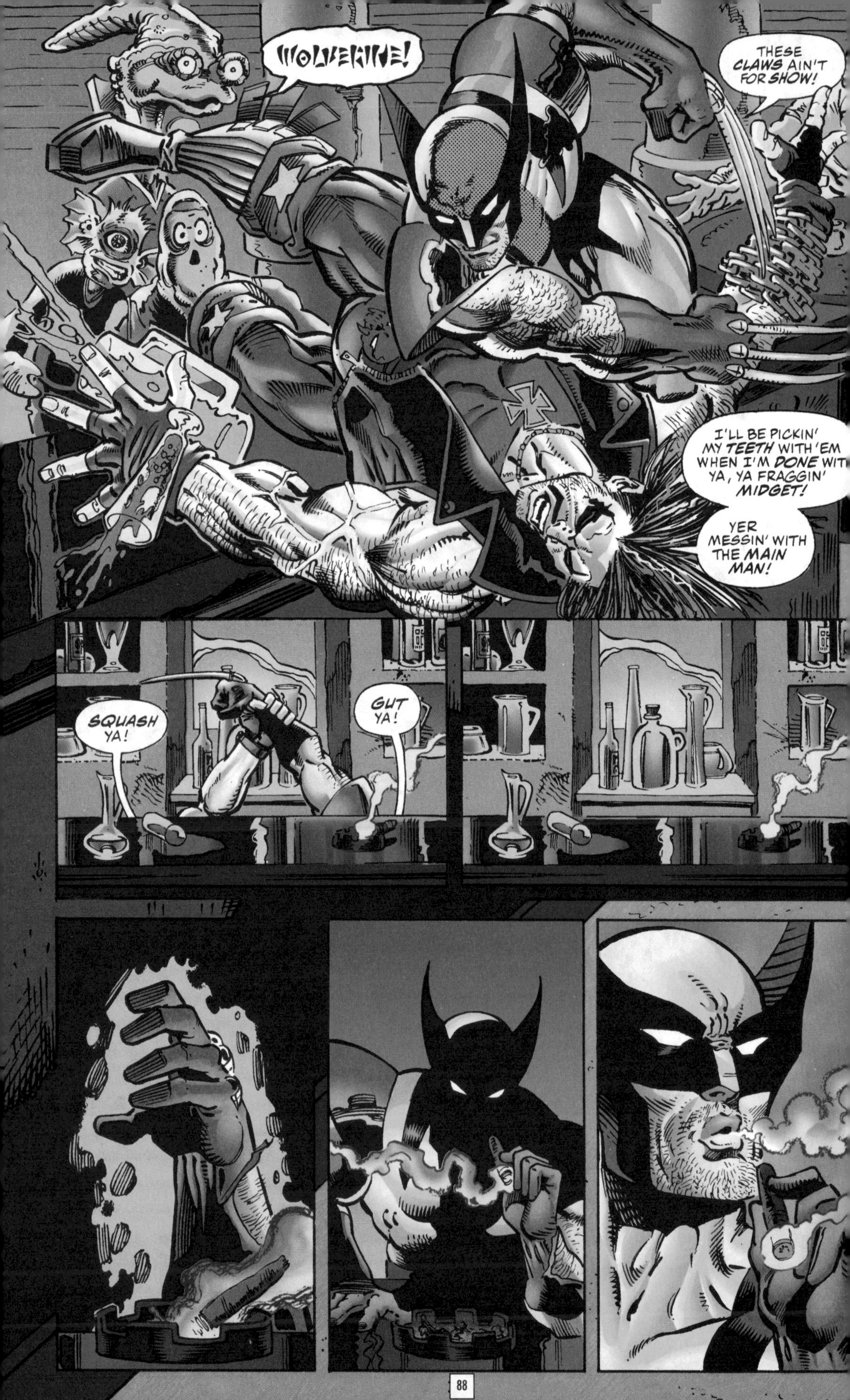
WOLVERINE!
THESE CLAWS AIN'T FOR SHOW!
I'LL BE PICKIN' MY TEETH WITH 'EM WHEN I'M DONE WIT YA, YA FRAGGIN' MIDGET!
YER MESSIN' WITH THE MAIN MAN!
SQUASH YA!
GUT YA!

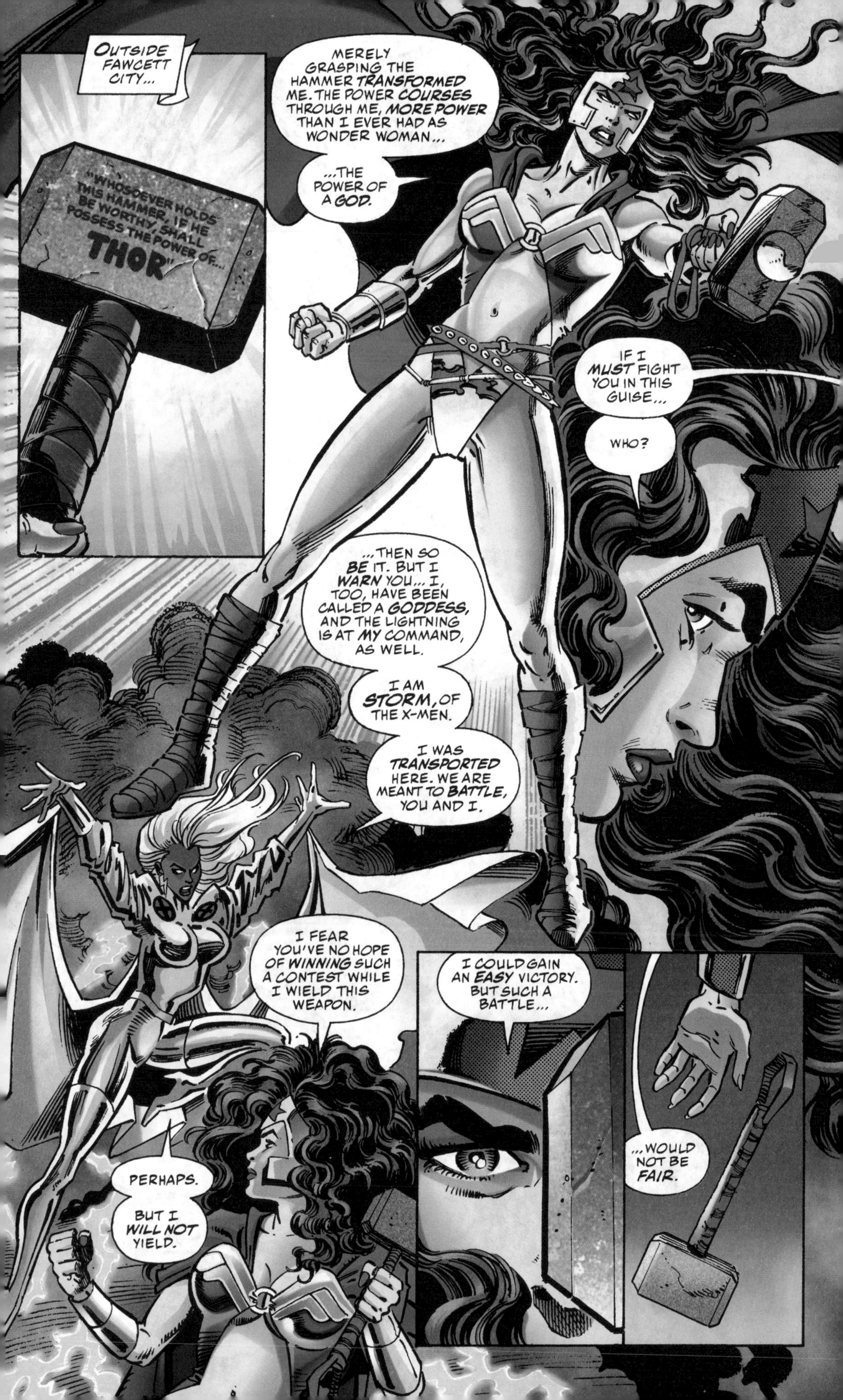

OUTSIDE FAWCETT CITY...
"WHOSOEVER HOLDS THIS HAMMER, IF HE BE WORTHY, SHALL POSSESS THE POWER OF... THOR"
MERELY GRASPING THE HAMMER TRANSFORMED ME. THE POWER COURSES THROUGH ME, MORE POWER THAN I EVER HAD AS WONDER WOMAN...
...THE POWER OF A GOD.
IF I MUST FIGHT YOU IN THIS GUISE...
WHO?
...THEN SO BE IT. BUT I WARN YOU... I, TOO, HAVE BEEN CALLED A GODDESS, AND THE LIGHTNING IS AT MY COMMAND, AS WELL.
I AM STORM, OF THE X-MEN.
I WAS TRANSPORTED HERE. WE ARE MEANT TO BATTLE, YOU AND I.
I FEAR YOU'VE NO HOPE OF WINNING SUCH A CONTEST WHILE I WIELD THIS WEAPON.
PERHAPS.
BUT I WILL NOT YIELD.
I COULD GAIN AN EASY VICTORY. BUT SUCH A BATTLE...
...WOULD NOT BE FAIR.

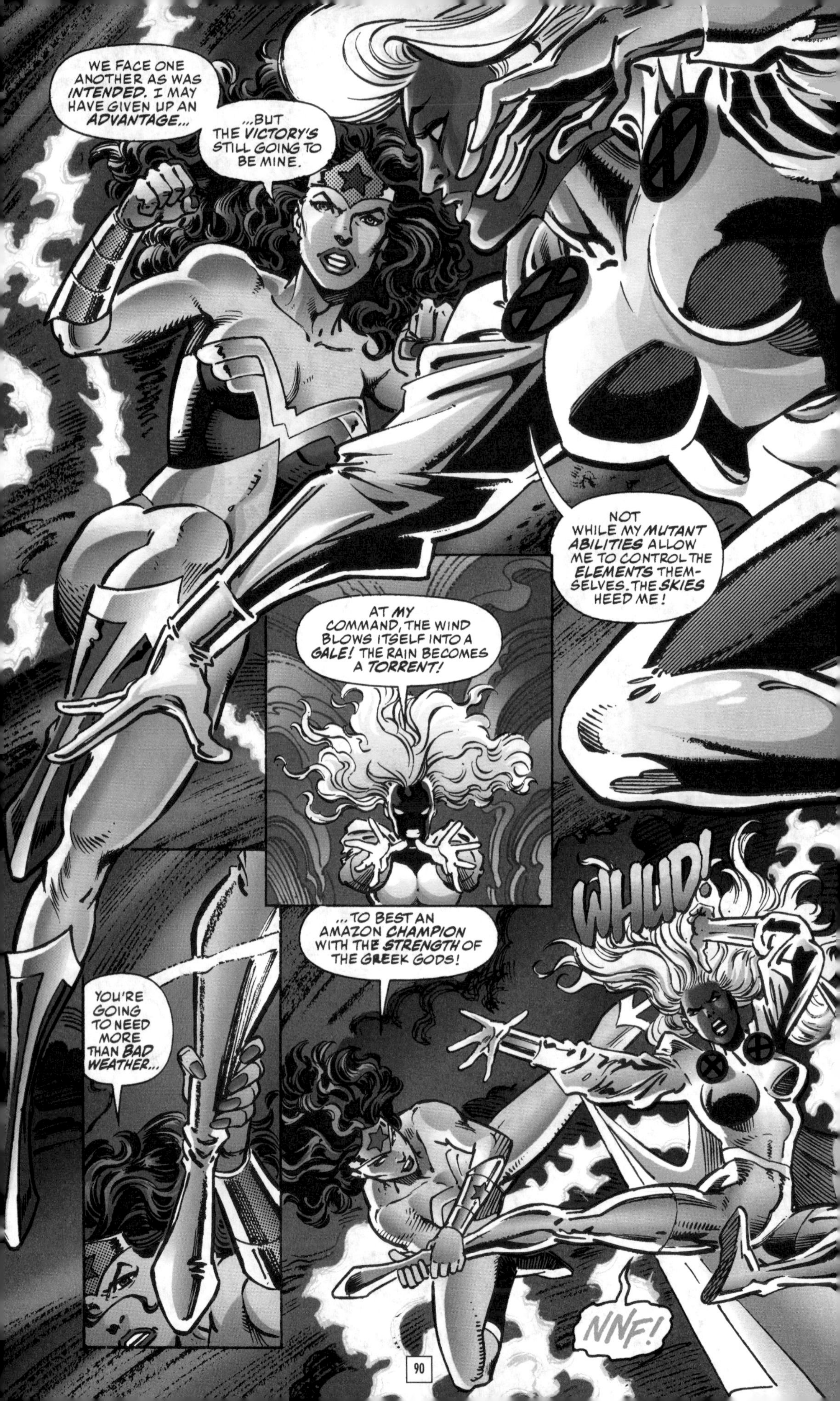

WE FACE ONE ANOTHER AS WAS INTENDED. I MAY HAVE GIVEN UP AN ADVANTAGE...
...BUT THE VICTORY'S STILL GOING TO BE MINE.
NOT WHILE MY MUTANT ABILITIES ALLOW ME TO CONTROL THE ELEMENTS THEMSELVES. THE SKIES HEED ME!
AT MY COMMAND, THE WIND BLOWS ITSELF INTO A GALE! THE RAIN BECOMES A TORRENT!
YOU'RE GOING TO NEED MORE THAN BAD WEATHER...
...TO BEST AN AMAZON CHAMPION WITH THE STRENGTH OF THE GREEK GODS!
WHUD!
NNF!

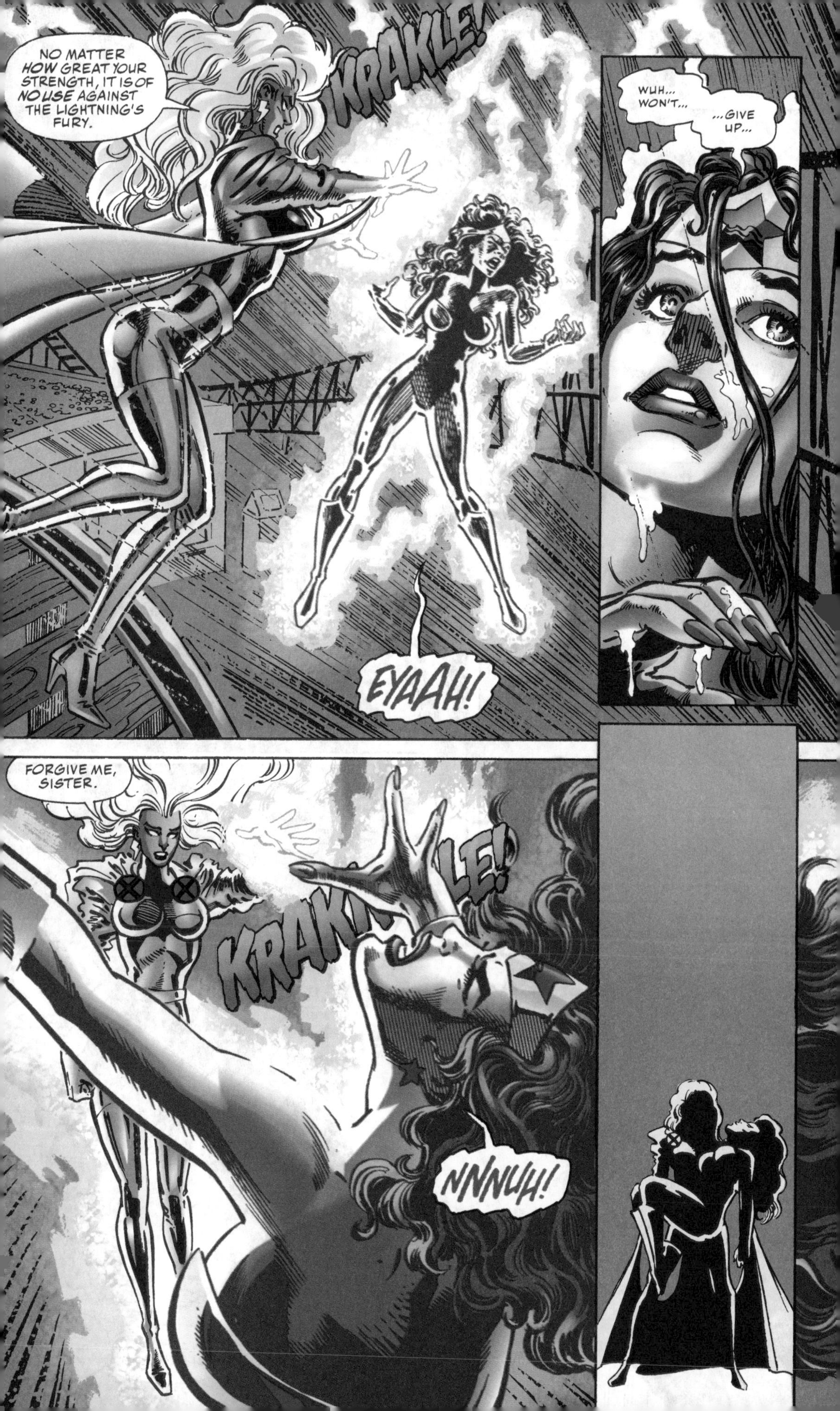

NO MATTER HOW GREAT YOUR STRENGTH, IT IS OF NO USE AGAINST THE LIGHTNING'S FURY.
KRAKLE!
EYAAH!
WUH... WON'T...
...GIVE UP...
FORGIVE ME, SISTER.
NNNUH!

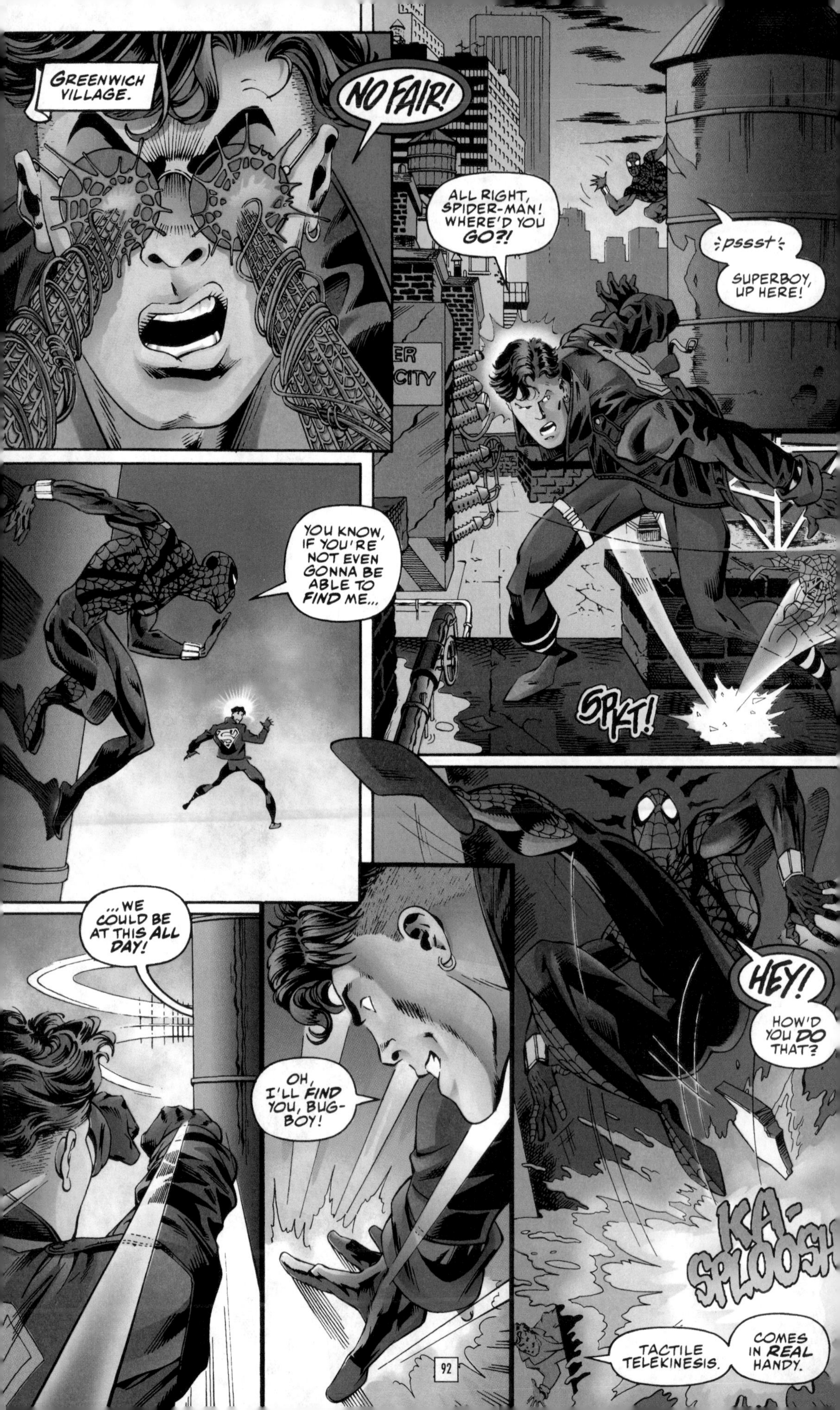
GREENWICH VILLAGE.
NO FAIR!
ALL RIGHT, SPIDER-MAN! WHERE'D YOU GO?!
pssst
SUPERBOY, UP HERE!
YOU KNOW, IF YOU'RE NOT EVEN GONNA BE ABLE TO FIND ME...
SPKT!
...WE COULD BE AT THIS ALL DAY!
OH, I'LL FIND YOU, BUG-BOY!
HEY!
HOW'D YOU DO THAT?
KA-SPLOOSH
TACTILE TELEKINESIS.
COMES IN REAL HANDY.

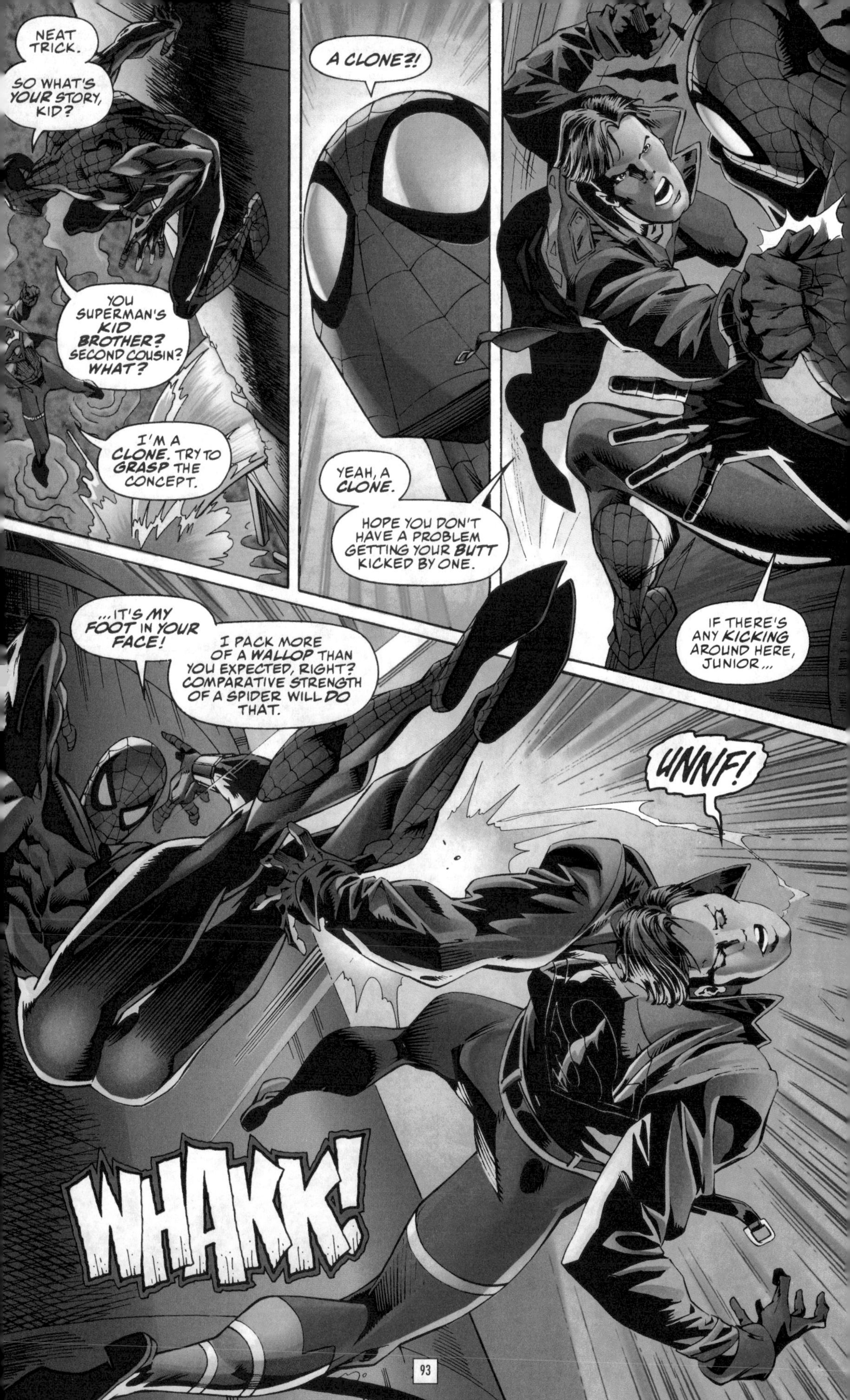
NEAT TRICK.
SO WHAT'S YOUR STORY, KID?
YOU SUPERMAN'S KID BROTHER? SECOND COUSIN? WHAT?
I'M A CLONE. TRY TO GRASP THE CONCEPT.
A CLONE?!
YEAH, A CLONE.
HOPE YOU DON'T HAVE A PROBLEM GETTING YOUR BUTT KICKED BY ONE.
IF THERE'S ANY KICKING AROUND HERE, JUNIOR...
...IT'S MY FOOT IN YOUR FACE!
I PACK MORE OF A WALLOP THAN YOU EXPECTED, RIGHT? COMPARATIVE STRENGTH OF A SPIDER WILL DO THAT.
UNNF!
WHAKK!

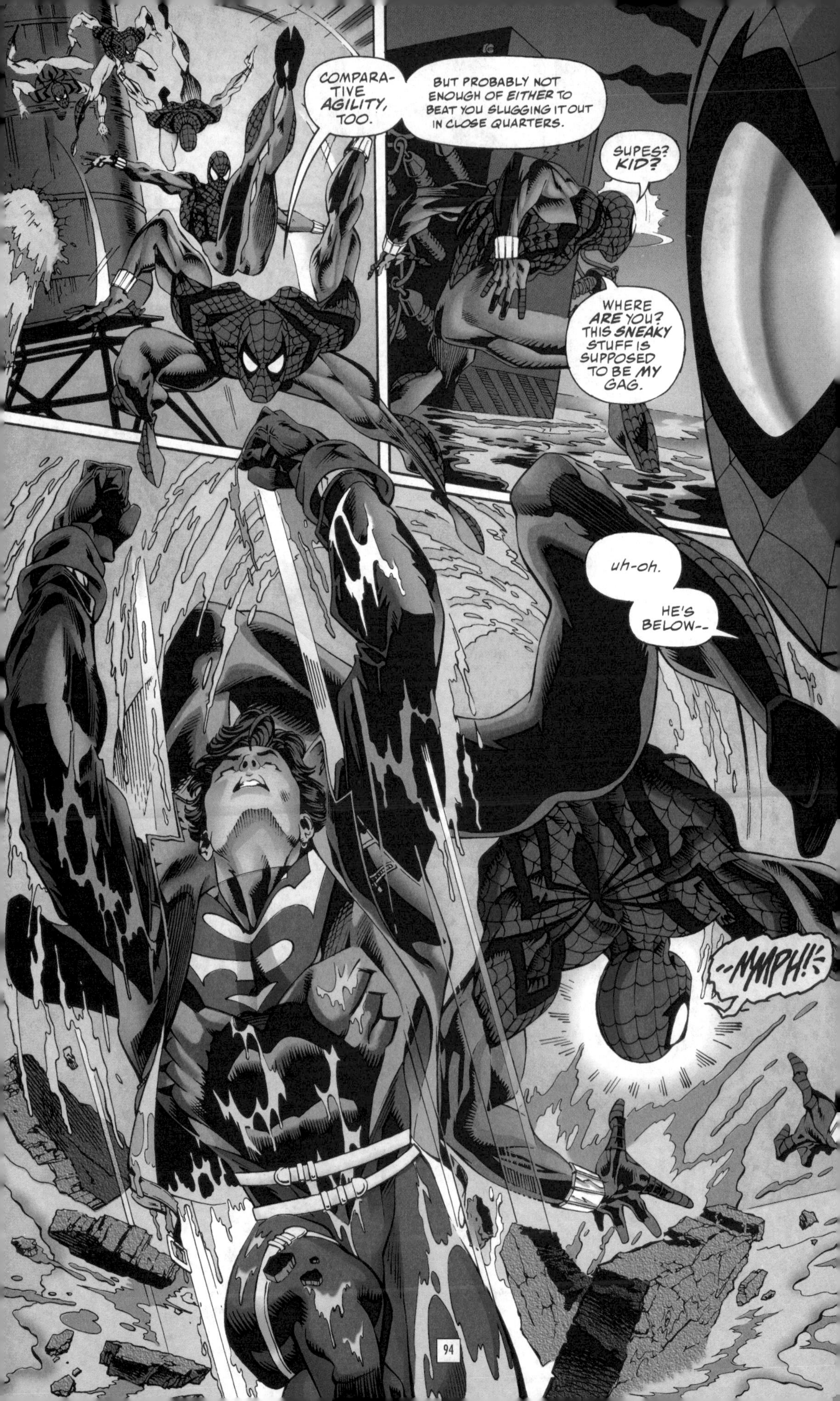
COMPARATIVE AGILITY, TOO.
BUT PROBABLY NOT ENOUGH OF EITHER TO BEAT YOU SLUGGING IT OUT IN CLOSE QUARTERS.
SUPES? KID?
WHERE ARE YOU? THIS SNEAKY STUFF IS SUPPOSED TO BE MY GAG.
uh-oh.
HE'S BELOW--
--MMPH!!

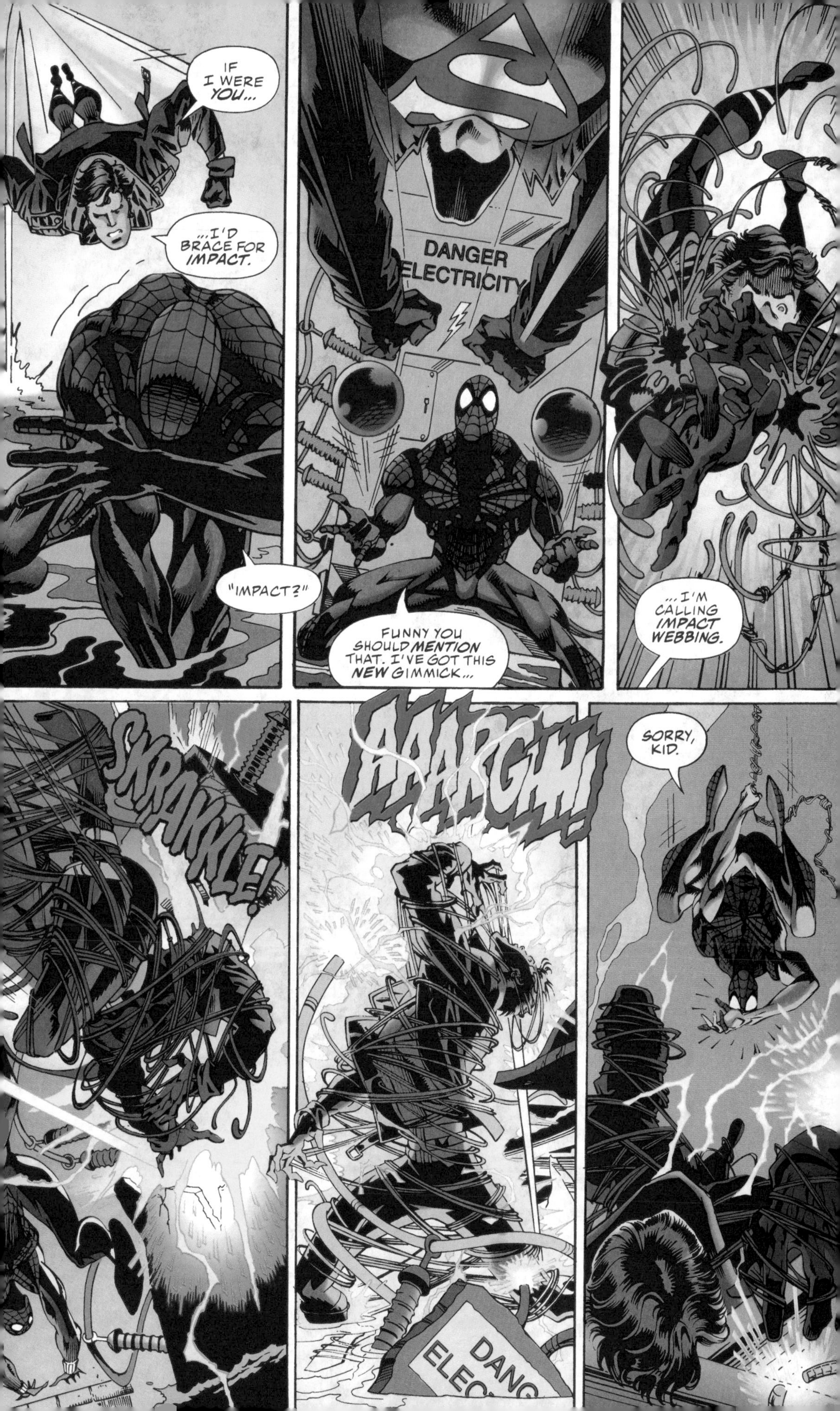
IF I WERE YOU...
...I'D BRACE FOR IMPACT.
"IMPACT?"
FUNNY YOU SHOULD MENTION THAT. I'VE GOT THIS NEW GIMMICK...
DANGER ELECTRICITY
...I'M CALLING IMPACT WEBBING.
SKRAKKLE!
AAARGH!
SORRY, KID.

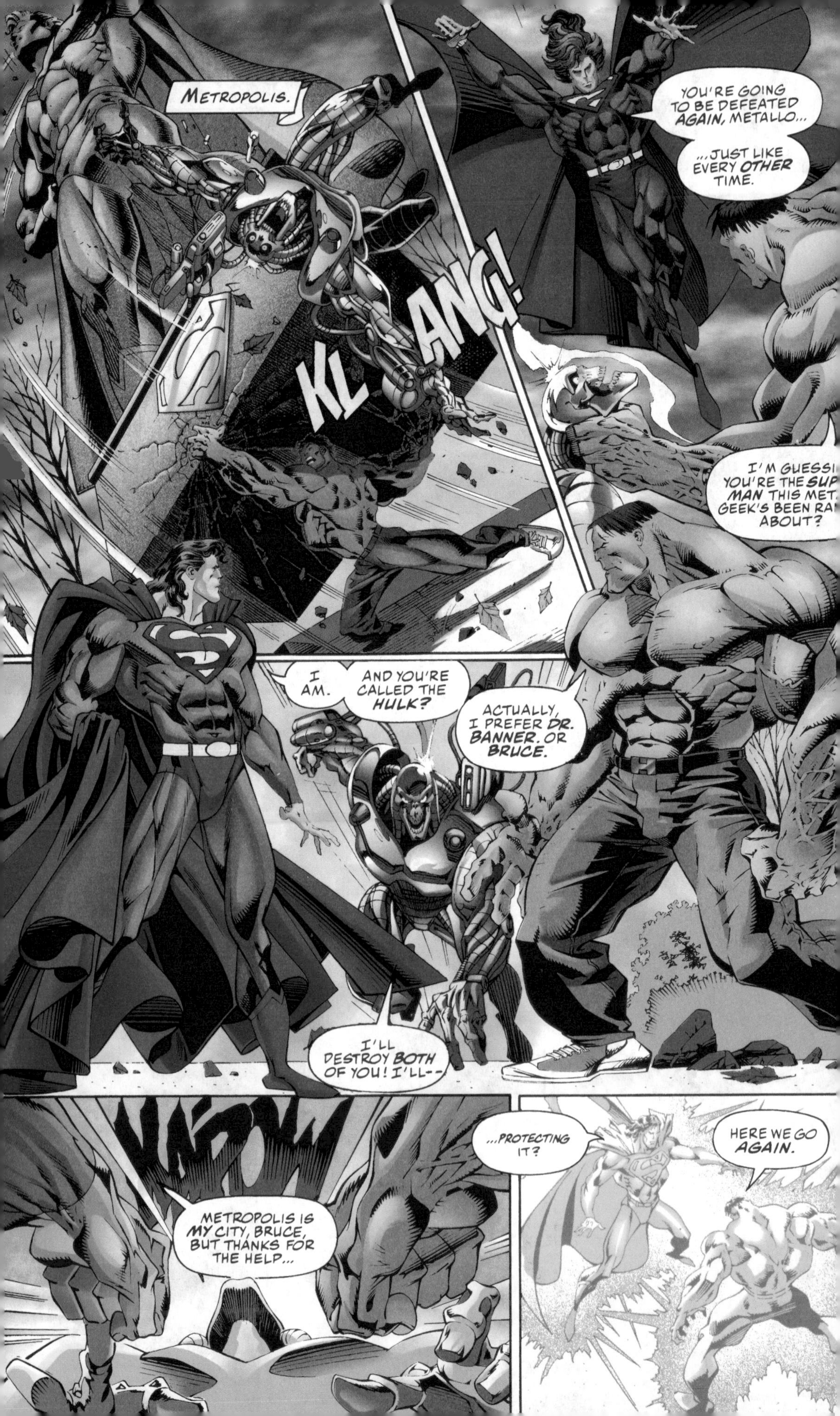

METROPOLIS.
KLANG!
YOU'RE GOING TO BE DEFEATED AGAIN, METALLO...
...JUST LIKE EVERY OTHER TIME.
I'M GUESSI YOU'RE THE SUP MAN THIS MET GEEK'S BEEN RA ABOUT?
I AM.
AND YOU'RE CALLED THE HULK?
ACTUALLY, I PREFER DR. BANNER. OR BRUCE.
I'LL DESTROY BOTH OF YOU! I'LL--
METROPOLIS IS MY CITY, BRUCE, BUT THANKS FOR THE HELP...
...PROTECTING IT?
HERE WE GO AGAIN.

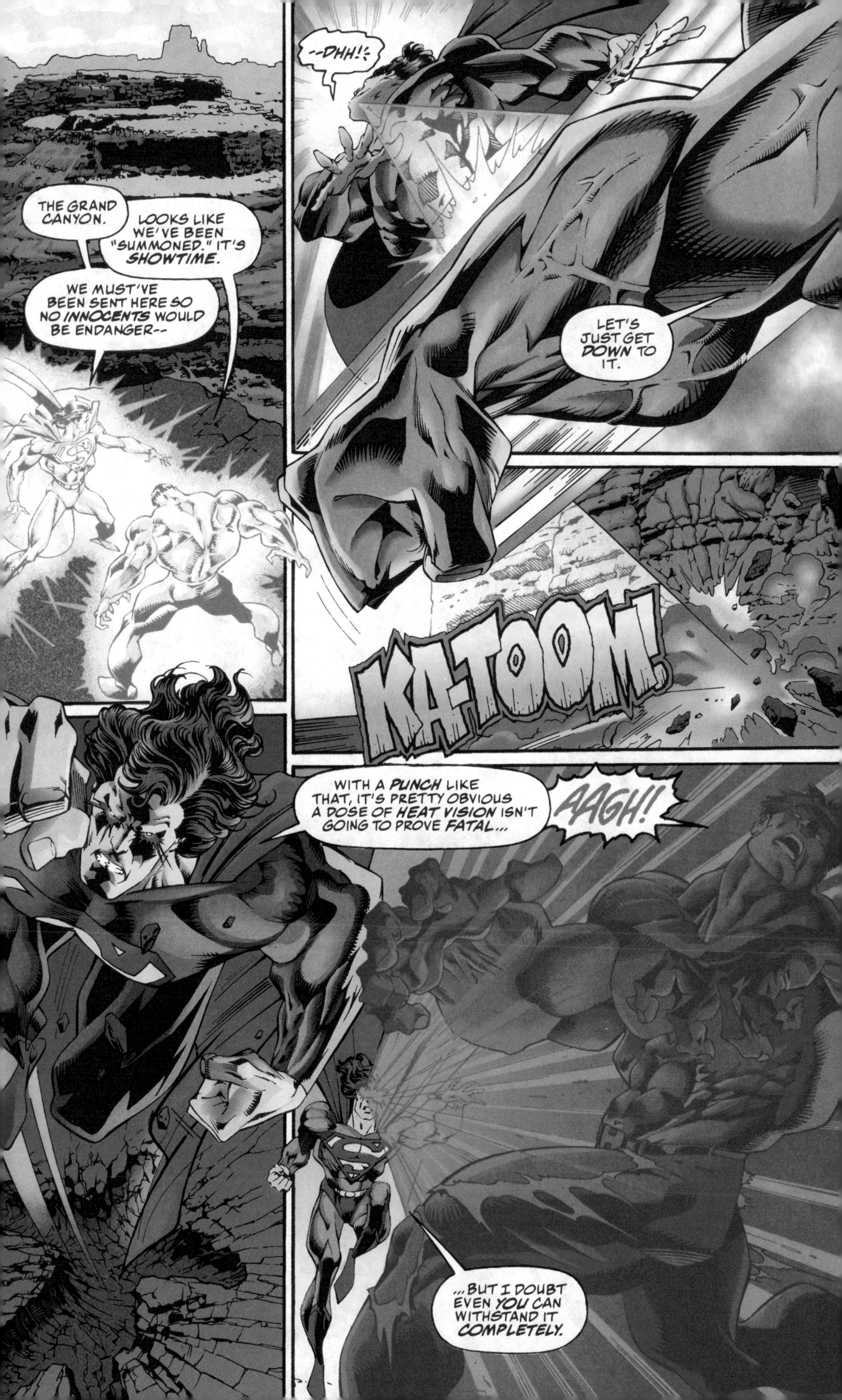

THE GRAND CANYON.
LOOKS LIKE WE'VE BEEN "SUMMONED." IT'S SHOWTIME.
WE MUST'VE BEEN SENT HERE SO NO INNOCENTS WOULD BE ENDANGER--
--DHH!!
LET'S JUST GET DOWN TO IT.
KA-TOOM!
WITH A PUNCH LIKE THAT, IT'S PRETTY OBVIOUS A DOSE OF HEAT VISION ISN'T GOING TO PROVE FATAL...
AAGH!
...BUT I DOUBT EVEN YOU CAN WITHSTAND IT COMPLETELY.

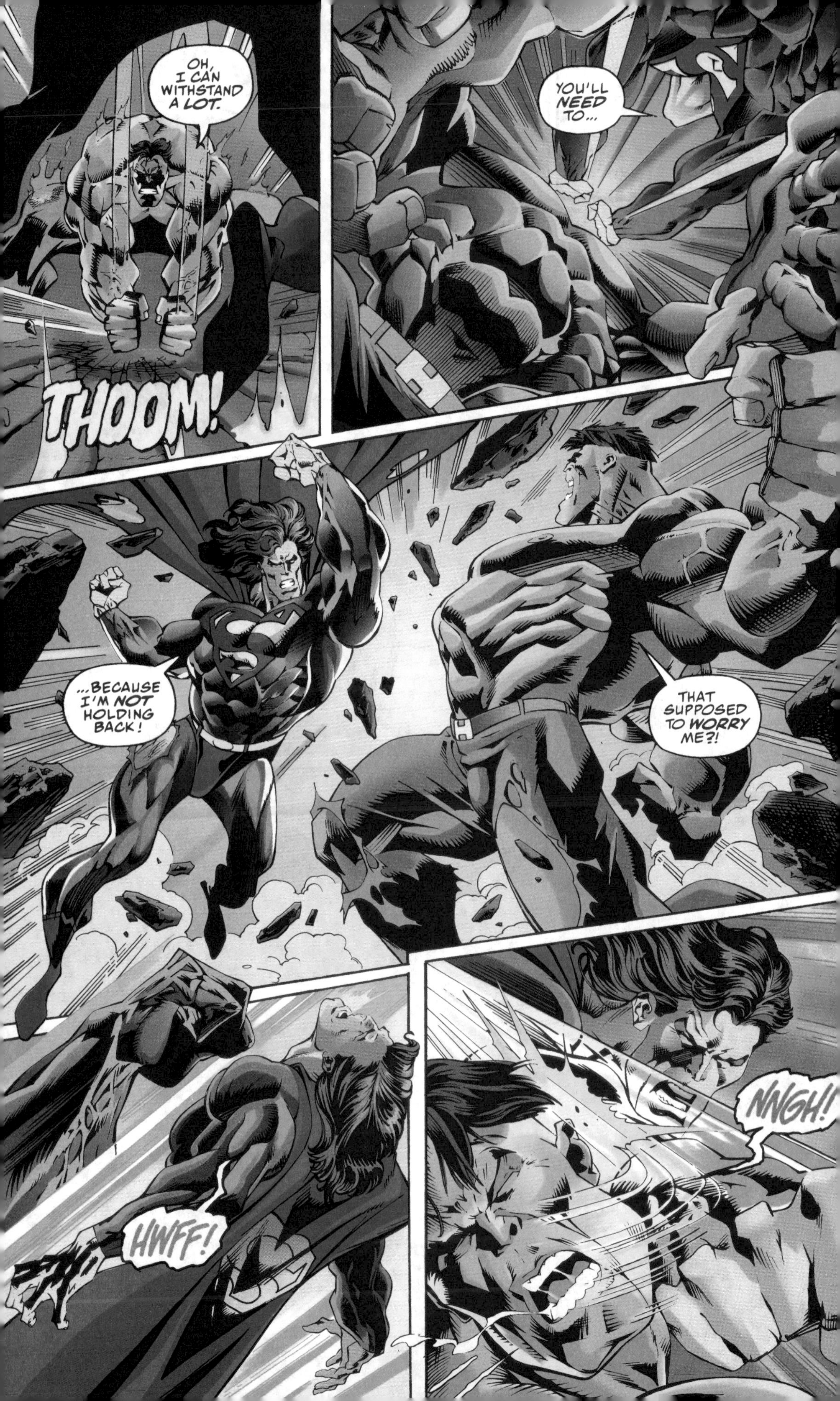
OH, I CAN WITHSTAND A LOT.
THOOM!
YOU'LL NEED TO...
...BECAUSE I'M NOT HOLDING BACK!
THAT SUPPOSED TO WORRY ME?!
HWFF!
NNGH!

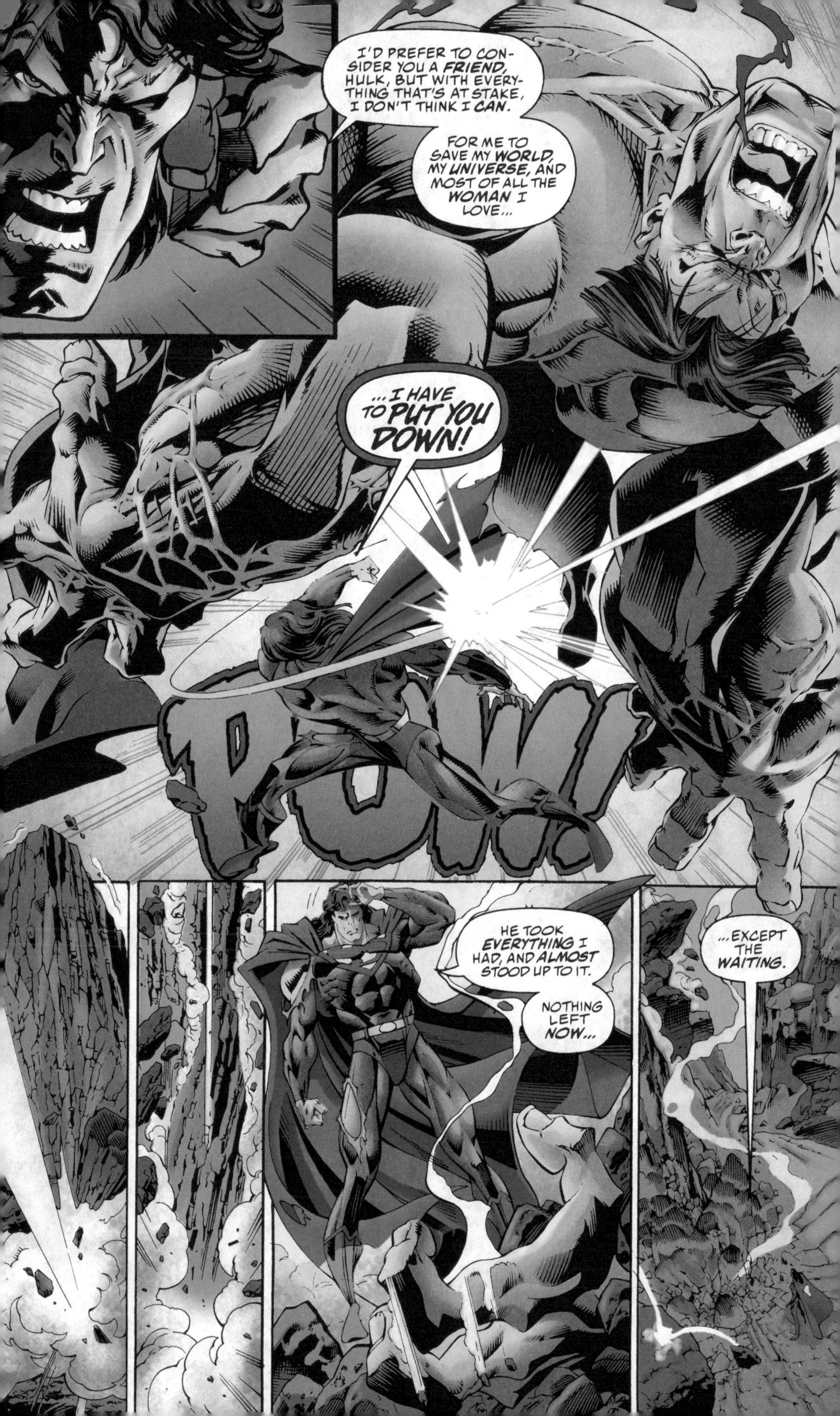
I'D PREFER TO CONSIDER YOU A FRIEND, HULK, BUT WITH EVERYTHING THAT'S AT STAKE, I DON'T THINK I CAN.
FOR ME TO SAVE MY WORLD, MY UNIVERSE, AND MOST OF ALL THE WOMAN I LOVE...
...I HAVE TO PUT YOU DOWN!
POW!
HE TOOK EVERYTHING I HAD, AND ALMOST STOOD UP TO IT.
NOTHING LEFT NOW...
...EXCEPT THE WAITING.

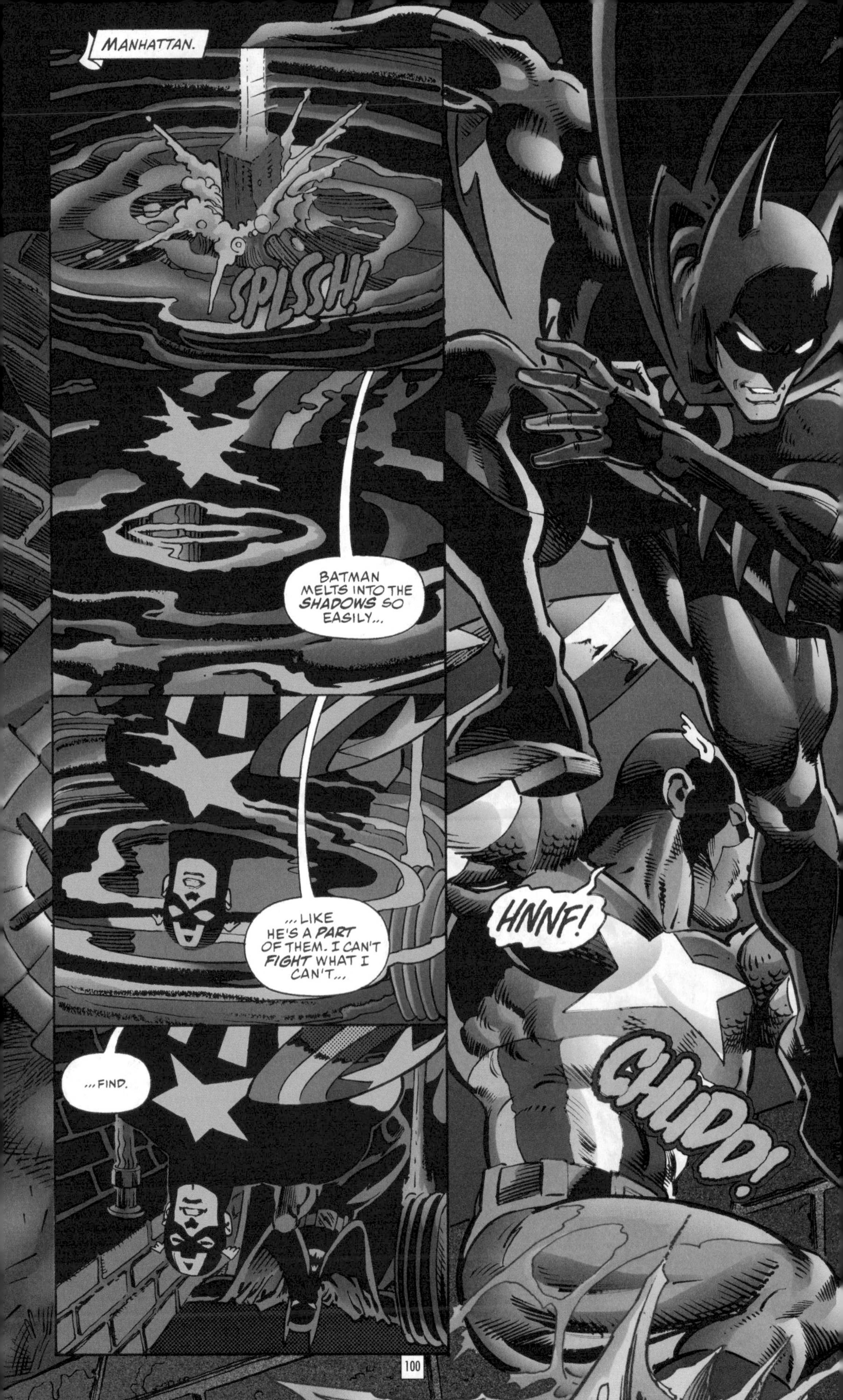
MANHATTAN.
SPLSSH!
BATMAN MELTS INTO THE SHADOWS SO EASILY...
...LIKE HE'S A PART OF THEM. I CAN'T FIGHT WHAT I CAN'T...
...FIND.
HNNF!
CHUDD!

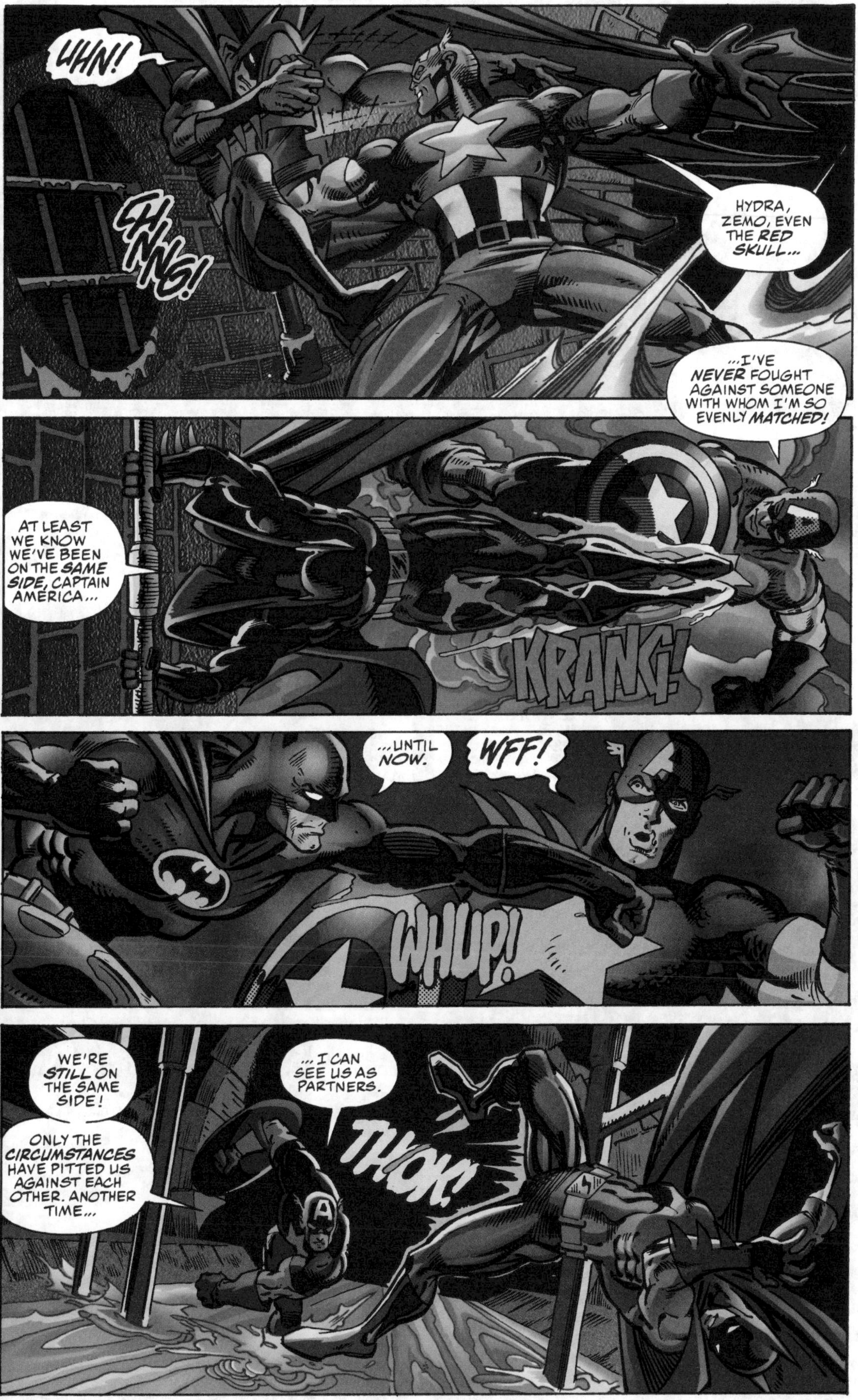
UHN!
CHNNG!
HYDRA, ZEMO, EVEN THE RED SKULL...
...I'VE NEVER FOUGHT AGAINST SOMEONE WITH WHOM I'M SO EVENLY MATCHED!
AT LEAST WE KNOW WE'VE BEEN ON THE SAME SIDE, CAPTAIN AMERICA...
KRANG!
...UNTIL NOW.
WFF!
WHUP!
WE'RE STILL ON THE SAME SIDE!
ONLY THE CIRCUMSTANCES HAVE PITTED US AGAINST EACH OTHER. ANOTHER TIME...
...I CAN SEE US AS PARTNERS.
THOK!

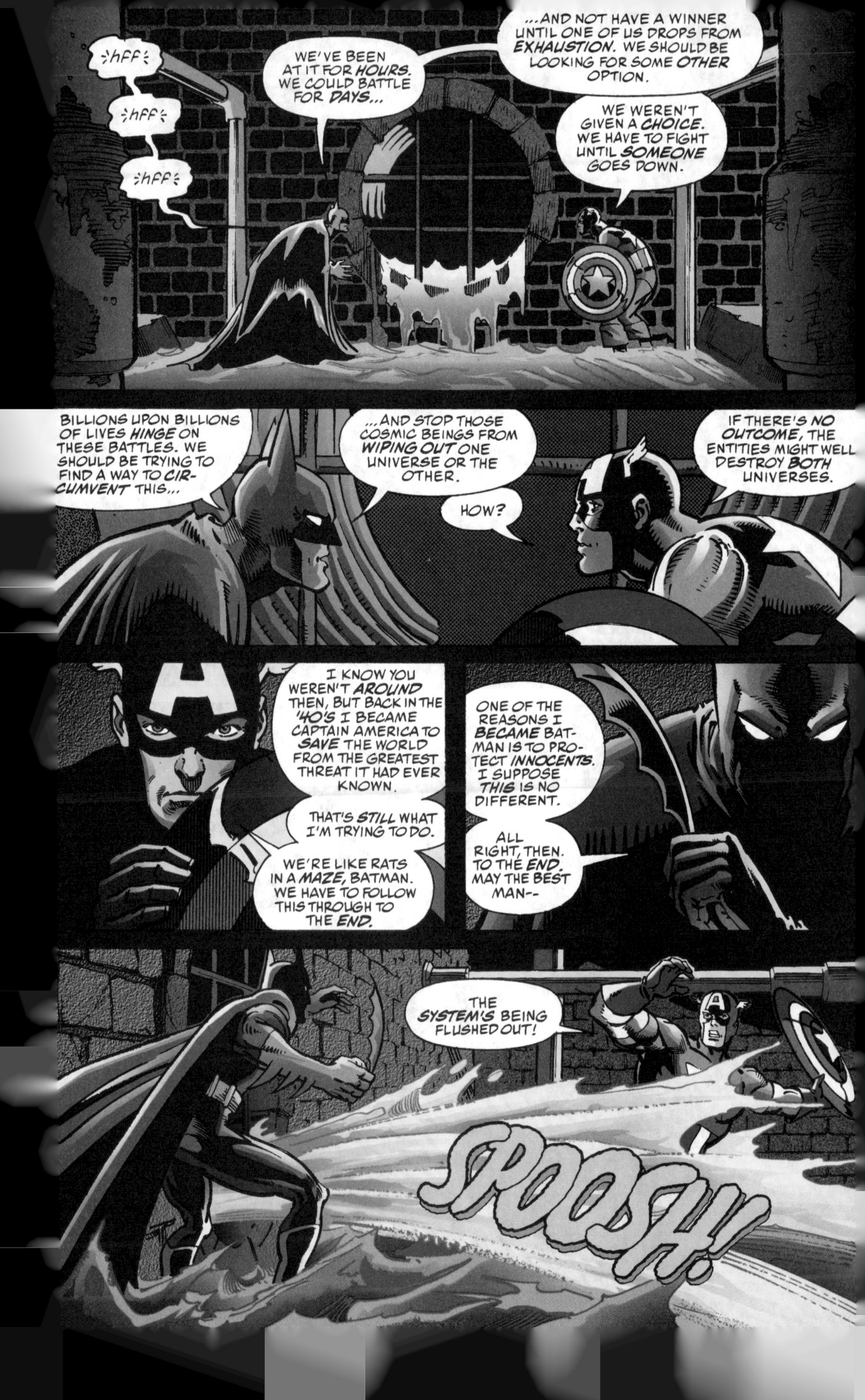
hff
hff
hff
WE'VE BEEN AT IT FOR HOURS. WE COULD BATTLE FOR DAYS...
...AND NOT HAVE A WINNER UNTIL ONE OF US DROPS FROM EXHAUSTION. WE SHOULD BE LOOKING FOR SOME OTHER OPTION.
WE WEREN'T GIVEN A CHOICE. WE HAVE TO FIGHT UNTIL SOMEONE GOES DOWN.
BILLIONS UPON BILLIONS OF LIVES HINGE ON THESE BATTLES. WE SHOULD BE TRYING TO FIND A WAY TO CIRCUMVENT THIS...
...AND STOP THOSE COSMIC BEINGS FROM WIPING OUT ONE UNIVERSE OR THE OTHER.
HOW?
IF THERE'S NO OUTCOME, THE ENTITIES MIGHT WELL DESTROY BOTH UNIVERSES.
I KNOW YOU WEREN'T AROUND THEN, BUT BACK IN THE '40'S I BECAME CAPTAIN AMERICA TO SAVE THE WORLD FROM THE GREATEST THREAT IT HAD EVER KNOWN.
THAT'S STILL WHAT I'M TRYING TO DO.
WE'RE LIKE RATS IN A MAZE, BATMAN. WE HAVE TO FOLLOW THIS THROUGH TO THE END.
ONE OF THE REASONS I BECAME BATMAN IS TO PROTECT INNOCENTS. I SUPPOSE THIS IS NO DIFFERENT.
ALL RIGHT, THEN. TO THE END. MAY THE BEST MAN--
THE SYSTEM'S BEING FLUSHED OUT!
SPOOSH!

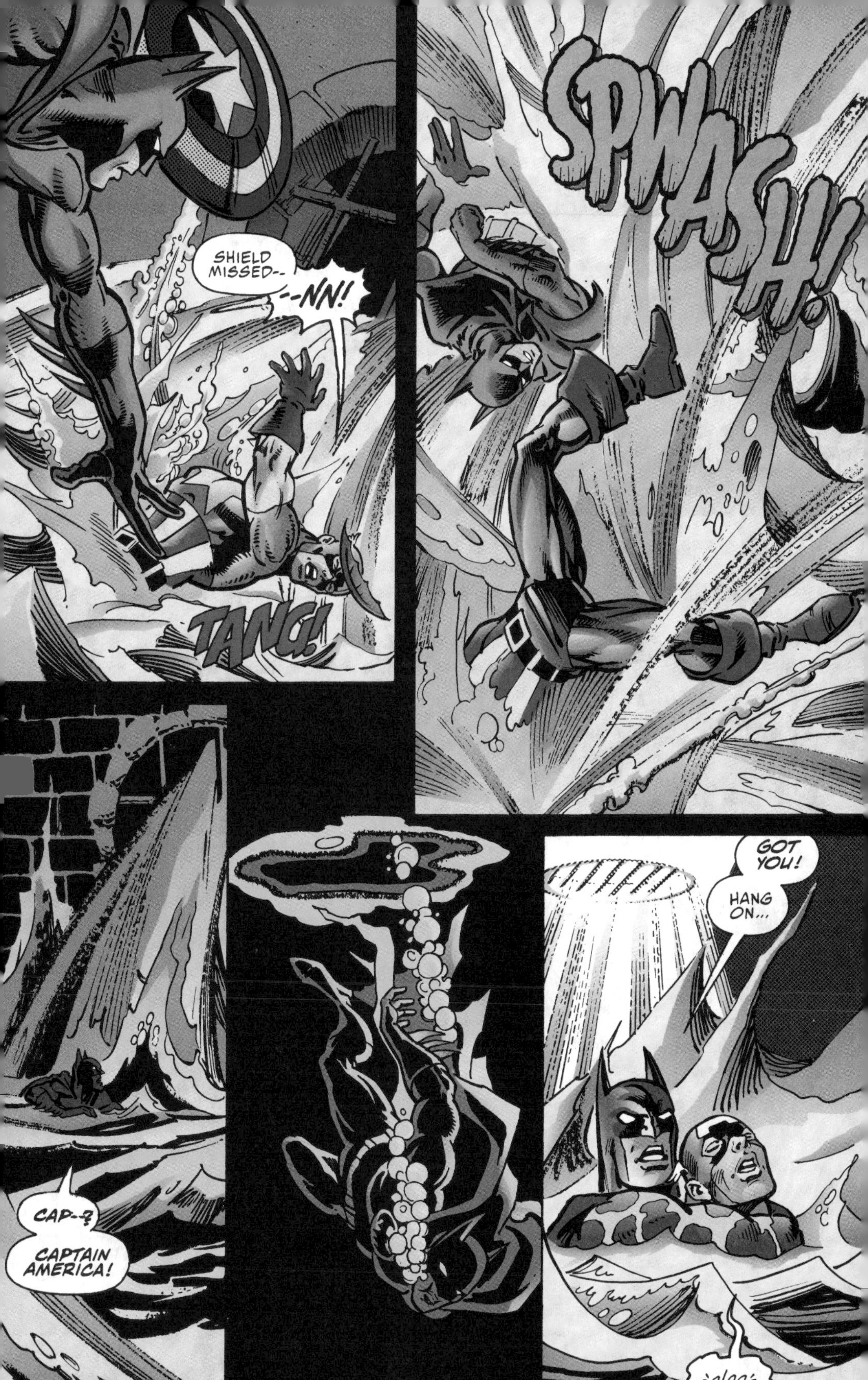
SHIELD MISSED--
--NN!
TANG!
SPWASH!!
CAP--?
CAPTAIN AMERICA!
GOT YOU!
HANG ON...
glgg

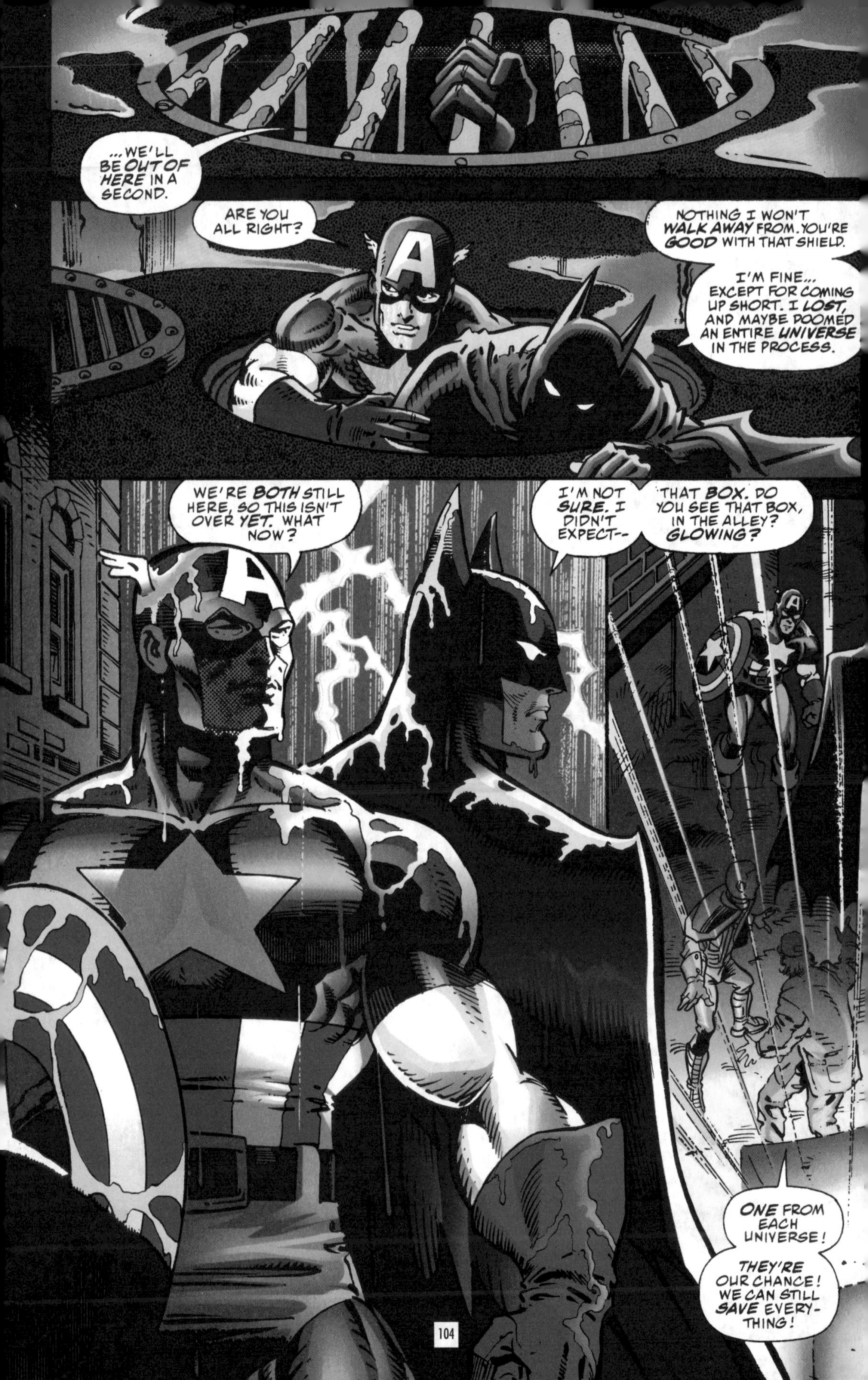
...WE'LL BE OUT OF HERE IN A SECOND.
ARE YOU ALL RIGHT?
NOTHING I WON'T WALK AWAY FROM. YOU'RE GOOD WITH THAT SHIELD.
I'M FINE... EXCEPT FOR COMING UP SHORT. I LOST, AND MAYBE DOOMED AN ENTIRE UNIVERSE IN THE PROCESS.
WE'RE BOTH STILL HERE, SO THIS ISN'T OVER YET. WHAT NOW?
I'M NOT SURE. I DIDN'T EXPECT--
THAT BOX. DO YOU SEE THAT BOX, IN THE ALLEY? GLOWING?
ONE FROM EACH UNIVERSE!
THEY'RE OUR CHANCE! WE CAN STILL SAVE EVERYTHING!

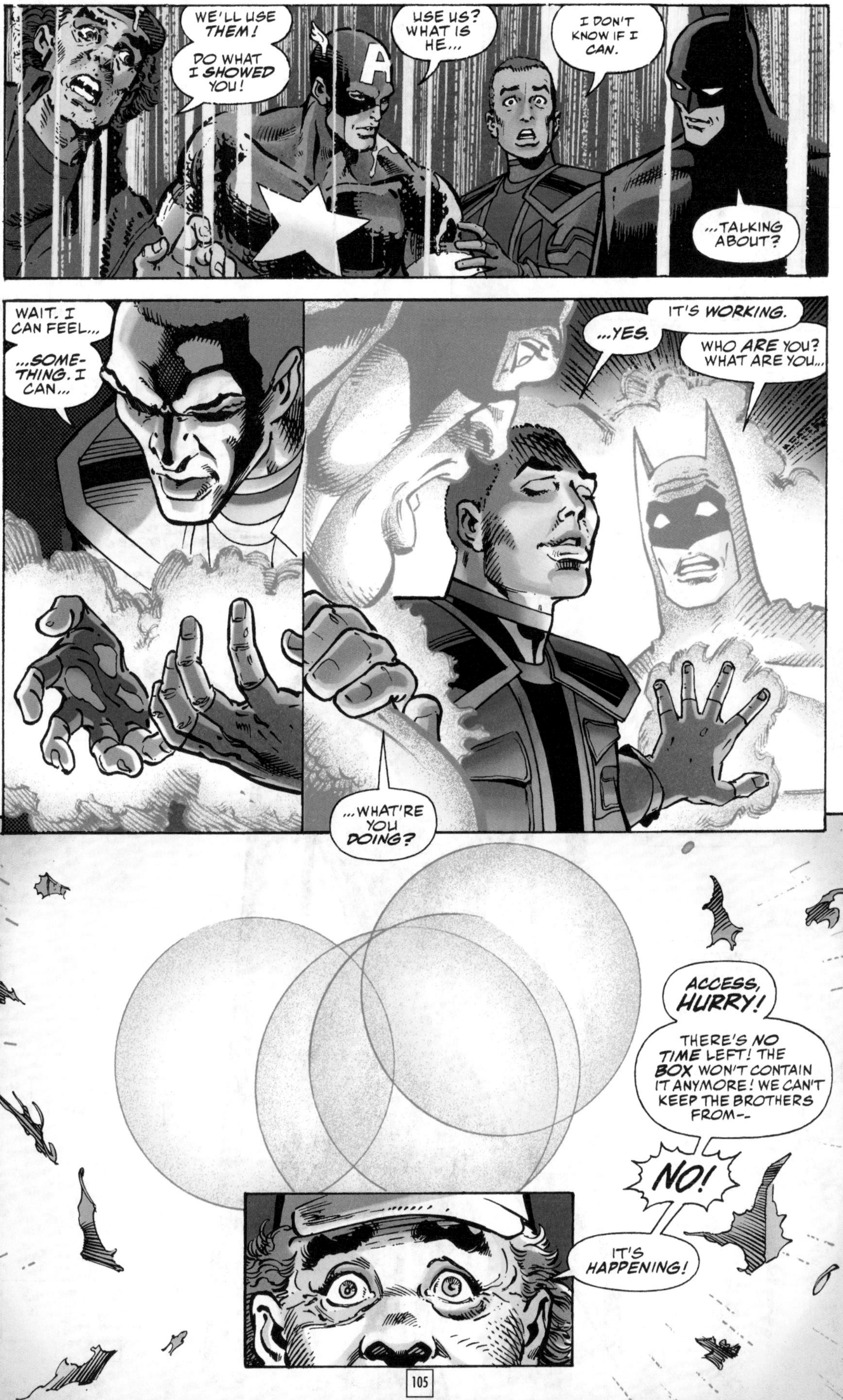
WE'LL USE THEM!
DO WHAT I SHOWED YOU!
USE US? WHAT IS HE...
I DON'T KNOW IF I CAN.
...TALKING ABOUT?
WAIT. I CAN FEEL...
...SOMETHING. I CAN...
...YES.
IT'S WORKING.
WHO ARE YOU? WHAT ARE YOU...
...WHAT'RE YOU DOING?
ACCESS, HURRY!
THERE'S NO TIME LEFT! THE BOX WON'T CONTAIN IT ANYMORE! WE CAN'T KEEP THE BROTHERS FROM--
NO!
IT'S HAPPENING!

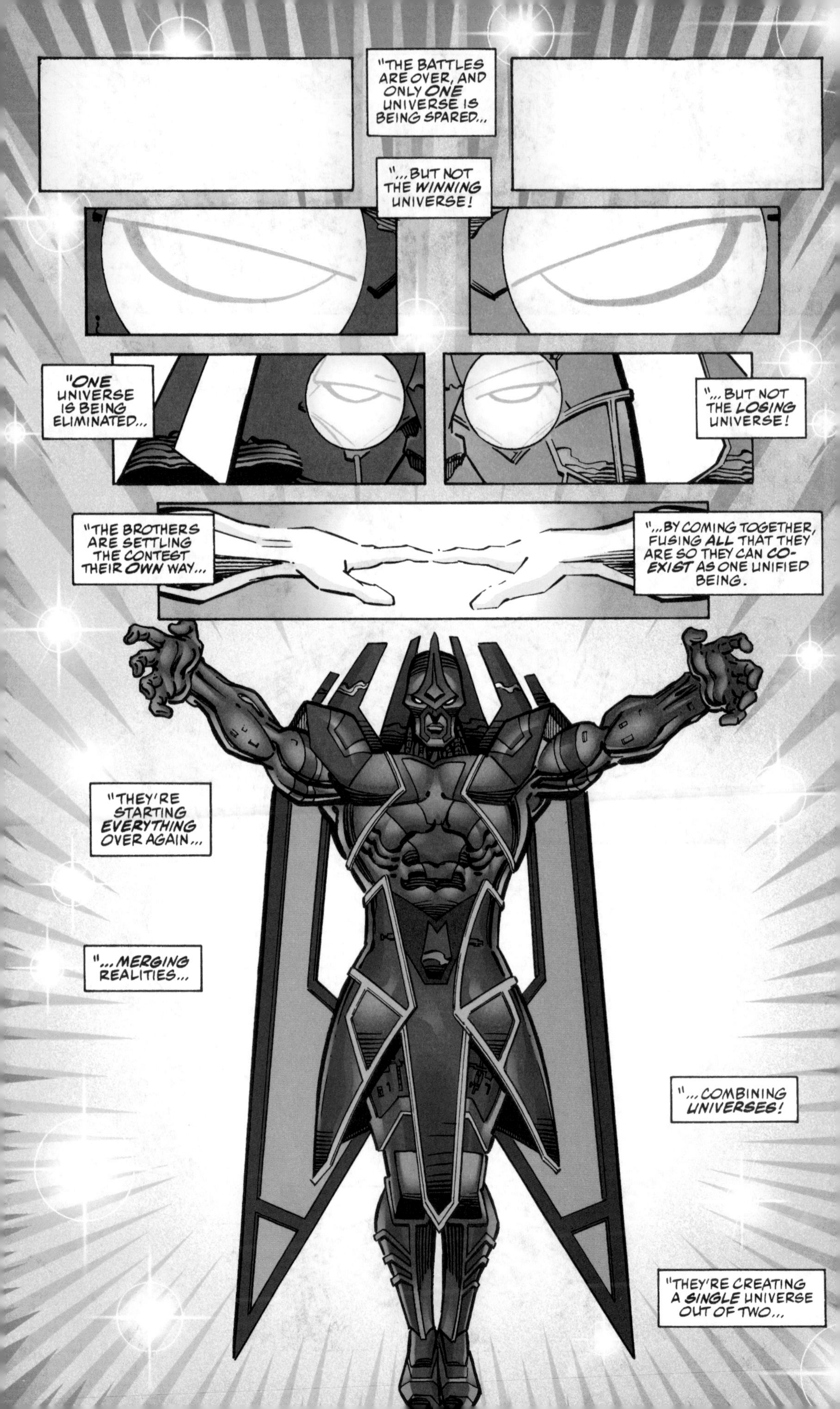
"THE BATTLES ARE OVER, AND ONLY ONE UNIVERSE IS BEING SPARED...
"...BUT NOT THE WINNING UNIVERSE!
"ONE UNIVERSE IS BEING ELIMINATED...
"...BUT NOT THE LOSING UNIVERSE!
"THE BROTHERS ARE SETTLING THE CONTEST THEIR OWN WAY...
"...BY COMING TOGETHER, FUSING ALL THAT THEY ARE SO THEY CAN CO-EXIST AS ONE UNIFIED BEING.
"THEY'RE STARTING EVERYTHING OVER AGAIN...
"...MERGING REALITIES...
"...COMBINING UNIVERSES!
"THEY'RE CREATING A SINGLE UNIVERSE OUT OF TWO...

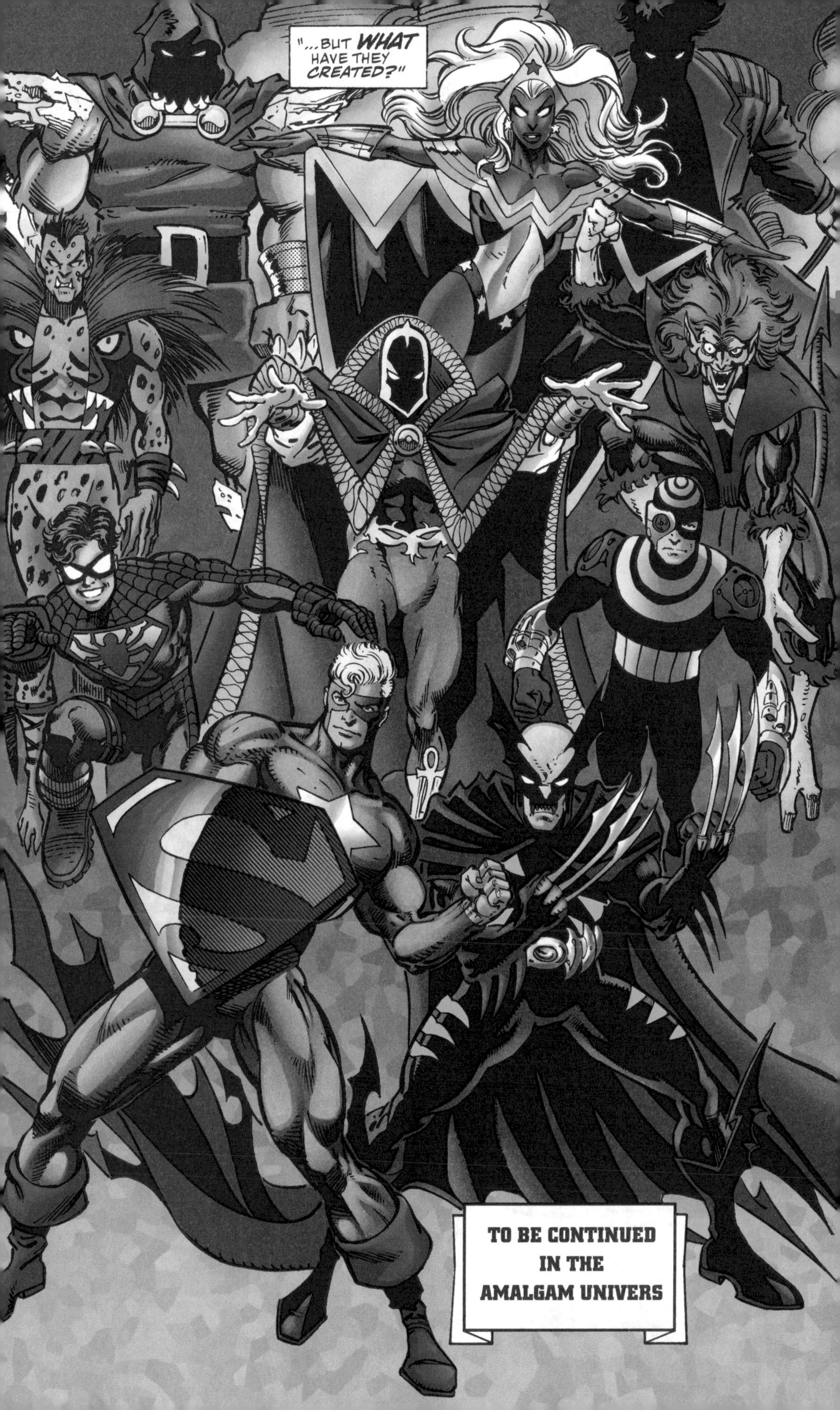
"...BUT WHAT HAVE THEY CREATED?"
TO BE CONTINUED IN THE AMALGAM UNIVERS

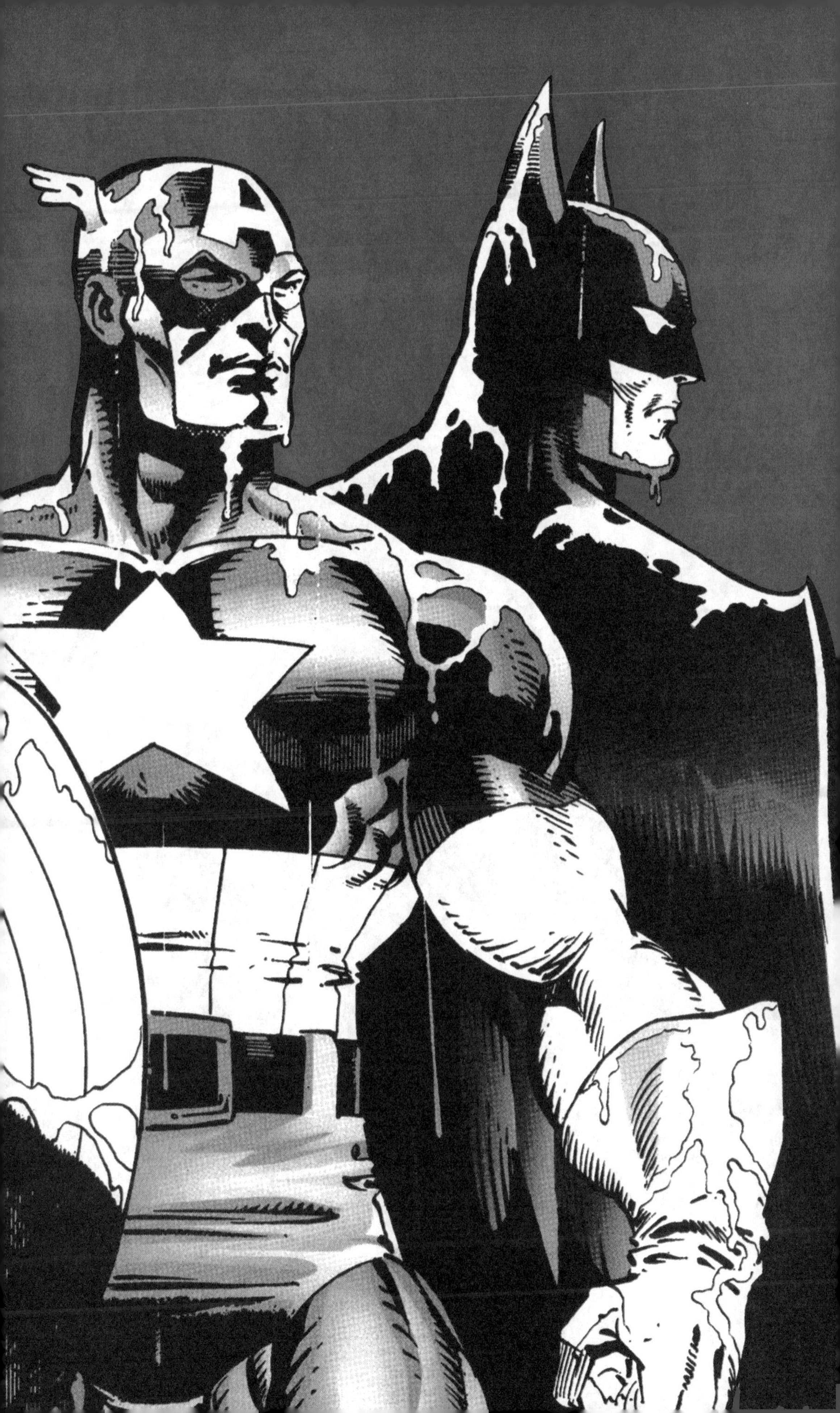

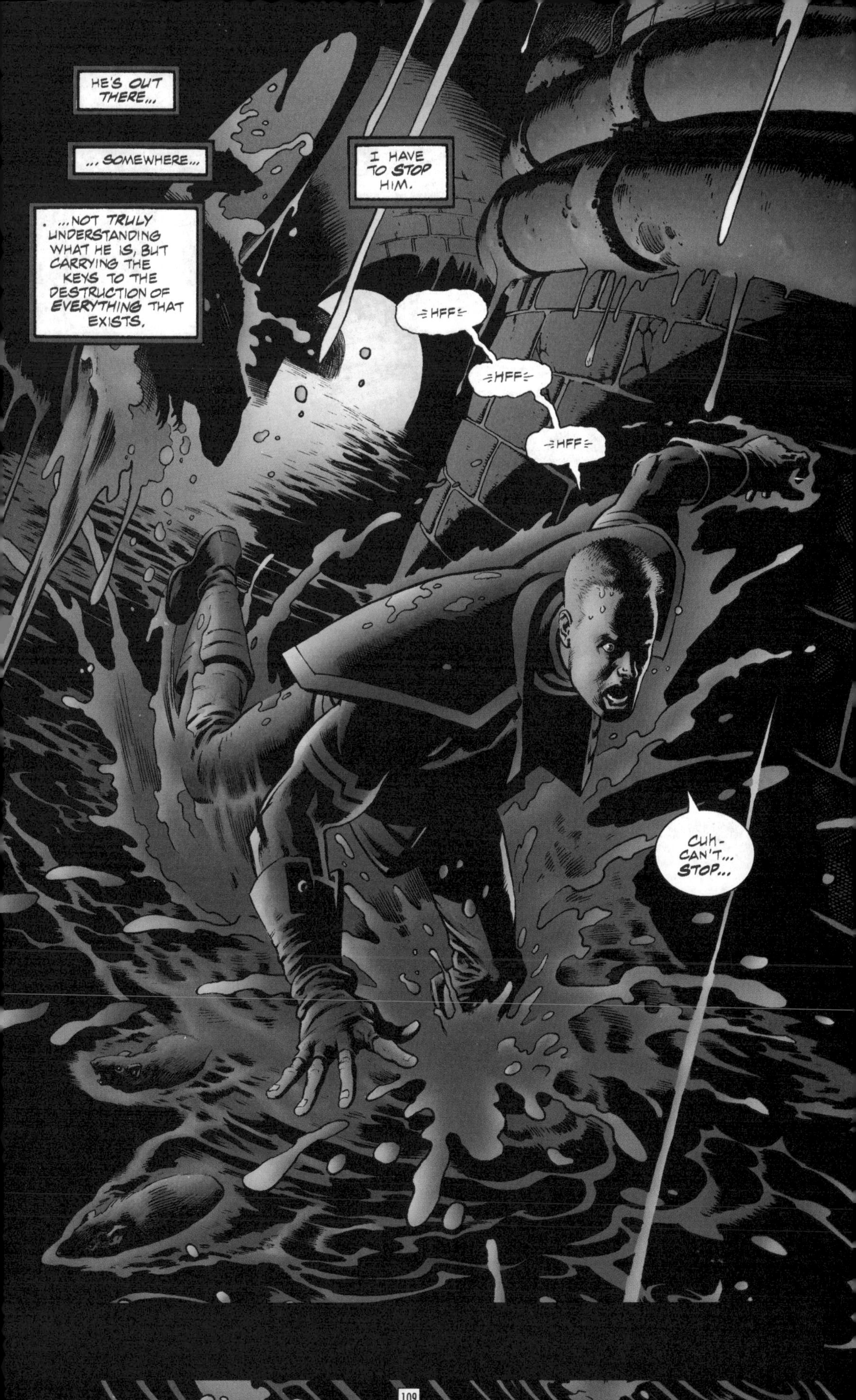
HE'S OUT THERE...
...SOMEWHERE...
...NOT TRULY UNDERSTANDING WHAT HE IS, BUT CARRYING THE KEYS TO THE DESTRUCTION OF EVERYTHING THAT EXISTS.
I HAVE TO STOP HIM.
HFF
HFF
HFF
CUH-CAN'T... STOP...

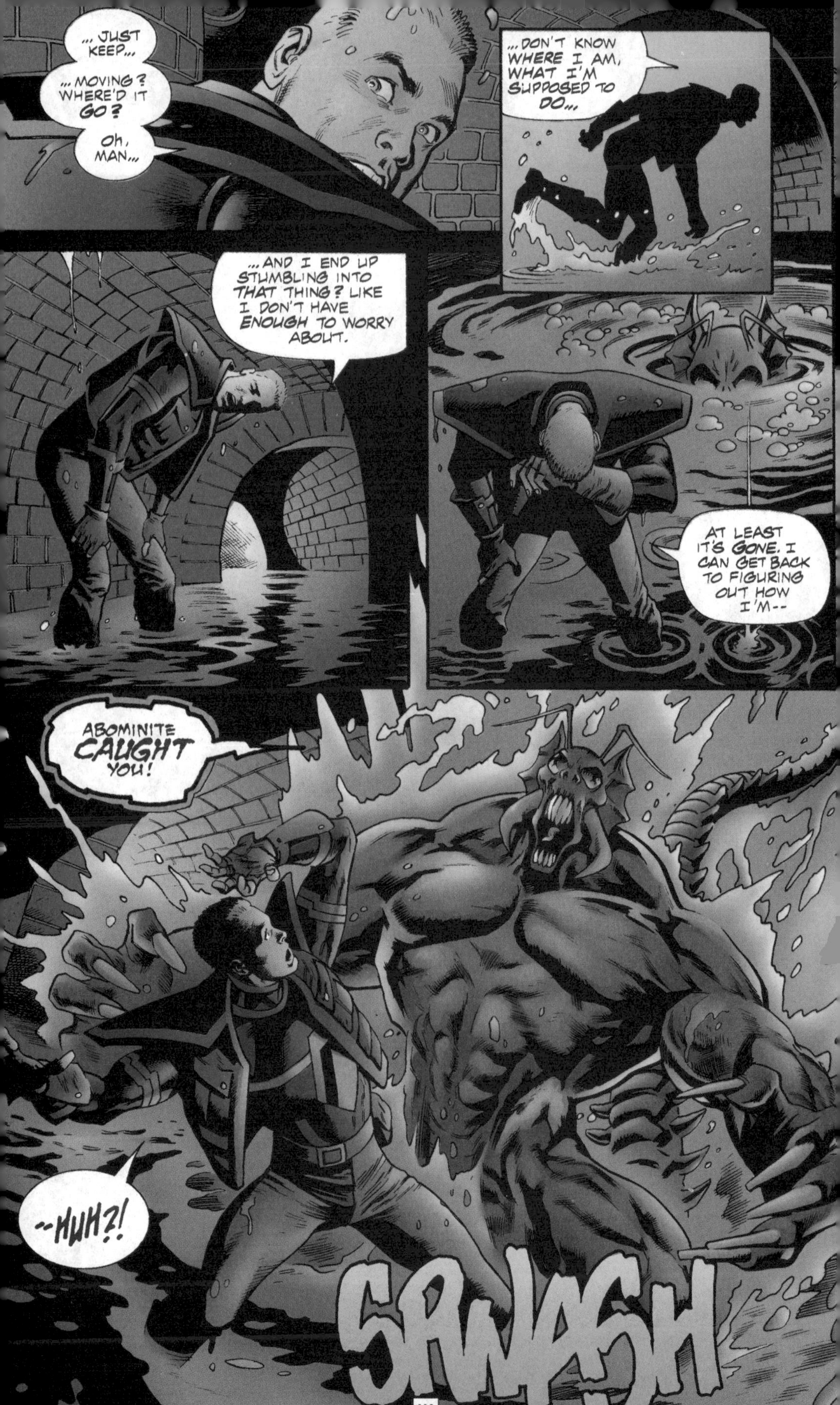
...JUST KEEP...
...MOVING? WHERE'D IT GO?
Oh, MAN...
...DON'T KNOW WHERE I AM, WHAT I'M SUPPOSED TO DO...
...AND I END UP STUMBLING INTO THAT THING? LIKE I DON'T HAVE ENOUGH TO WORRY ABOUT.
AT LEAST IT'S GONE. I CAN GET BACK TO FIGURING OUT HOW I'M--
ABOMINITE CAUGHT YOU!
--HUH?!
SPLASH

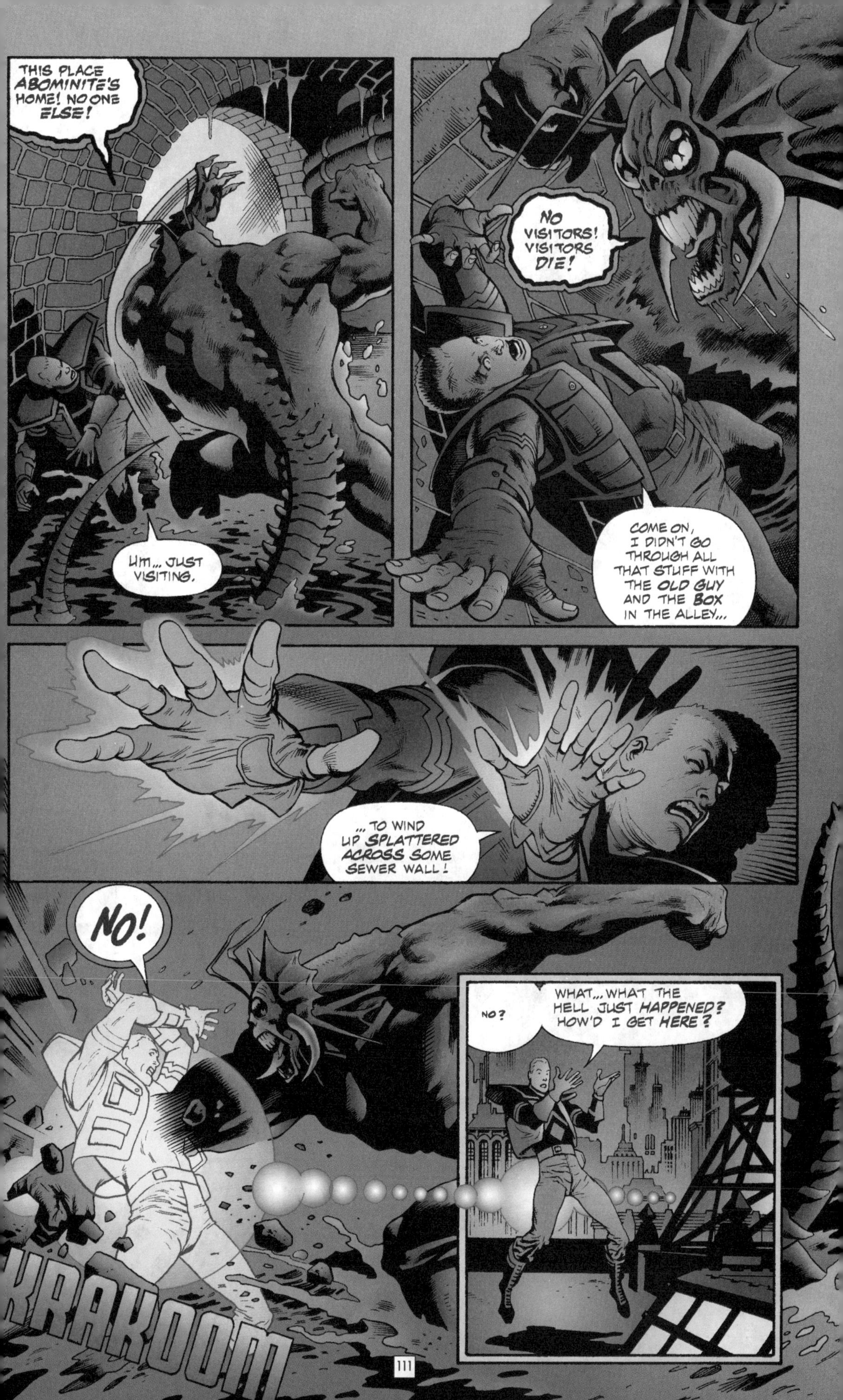
THIS PLACE ABOMINITE'S HOME! NO ONE ELSE!
UM... JUST VISITING.
NO VISITORS! VISITORS DIE!
COME ON, I DIDN'T GO THROUGH ALL THAT STUFF WITH THE OLD GUY AND THE BOX IN THE ALLEY...
... TO WIND UP SPLATTERED ACROSS SOME SEWER WALL!
NO!
KRAKOOM
NO?
WHAT... WHAT THE HELL JUST HAPPENED? HOW'D I GET HERE?

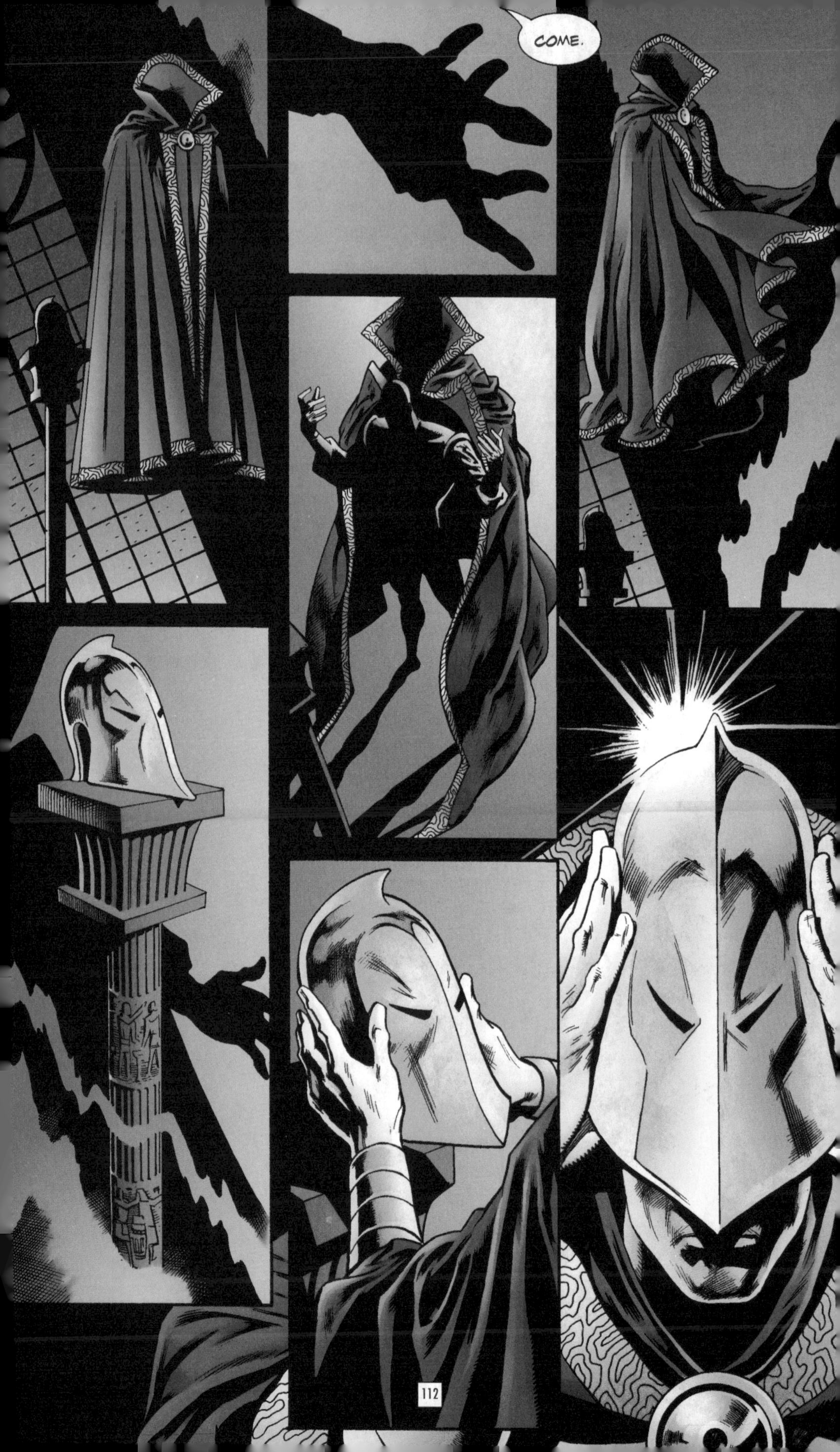
COME.

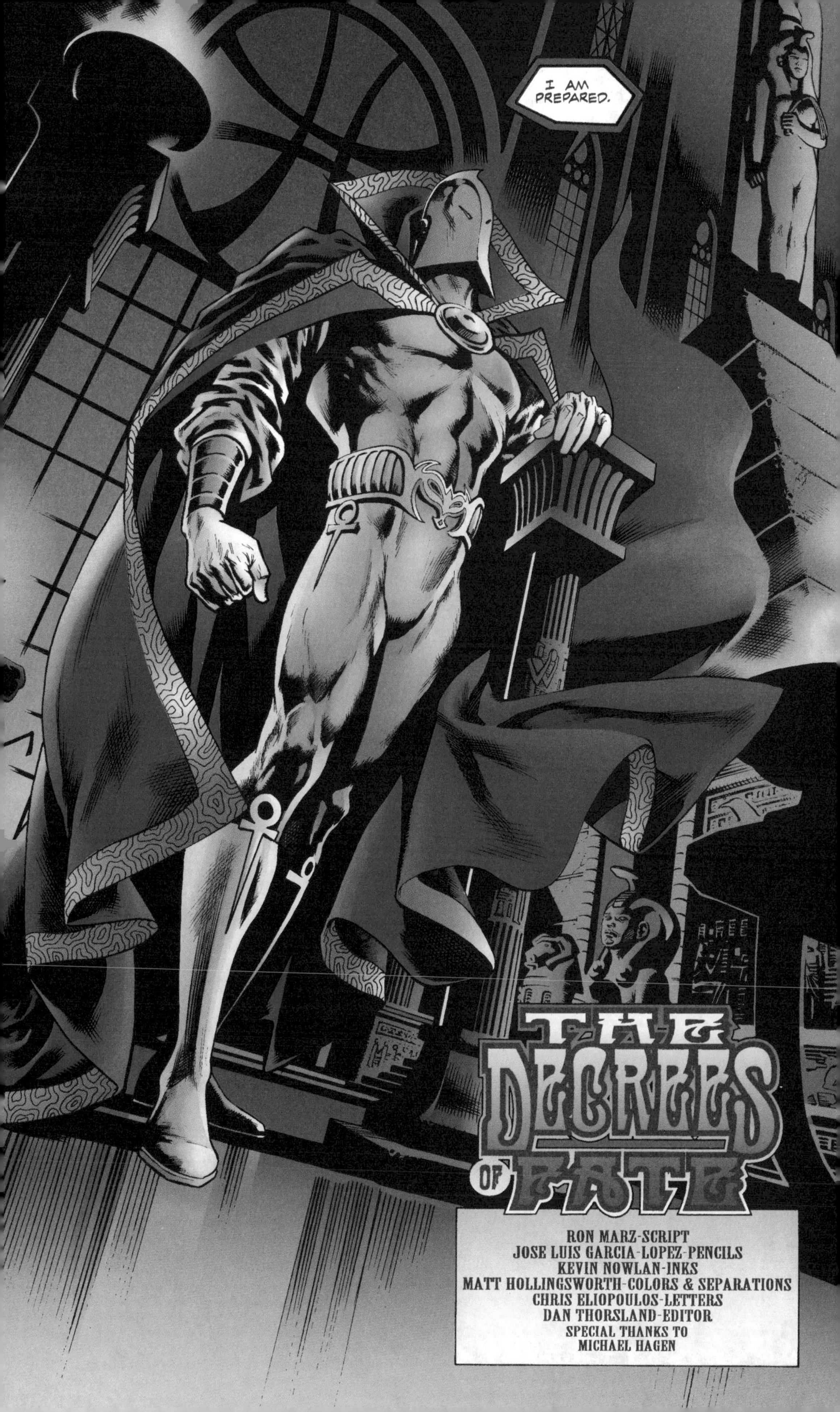
I AM PREPARED.
THE DEGREES OF FATE
RON MARZ-SCRIPT
JOSE LUIS GARCIA-LOPEZ-PENCILS
KEVIN NOWLAN-INKS
MATT HOLLINGSWORTH-COLORS & SEPARATIONS
CHRIS ELIOPOULOS-LETTERS
DAN THORSLAND-EDITOR
SPECIAL THANKS TO
MICHAEL HAGEN

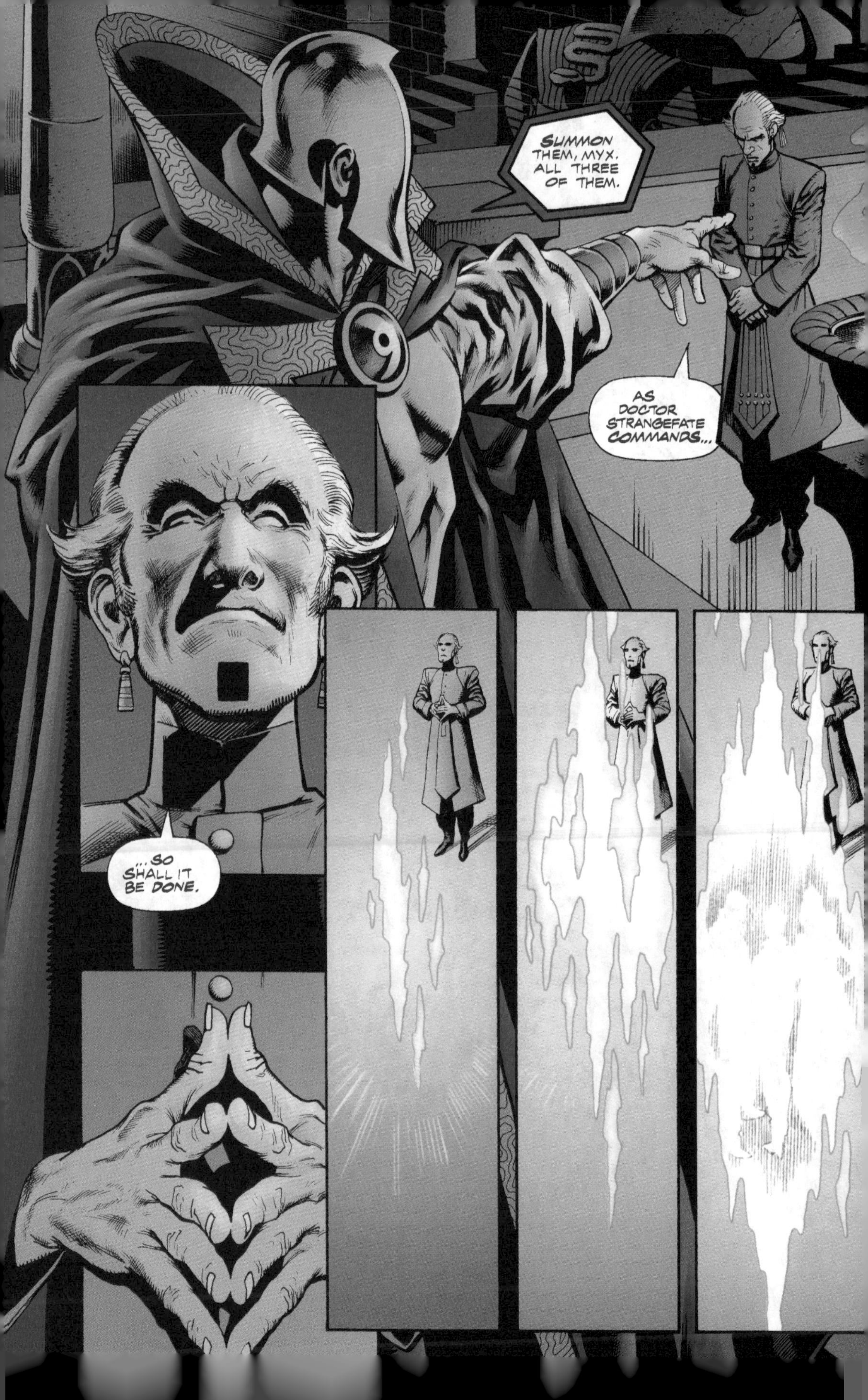
SUMMON THEM, MYX. ALL THREE OF THEM.
AS DOCTOR STRANGEFATE COMMANDS...
...SO SHALL IT BE DONE.

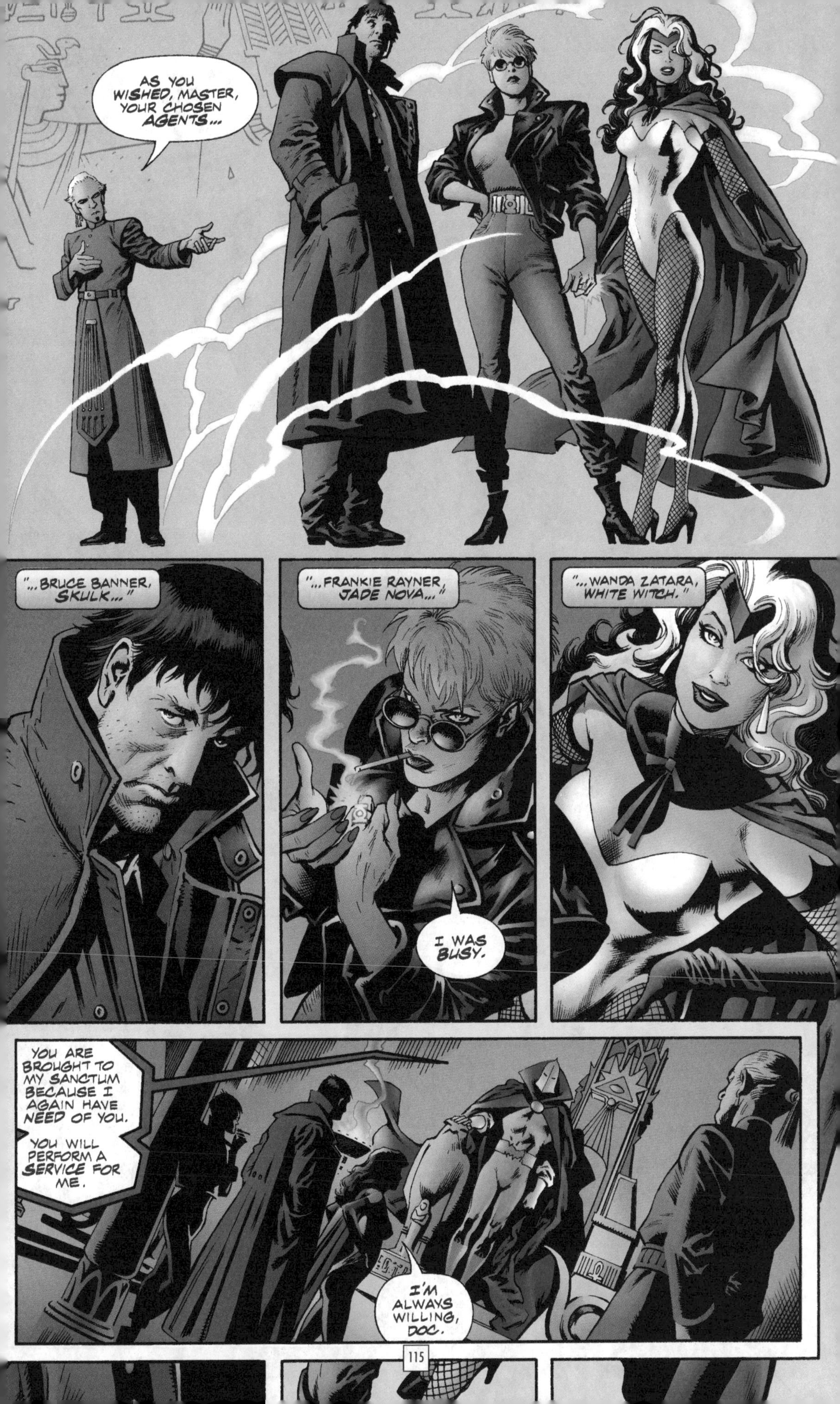
AS YOU WISHED, MASTER, YOUR CHOSEN AGENTS...
"...BRUCE BANNER, SKULK..."
"...FRANKIE RAYNER, JADE NOVA..."
I WAS BUSY.
"...WANDA ZATARA, WHITE WITCH."
YOU ARE BROUGHT TO MY SANCTUM BECAUSE I AGAIN HAVE NEED OF YOU.
YOU WILL PERFORM A SERVICE FOR ME.
I'M ALWAYS WILLING, DOC.

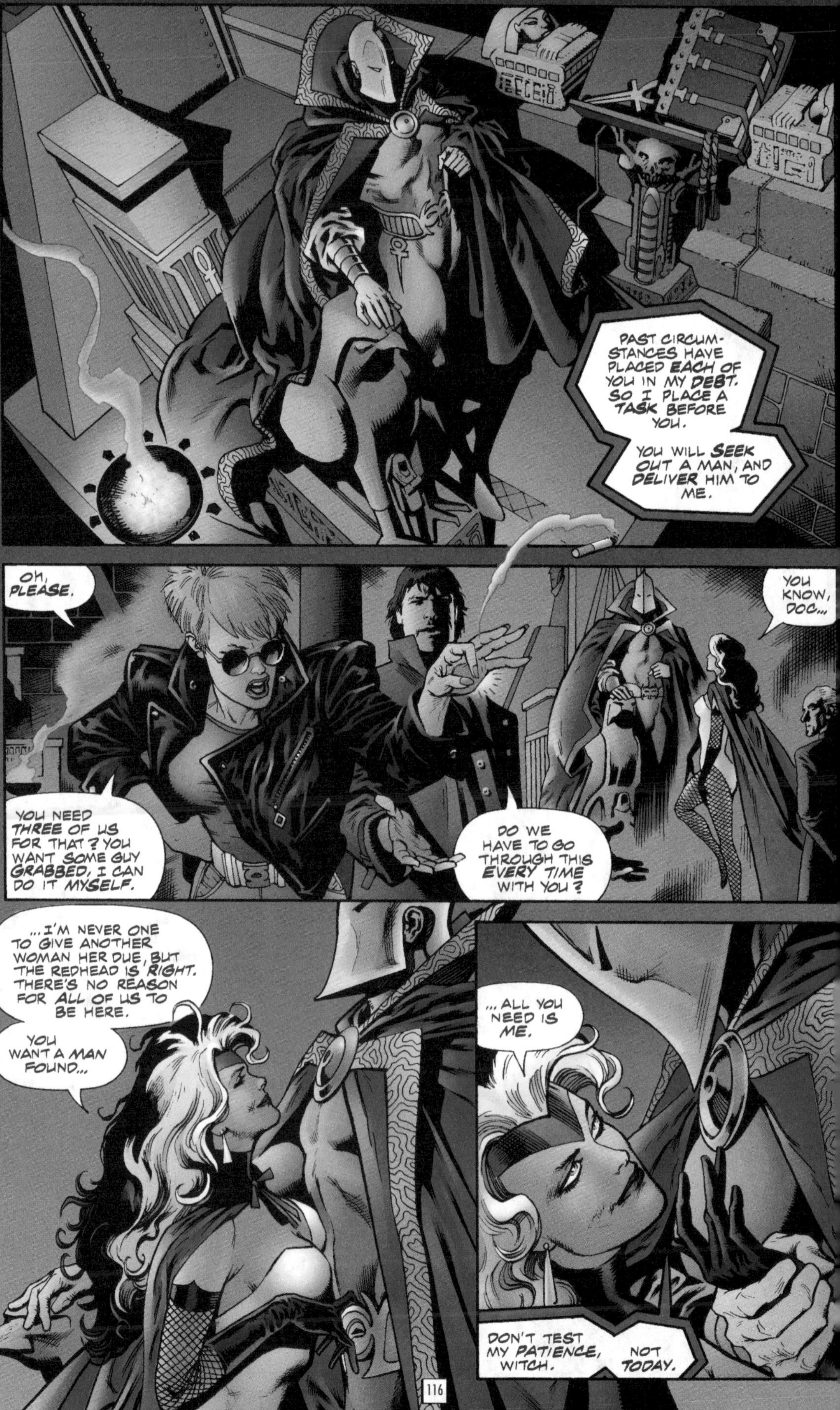
PAST CIRCUMSTANCES HAVE PLACED EACH OF YOU IN MY DEBT. SO I PLACE A TASK BEFORE YOU.
YOU WILL SEEK OUT A MAN, AND DELIVER HIM TO ME.
OH, PLEASE.
YOU KNOW, DOC...
YOU NEED THREE OF US FOR THAT? YOU WANT SOME GUY GRABBED, I CAN DO IT MYSELF.
DO WE HAVE TO GO THROUGH THIS EVERY TIME WITH YOU?
...I'M NEVER ONE TO GIVE ANOTHER WOMAN HER DUE, BUT THE REDHEAD IS RIGHT. THERE'S NO REASON FOR ALL OF US TO BE HERE.
YOU WANT A MAN FOUND...
...ALL YOU NEED IS ME.
DON'T TEST MY PATIENCE, WITCH.
NOT TODAY.

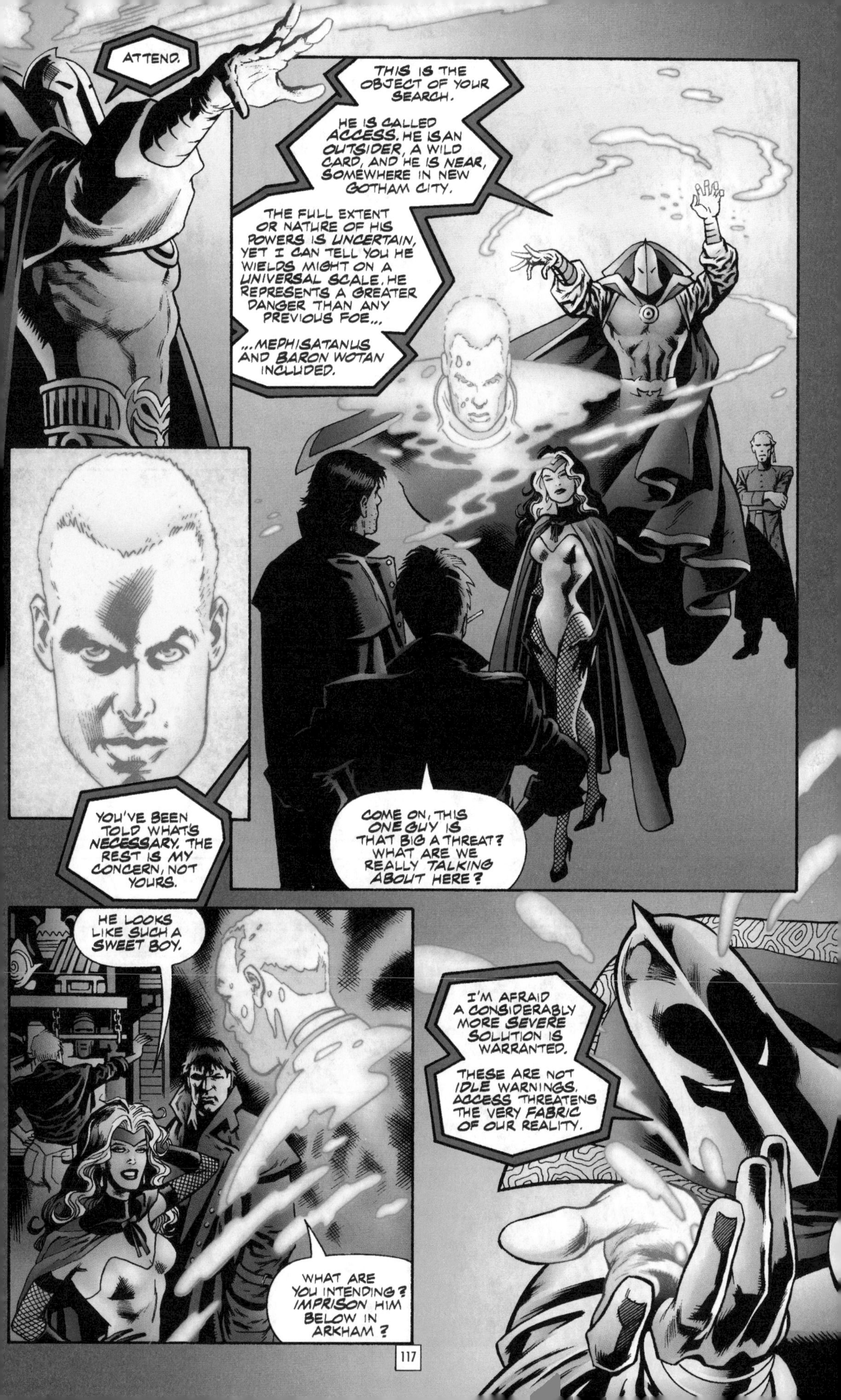
ATTEND.
THIS IS THE OBJECT OF YOUR SEARCH.
HE IS CALLED ACCESS. HE IS AN OUTSIDER, A WILD CARD, AND HE IS NEAR, SOMEWHERE IN NEW GOTHAM CITY.
THE FULL EXTENT OR NATURE OF HIS POWERS IS UNCERTAIN, YET I CAN TELL YOU HE WIELDS MIGHT ON A UNIVERSAL SCALE. HE REPRESENTS A GREATER DANGER THAN ANY PREVIOUS FOE...
...MEPHISATANUS AND BARON WOTAN INCLUDED.
COME ON, THIS ONE GUY IS THAT BIG A THREAT? WHAT ARE WE REALLY TALKING ABOUT HERE?
YOU'VE BEEN TOLD WHAT'S NECESSARY. THE REST IS MY CONCERN, NOT YOURS.
HE LOOKS LIKE SUCH A SWEET BOY.
WHAT ARE YOU INTENDING? IMPRISON HIM BELOW IN ARKHAM?
I'M AFRAID A CONSIDERABLY MORE SEVERE SOLUTION IS WARRANTED.
THESE ARE NOT IDLE WARNINGS. ACCESS THREATENS THE VERY FABRIC OF OUR REALITY.

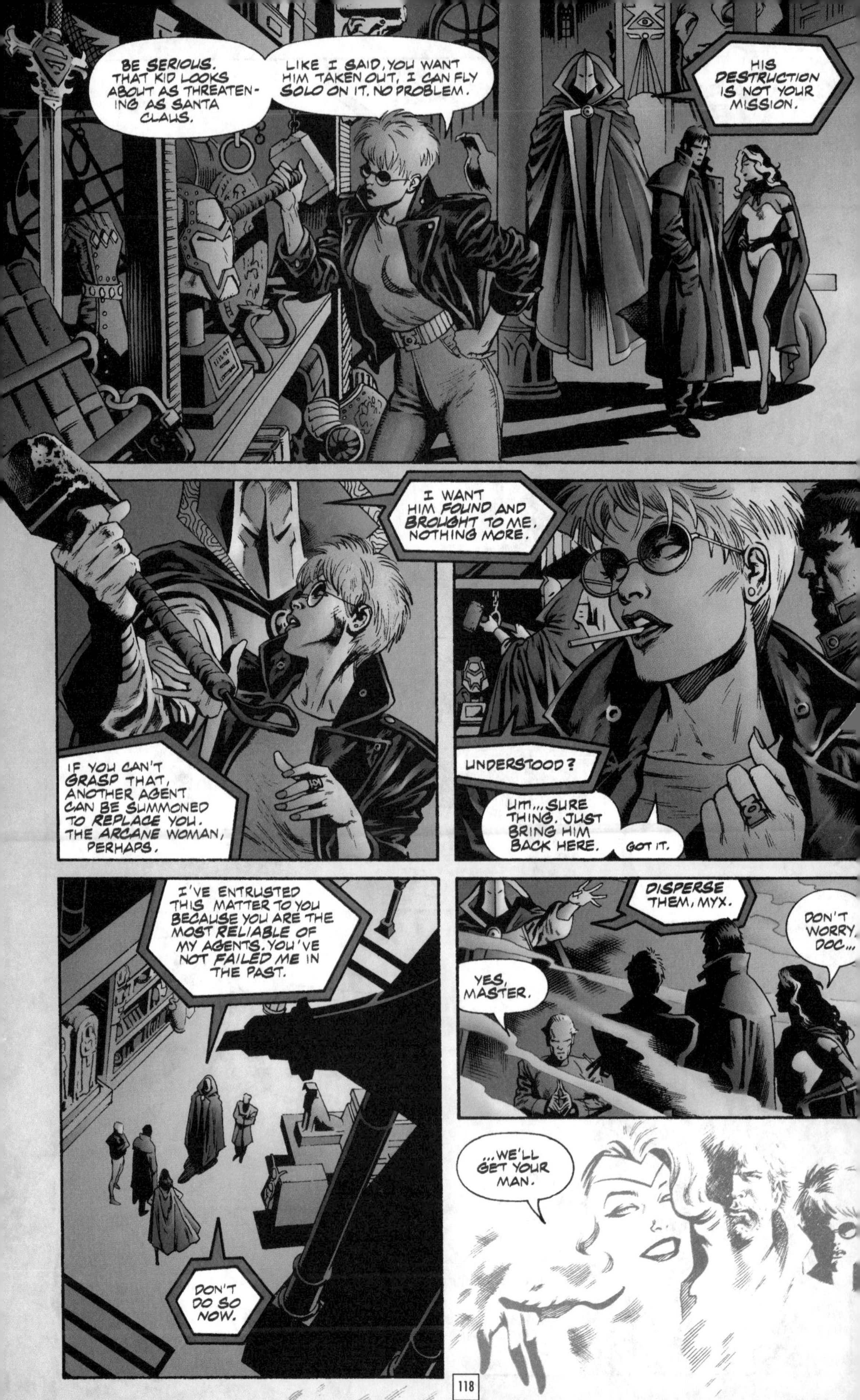

BE SERIOUS. THAT KID LOOKS ABOUT AS THREATEN-ING AS SANTA CLAUS.
LIKE I SAID, YOU WANT HIM TAKEN OUT, I CAN FLY SOLO ON IT. NO PROBLEM.
HIS DESTRUCTION IS NOT YOUR MISSION.
I WANT HIM FOUND AND BROUGHT TO ME. NOTHING MORE.
IF YOU CAN'T GRASP THAT, ANOTHER AGENT CAN BE SUMMONED TO REPLACE YOU. THE ARCANE WOMAN, PERHAPS.
UNDERSTOOD?
UM... SURE THING. JUST BRING HIM BACK HERE.
GOT IT.
I'VE ENTRUSTED THIS MATTER TO YOU BECAUSE YOU ARE THE MOST RELIABLE OF MY AGENTS. YOU'VE NOT FAILED ME IN THE PAST.
DON'T DO SO NOW.
DISPERSE THEM, MYX.
YES, MASTER.
DON'T WORRY, DOC...
...WE'LL GET YOUR MAN.

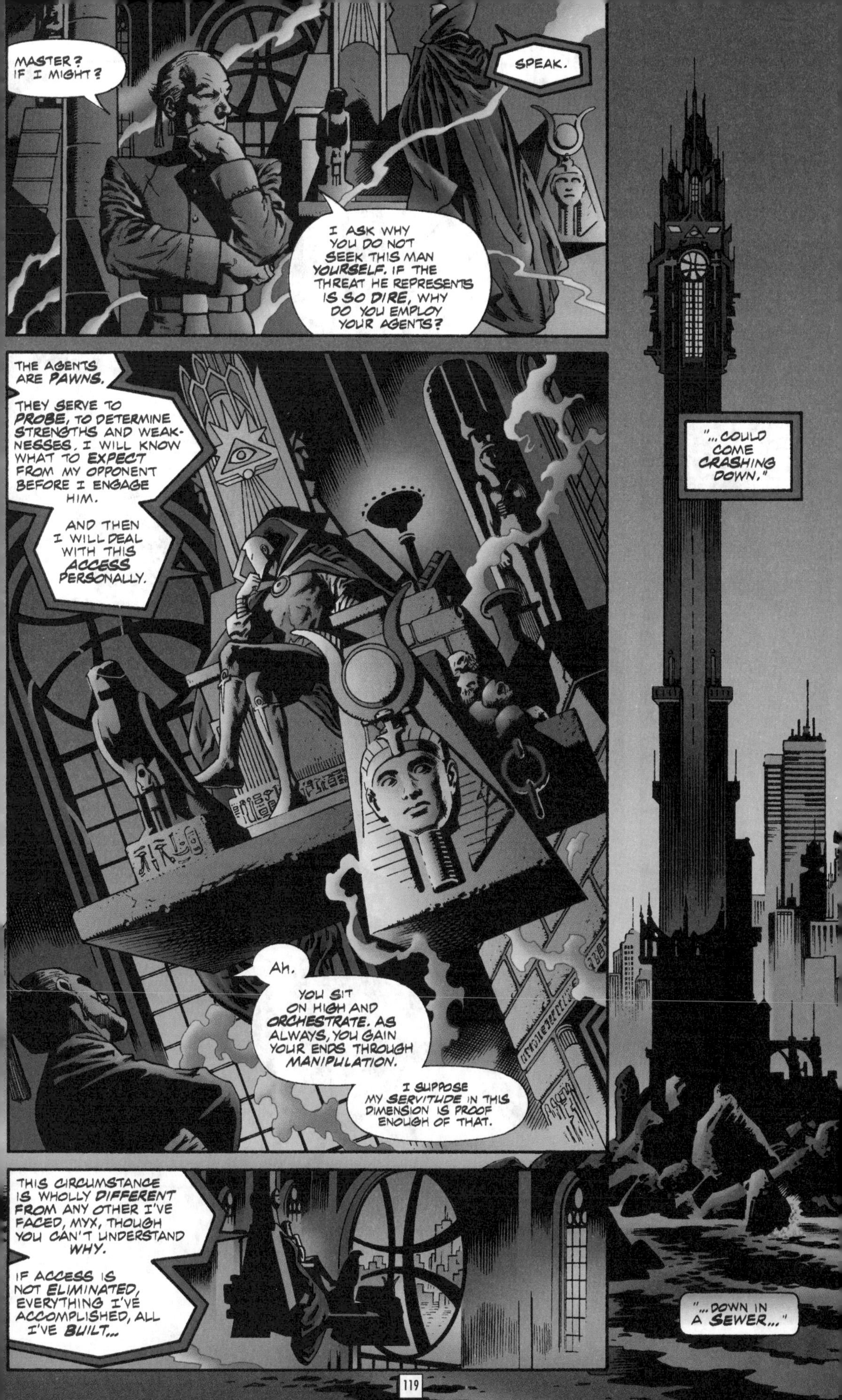
MASTER? IF I MIGHT?
SPEAK.
I ASK WHY YOU DO NOT SEEK THIS MAN YOURSELF. IF THE THREAT HE REPRESENTS IS SO DIRE, WHY DO YOU EMPLOY YOUR AGENTS?
THE AGENTS ARE PAWNS.
THEY SERVE TO PROBE, TO DETERMINE STRENGTHS AND WEAK-NESSES. I WILL KNOW WHAT TO EXPECT FROM MY OPPONENT BEFORE I ENGAGE HIM.
AND THEN I WILL DEAL WITH THIS ACCESS PERSONALLY.
Ah.
YOU SIT ON HIGH AND ORCHESTRATE. AS ALWAYS, YOU GAIN YOUR ENDS THROUGH MANIPULATION.
I SUPPOSE MY SERVITUDE IN THIS DIMENSION IS PROOF ENOUGH OF THAT.
THIS CIRCUMSTANCE IS WHOLLY DIFFERENT FROM ANY OTHER I'VE FACED, MYX, THOUGH YOU CAN'T UNDERSTAND WHY.
IF ACCESS IS NOT ELIMINATED, EVERYTHING I'VE ACCOMPLISHED, ALL I'VE BUILT...
"...COULD COME CRASHING DOWN."
"...DOWN IN A SEWER..."

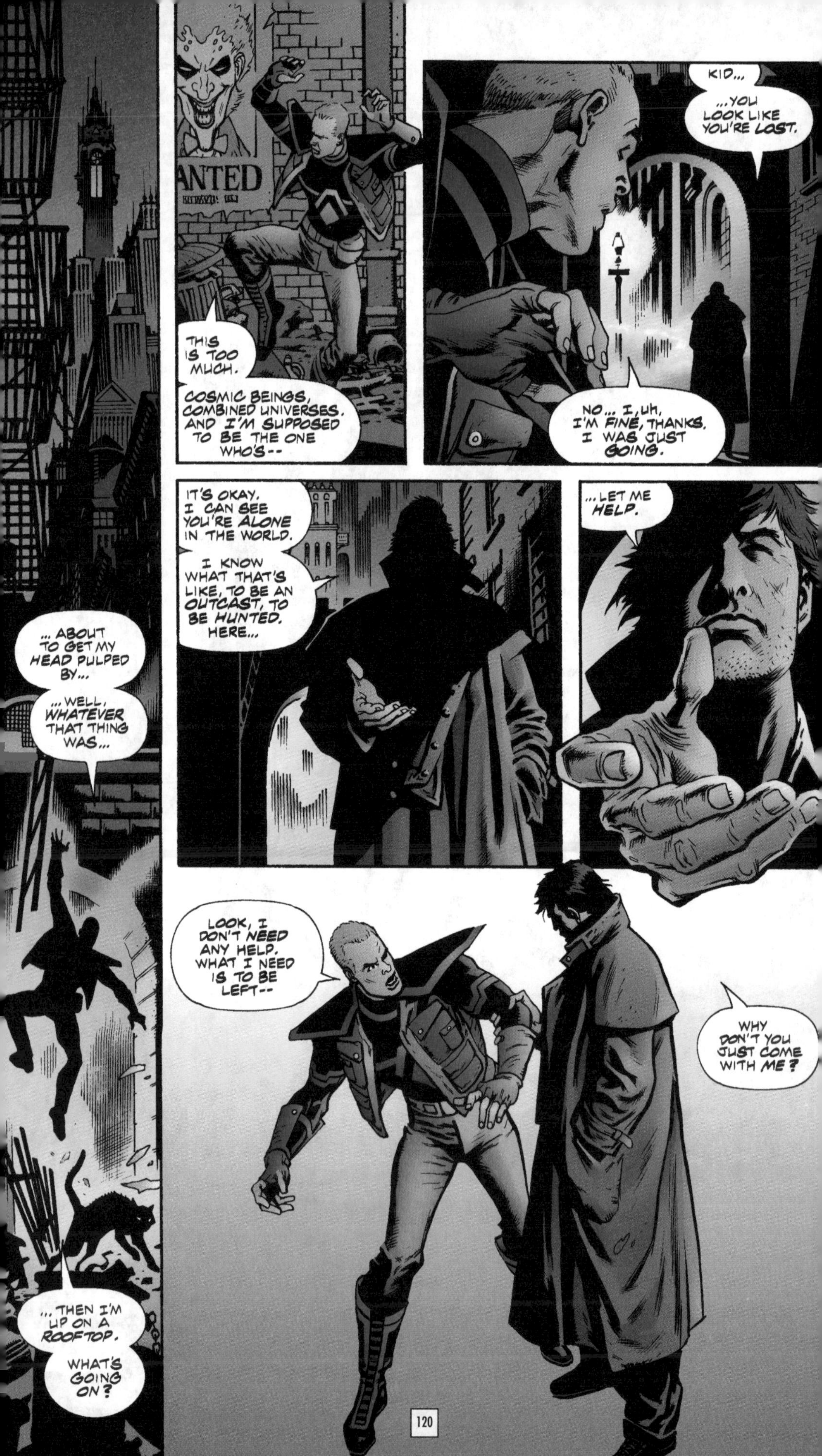
THIS IS TOO MUCH.
COSMIC BEINGS, COMBINED UNIVERSES. AND I'M SUPPOSED TO BE THE ONE WHO'S--
... ABOUT TO GET MY HEAD PULPED BY...
...WELL, WHATEVER THAT THING WAS...
... THEN I'M UP ON A ROOFTOP.
WHAT'S GOING ON?
WANTED
KID...
...YOU LOOK LIKE YOU'RE LOST.
NO... I, uh, I'M FINE, THANKS. I WAS JUST GOING.
IT'S OKAY. I CAN SEE YOU'RE ALONE IN THE WORLD.
I KNOW WHAT THAT'S LIKE, TO BE AN OUTCAST, TO BE HUNTED. HERE...
...LET ME HELP.
LOOK, I DON'T NEED ANY HELP. WHAT I NEED IS TO BE LEFT--
WHY DON'T YOU JUST COME WITH ME?

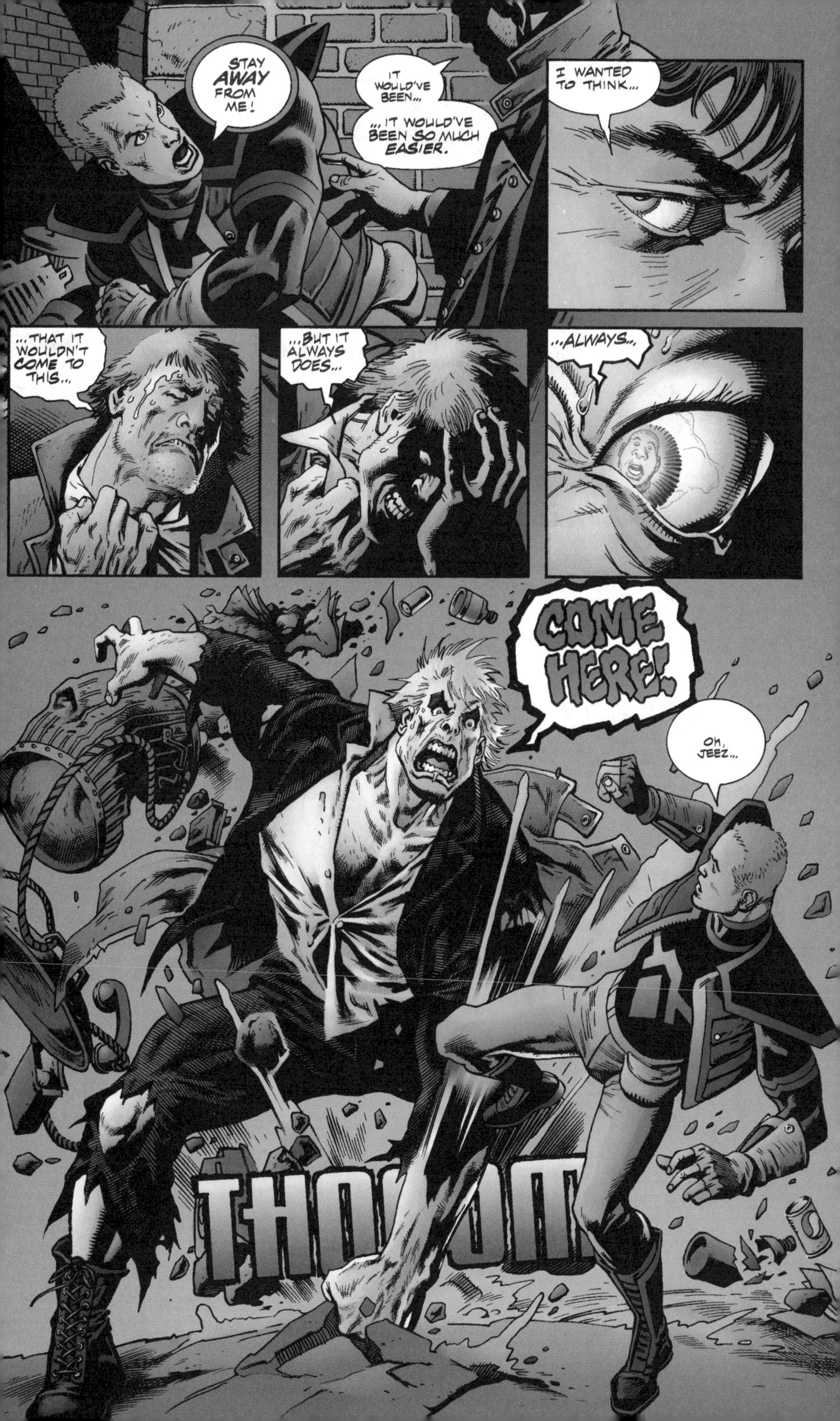
STAY AWAY FROM ME!
IT WOULD'VE BEEN...
...IT WOULD'VE BEEN SO MUCH EASIER.
I WANTED TO THINK...
...THAT IT WOULDN'T COME TO THIS...
...BUT IT ALWAYS DOES...
...ALWAYS...
COME HERE!
OH, JEEZ...
THOOOM

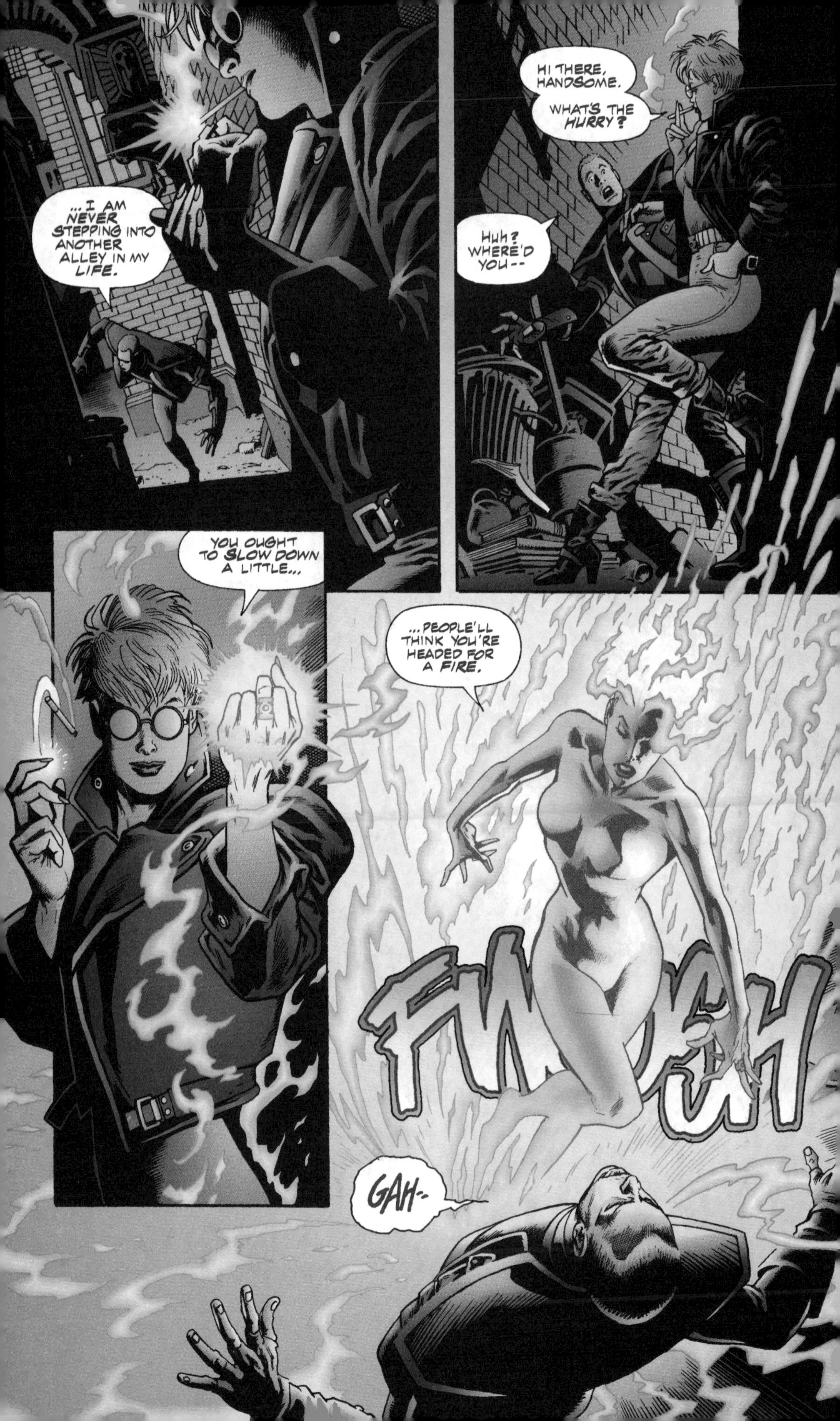
...I AM NEVER STEPPING INTO ANOTHER ALLEY IN MY LIFE.
HI THERE, HANDSOME.
WHAT'S THE HURRY?
Huh? WHERE'D YOU--
YOU OUGHT TO SLOW DOWN A LITTLE...
...PEOPLE'LL THINK YOU'RE HEADED FOR A FIRE.
FWOOSH
GAH--

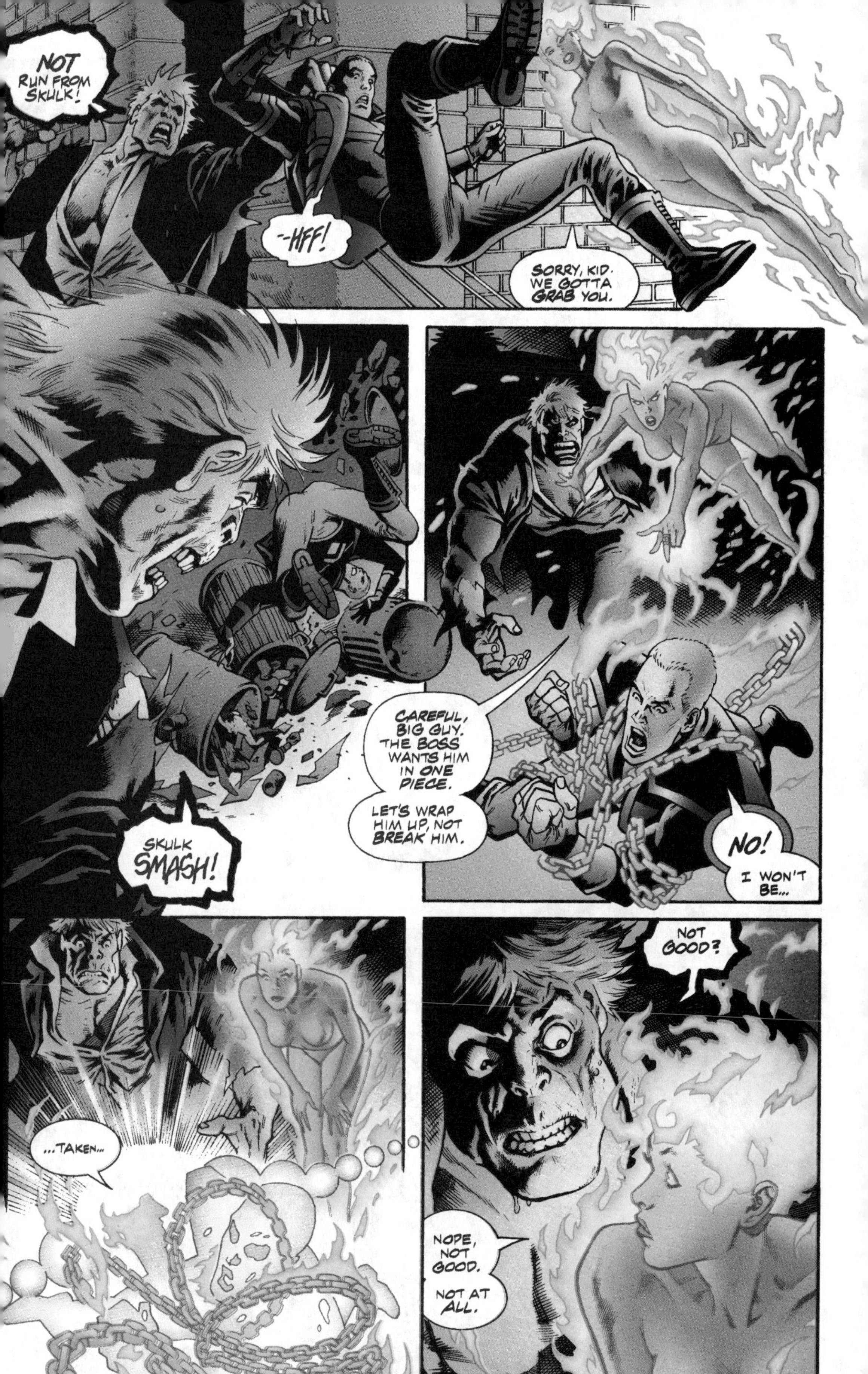
NOT RUN FROM SKULK!
--HFF!
SORRY, KID. WE GOTTA GRAB YOU.
SKULK SMASH!
CAREFUL, BIG GUY. THE BOSS WANTS HIM IN ONE PIECE.
LET'S WRAP HIM UP, NOT BREAK HIM.
NO!
I WON'T BE...
...TAKEN...
NOT GOOD?
NOPE, NOT GOOD.
NOT AT ALL.

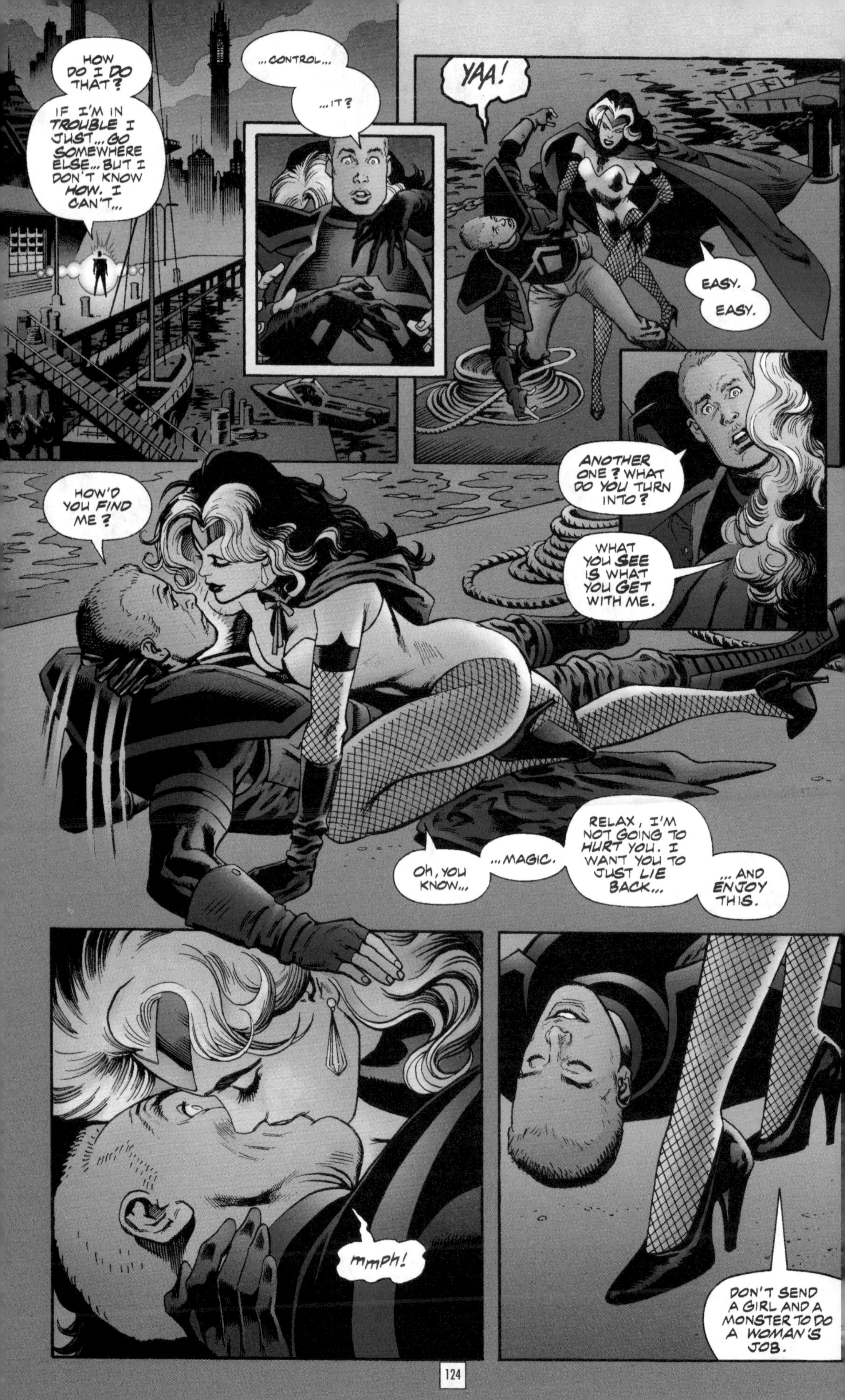

HOW DO I DO THAT?
IF I'M IN TROUBLE I JUST... GO SOMEWHERE ELSE... BUT I DON'T KNOW HOW. I CAN'T...
...CONTROL...
...IT?
YAA!
EASY.
EASY.
ANOTHER ONE? WHAT DO YOU TURN INTO?
WHAT YOU SEE IS WHAT YOU GET WITH ME.
HOW'D YOU FIND ME?
Oh, YOU KNOW...
...MAGIC.
RELAX, I'M NOT GOING TO HURT YOU. I WANT YOU TO JUST LIE BACK...
...AND ENJOY THIS.
mmph!
DON'T SEND A GIRL AND A MONSTER TO DO A WOMAN'S JOB.

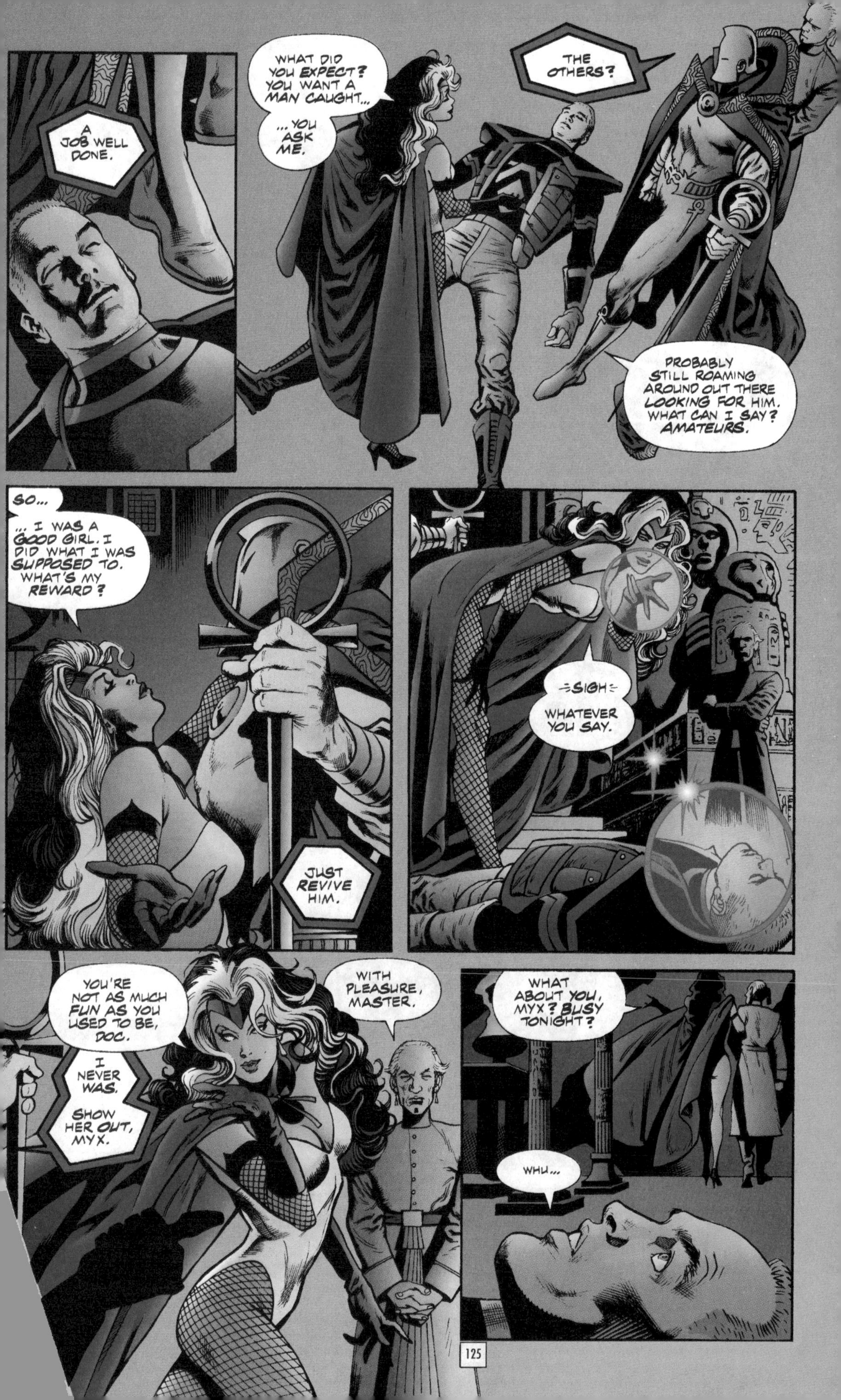
A JOB WELL DONE.
WHAT DID YOU EXPECT? YOU WANT A MAN CAUGHT...
...YOU ASK ME.
THE OTHERS?
PROBABLY STILL ROAMING AROUND OUT THERE LOOKING FOR HIM. WHAT CAN I SAY? AMATEURS.
SO...
...I WAS A GOOD GIRL. I DID WHAT I WAS SUPPOSED TO. WHAT'S MY REWARD?
JUST REVIVE HIM.
=SIGH=
WHATEVER YOU SAY.
YOU'RE NOT AS MUCH FUN AS YOU USED TO BE, DOC.
I NEVER WAS.
SHOW HER OUT, MYX.
WITH PLEASURE, MASTER.
WHAT ABOUT YOU, MYX? BUSY TONIGHT?
WHU...

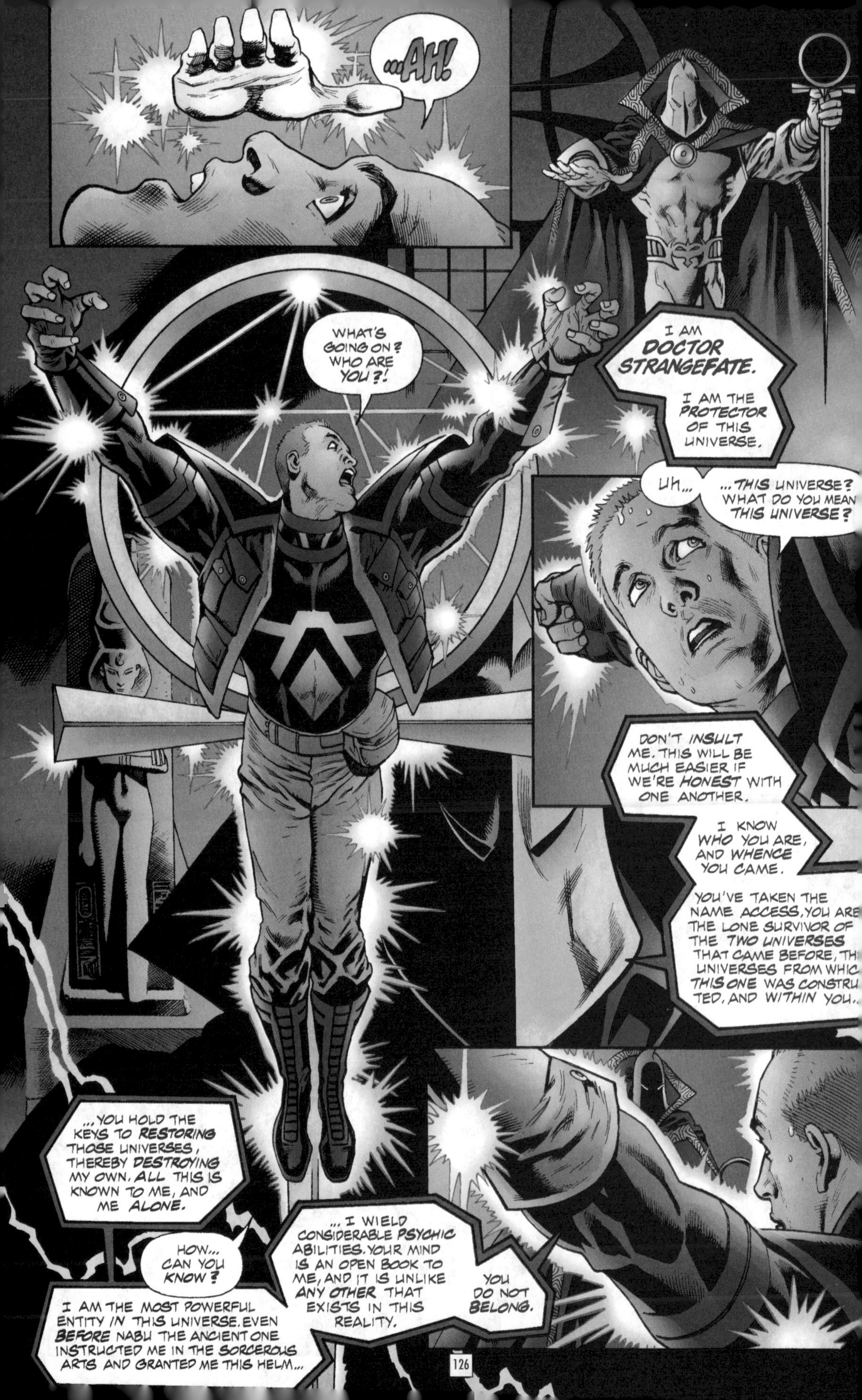
...AH!
I AM DOCTOR STRANGEFATE.
I AM THE PROTECTOR OF THIS UNIVERSE.
WHAT'S GOING ON? WHO ARE YOU?!
UH...
...THIS UNIVERSE? WHAT DO YOU MEAN THIS UNIVERSE?
DON'T INSULT ME. THIS WILL BE MUCH EASIER IF WE'RE HONEST WITH ONE ANOTHER.
I KNOW WHO YOU ARE, AND WHENCE YOU CAME.
YOU'VE TAKEN THE NAME ACCESS, YOU ARE THE LONE SURVIVOR OF THE TWO UNIVERSES THAT CAME BEFORE, TH UNIVERSES FROM WHIC THIS ONE WAS CONSTRU TED, AND WITHIN YOU...
...YOU HOLD THE KEYS TO RESTORING THOSE UNIVERSES, THEREBY DESTROYING MY OWN. ALL THIS IS KNOWN TO ME, AND ME ALONE.
HOW... CAN YOU KNOW?
I AM THE MOST POWERFUL ENTITY IN THIS UNIVERSE. EVEN BEFORE NABU THE ANCIENT ONE INSTRUCTED ME IN THE SORCEROUS ARTS AND GRANTED ME THIS HELM...
...I WIELD CONSIDERABLE PSYCHIC ABILITIES. YOUR MIND IS AN OPEN BOOK TO ME, AND IT IS UNLIKE ANY OTHER THAT EXISTS IN THIS REALITY.
YOU DO NOT BELONG.

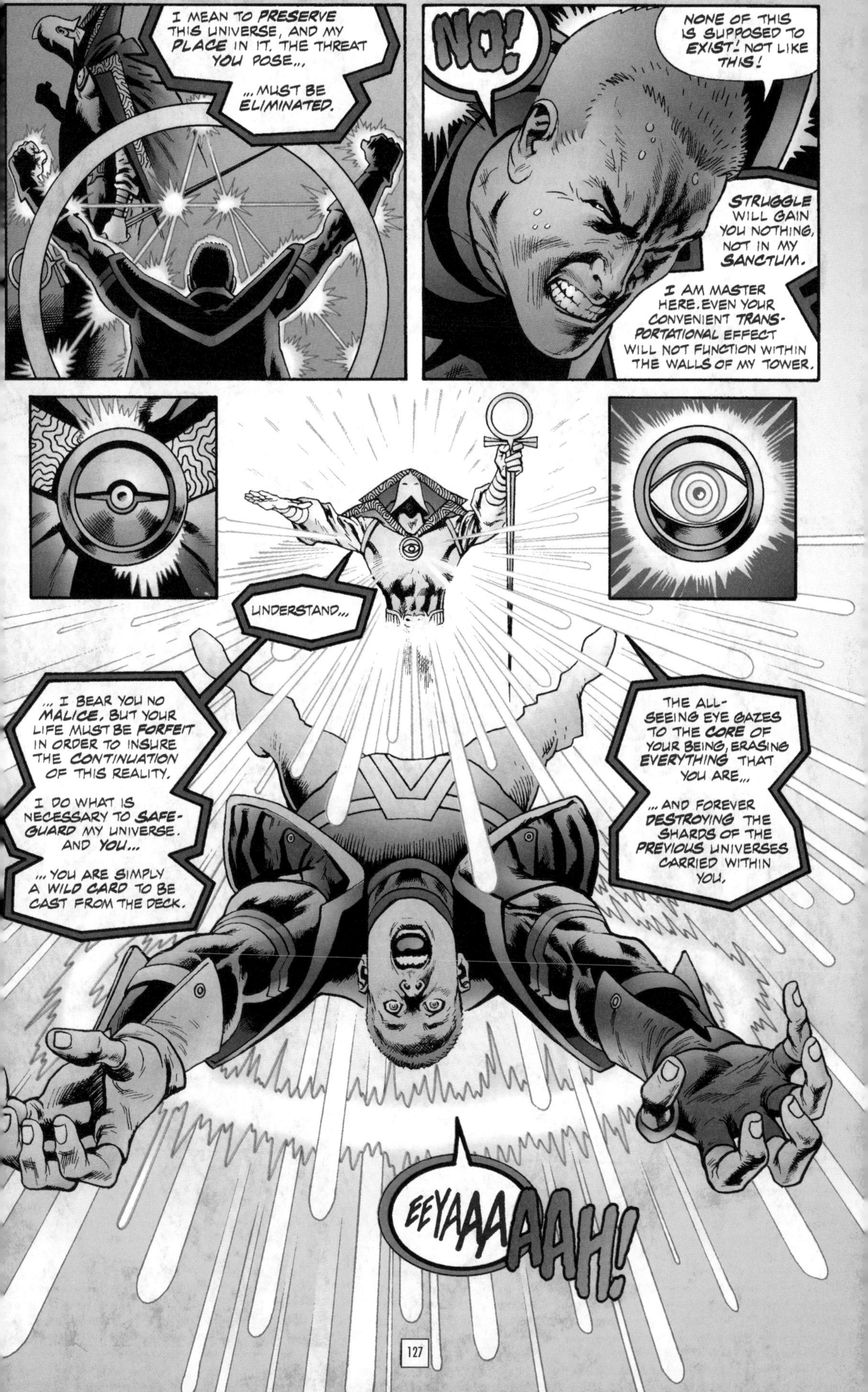

I MEAN TO PRESERVE THIS UNIVERSE, AND MY PLACE IN IT. THE THREAT YOU POSE...
...MUST BE ELIMINATED.
NO!
NONE OF THIS IS SUPPOSED TO EXIST! NOT LIKE THIS!
STRUGGLE WILL GAIN YOU NOTHING, NOT IN MY SANCTUM.
I AM MASTER HERE. EVEN YOUR CONVENIENT TRANSPORTATIONAL EFFECT WILL NOT FUNCTION WITHIN THE WALLS OF MY TOWER.
UNDERSTAND...
... I BEAR YOU NO MALICE. BUT YOUR LIFE MUST BE FORFEIT IN ORDER TO INSURE THE CONTINUATION OF THIS REALITY.
I DO WHAT IS NECESSARY TO SAFEGUARD MY UNIVERSE. AND YOU...
...YOU ARE SIMPLY A WILD CARD TO BE CAST FROM THE DECK.
THE ALL-SEEING EYE GAZES TO THE CORE OF YOUR BEING, ERASING EVERYTHING THAT YOU ARE...
...AND FOREVER DESTROYING THE SHARDS OF THE PREVIOUS UNIVERSES CARRIED WITHIN YOU.
EEYAAAAAH!

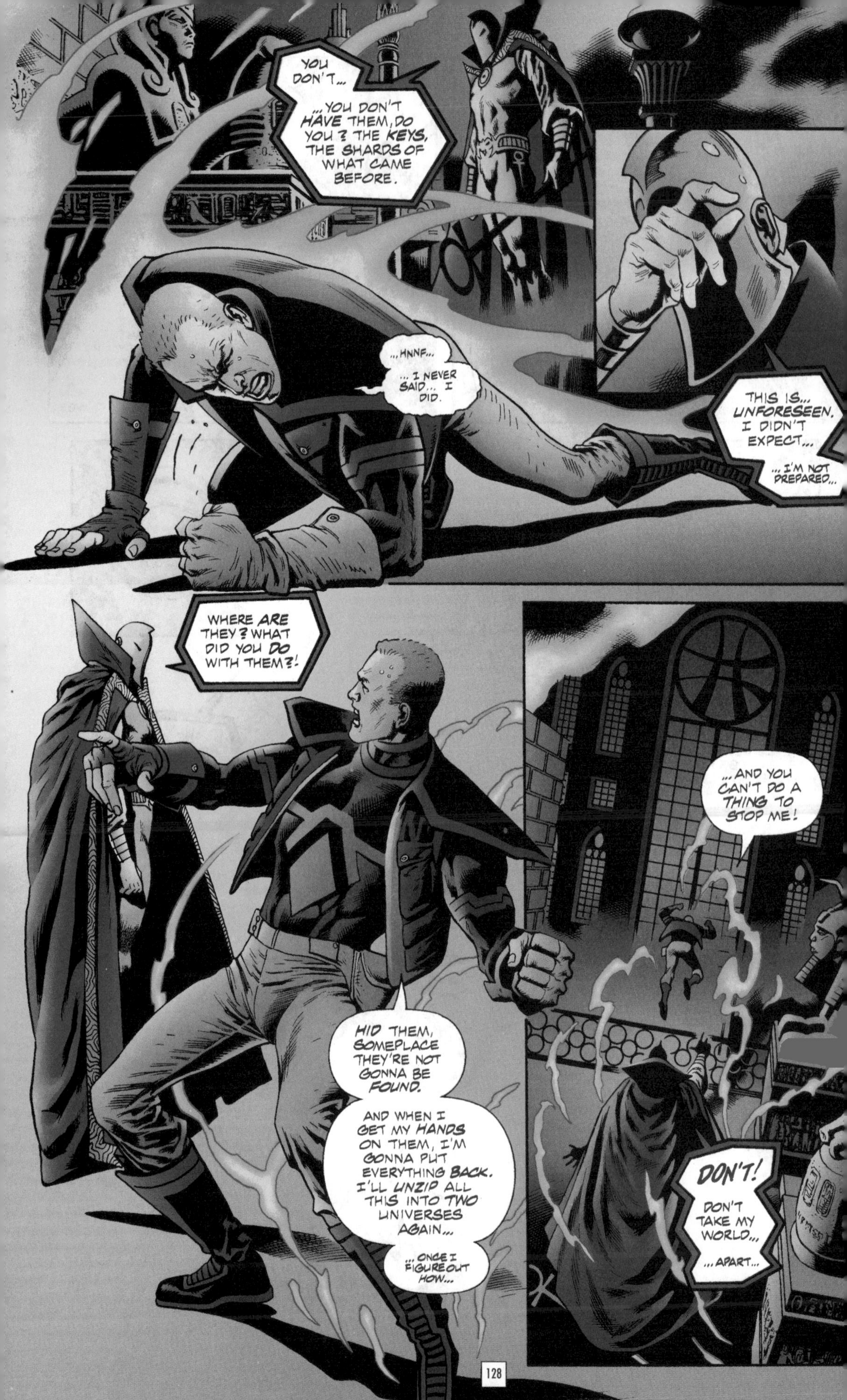
YOU DON'T...
...YOU DON'T HAVE THEM, DO YOU? THE KEYS, THE SHARDS OF WHAT CAME BEFORE.
...HNNF...
...I NEVER SAID... I DID.
THIS IS... UNFORESEEN. I DIDN'T EXPECT...
...I'M NOT PREPARED...
WHERE ARE THEY? WHAT DID YOU DO WITH THEM?!
HID THEM, SOMEPLACE THEY'RE NOT GONNA BE FOUND.
AND WHEN I GET MY HANDS ON THEM, I'M GONNA PUT EVERYTHING BACK. I'LL UNZIP ALL THIS INTO TWO UNIVERSES AGAIN...
...ONCE I FIGURE OUT HOW...
...AND YOU CAN'T DO A THING TO STOP ME!
DON'T!
DON'T TAKE MY WORLD...
...APART...

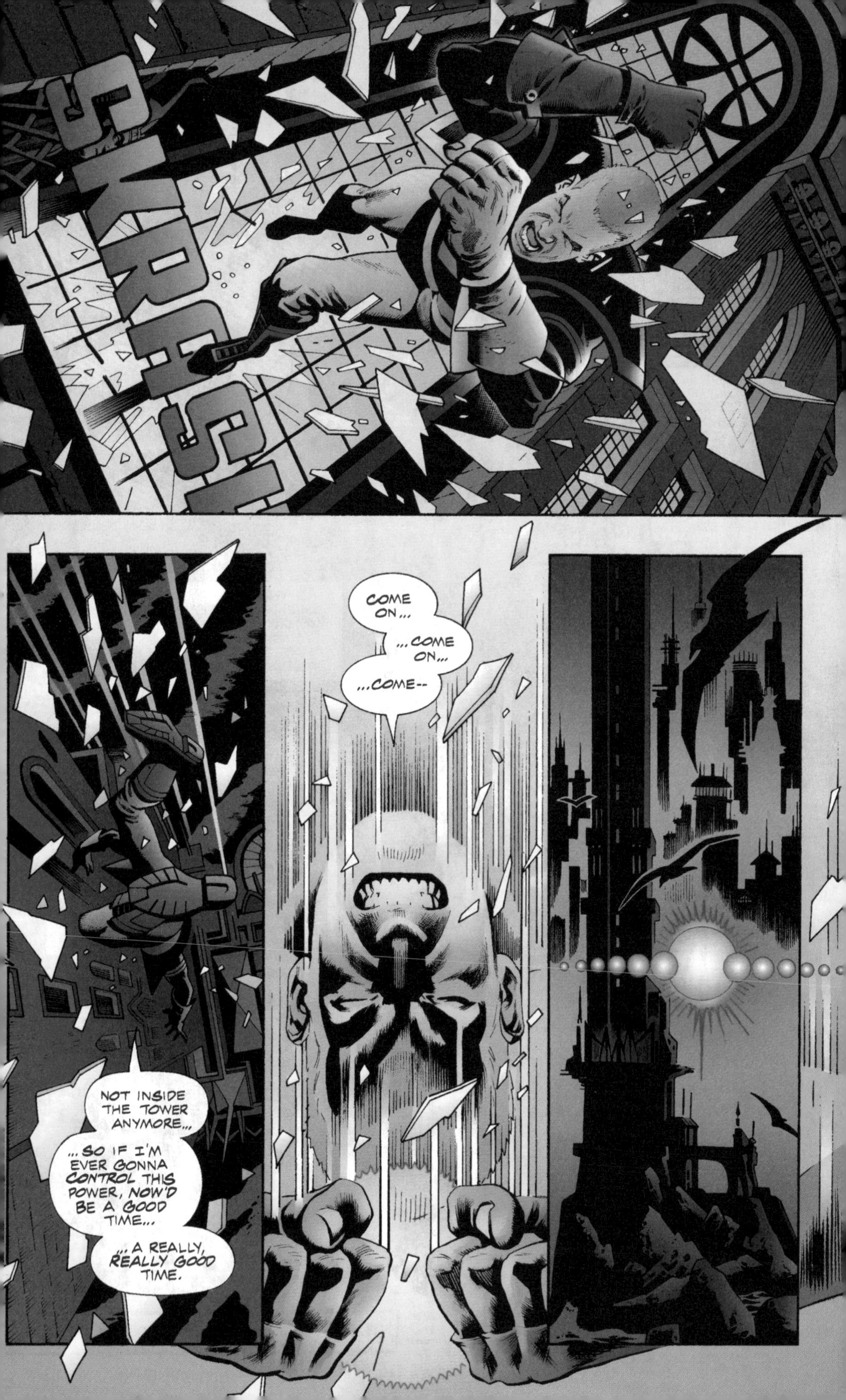
COME ON...
...COME ON...
...COME--
NOT INSIDE THE TOWER ANYMORE...
...SO IF I'M EVER GONNA CONTROL THIS POWER, NOW'D BE A GOOD TIME...
...A REALLY, REALLY GOOD TIME.

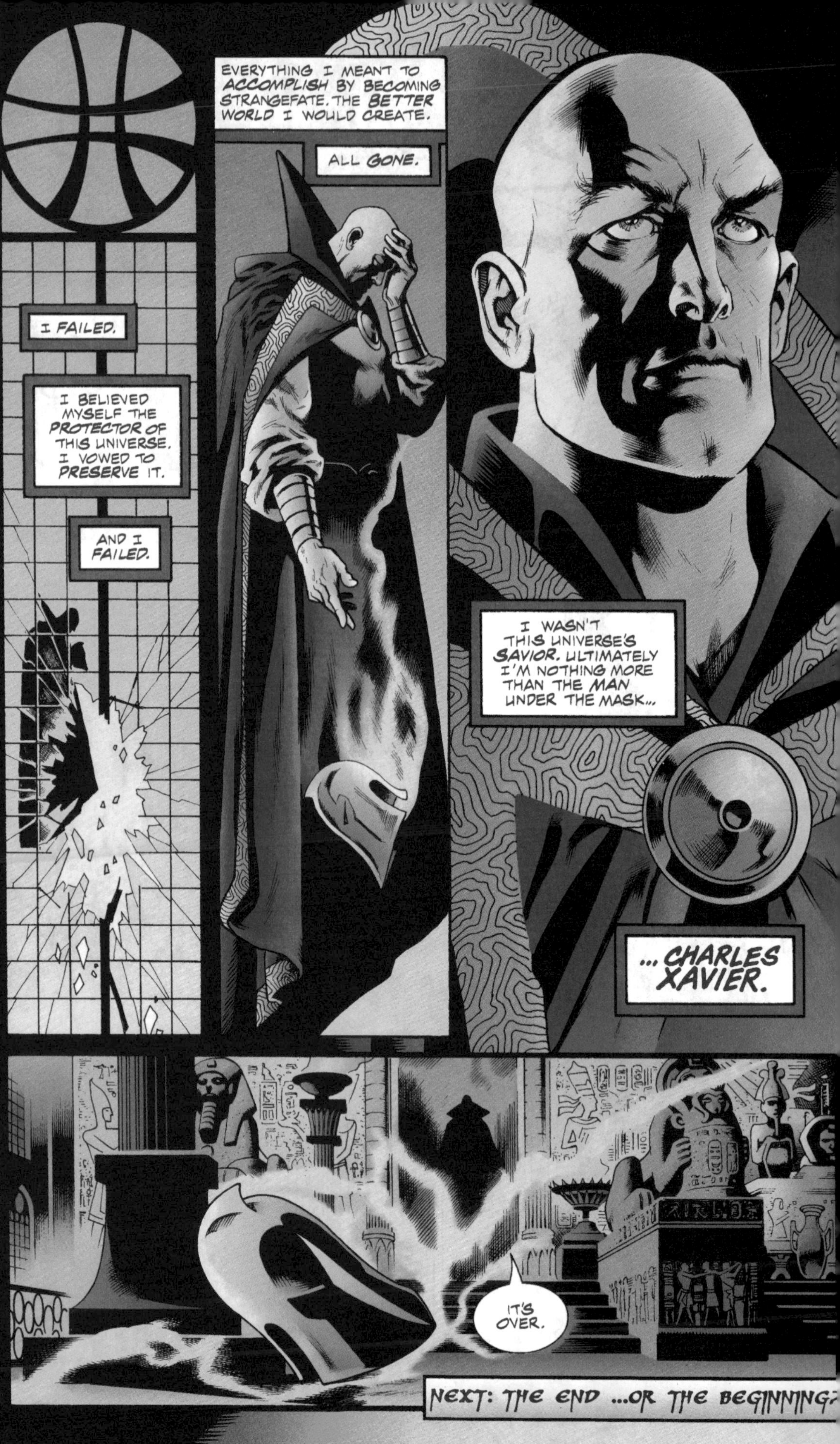
EVERYTHING I MEANT TO ACCOMPLISH BY BECOMING STRANGEFATE. THE BETTER WORLD I WOULD CREATE.
ALL GONE.
I FAILED.
I BELIEVED MYSELF THE PROTECTOR OF THIS UNIVERSE. I VOWED TO PRESERVE IT.
AND I FAILED.
I WASN'T THIS UNIVERSE'S SAVIOR. ULTIMATELY I'M NOTHING MORE THAN THE MAN UNDER THE MASK...
...CHARLES XAVIER.
IT'S OVER.
NEXT: THE END ...OR THE BEGINNING?

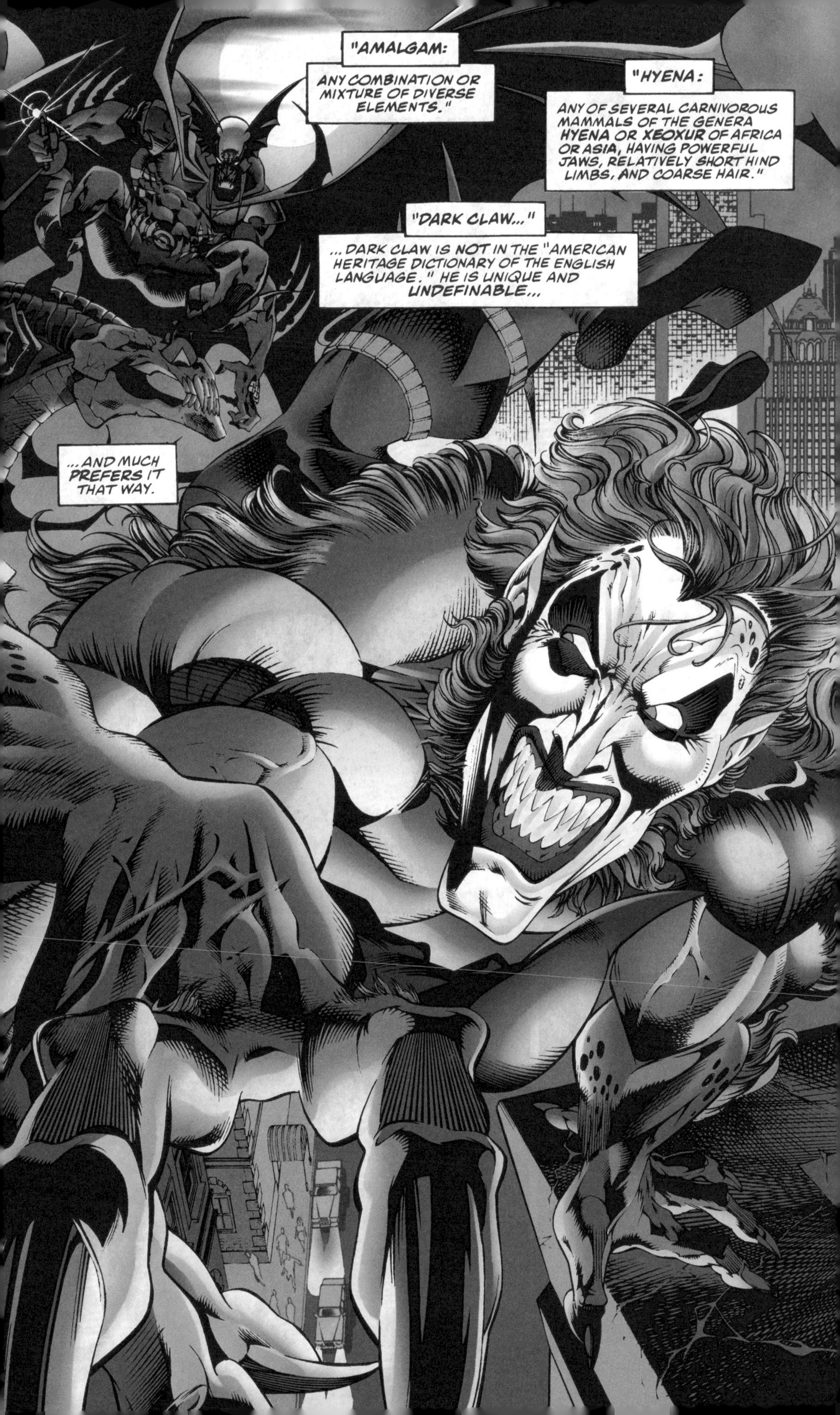
"AMALGAM:
ANY COMBINATION OR MIXTURE OF DIVERSE ELEMENTS."
"HYENA:
ANY OF SEVERAL CARNIVOROUS MAMMALS OF THE GENERA HYENA OR XEOXUR OF AFRICA OR ASIA, HAVING POWERFUL JAWS, RELATIVELY SHORT HIND LIMBS, AND COARSE HAIR."
"DARK CLAW..."
...DARK CLAW IS NOT IN THE "AMERICAN HERITAGE DICTIONARY OF THE ENGLISH LANGUAGE." HE IS UNIQUE AND UNDEFINABLE...
...AND MUCH PREFERS IT THAT WAY.

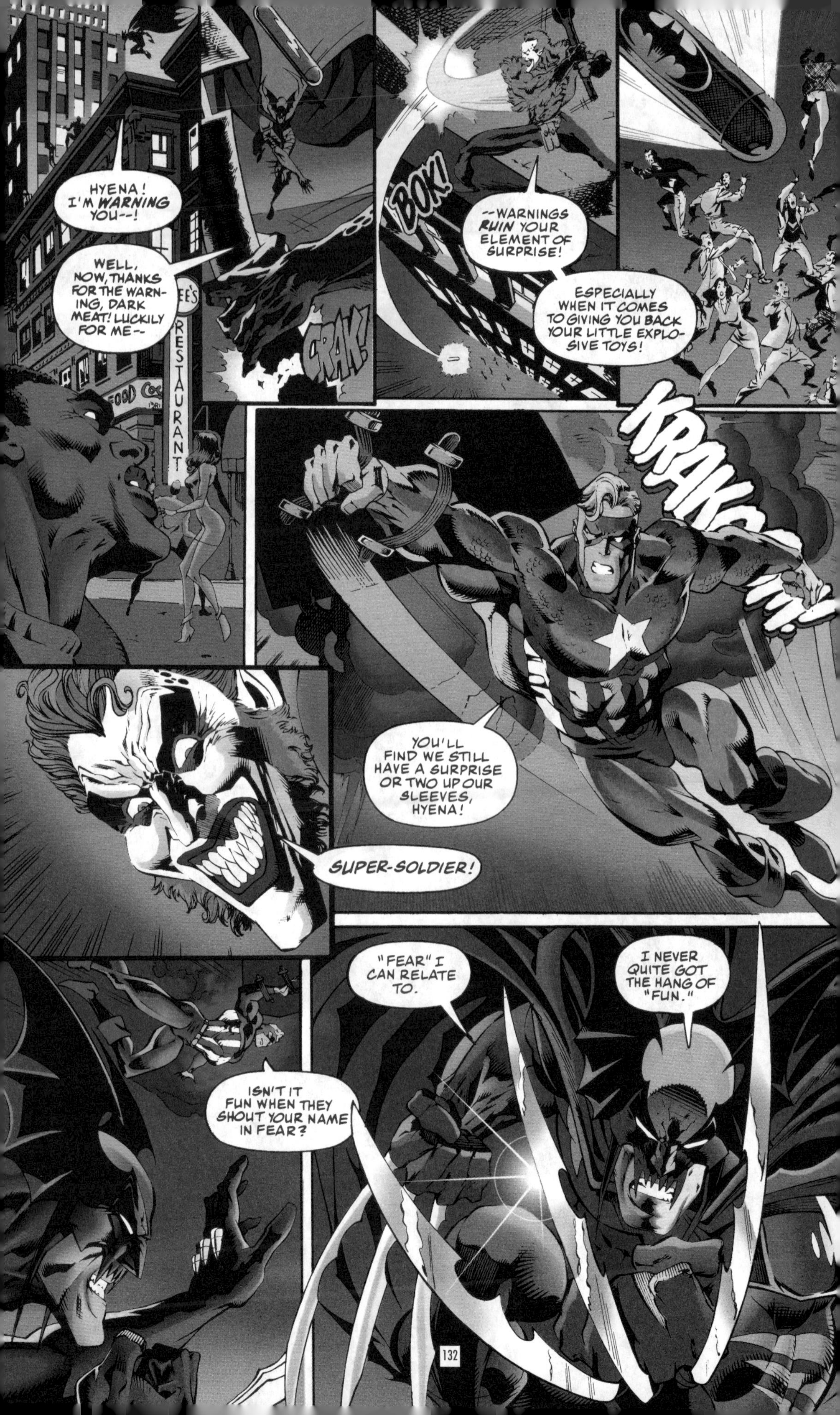
HYENA! I'M WARNING YOU--!
WELL, NOW, THANKS FOR THE WARNING, DARK MEAT! LUCKILY FOR ME--
RESTAURANT
CRAK!
BOK!
--WARNINGS RUIN YOUR ELEMENT OF SURPRISE!
ESPECIALLY WHEN IT COMES TO GIVING YOU BACK YOUR LITTLE EXPLOSIVE TOYS!
KRAK
YOU'LL FIND WE STILL HAVE A SURPRISE OR TWO UP OUR SLEEVES, HYENA!
SUPER-SOLDIER!
ISN'T IT FUN WHEN THEY SHOUT YOUR NAME IN FEAR?
"FEAR" I CAN RELATE TO.
I NEVER QUITE GOT THE HANG OF "FUN."

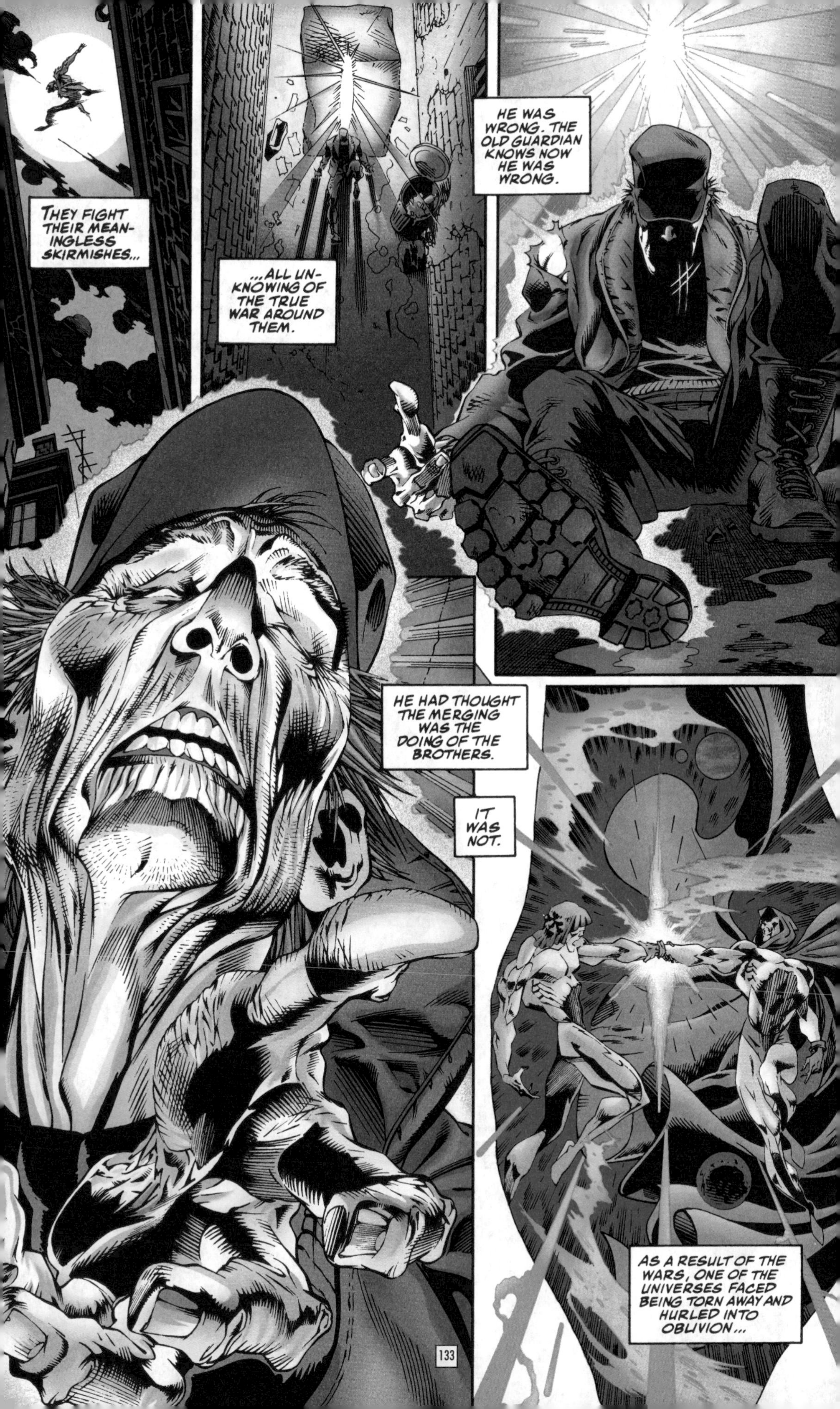
THEY FIGHT THEIR MEAN-INGLESS SKIRMISHES...
...ALL UN-KNOWING OF THE TRUE WAR AROUND THEM.
HE WAS WRONG. THE OLD GUARDIAN KNOWS NOW HE WAS WRONG.
HE HAD THOUGHT THE MERGING WAS THE DOING OF THE BROTHERS.
IT WAS NOT.
AS A RESULT OF THE WARS, ONE OF THE UNIVERSES FACED BEING TORN AWAY AND HURLED INTO OBLIVION...

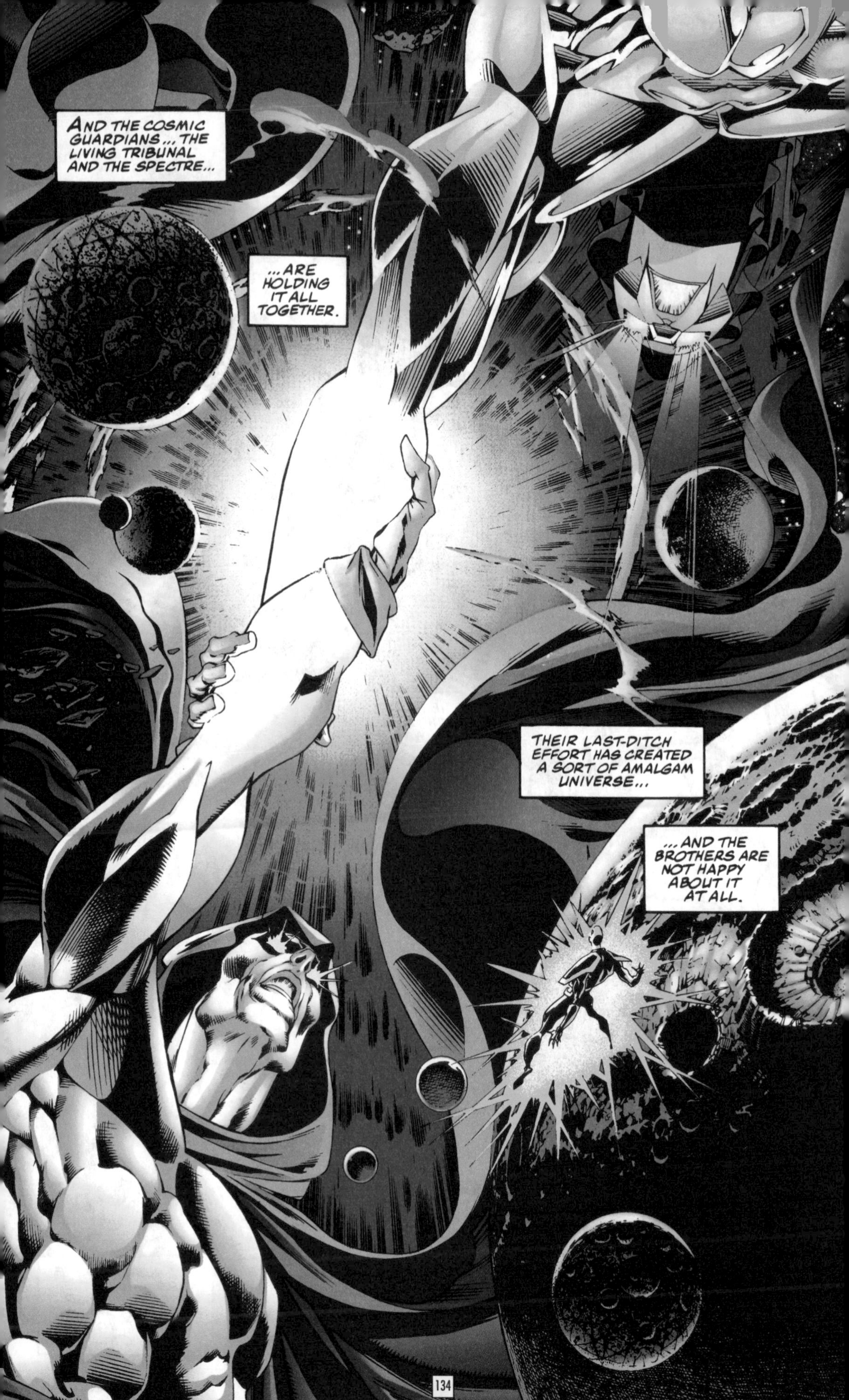
AND THE COSMIC GUARDIANS... THE LIVING TRIBUNAL AND THE SPECTRE...
...ARE HOLDING IT ALL TOGETHER.
THEIR LAST-DITCH EFFORT HAS CREATED A SORT OF AMALGAM UNIVERSE...
...AND THE BROTHERS ARE NOT HAPPY ABOUT IT AT ALL.

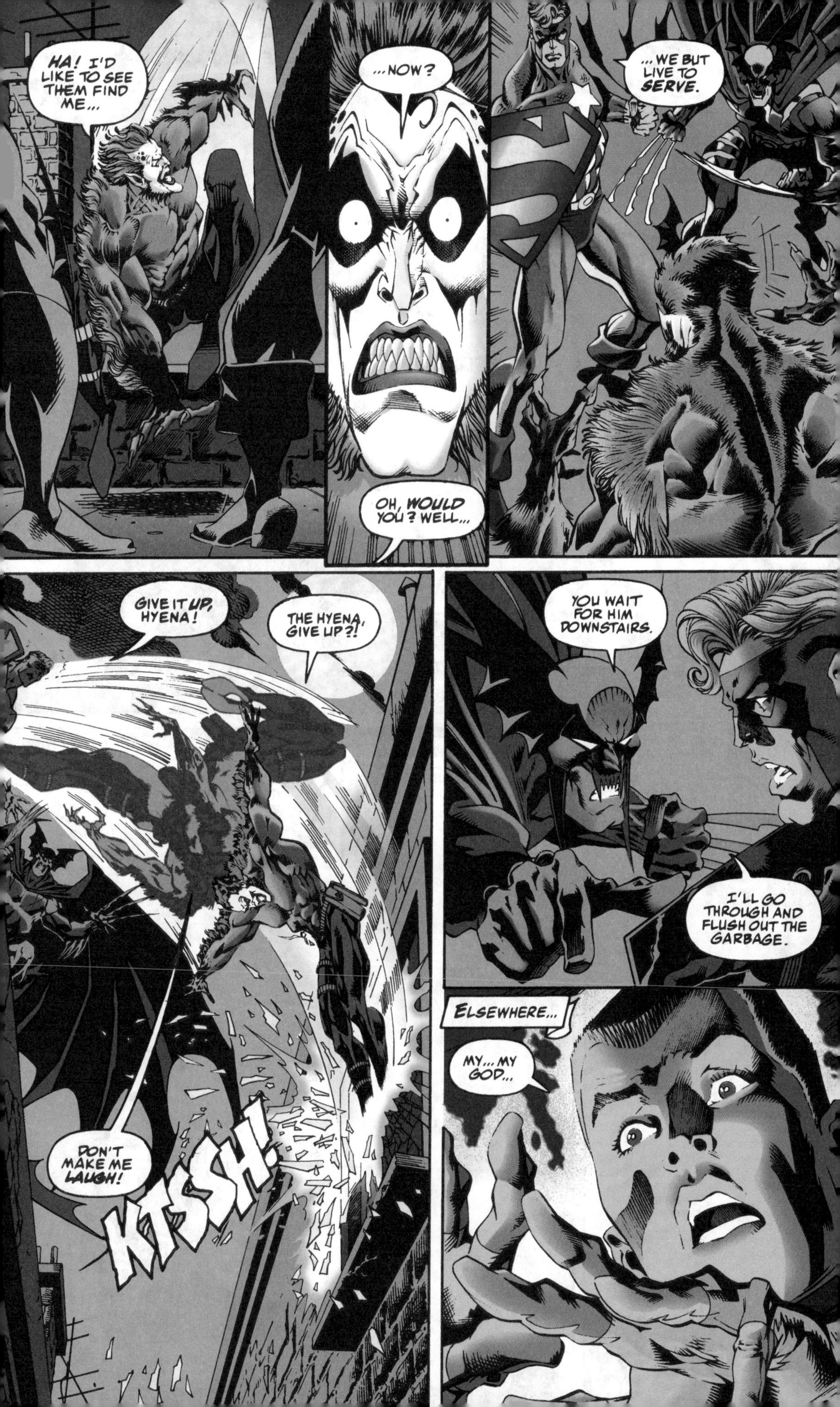
HA! I'D LIKE TO SEE THEM FIND ME...
...NOW?
OH, WOULD YOU? WELL,...
...WE BUT LIVE TO SERVE.
GIVE IT UP, HYENA!
THE HYENA, GIVE UP?!
DON'T MAKE ME LAUGH!
KTSSH!
YOU WAIT FOR HIM DOWNSTAIRS.
I'LL GO THROUGH AND FLUSH OUT THE GARBAGE.
ELSEWHERE...
MY... MY GOD...

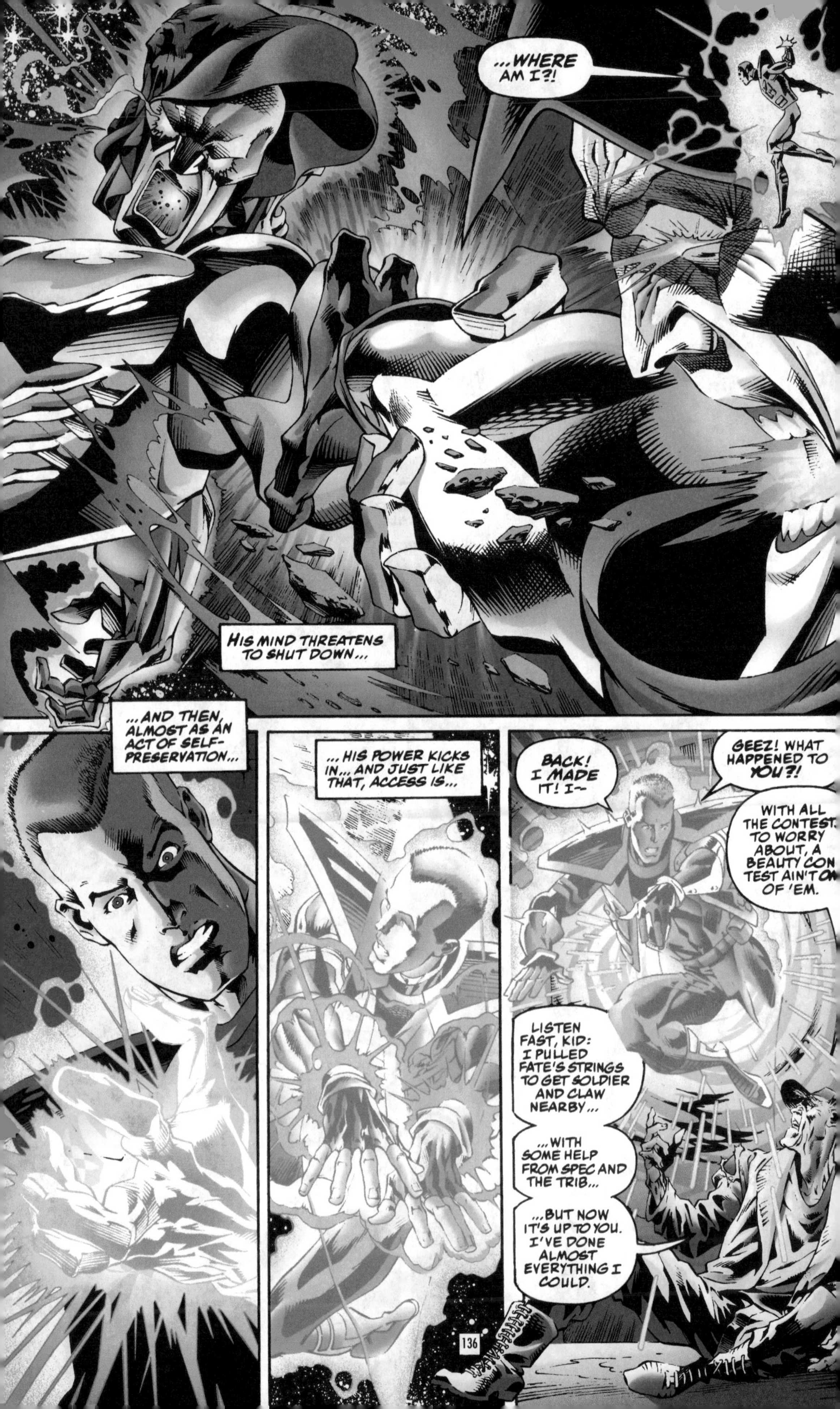

...WHERE AM I?!
HIS MIND THREATENS TO SHUT DOWN...
...AND THEN, ALMOST AS AN ACT OF SELF-PRESERVATION...
...HIS POWER KICKS IN... AND JUST LIKE THAT, ACCESS IS...
BACK! I MADE IT! I--
GEEZ! WHAT HAPPENED TO YOU?!
WITH ALL THE CONTEST TO WORRY ABOUT, A BEAUTY CONTEST AIN'T ONE OF 'EM.
LISTEN FAST, KID: I PULLED FATE'S STRINGS TO GET SOLDIER AND CLAW NEARBY...
...WITH SOME HELP FROM SPEC AND THE TRIB...
...BUT NOW IT'S UP TO YOU. I'VE DONE ALMOST EVERYTHING I COULD.

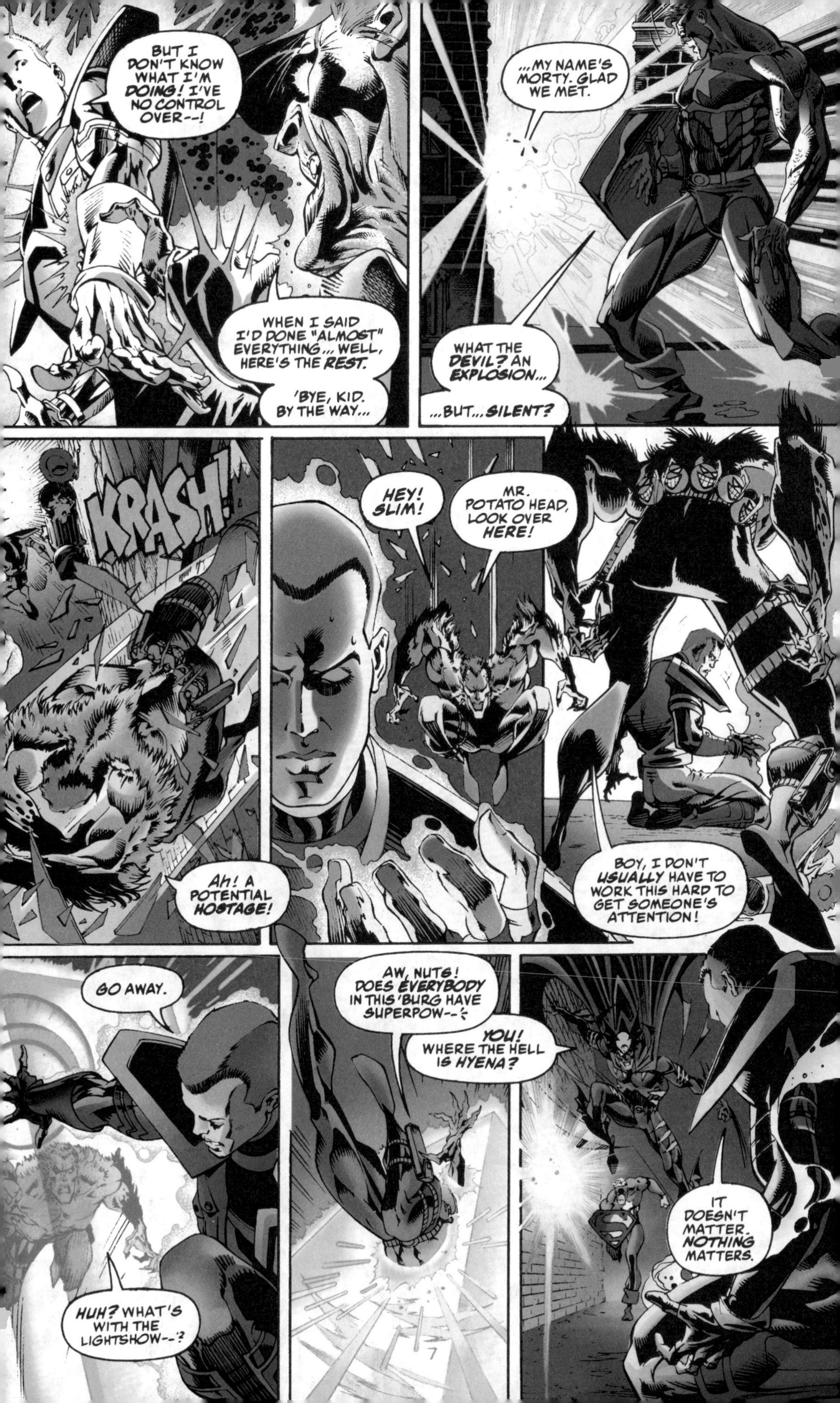
BUT I DON'T KNOW WHAT I'M DOING! I'VE NO CONTROL OVER--!
WHEN I SAID I'D DONE "ALMOST" EVERYTHING... WELL, HERE'S THE REST.
'BYE, KID. BY THE WAY...
...MY NAME'S MORTY. GLAD WE MET.
WHAT THE DEVIL? AN EXPLOSION...
...BUT... SILENT?
KRASH!
Ah! A POTENTIAL HOSTAGE!
HEY! SLIM!
MR. POTATO HEAD, LOOK OVER HERE!
BOY, I DON'T USUALLY HAVE TO WORK THIS HARD TO GET SOMEONE'S ATTENTION!
GO AWAY.
HUH? WHAT'S WITH THE LIGHTSHOW--?
AW, NUTS! DOES EVERYBODY IN THIS 'BURG HAVE SUPERPOW--!
YOU! WHERE THE HELL IS HYENA?
IT DOESN'T MATTER. NOTHING MATTERS.

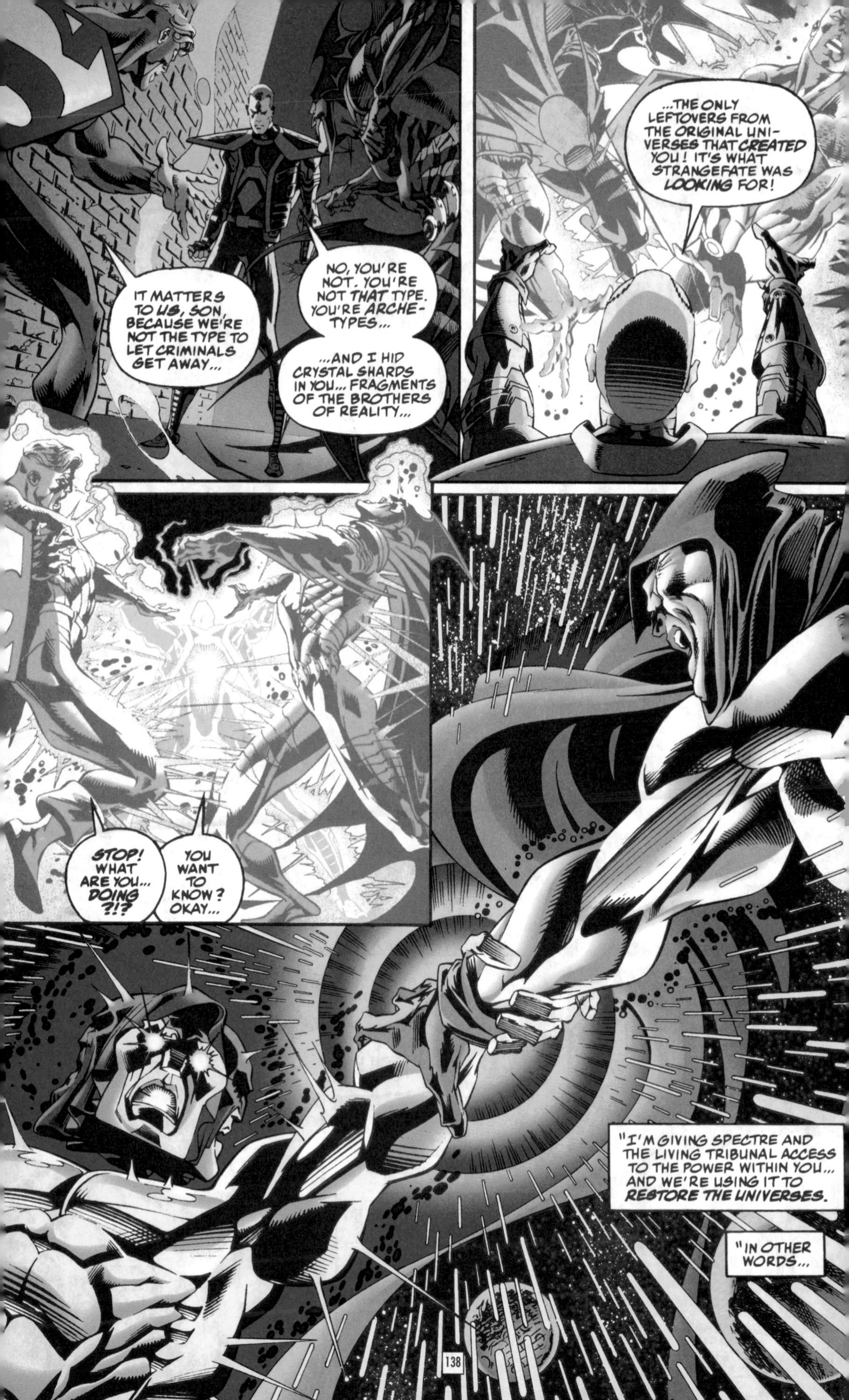
IT MATTERS TO US, SON, BECAUSE WE'RE NOT THE TYPE TO LET CRIMINALS GET AWAY...
NO, YOU'RE NOT. YOU'RE NOT THAT TYPE. YOU'RE ARCHE-TYPES...
...AND I HID CRYSTAL SHARDS IN YOU... FRAGMENTS OF THE BROTHERS OF REALITY...
...THE ONLY LEFTOVERS FROM THE ORIGINAL UNI-VERSES THAT CREATED YOU! IT'S WHAT STRANGEFATE WAS LOOKING FOR!
STOP! WHAT ARE YOU... DOING ?!?
YOU WANT TO KNOW? OKAY...
"I'M GIVING SPECTRE AND THE LIVING TRIBUNAL ACCESS TO THE POWER WITHIN YOU... AND WE'RE USING IT TO RESTORE THE UNIVERSES.
"IN OTHER WORDS...

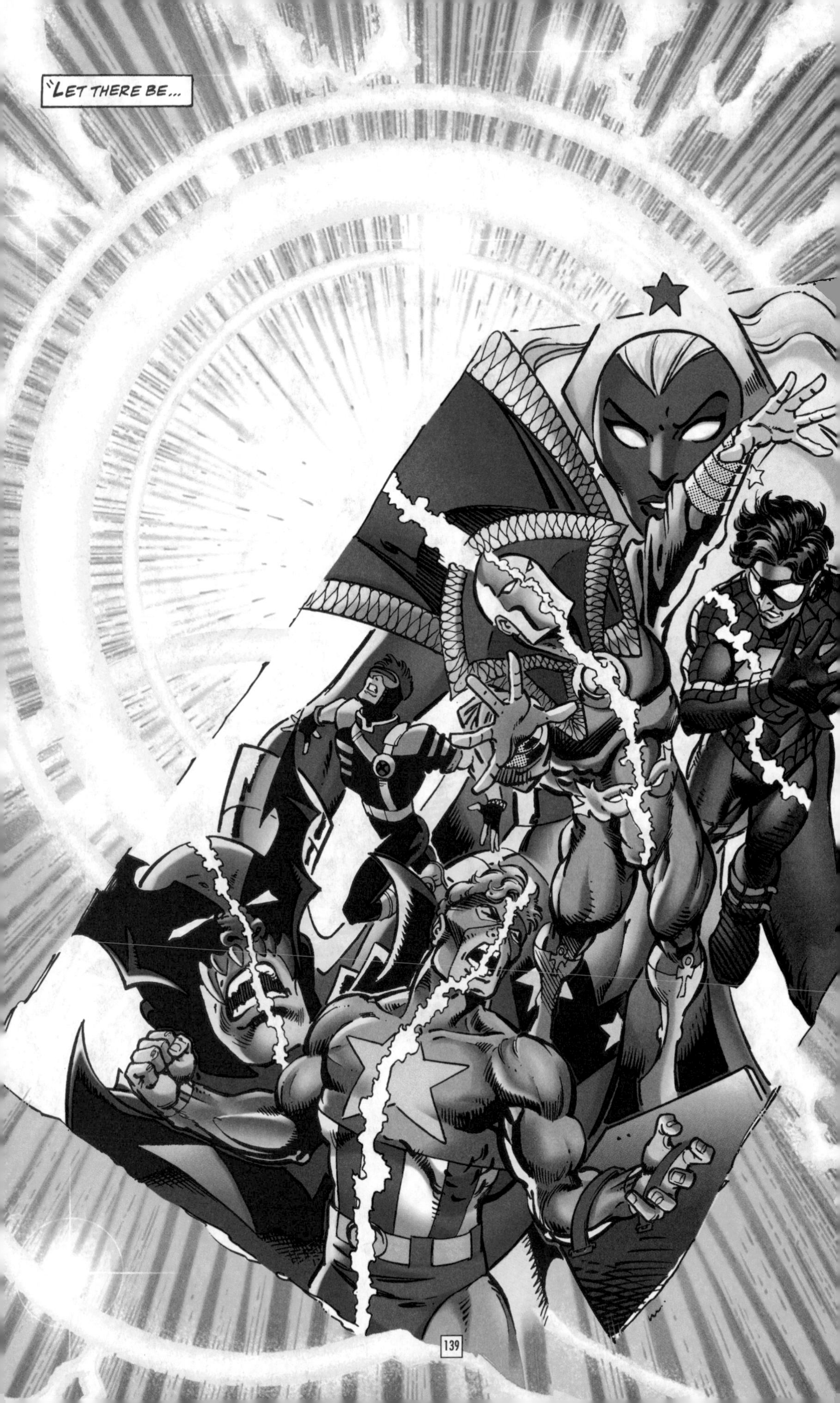
"LET THERE BE...

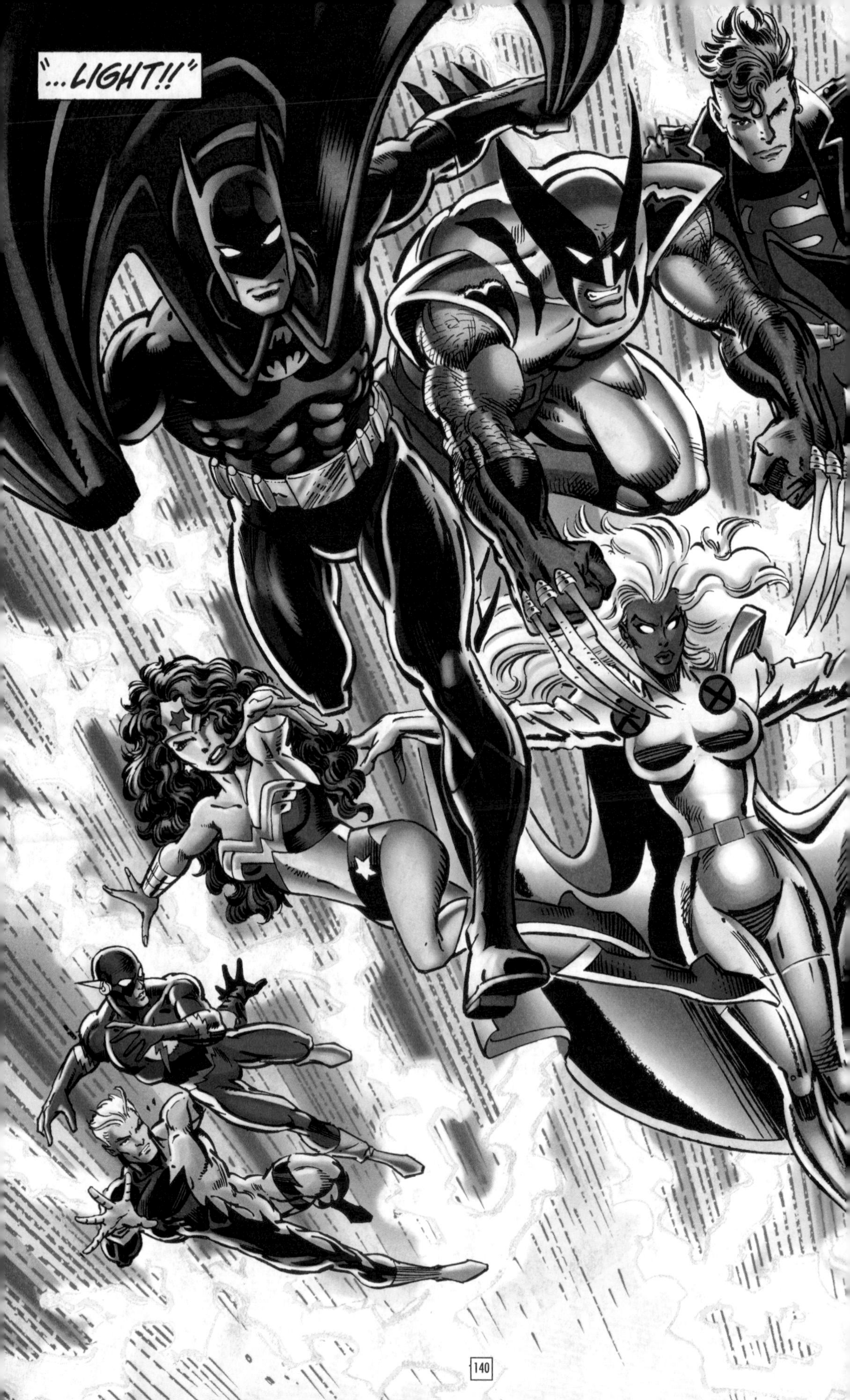
"...LIGHT!!"

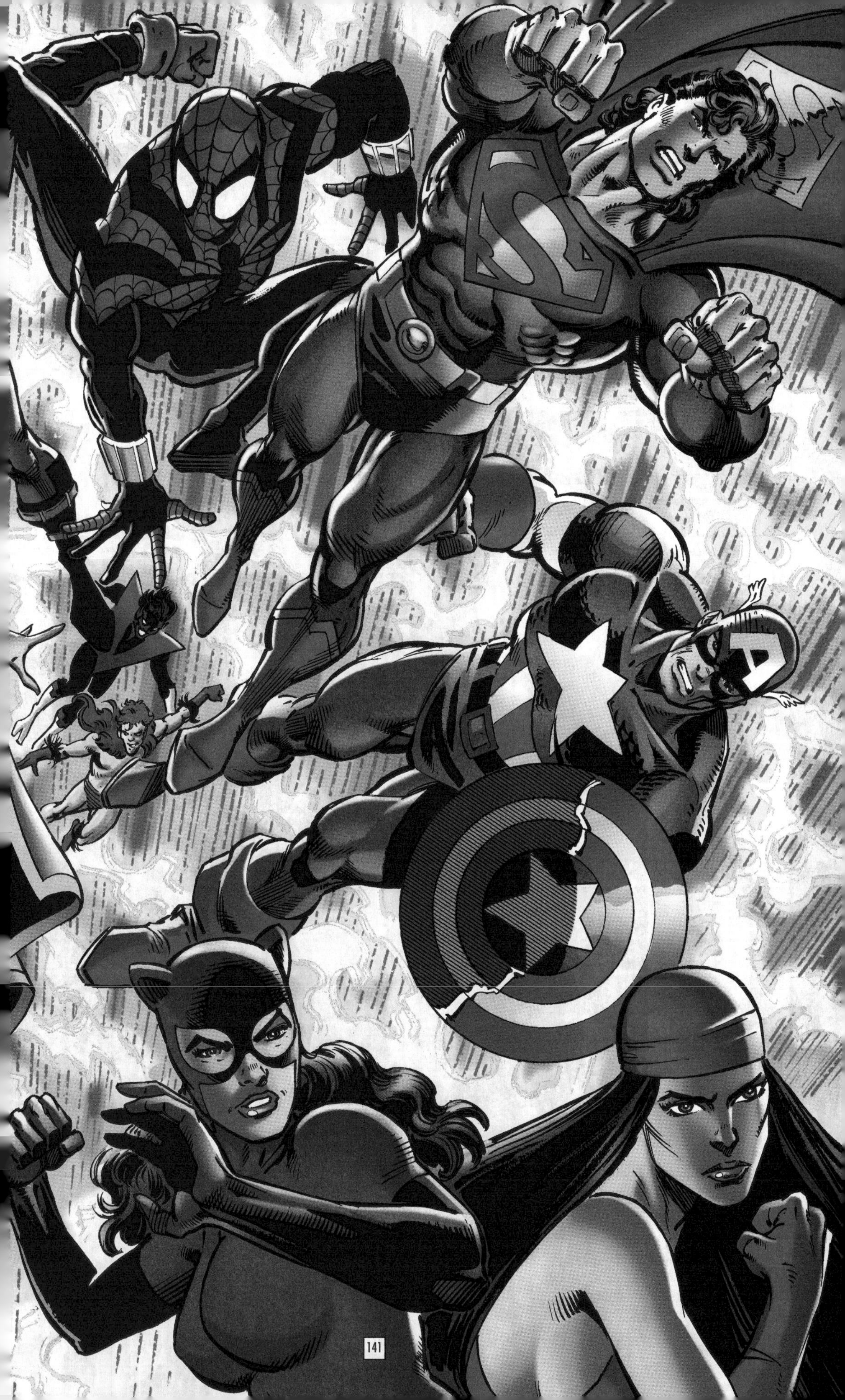

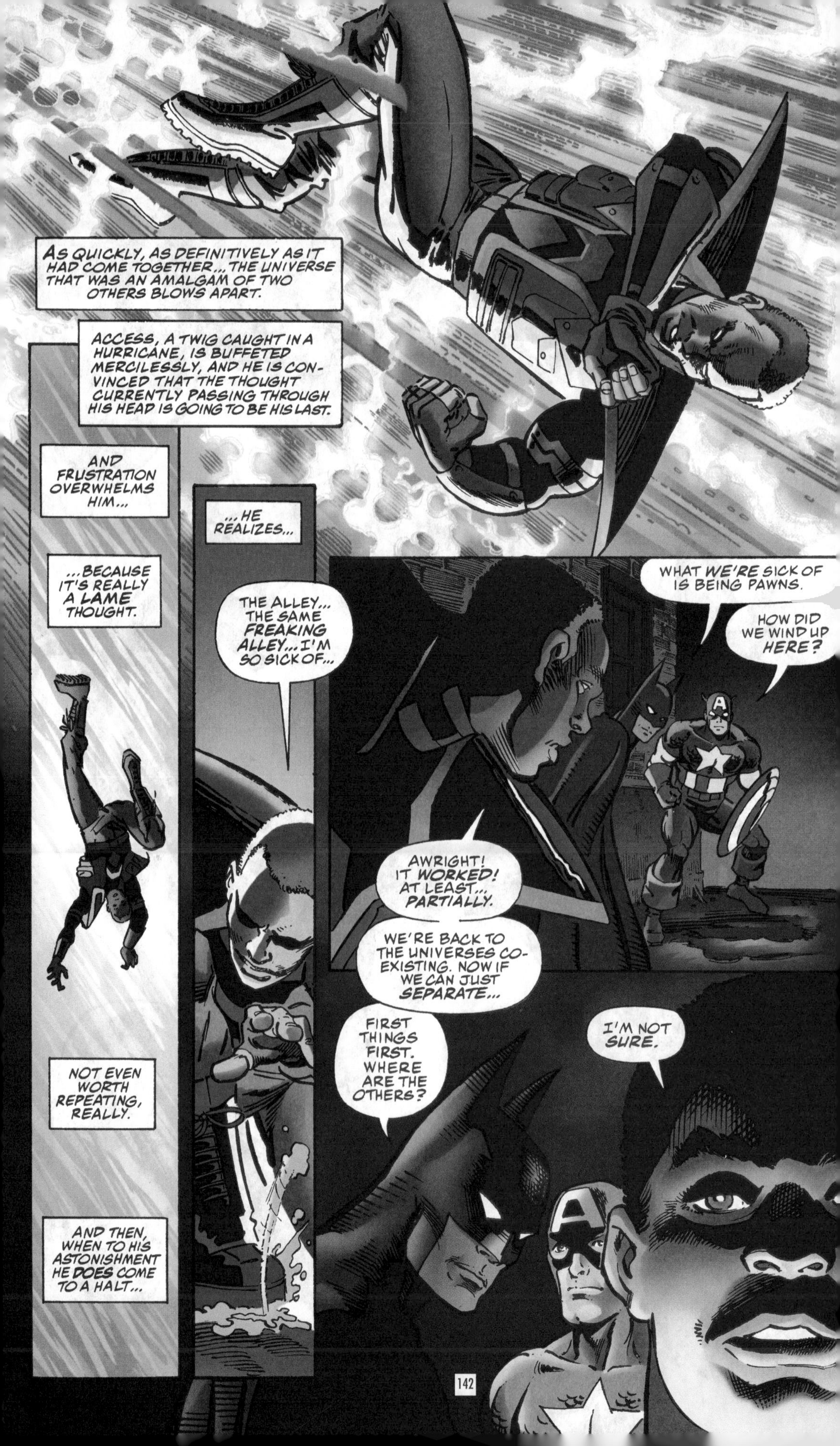
AS QUICKLY, AS DEFINITIVELY AS IT HAD COME TOGETHER... THE UNIVERSE THAT WAS AN AMALGAM OF TWO OTHERS BLOWS APART.
ACCESS, A TWIG CAUGHT IN A HURRICANE, IS BUFFETED MERCILESSLY, AND HE IS CONVINCED THAT THE THOUGHT CURRENTLY PASSING THROUGH HIS HEAD IS GOING TO BE HIS LAST.
AND FRUSTRATION OVERWHELMS HIM...
...BECAUSE IT'S REALLY A LAME THOUGHT.
NOT EVEN WORTH REPEATING, REALLY.
AND THEN, WHEN TO HIS ASTONISHMENT HE DOES COME TO A HALT...
...HE REALIZES...
THE ALLEY... THE SAME FREAKING ALLEY... I'M SO SICK OF...
WHAT WE'RE SICK OF IS BEING PAWNS.
HOW DID WE WIND UP HERE?
AWRIGHT! IT WORKED! AT LEAST... PARTIALLY.
WE'RE BACK TO THE UNIVERSES CO-EXISTING. NOW IF WE CAN JUST SEPARATE...
FIRST THINGS FIRST. WHERE ARE THE OTHERS?
I'M NOT SURE.

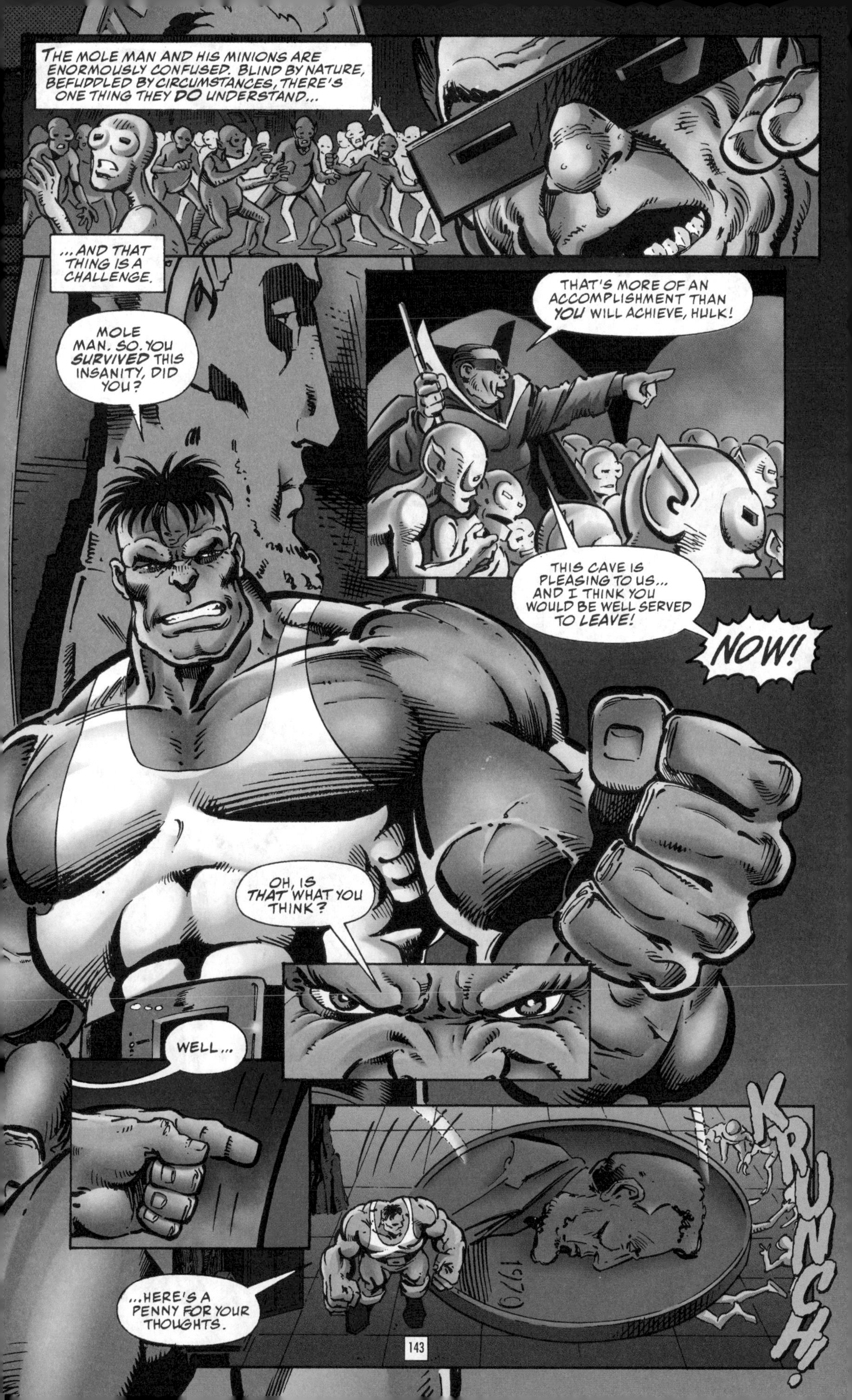
THE MOLE MAN AND HIS MINIONS ARE ENORMOUSLY CONFUSED. BLIND BY NATURE, BEFUDDLED BY CIRCUMSTANCES, THERE'S ONE THING THEY DO UNDERSTAND...
...AND THAT THING IS A CHALLENGE.
MOLE MAN. SO. YOU SURVIVED THIS INSANITY, DID YOU?
THAT'S MORE OF AN ACCOMPLISHMENT THAN YOU WILL ACHIEVE, HULK!
THIS CAVE IS PLEASING TO US... AND I THINK YOU WOULD BE WELL SERVED TO LEAVE!
NOW!
OH, IS THAT WHAT YOU THINK?
WELL...
...HERE'S A PENNY FOR YOUR THOUGHTS.
KRUNCH!
1970

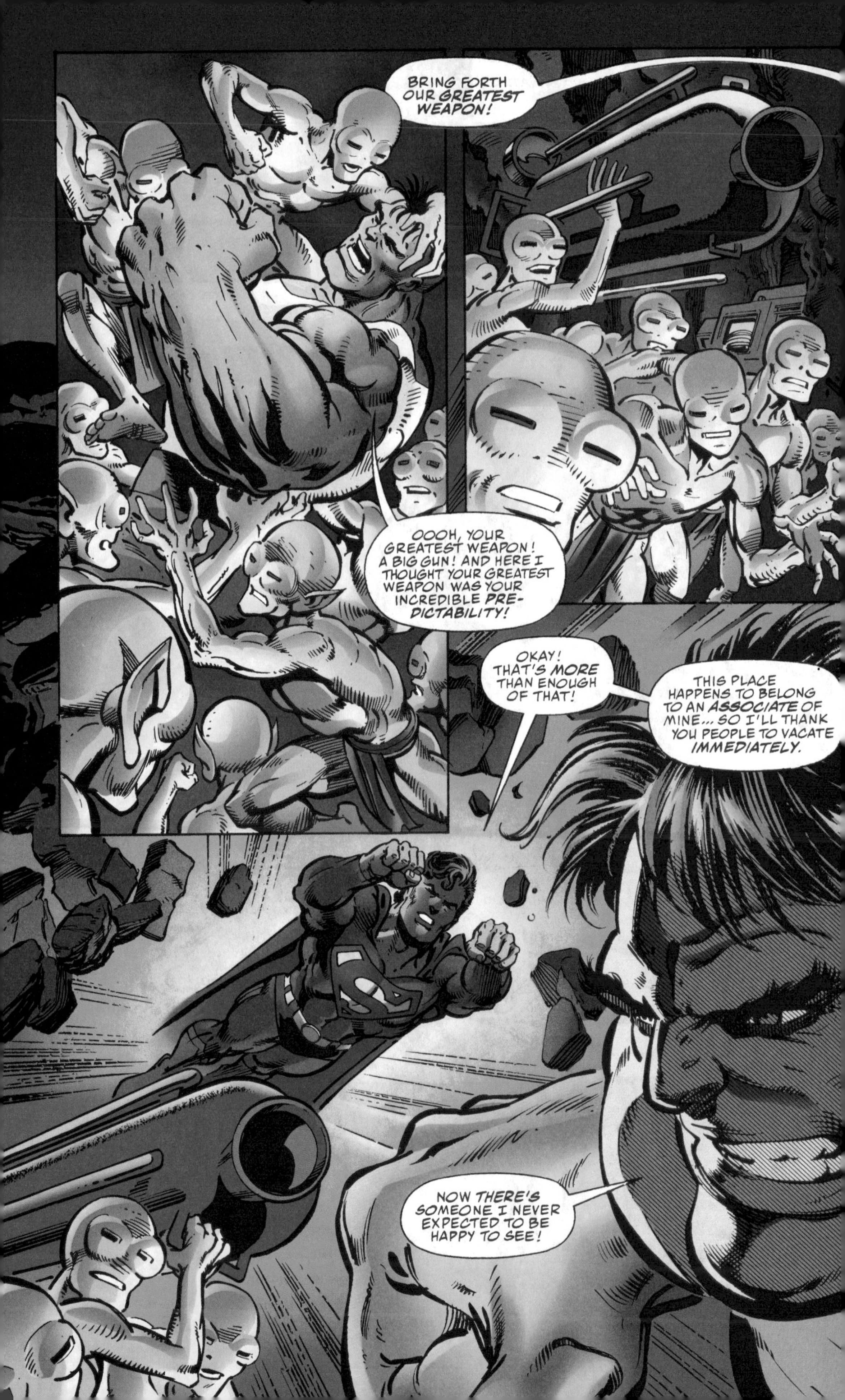
BRING FORTH OUR GREATEST WEAPON!
OOOH, YOUR GREATEST WEAPON! A BIG GUN! AND HERE I THOUGHT YOUR GREATEST WEAPON WAS YOUR INCREDIBLE PRE-DICTABILITY!
OKAY! THAT'S MORE THAN ENOUGH OF THAT!
THIS PLACE HAPPENS TO BELONG TO AN ASSOCIATE OF MINE... SO I'LL THANK YOU PEOPLE TO VACATE IMMEDIATELY.
NOW THERE'S SOMEONE I NEVER EXPECTED TO BE HAPPY TO SEE!

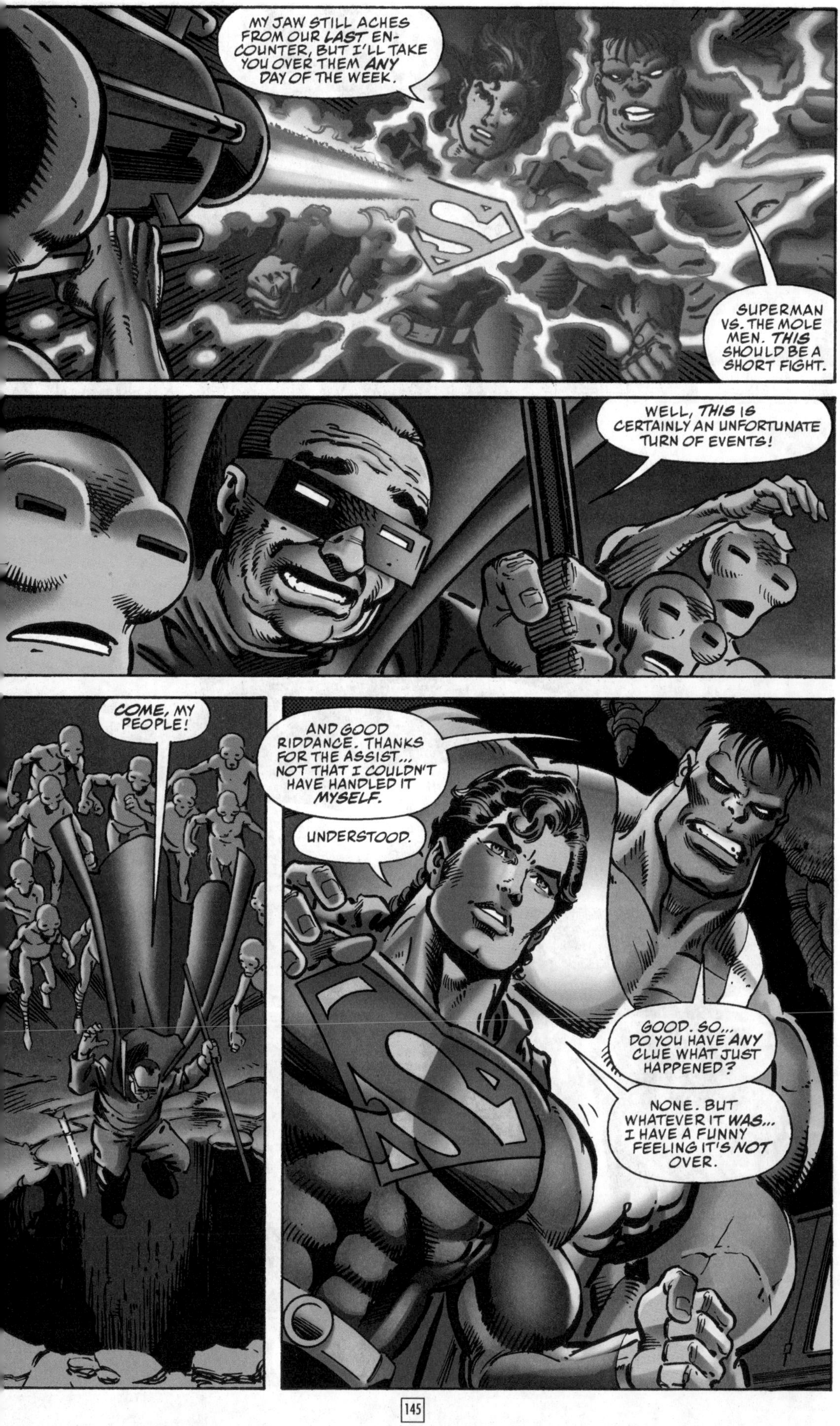
MY JAW STILL ACHES FROM OUR LAST ENCOUNTER, BUT I'LL TAKE YOU OVER THEM ANY DAY OF THE WEEK.
SUPERMAN VS. THE MOLE MEN. THIS SHOULD BE A SHORT FIGHT.
WELL, THIS IS CERTAINLY AN UNFORTUNATE TURN OF EVENTS!
COME, MY PEOPLE!
AND GOOD RIDDANCE. THANKS FOR THE ASSIST... NOT THAT I COULDN'T HAVE HANDLED IT MYSELF.
UNDERSTOOD.
GOOD. SO... DO YOU HAVE ANY CLUE WHAT JUST HAPPENED?
NONE. BUT WHATEVER IT WAS... I HAVE A FUNNY FEELING IT'S NOT OVER.

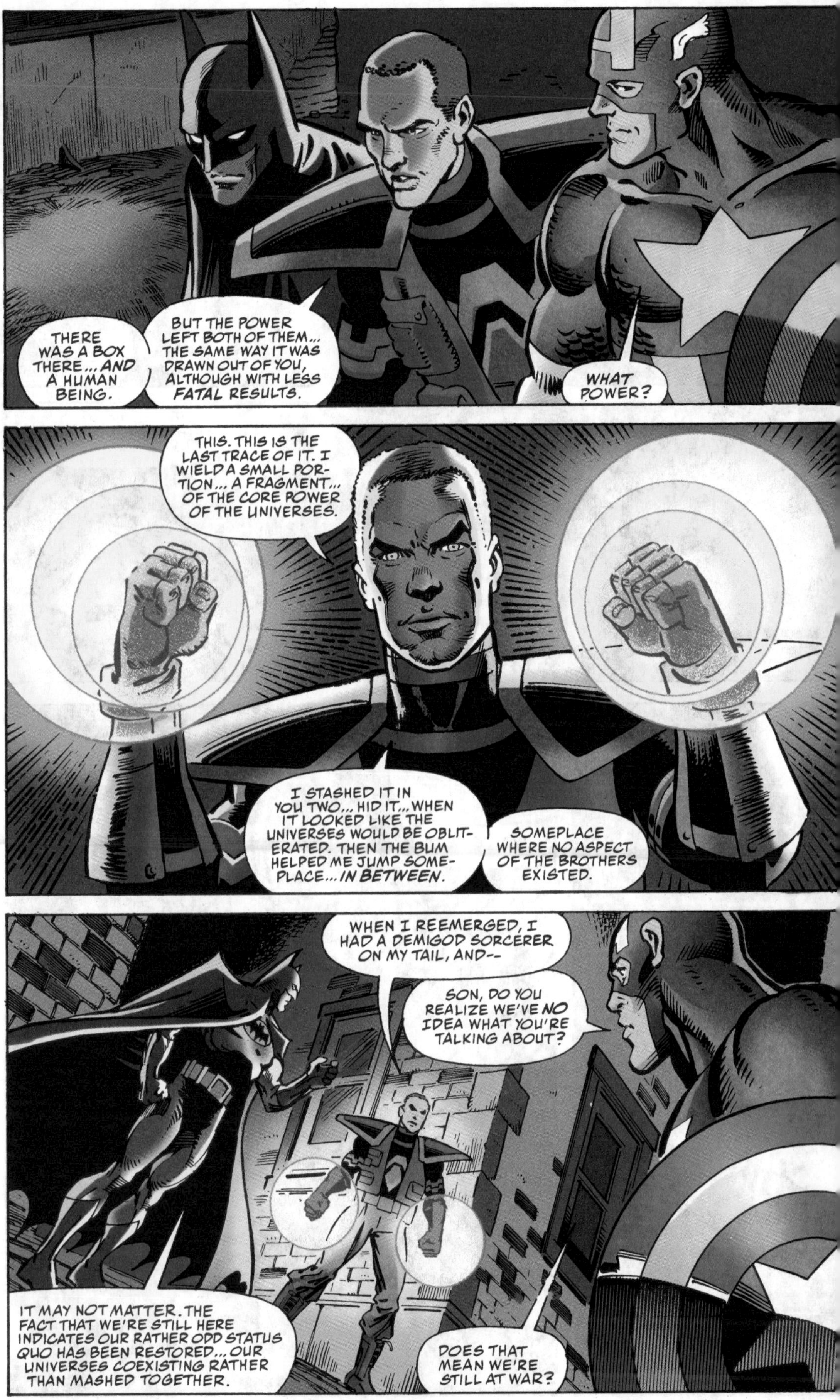
THERE WAS A BOX THERE... AND A HUMAN BEING.
BUT THE POWER LEFT BOTH OF THEM... THE SAME WAY IT WAS DRAWN OUT OF YOU, ALTHOUGH WITH LESS FATAL RESULTS.
WHAT POWER?
THIS. THIS IS THE LAST TRACE OF IT. I WIELD A SMALL PORTION... A FRAGMENT... OF THE CORE POWER OF THE UNIVERSES.
I STASHED IT IN YOU TWO... HID IT... WHEN IT LOOKED LIKE THE UNIVERSES WOULD BE OBLITERATED. THEN THE BUM HELPED ME JUMP SOMEPLACE... IN BETWEEN.
SOMEPLACE WHERE NO ASPECT OF THE BROTHERS EXISTED.
WHEN I REEMERGED, I HAD A DEMIGOD SORCERER ON MY TAIL, AND--
SON, DO YOU REALIZE WE'VE NO IDEA WHAT YOU'RE TALKING ABOUT?
IT MAY NOT MATTER. THE FACT THAT WE'RE STILL HERE INDICATES OUR RATHER ODD STATUS QUO HAS BEEN RESTORED... OUR UNIVERSES COEXISTING RATHER THAN MASHED TOGETHER.
DOES THAT MEAN WE'RE STILL AT WAR?

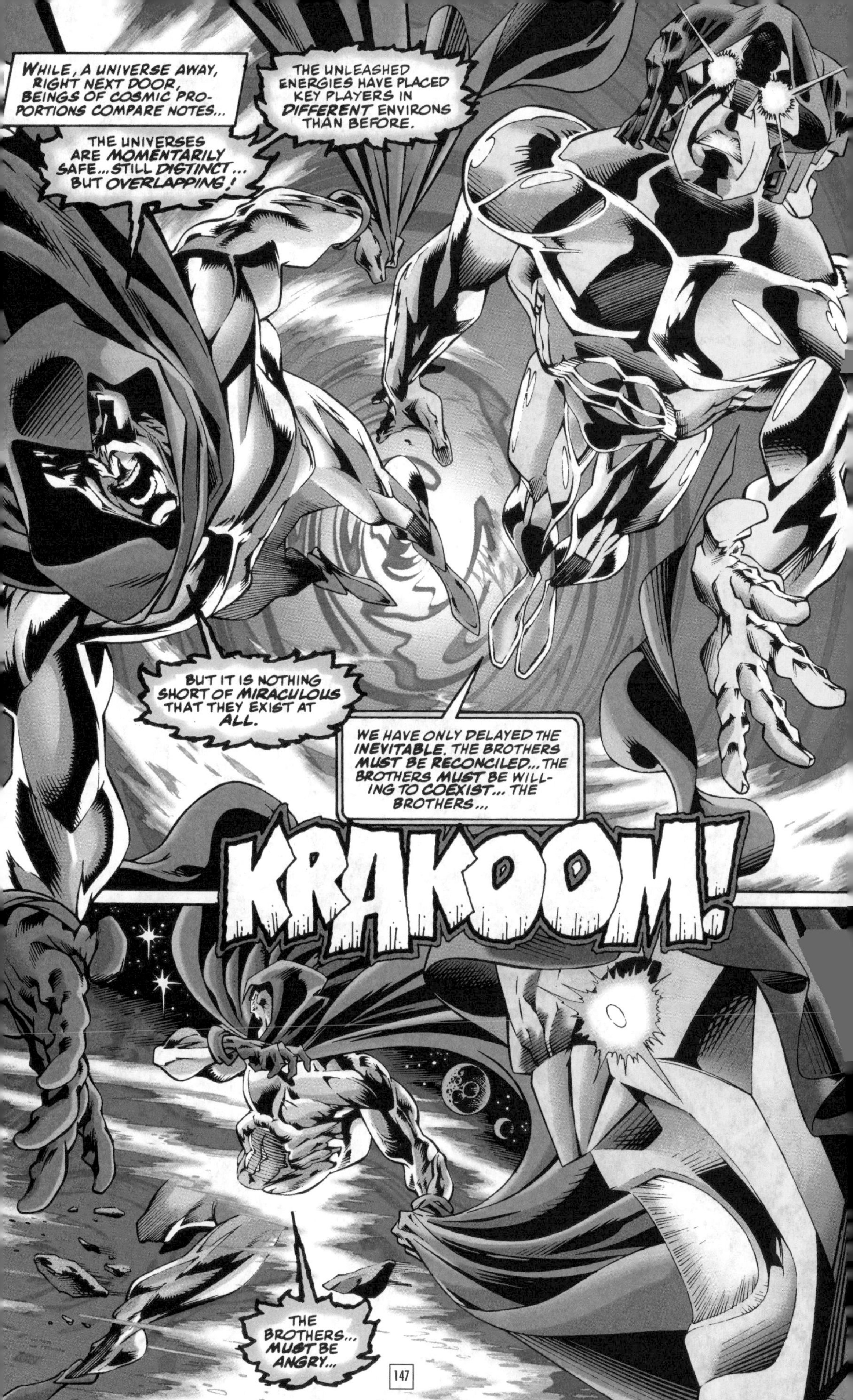

WHILE, A UNIVERSE AWAY, RIGHT NEXT DOOR, BEINGS OF COSMIC PROPORTIONS COMPARE NOTES...
THE UNIVERSES ARE MOMENTARILY SAFE... STILL DISTINCT... BUT OVERLAPPING!
THE UNLEASHED ENERGIES HAVE PLACED KEY PLAYERS IN DIFFERENT ENVIRONS THAN BEFORE.
BUT IT IS NOTHING SHORT OF MIRACULOUS THAT THEY EXIST AT ALL.
WE HAVE ONLY DELAYED THE INEVITABLE. THE BROTHERS MUST BE RECONCILED... THE BROTHERS MUST BE WILLING TO COEXIST... THE BROTHERS...
KRAKOOM!
THE BROTHERS... MUST BE ANGRY...

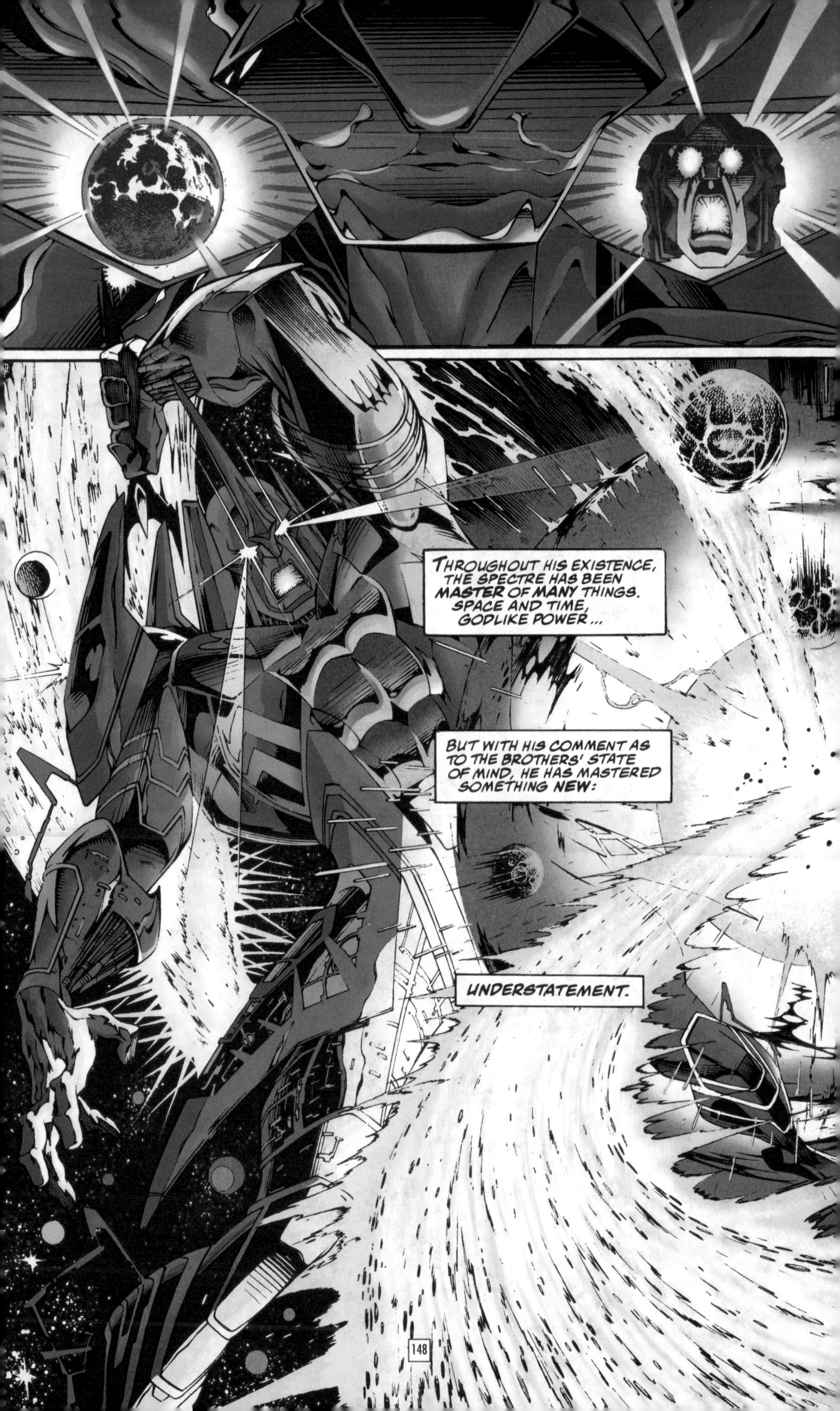
THROUGHOUT HIS EXISTENCE, THE SPECTRE HAS BEEN MASTER OF MANY THINGS. SPACE AND TIME, GODLIKE POWER...
BUT WITH HIS COMMENT AS TO THE BROTHERS' STATE OF MIND, HE HAS MASTERED SOMETHING NEW:
UNDERSTATEMENT.

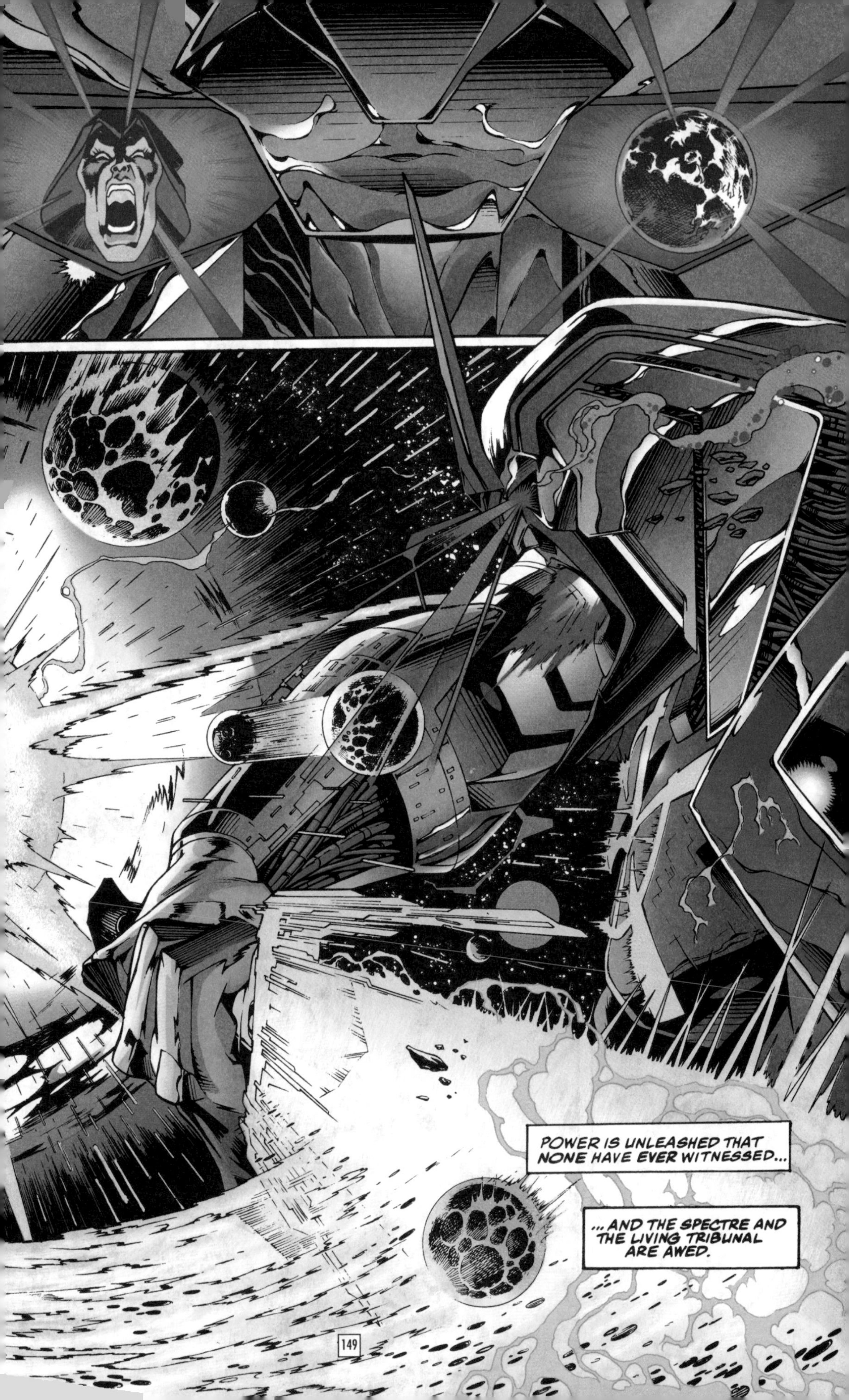
POWER IS UNLEASHED THAT NONE HAVE EVER WITNESSED...
...AND THE SPECTRE AND THE LIVING TRIBUNAL ARE AWED.

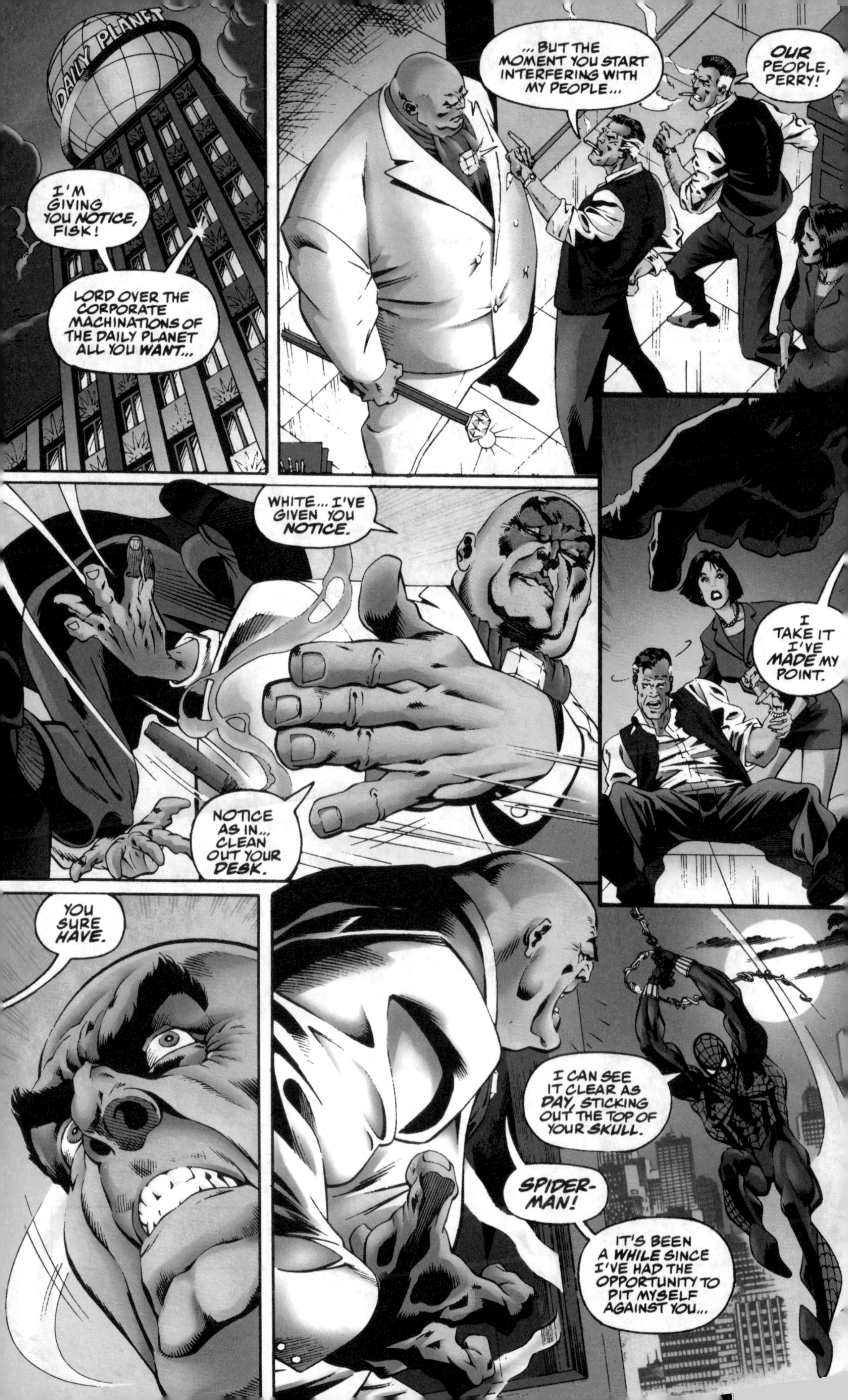

DAILY PLANET
I'M GIVING YOU NOTICE, FISK!
LORD OVER THE CORPORATE MACHINATIONS OF THE DAILY PLANET ALL YOU WANT...
... BUT THE MOMENT YOU START INTERFERING WITH MY PEOPLE...
OUR PEOPLE, PERRY!
WHITE... I'VE GIVEN YOU NOTICE.
NOTICE AS IN... CLEAN OUT YOUR DESK.
I TAKE IT I'VE MADE MY POINT.
YOU SURE HAVE.
I CAN SEE IT CLEAR AS DAY, STICKING OUT THE TOP OF YOUR SKULL.
SPIDER-MAN!
IT'S BEEN A WHILE SINCE I'VE HAD THE OPPORTUNITY TO PIT MYSELF AGAINST YOU...

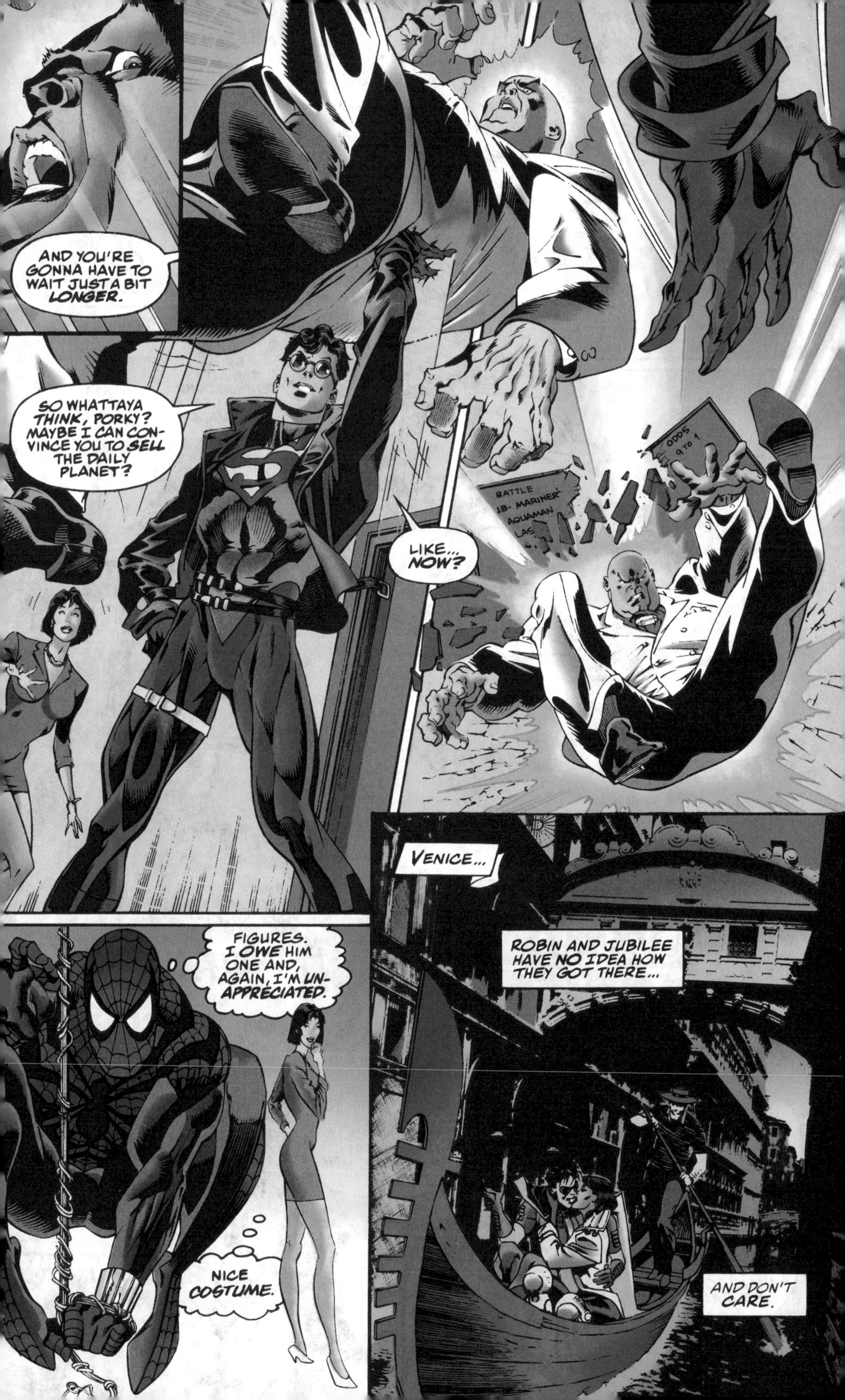
AND YOU'RE GONNA HAVE TO WAIT JUST A BIT LONGER.
SO WHATTAYA THINK, PORKY? MAYBE I CAN CONVINCE YOU TO SELL THE DAILY PLANET?
LIKE... NOW?
FIGURES. I OWE HIM ONE AND, AGAIN, I'M UNAPPRECIATED.
NICE COSTUME.
VENICE...
ROBIN AND JUBILEE HAVE NO IDEA HOW THEY GOT THERE...
AND DON'T CARE.

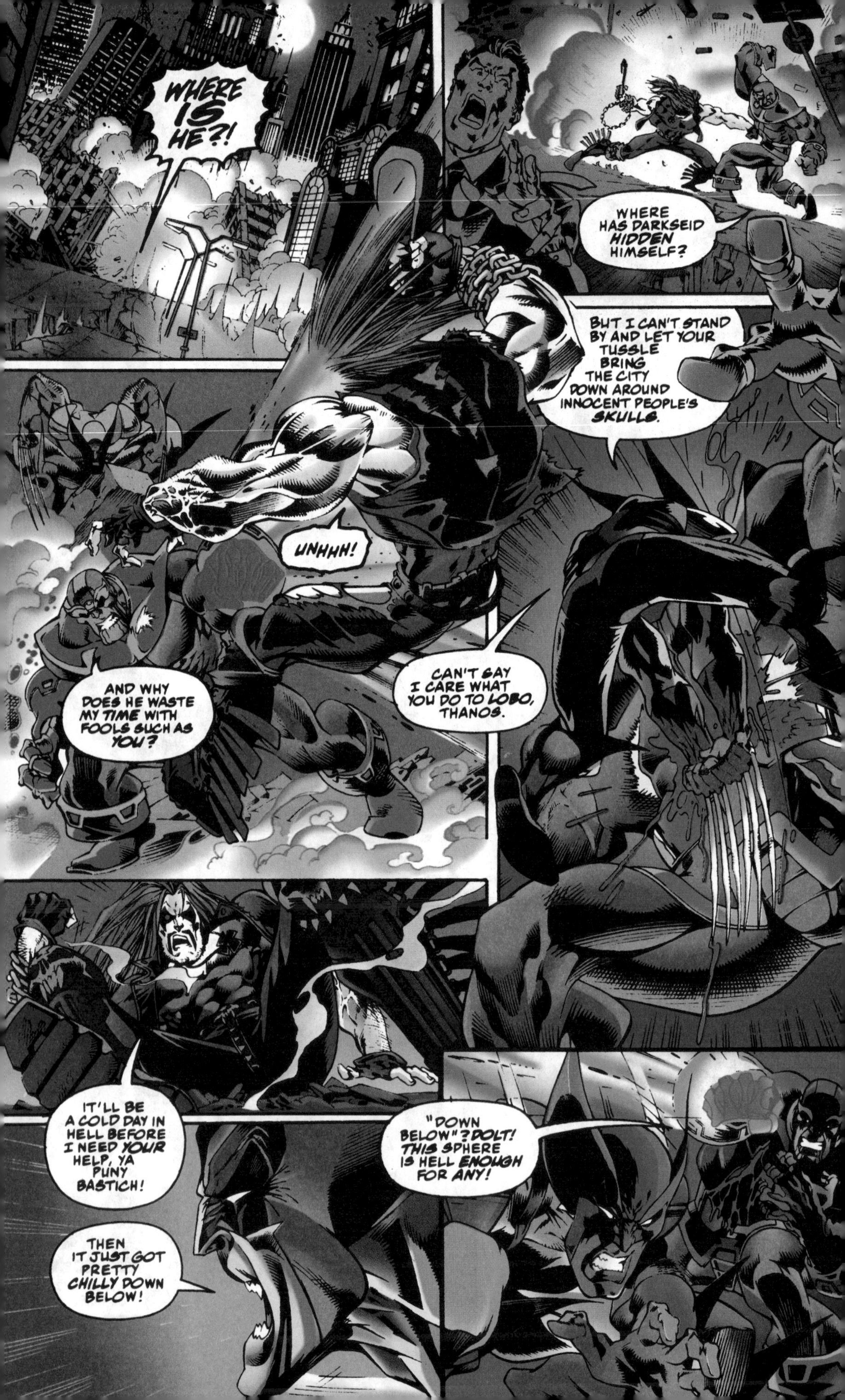
WHERE IS HE?!
WHERE HAS DARKSEID HIDDEN HIMSELF?
BUT I CAN'T STAND BY AND LET YOUR TUSSLE BRING THE CITY DOWN AROUND INNOCENT PEOPLE'S SKULLS.
UNHHH!
AND WHY DOES HE WASTE MY TIME WITH FOOLS SUCH AS YOU?
CAN'T SAY I CARE WHAT YOU DO TO LOBO, THANOS.
IT'LL BE A COLD DAY IN HELL BEFORE I NEED YOUR HELP, YA PUNY BASTICH!
THEN IT JUST GOT PRETTY CHILLY DOWN BELOW!
"DOWN BELOW"? DOLT! THIS SPHERE IS HELL ENOUGH FOR ANY!

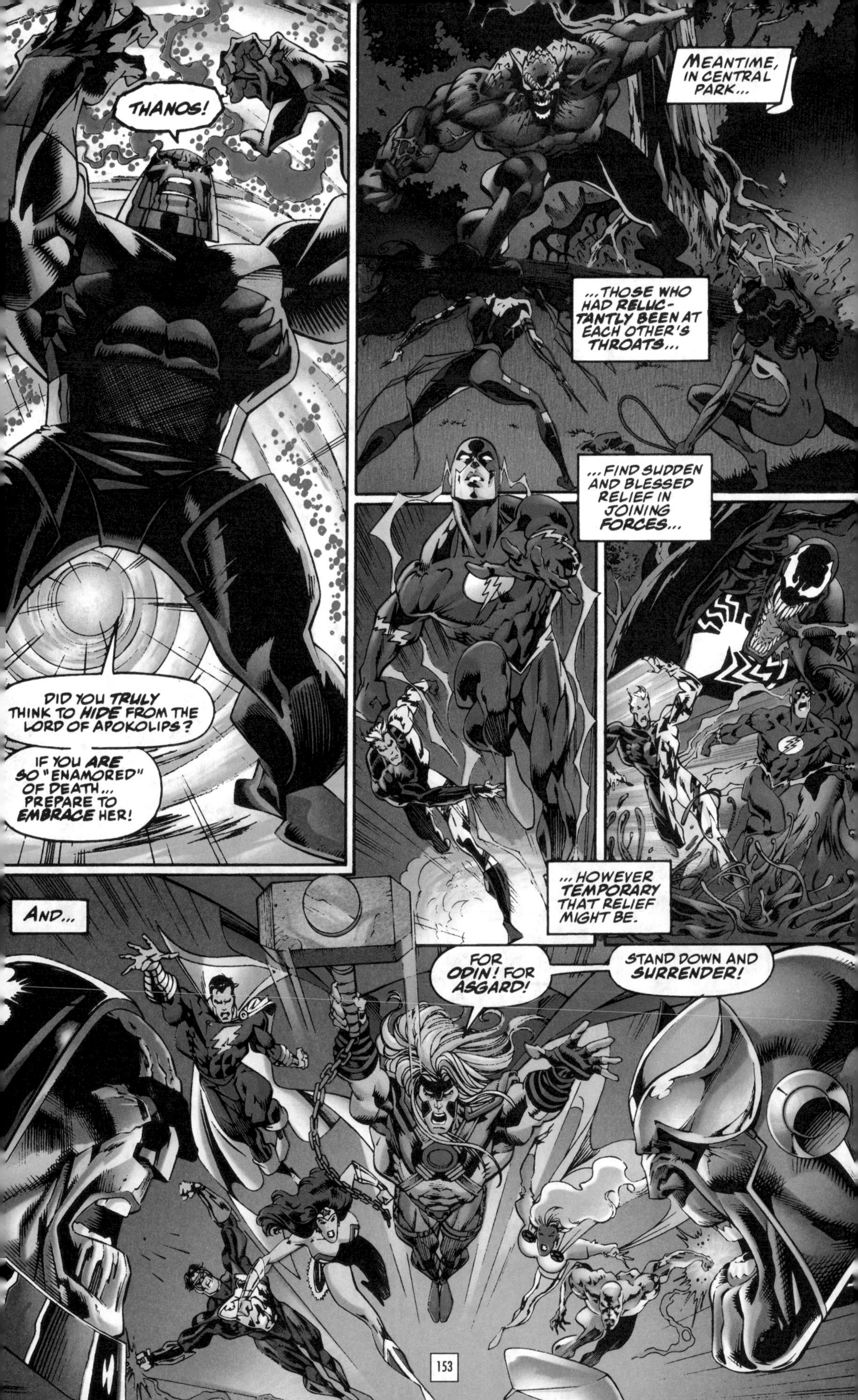
THANOS!
DID YOU TRULY THINK TO HIDE FROM THE LORD OF APOKOLIPS?
IF YOU ARE SO "ENAMORED" OF DEATH... PREPARE TO EMBRACE HER!
MEANTIME, IN CENTRAL PARK...
...THOSE WHO HAD RELUCTANTLY BEEN AT EACH OTHER'S THROATS...
...FIND SUDDEN AND BLESSED RELIEF IN JOINING FORCES...
...HOWEVER TEMPORARY THAT RELIEF MIGHT BE.
AND...
FOR ODIN! FOR ASGARD!
STAND DOWN AND SURRENDER!

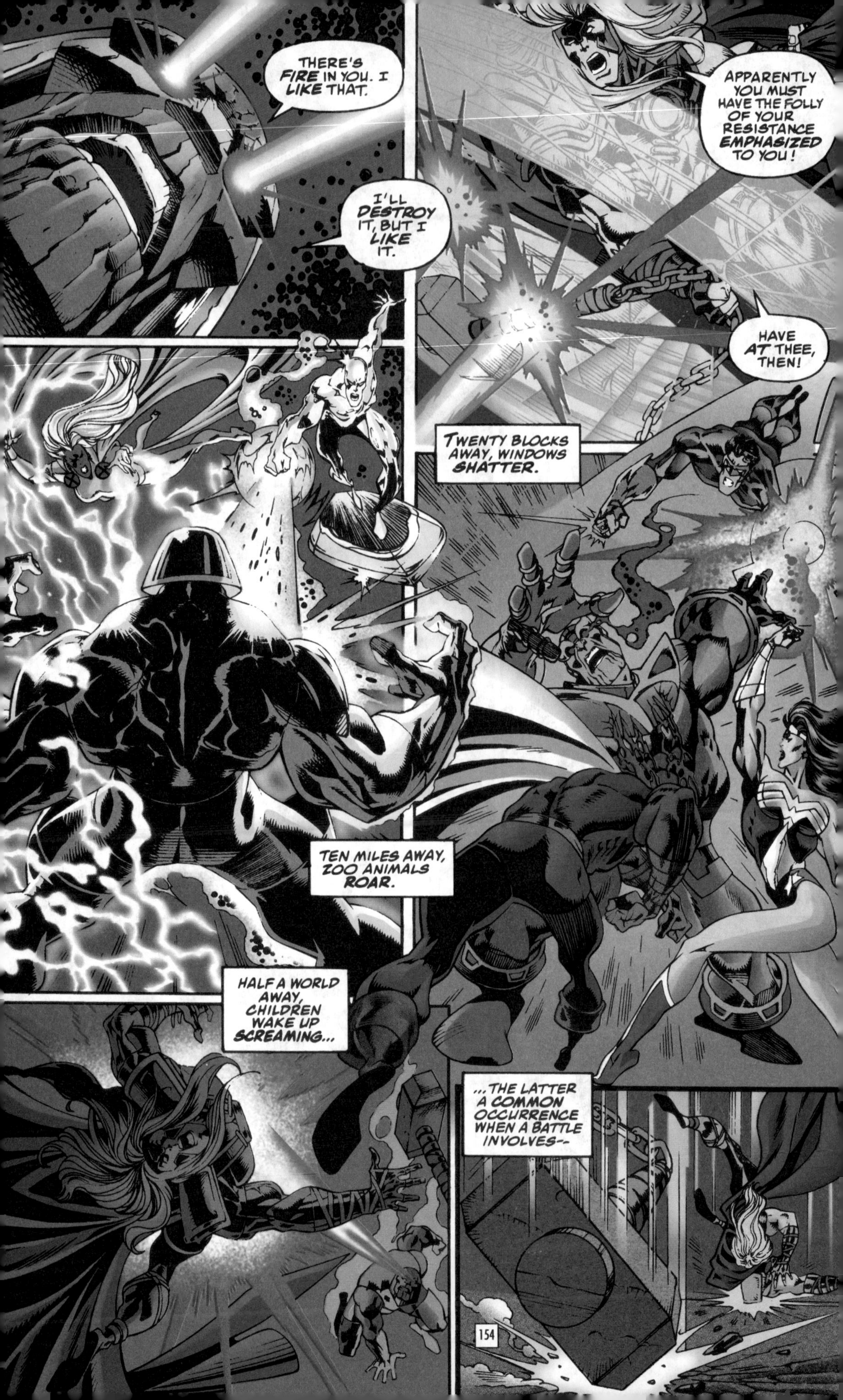
THERE'S FIRE IN YOU. I LIKE THAT.
I'LL DESTROY IT, BUT I LIKE IT.
APPARENTLY YOU MUST HAVE THE FOLLY OF YOUR RESISTANCE EMPHASIZED TO YOU!
HAVE AT THEE, THEN!
TWENTY BLOCKS AWAY, WINDOWS SHATTER.
TEN MILES AWAY, ZOO ANIMALS ROAR.
HALF A WORLD AWAY, CHILDREN WAKE UP SCREAMING...
...THE LATTER A COMMON OCCURRENCE WHEN A BATTLE INVOLVES--

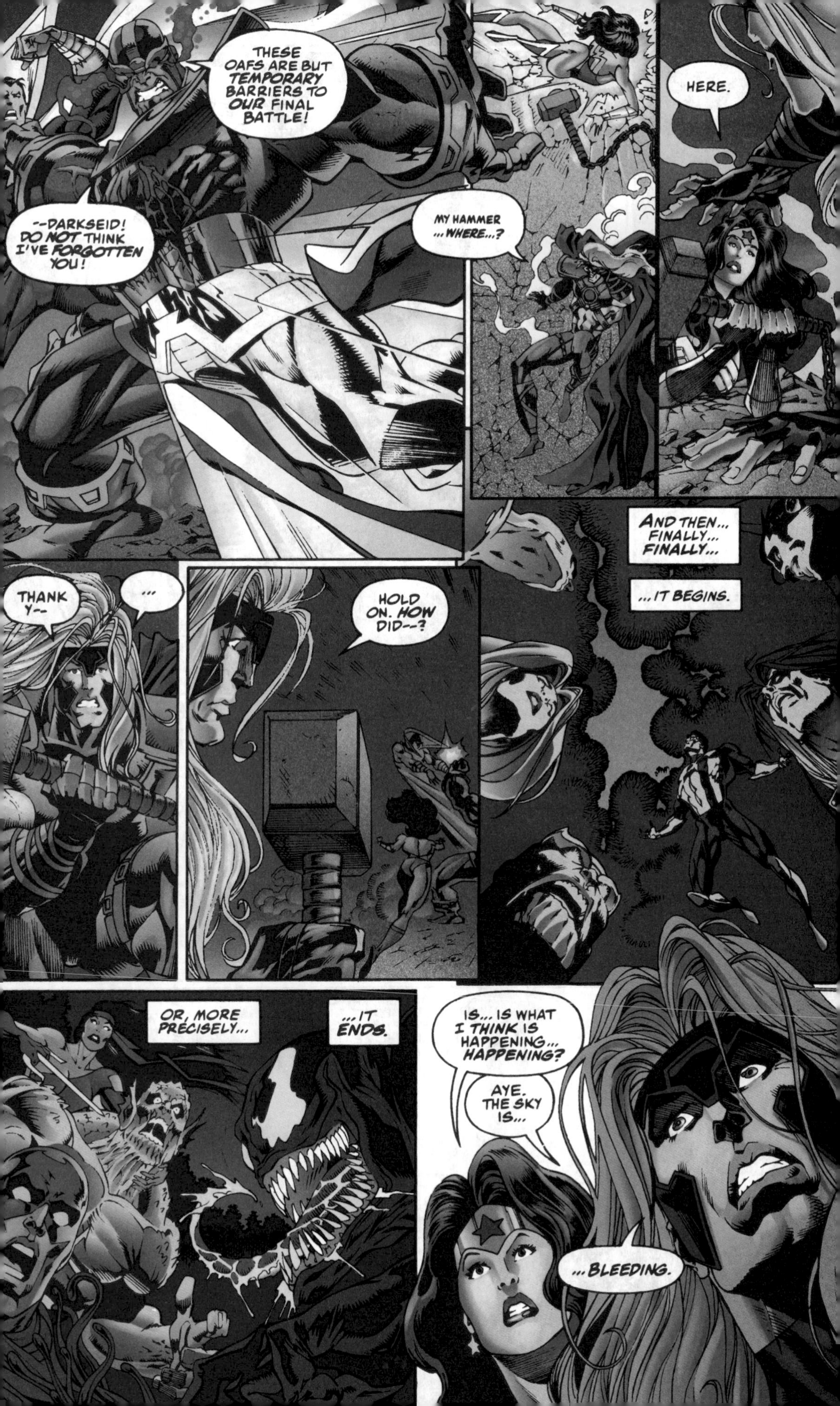
THESE OAFS ARE BUT TEMPORARY BARRIERS TO OUR FINAL BATTLE!
--DARKSEID! DO NOT THINK I'VE FORGOTTEN YOU!
MY HAMMER ...WHERE...?
HERE.
THANK Y--
...
HOLD ON. HOW DID--?
AND THEN... FINALLY... FINALLY...
...IT BEGINS.
OR, MORE PRECISELY...
...IT ENDS.
IS... IS WHAT I THINK IS HAPPENING... HAPPENING?
AYE. THE SKY IS...
...BLEEDING.

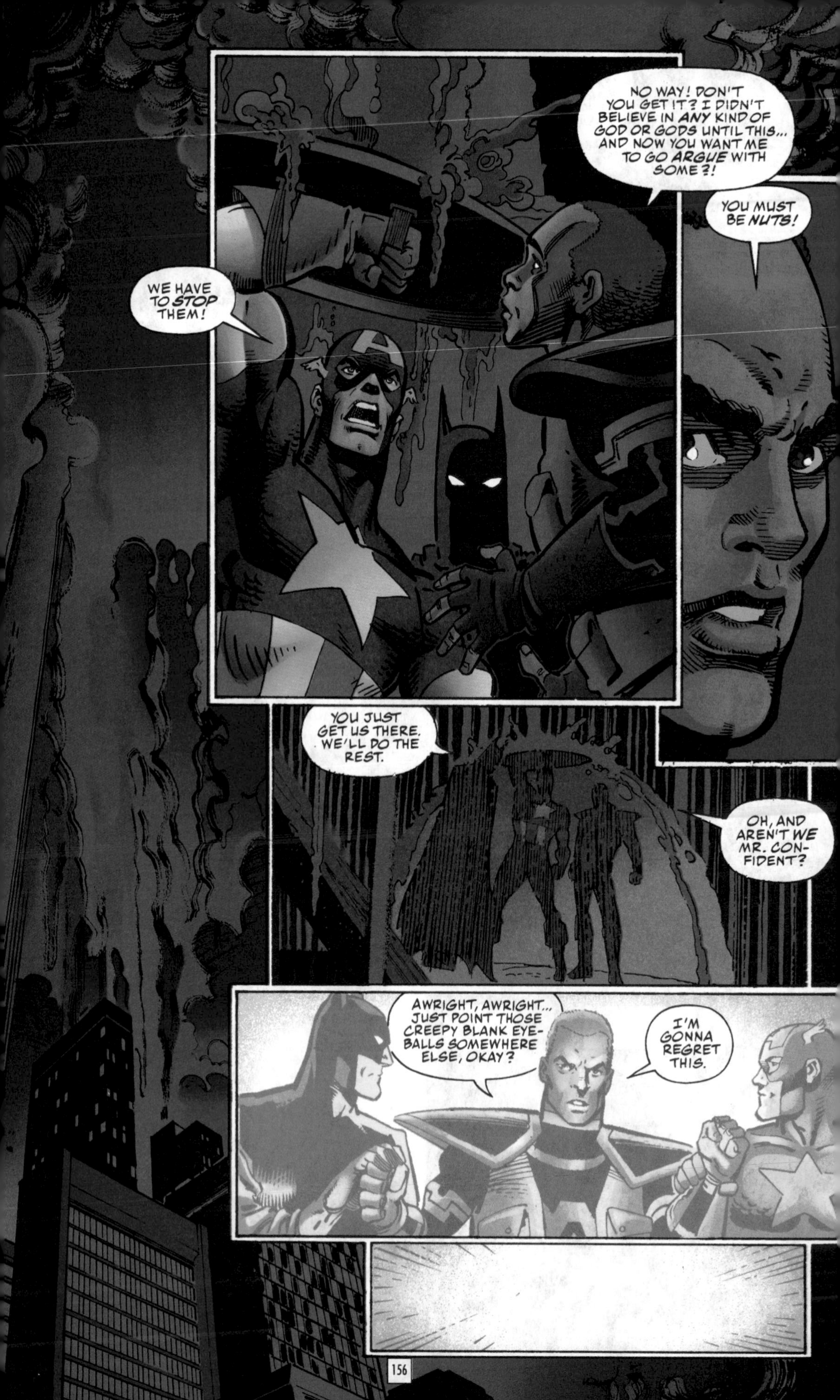
NO WAY! DON'T YOU GET IT? I DIDN'T BELIEVE IN ANY KIND OF GOD OR GODS UNTIL THIS... AND NOW YOU WANT ME TO GO ARGUE WITH SOME?!
YOU MUST BE NUTS!
WE HAVE TO STOP THEM!
YOU JUST GET US THERE. WE'LL DO THE REST.
OH, AND AREN'T WE MR. CONFIDENT?
AWRIGHT, AWRIGHT... JUST POINT THOSE CREEPY BLANK EYEBALLS SOMEWHERE ELSE, OKAY?
I'M GONNA REGRET THIS.

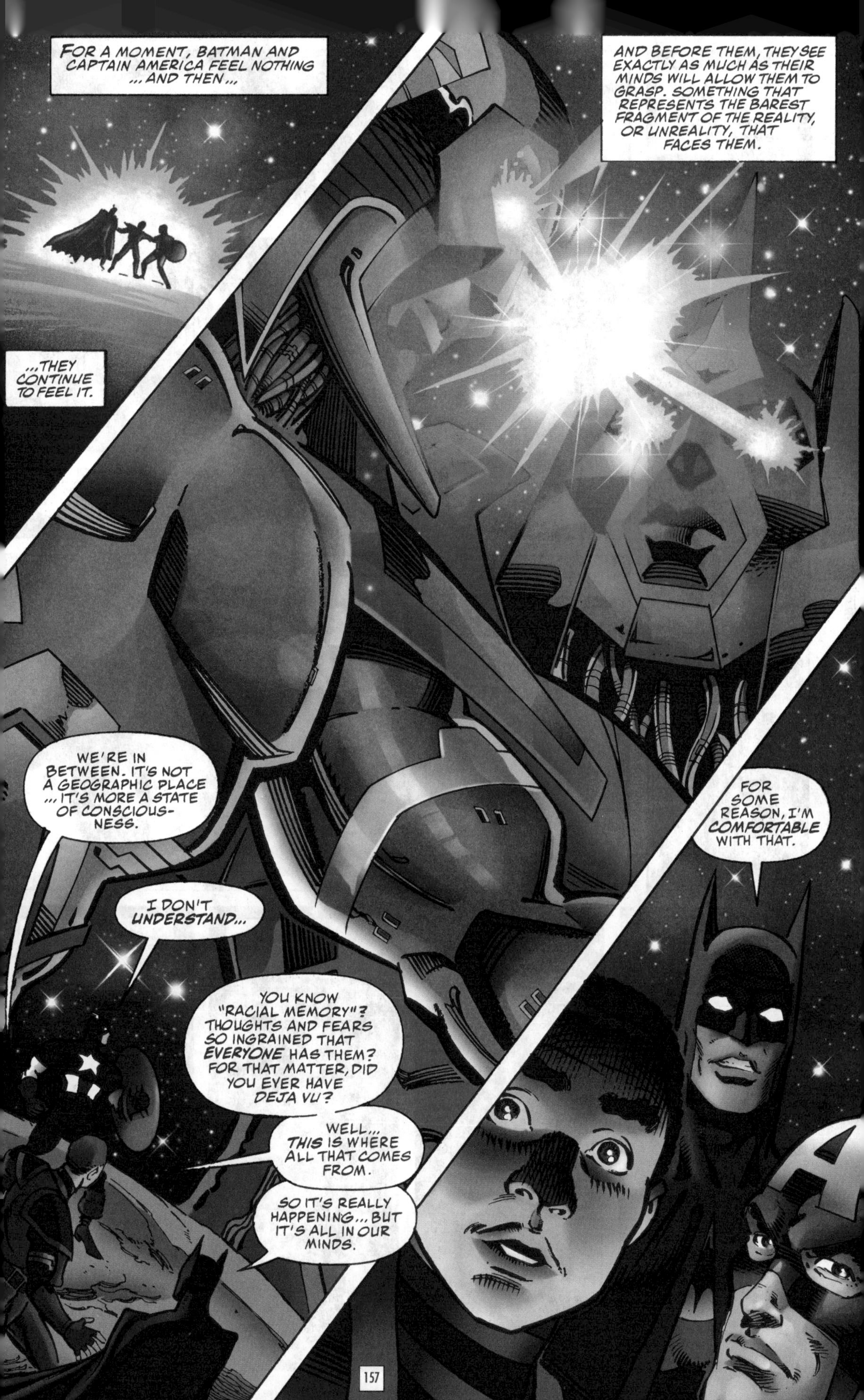

FOR A MOMENT, BATMAN AND CAPTAIN AMERICA FEEL NOTHING ...AND THEN...
...THEY CONTINUE TO FEEL IT.
AND BEFORE THEM, THEY SEE EXACTLY AS MUCH AS THEIR MINDS WILL ALLOW THEM TO GRASP. SOMETHING THAT REPRESENTS THE BAREST FRAGMENT OF THE REALITY, OR UNREALITY, THAT FACES THEM.
WE'RE IN BETWEEN. IT'S NOT A GEOGRAPHIC PLACE ...IT'S MORE A STATE OF CONSCIOUS-NESS.
I DON'T UNDERSTAND...
YOU KNOW "RACIAL MEMORY"? THOUGHTS AND FEARS SO INGRAINED THAT EVERYONE HAS THEM? FOR THAT MATTER, DID YOU EVER HAVE DEJA VU?
WELL... THIS IS WHERE ALL THAT COMES FROM.
SO IT'S REALLY HAPPENING... BUT IT'S ALL IN OUR MINDS.
FOR SOME REASON, I'M COMFORTABLE WITH THAT.

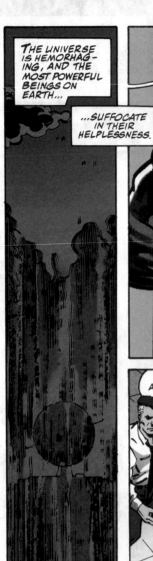

THE UNIVERSE IS HEMORHAGING, AND THE MOST POWERFUL BEINGS ON EARTH...

...SUFFOCATE IN THEIR HELPLESSNESS.

LOIS...?

CLARK! I... I WAS AFRAID YOU WERE OFF DOING...

...DOING WHO *KNOWS* WHAT?

IF THERE WAS... ANYTHING I *COULD* DO... I'D BE DOING IT.

AS IT IS... THE BEST PLACE FOR ME TO BE IS WITH YOU.

WELL, JAMESON? GOING TO TAKE ONE LAST POTSHOT AT ME?

FOR WHAT IT'S WORTH...

...I'M SORRY.

... oh.

ACROSS THE COUNTRY...

...OLD LOVERS AND YOUNG ONES WATCH HELPLESSLY.

...ACROSS THE WORLD...

AND IN BETWEEN... THE WOULD-BE SAVIORS FEEL EQUALLY HELPLESS.

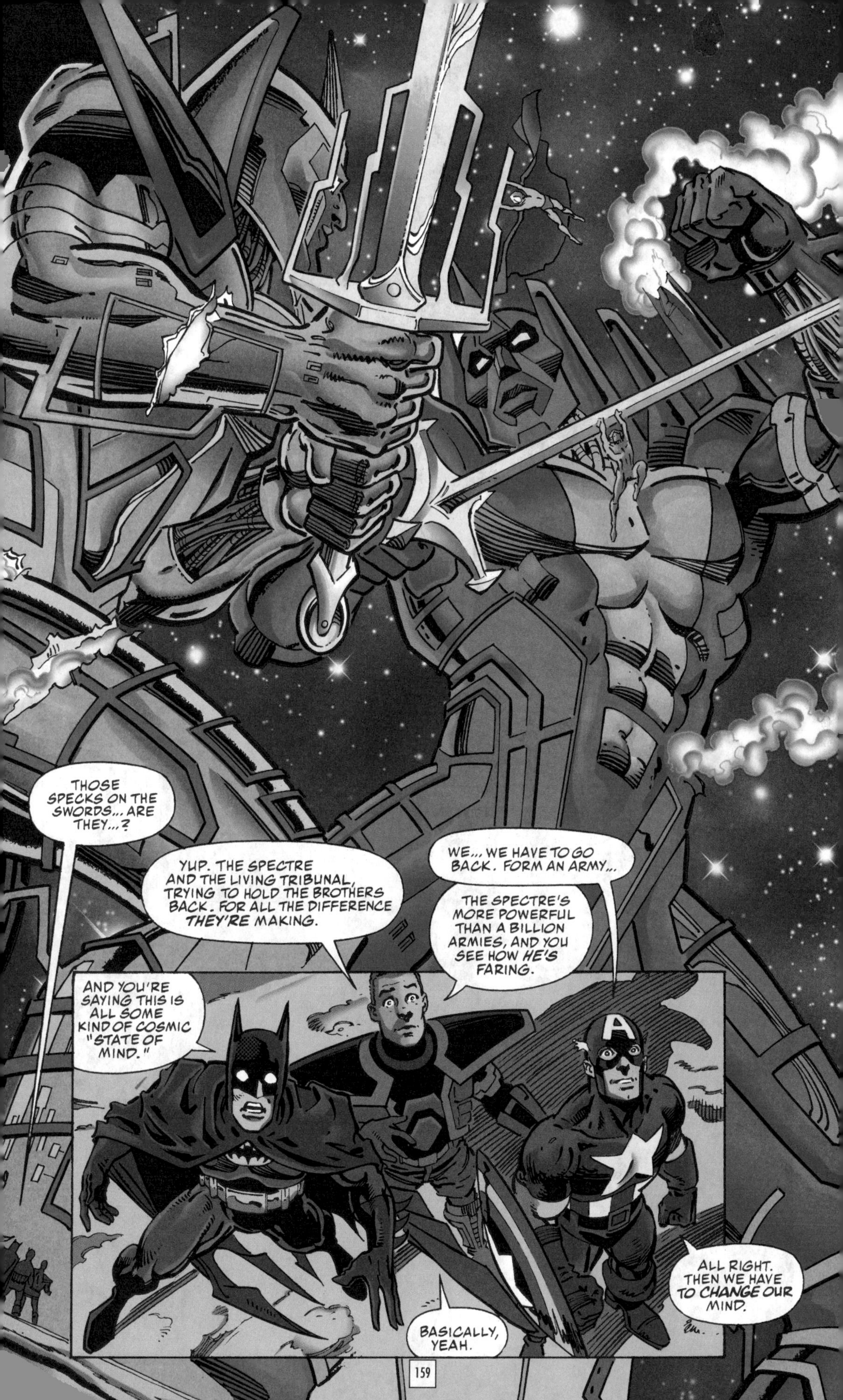
THOSE SPECKS ON THE SWORDS... ARE THEY...?
YUP. THE SPECTRE AND THE LIVING TRIBUNAL, TRYING TO HOLD THE BROTHERS BACK. FOR ALL THE DIFFERENCE THEY'RE MAKING.
WE... WE HAVE TO GO BACK. FORM AN ARMY...
THE SPECTRE'S MORE POWERFUL THAN A BILLION ARMIES, AND YOU SEE HOW HE'S FARING.
AND YOU'RE SAYING THIS IS ALL SOME KIND OF COSMIC "STATE OF MIND."
BASICALLY, YEAH.
ALL RIGHT. THEN WE HAVE TO CHANGE OUR MIND.

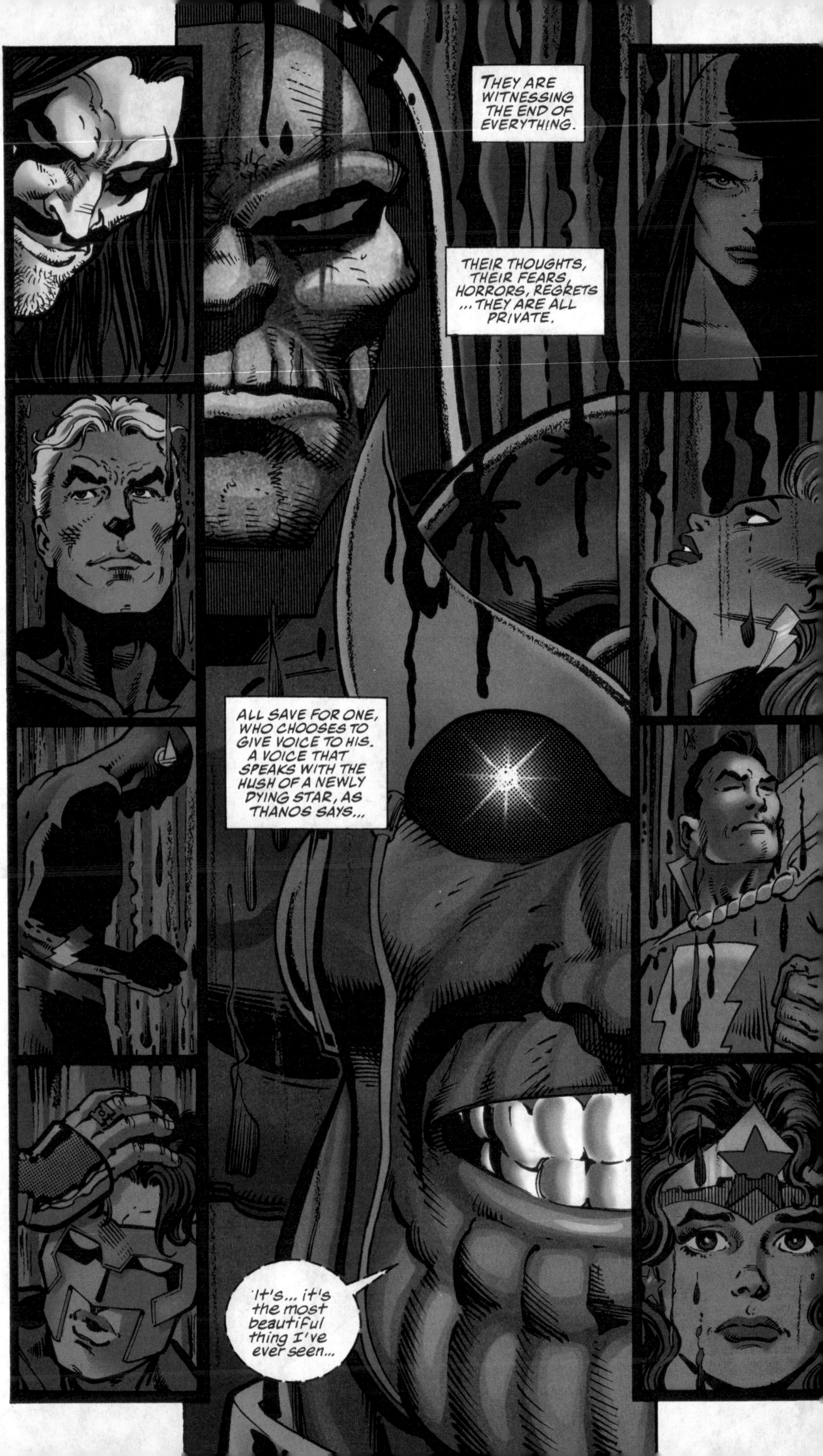

THEY ARE WITNESSING THE END OF EVERYTHING.
THEIR THOUGHTS, THEIR FEARS, HORRORS, REGRETS ...THEY ARE ALL PRIVATE.
ALL SAVE FOR ONE, WHO CHOOSES TO GIVE VOICE TO HIS. A VOICE THAT SPEAKS WITH THE HUSH OF A NEWLY DYING STAR, AS THANOS SAYS...
It's... it's the most beautiful thing I've ever seen...

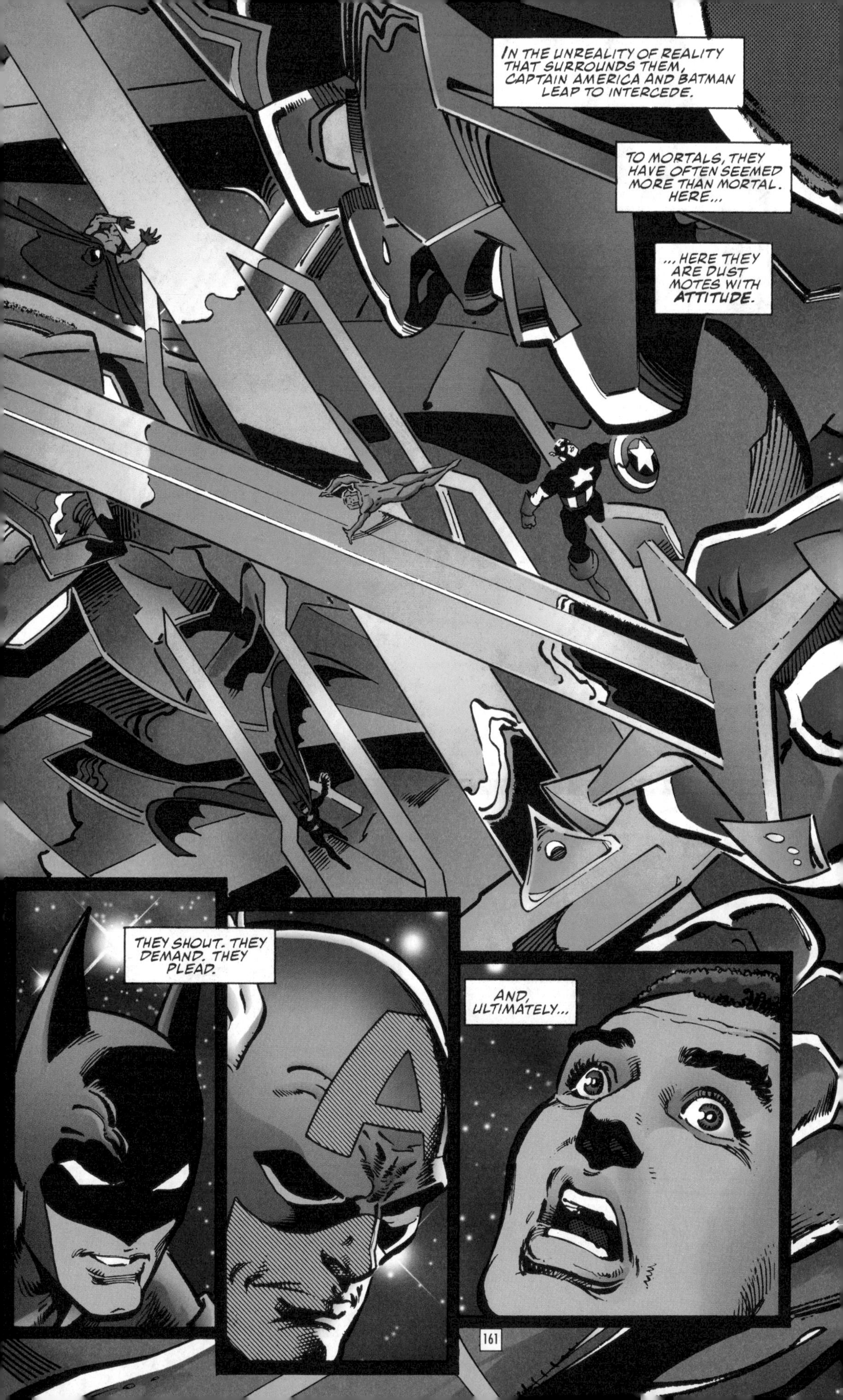
IN THE UNREALITY OF REALITY THAT SURROUNDS THEM, CAPTAIN AMERICA AND BATMAN LEAP TO INTERCEDE.
TO MORTALS, THEY HAVE OFTEN SEEMED MORE THAN MORTAL. HERE...
...HERE THEY ARE DUST MOTES WITH ATTITUDE.
THEY SHOUT. THEY DEMAND. THEY PLEAD.
AND, ULTIMATELY...

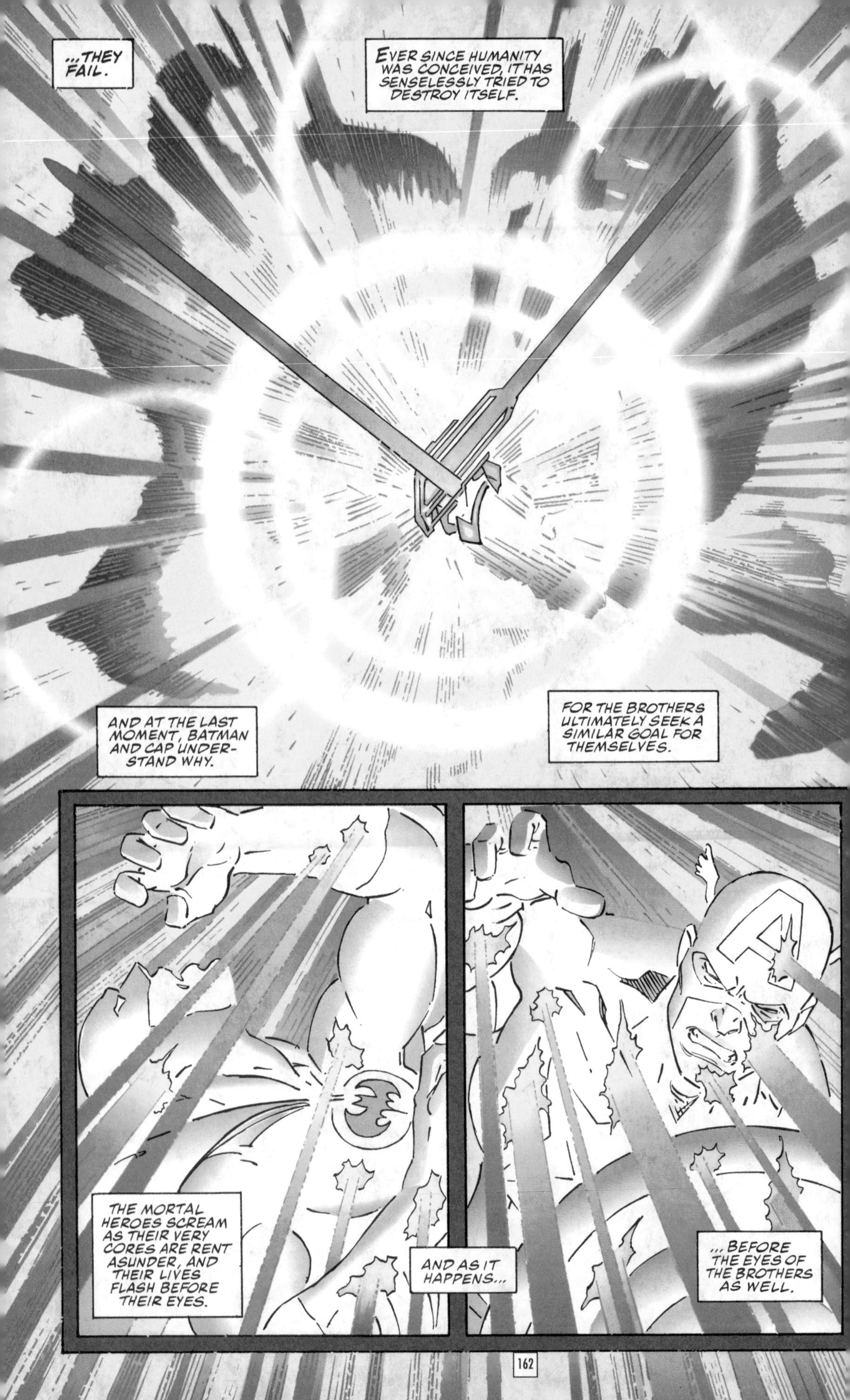
...THEY FAIL.
EVER SINCE HUMANITY WAS CONCEIVED, IT HAS SENSELESSLY TRIED TO DESTROY ITSELF.
AND AT THE LAST MOMENT, BATMAN AND CAP UNDER-STAND WHY.
FOR THE BROTHERS ULTIMATELY SEEK A SIMILAR GOAL FOR THEMSELVES.
THE MORTAL HEROES SCREAM AS THEIR VERY CORES ARE RENT ASUNDER, AND THEIR LIVES FLASH BEFORE THEIR EYES.
AND AS IT HAPPENS...
...BEFORE THE EYES OF THE BROTHERS AS WELL.

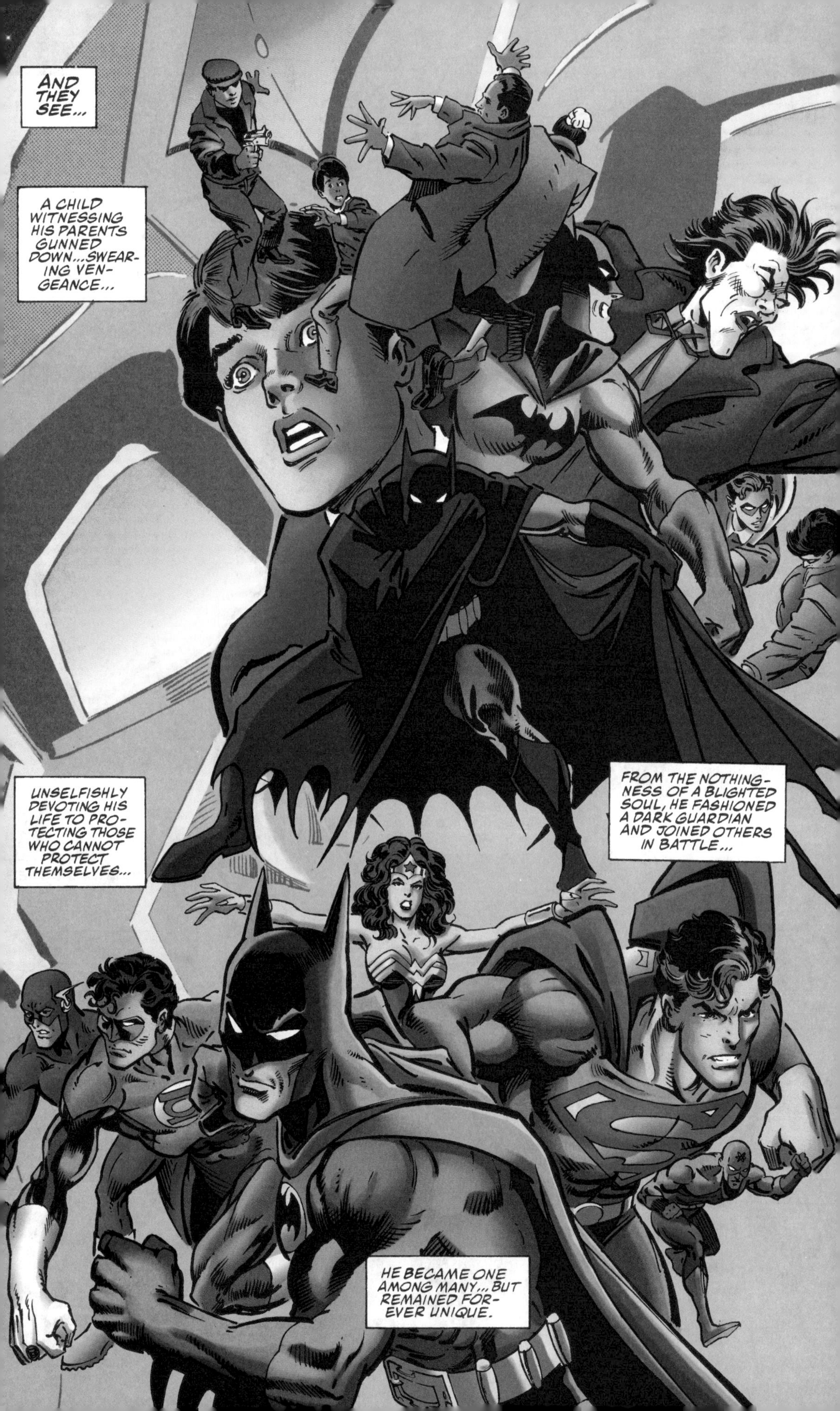
AND THEY SEE...
A CHILD WITNESSING HIS PARENTS GUNNED DOWN...SWEARING VENGEANCE...
UNSELFISHLY DEVOTING HIS LIFE TO PROTECTING THOSE WHO CANNOT PROTECT THEMSELVES...
FROM THE NOTHINGNESS OF A BLIGHTED SOUL, HE FASHIONED A DARK GUARDIAN AND JOINED OTHERS IN BATTLE...
HE BECAME ONE AMONG MANY... BUT REMAINED FOREVER UNIQUE.

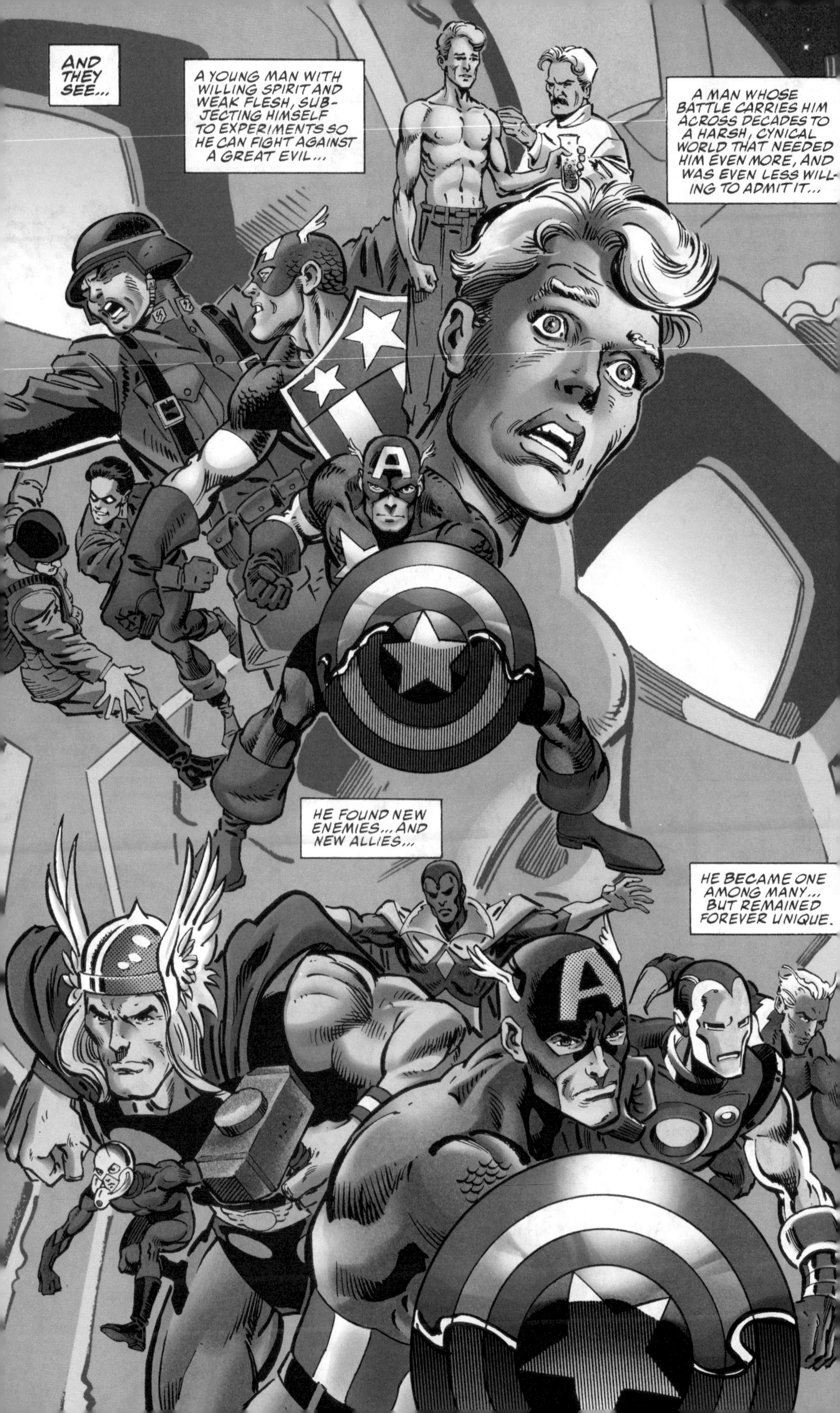
AND THEY SEE...
A YOUNG MAN WITH WILLING SPIRIT AND WEAK FLESH, SUB-JECTING HIMSELF TO EXPERIMENTS SO HE CAN FIGHT AGAINST A GREAT EVIL...
A MAN WHOSE BATTLE CARRIES HIM ACROSS DECADES TO A HARSH, CYNICAL WORLD THAT NEEDED HIM EVEN MORE, AND WAS EVEN LESS WILL-ING TO ADMIT IT...
HE FOUND NEW ENEMIES... AND NEW ALLIES...
HE BECAME ONE AMONG MANY... BUT REMAINED FOREVER UNIQUE.

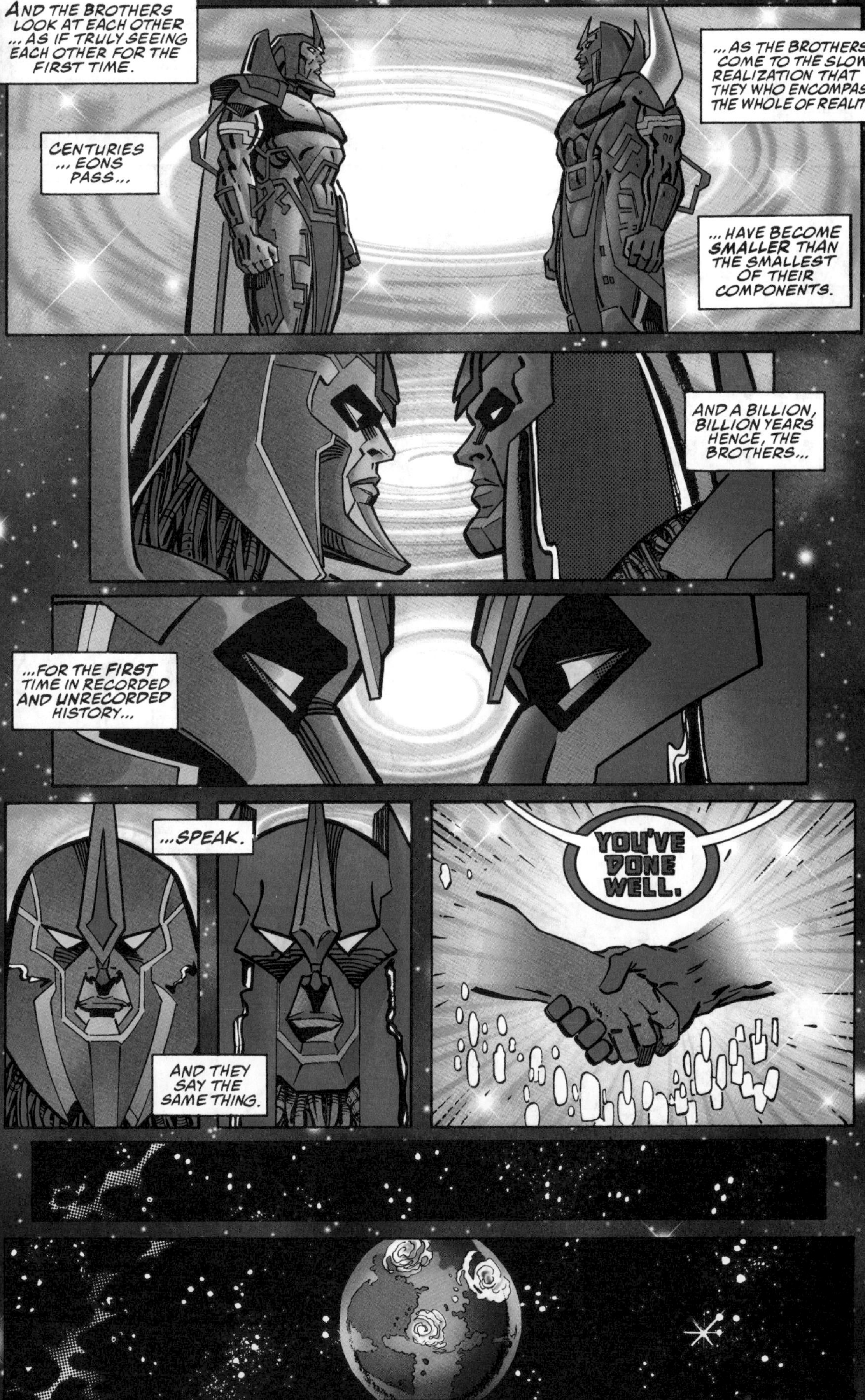
AND THE BROTHERS LOOK AT EACH OTHER ...AS IF TRULY SEEING EACH OTHER FOR THE FIRST TIME.
...AS THE BROTHERS COME TO THE SLOW REALIZATION THAT THEY WHO ENCOMPASS THE WHOLE OF REALITY...
CENTURIES ...EONS PASS...
...HAVE BECOME SMALLER THAN THE SMALLEST OF THEIR COMPONENTS.
AND A BILLION, BILLION YEARS HENCE, THE BROTHERS...
...FOR THE FIRST TIME IN RECORDED AND UNRECORDED HISTORY...
...SPEAK.
AND THEY SAY THE SAME THING.
YOU'VE DONE WELL.

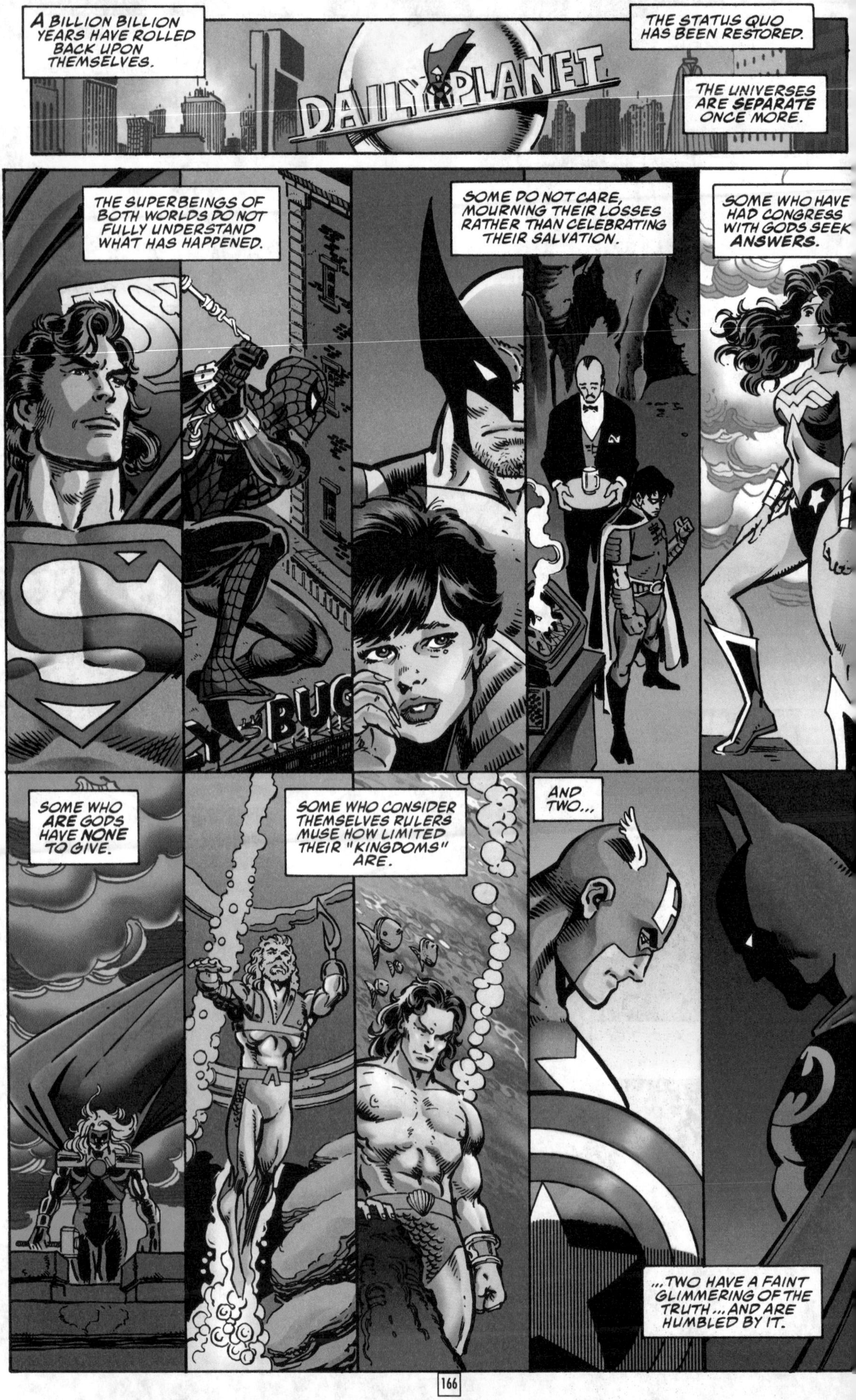
A BILLION BILLION YEARS HAVE ROLLED BACK UPON THEMSELVES.
THE STATUS QUO HAS BEEN RESTORED.
DAILY PLANET
THE UNIVERSES ARE SEPARATE ONCE MORE.
THE SUPERBEINGS OF BOTH WORLDS DO NOT FULLY UNDERSTAND WHAT HAS HAPPENED.
SOME DO NOT CARE, MOURNING THEIR LOSSES RATHER THAN CELEBRATING THEIR SALVATION.
SOME WHO HAVE HAD CONGRESS WITH GODS SEEK ANSWERS.
SOME WHO ARE GODS HAVE NONE TO GIVE.
SOME WHO CONSIDER THEMSELVES RULERS MUSE HOW LIMITED THEIR "KINGDOMS" ARE.
AND TWO...
...TWO HAVE A FAINT GLIMMERING OF THE TRUTH... AND ARE HUMBLED BY IT.

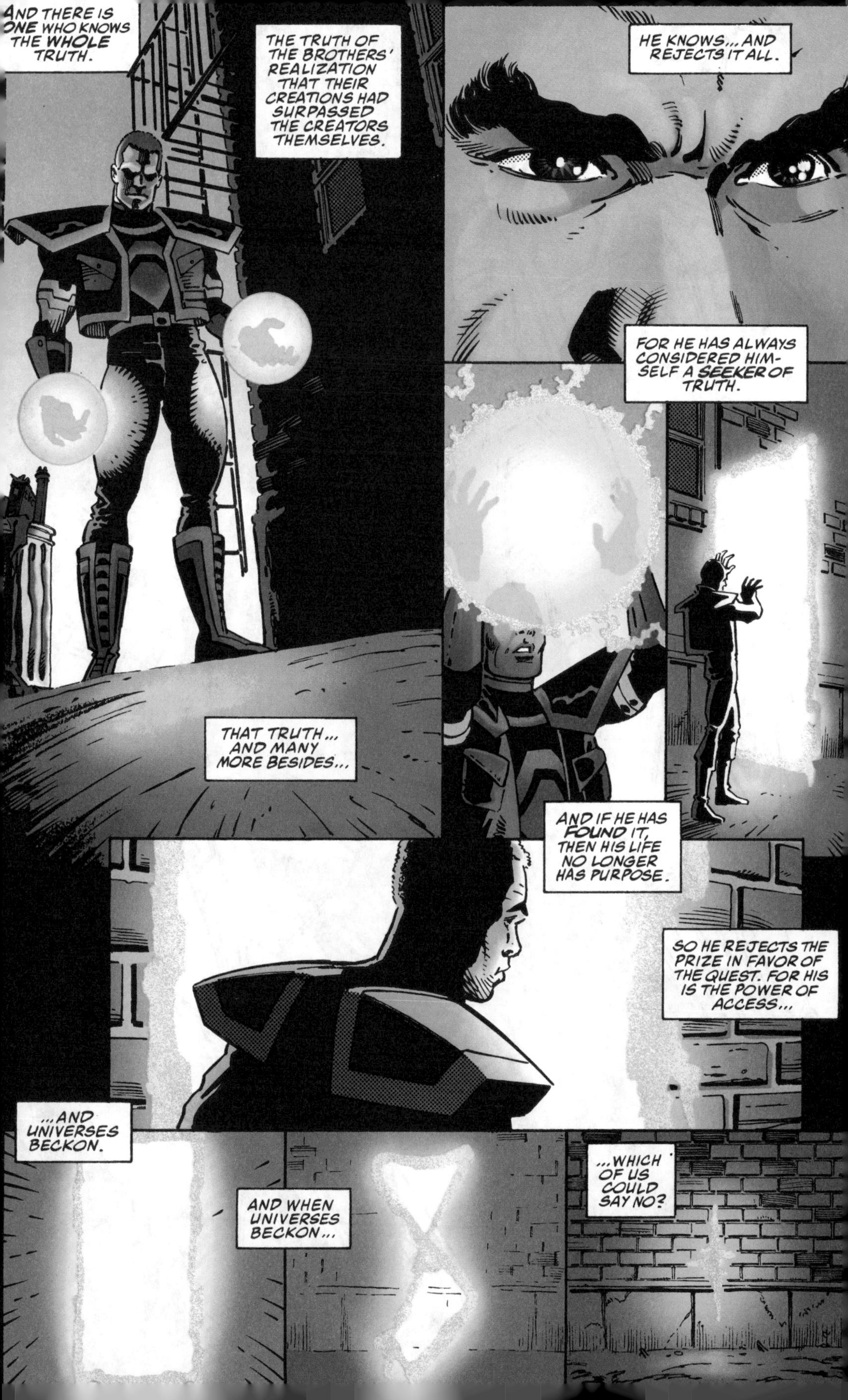
AND THERE IS ONE WHO KNOWS THE WHOLE TRUTH.
THE TRUTH OF THE BROTHERS' REALIZATION THAT THEIR CREATIONS HAD SURPASSED THE CREATORS THEMSELVES.
THAT TRUTH... AND MANY MORE BESIDES...
HE KNOWS... AND REJECTS IT ALL.
FOR HE HAS ALWAYS CONSIDERED HIM-SELF A SEEKER OF TRUTH.
AND IF HE HAS FOUND IT, THEN HIS LIFE NO LONGER HAS PURPOSE.
SO HE REJECTS THE PRIZE IN FAVOR OF THE QUEST. FOR HIS IS THE POWER OF ACCESS...
...AND UNIVERSES BECKON.
AND WHEN UNIVERSES BECKON...
...WHICH OF US COULD SAY NO?

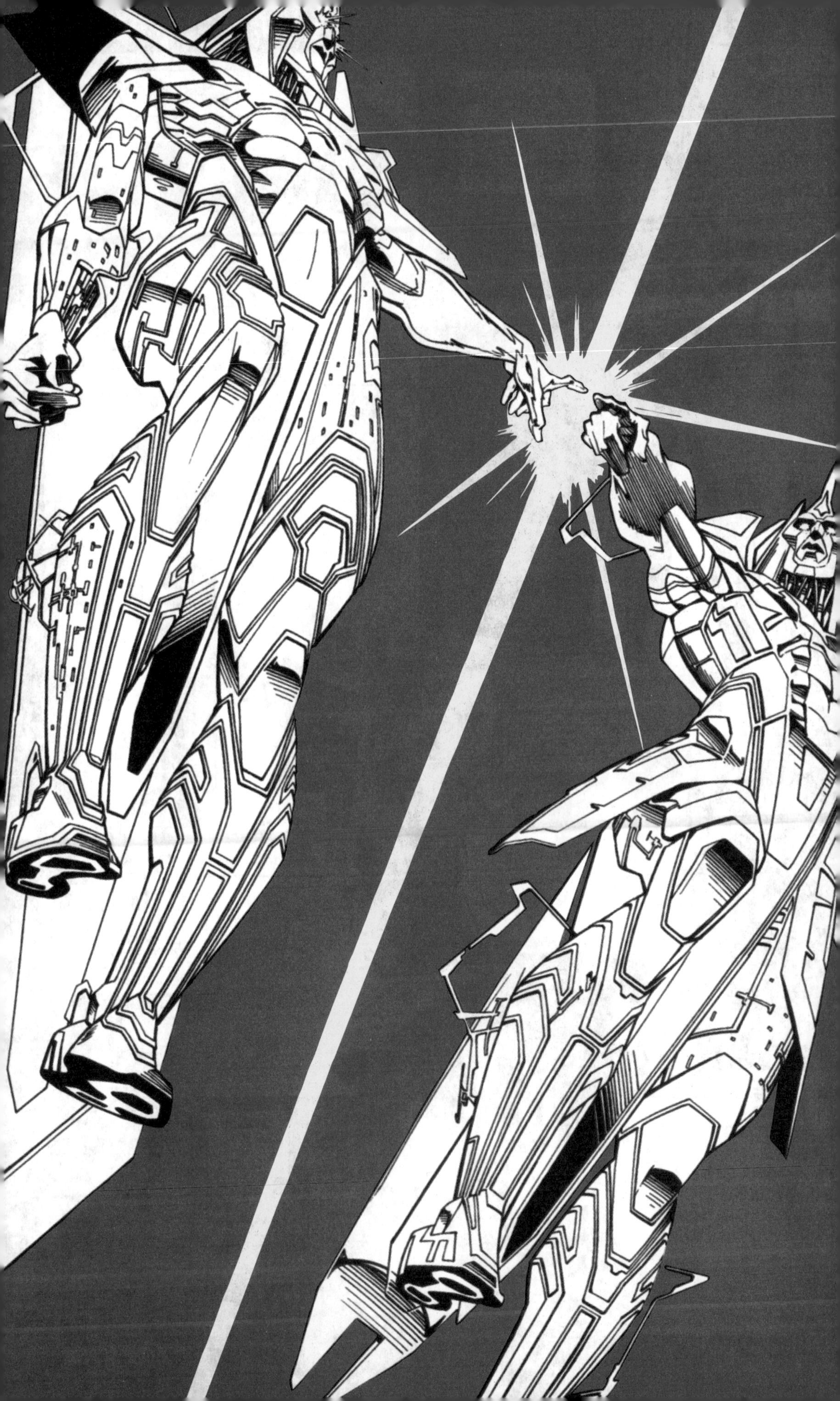

SUPERMAN

Created by Jerry Siegel & Joe Shuster

REAL NAME: Clark Kent
OTHER CURRENT ALIASES: None
DUAL IDENTITY: Secret
CURRENT OCCUPATION: Reporter, columnist, novelist
FORMER OCCUPATIONS: Editor of Newstime magazine
PLACE OF BIRTH: Conceived on planet Krypton, "born" out of birthing matrix in Smallville, Kansas, U.S.A., DC-Earth
MARITAL STATUS: Engaged to Lois Lane
USUAL BASE OF OPERATIONS: Metropolis
CURRENT GROUP MEMBERSHIP: None
HEIGHT: 6' 3"   **WEIGHT:** 225 lbs.
EYES: Blue   **HAIR:** Black
SUPERHUMAN POWERS: Vast superhuman strength; invulnerability; able to move, fly and react at superhuman speeds; X-ray vision, telescopic vision, microscopic vision, heat vision, superhuman senses
SOURCE OF POWERS: Kryptonian physiology charged by solar radiation
SPECIAL SKILLS: None
WEAPONS: None
FIRST APPEARANCE: ACTION COMICS #1 (1938)

DC VERSUS MARVEL COMICS

THE HULK

REAL NAME: Robert Bruce Banner
OTHER CURRENT ALIASES: Bob Danner
DUAL IDENTITY: Publicly known
CURRENT OCCUPATION: Unemployed
FORMER OCCUPATIONS: Nuclear physicist, enforcer, covert operations leader, auto mechanic
PLACE OF BIRTH: Dayton, Ohio, U.S.A., Marvel-Earth
MARITAL STATUS: Married to Elizabeth "Betty" Ross
USUAL BASE OF OPERATIONS: Mobile
CURRENT GROUP MEMBERSHIP: None
HEIGHT: 6' 6"   **WEIGHT:** 1,150 lbs.
EYES: Green   **HAIR:** Black
SUPERHUMAN POWERS: Vast superhuman strength, stamina, and resistance to injury; ability to leap miles in a single bound
SOURCE OF POWERS: Gamma radiation mutated physique
SPECIAL SKILLS: None
WEAPONS: None
FIRST APPEARANCE: INCREDIBLE HULK #1 (1962)

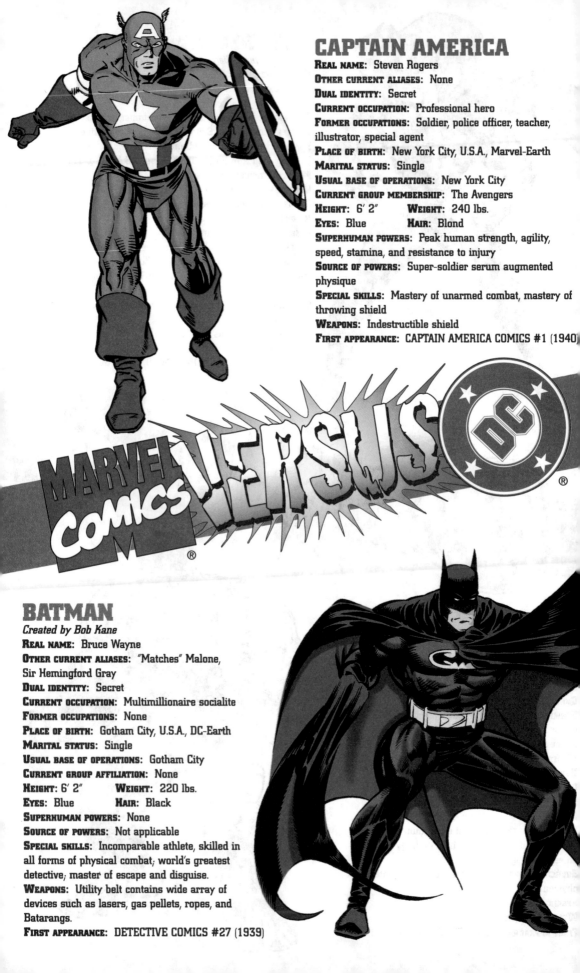

CAPTAIN AMERICA

REAL NAME: Steven Rogers
OTHER CURRENT ALIASES: None
DUAL IDENTITY: Secret
CURRENT OCCUPATION: Professional hero
FORMER OCCUPATIONS: Soldier, police officer, teacher, illustrator, special agent
PLACE OF BIRTH: New York City, U.S.A., Marvel-Earth
MARITAL STATUS: Single
USUAL BASE OF OPERATIONS: New York City
CURRENT GROUP MEMBERSHIP: The Avengers
HEIGHT: 6′ 2″   **WEIGHT:** 240 lbs.
EYES: Blue   **HAIR:** Blond
SUPERHUMAN POWERS: Peak human strength, agility, speed, stamina, and resistance to injury
SOURCE OF POWERS: Super-soldier serum augmented physique
SPECIAL SKILLS: Mastery of unarmed combat, mastery of throwing shield
WEAPONS: Indestructible shield
FIRST APPEARANCE: CAPTAIN AMERICA COMICS #1 (1940)

MARVEL COMICS VERSUS DC

BATMAN

Created by Bob Kane
REAL NAME: Bruce Wayne
OTHER CURRENT ALIASES: "Matches" Malone, Sir Hemingford Gray
DUAL IDENTITY: Secret
CURRENT OCCUPATION: Multimillionaire socialite
FORMER OCCUPATIONS: None
PLACE OF BIRTH: Gotham City, U.S.A., DC-Earth
MARITAL STATUS: Single
USUAL BASE OF OPERATIONS: Gotham City
CURRENT GROUP AFFILIATION: None
HEIGHT: 6′ 2″   **WEIGHT:** 220 lbs.
EYES: Blue   **HAIR:** Black
SUPERHUMAN POWERS: None
SOURCE OF POWERS: Not applicable
SPECIAL SKILLS: Incomparable athlete, skilled in all forms of physical combat; world's greatest detective; master of escape and disguise.
WEAPONS: Utility belt contains wide array of devices such as lasers, gas pellets, ropes, and Batarangs.
FIRST APPEARANCE: DETECTIVE COMICS #27 (1939)

WONDER WOMAN

Created by William Moulton Marston

Real name: Diana
Other current aliases: None
Current occupation: Ambassador, visiting lecturer
Former occupations: Princess
Place of birth: Themyscira, DC-Earth
Marital status: Single
Usual base of operations: Gateway City
Current group membership: Justice League America
Height: 5′ 11″ **Weight:** 135 lbs.
Eyes: Blue **Hair:** Black
Superhuman powers: Vast superhuman strength, able to fly and move fast enough to deflect bullets with her silver bracelets
Source of powers: Gift of the ancient Greek gods
Special skills: Trained in all ancient Greek methods of armed and unarmed combat
Weapons: Wields the unbreakable Lasso of Truth, forged from the girdle of Gaea, which forces anyone held by it to tell the absolute truth
First appearance: ALL-STAR COMICS #8 (1941)

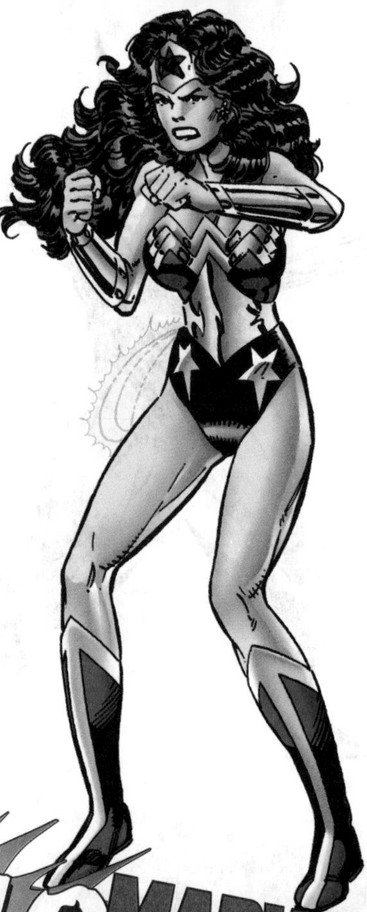

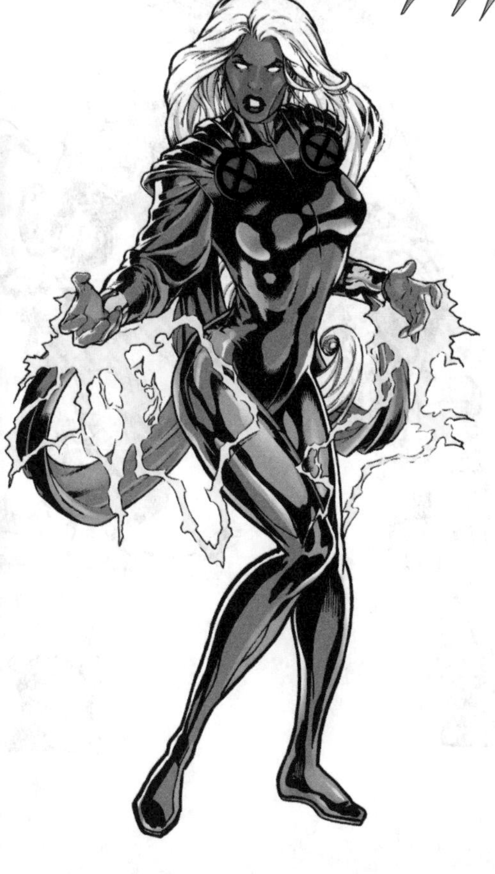

STORM

Real name: Ororo Munroe
Other current aliases: None
Dual identity: Secret
Current occupation: Professional hero
Former occupations: Rain goddess, thief
Place of birth: New York City, U.S.A.–Marvel-Earth
Marital status: Single
Usual base of operations: Salem Center, New York
Current group membership: The X-Men
Height: 5′ 11″ **Weight:** 127 lbs.
Eyes: Blue **Hair:** White
Superhuman powers: Psionic manipulation of the weather, including rain, fog, lightning, and wind; she can fly by riding wind currents
Source of powers: Benevolent mutation
Special skills: Mastery of lockpicking, escape arts, and battle strategies
Weapons: None
First appearance: GIANT-SIZE X-MEN #1 (1975)

WOLVERINE

REAL NAME: Logan (no known first name)
OTHER CURRENT ALIASES: None
DUAL IDENTITY: Secret
CURRENT OCCUPATION: Professional hero
FORMER OCCUPATIONS: Soldier, covert operative
PLACE OF BIRTH: Somewhere in Canada, Marvel-Earth
MARITAL STATUS: Single
USUAL BASE OF OPERATIONS: Salem Center, New York
CURRENT GROUP MEMBERSHIP: The X-Men
HEIGHT: 5′ 3″   **WEIGHT:** 195 lbs.
EYES: Brown   **HAIR:** Black
SUPERHUMAN POWERS: Superhuman strength, agility, reflexes, and stamina, heightened senses, rapid healing powers, possesses retractable claws on each hand
SOURCE OF POWERS: Benevolent mutation
SPECIAL SKILLS: Mastery of many forms of unarmed combat
WEAPONS: None
FIRST APPEARANCE: INCREDIBLE HULK #180 (1974)

MARVEL COMICS VERSUS DC

LOBO

Created by Keith Giffen and Roger Slifer
REAL NAME: Just Lobo
OTHER CURRENT ALIASES: The Main Man, the Master of Frag
DUAL IDENTITY: Just Lobo, okay?
CURRENT OCCUPATION: Bounty hunter, assassin, scourge of th' cosmos, thug
FORMER OCCUPATIONS: Bounty hunter, assassin, scourge of th' cosmos, thug
PLACE OF BIRTH: The formerly delightful planet of Czarnia
MARITAL STATUS: Confirmed bachelor
USUAL BASE OF OPERATIONS: At large on his spazzfrag spacehawg or in some divey space bar
CURRENT GROUP AFFILIATION: No one would have him!
HEIGHT: 6′ 4″   **WEIGHT:** 305 lbs.
EYES: Blood red   **HAIR:** Sepulchre black
SUPERHUMAN POWERS: Vast superhuman strength, intergalactic tracking ability, healing factor, deal with heaven that makes him immortal
SOURCE OF POWERS: Hideous twist of fate
SPECIAL SKILLS: Good with his hook and chain, good brawler, mean biker
WEAPONS: Gutting hook with chain, various sidearms
FIRST APPEARANCE: Goofy version: OMEGA MEN #3 (1983); cooler version: JLA #18 (1988)

SUPERBOY

Real name: Superboy
Other current aliases: None
Dual identity: None
Current occupation: Hero and student
Former occupations: Defender of Metropolis
Place of birth: Project Cadmus, U.S.A.–DC-Earth
Marital status: He's single and likes it that way.
Usual base of operations: Hawaii
Current group membership: Honorary Legionnaire
Height: 5′ 7″ **Weight:** 150 lbs.
Eyes: Blue **Hair:** Black
Superhuman powers: Tactile telekinesis power enables him to fly, lift anything he touches, and protect himself and those he touches from direct physical harm. He can also extend t.k. causing objects to break apart, move, or explode.
Source of powers: Genetically altered clone
Special skills: Popular with the ladies
Weapons: None
First appearance: ADVENTURES OF SUPERMAN #500 (1993)

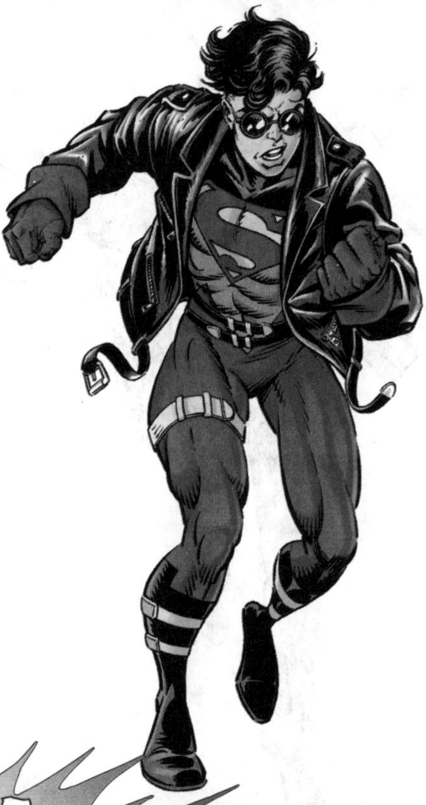

DC VERSUS MARVEL COMICS

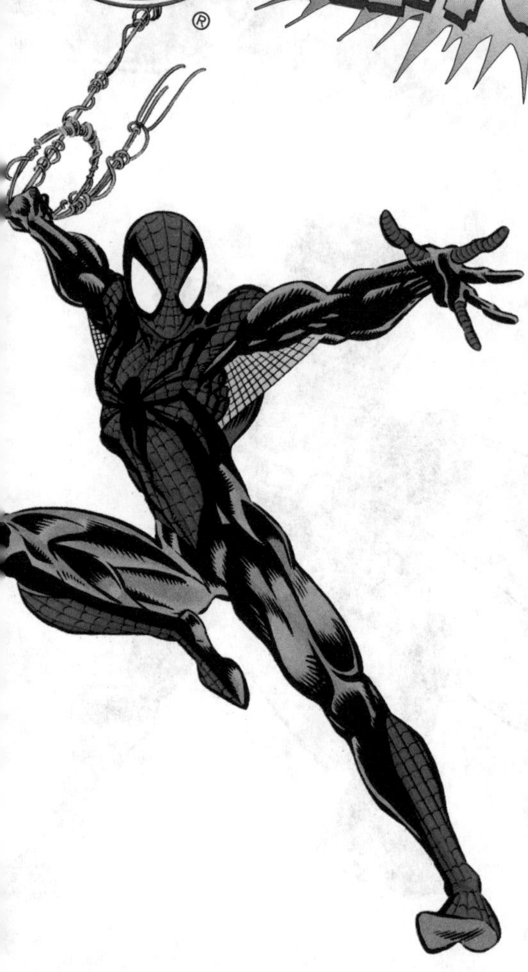

SPIDER-MAN

Real name: Peter Parker
Other current aliases: Ben Reilly
Dual identity: Secret
Current occupation: Waiter
Former occupations: Newspaper photographer
Place of birth: New York City, U.S.A.–Marvel-Earth
Marital status: Single
Usual base of operations: New York City
Current group membership: None
Height: 5′ 10″ ***Weight:*** 165 lbs.
Eyes: Hazel **Hair:** Brown (dyed blond)
Superhuman powers: Superhuman strength, stamina, and resistance to injury, ability to leap 20 feet in a single bound, ability to stick to walls
Source of powers: Irradiated blood
Special skills: Inventive genius
Weapons: Wrist-worn web-shooters projecting strong, fast-drying web for a variety of uses, including impact webbing, stingers
First appearance: AMAZING FANTASY #15 (1962)

JUBILEE

REAL NAME: Jubilation Lee
OTHER CURRENT ALIASES: None
DUAL IDENTITY: Publicly known
CURRENT OCCUPATION: Adventurer
FORMER OCCUPATIONS: High school student
PLACE OF BIRTH: Beverly Hills, California, Marvel-Earth
MARITAL STATUS: Single
USUAL BASE OF OPERATIONS: Professor Xavier's School for Gifted Youngsters, Massachusetts Academy, Marvel-Earth
CURRENT GROUP MEMBERSHIP: Generation X
HEIGHT: 5' 5"   **WEIGHT:** 105 lbs.
EYES: Blue   **HAIR:** Black
SUPERHUMAN POWERS: Superhuman ability to generate energy globules called "fireworks," capable of various effects including dazzling light and explosive concussions
SOURCE OF POWERS: Benevolent mutation
SPECIAL SKILLS: Better-than-average unarmed combatant
WEAPONS: None
FIRST APPEARANCE: UNCANNY X-MEN #244 (1989)

MARVEL COMICS **VERSUS** DC

ROBIN

REAL NAME: Tim Drake
OTHER CURRENT ALIASES: Alvin Draper
DUAL IDENTITY: Secret
CURRENT OCCUPATION: High school student
FORMER OCCUPATIONS: None
PLACE OF BIRTH: Gotham City, U.S.A.–DC-Earth
MARITAL STATUS: Single
USUAL BASE OF OPERATIONS: Gotham City
CURRENT GROUP MEMBERSHIP: None
HEIGHT: 5' 3"   **WEIGHT:** 120 lbs.
EYES: Blue   **HAIR:** Black
SUPERHUMAN POWERS: None
SOURCE OF POWERS: Not applicable
SPECIAL SKILLS: A superb martial artist and acrobat, incredibly well-versed in detection and computer science
WEAPONS: Robin's costume is virtually fireproof and bulletproof and contains numerous devices such as gas pellets, lasers, and throwing darts. He also carries a sling and a collapsible bo staff.
FIRST APPEARANCE: BATMAN #457 (1990)

THE FLASH

REAL NAME: Wallace West
OTHER CURRENT ALIASES: None
DUAL IDENTITY: Generally known
CURRENT OCCUPATION: Super hero
FORMER OCCUPATIONS: Student, I.R.S. agent, overnight courier
PLACE OF BIRTH: Blue Valley, Nebraska, USA, DC-Earth
MARITAL STATUS: Single
USUAL BASE OF OPERATIONS: Keystone City
CURRENT GROUP MEMBERSHIP: The Justice League
HEIGHT: 6' 0"   **WEIGHT:** 175 lbs.
EYES: Green   **HAIR:** Red
SUPERHUMAN POWERS: The fastest man alive, he can propel himself at speeds approaching the speed of light; can "lend" speed to already moving objects and people; vibrate through barriers, leaving an explosive, kinetic charge in his wake; using speed can generate heat and destructive vibration
SOURCE OF POWERS: Directly channels power from an extra dimensional energy source known as the "speed field"
SPECIAL SKILLS: (see Superhuman Powers)
WEAPONS: None
FIRST APPEARENCE: As teen hero, Kid Flash—FLASH #110 (1959). As Flash—CRISIS ON INFINITE EARTHS #12 (1986)

DC VERSUS MARVEL COMICS

QUICKSILVER

REAL NAME: Pietro Maximoff
OTHER CURRENT ALIASES: None
DUAL IDENTITY: Publicly known
CURRENT OCCUPATION: Adventurer
FORMER OCCUPATIONS: Terrorist, government operative
PLACE OF BIRTH: Wundagore Mountain, Transia, Marvel-Earth
MARITAL STATUS: Married (wife: Crystal)
USUAL BASE OF OPERATIONS: Avengers Mansion, New York City
CURRENT GROUP MEMBERSHIP: The Avengers
HEIGHT: 6' 0"   **WEIGHT:** 175 lbs.
EYES: Blue   **HAIR:** Silver
SUPERHUMAN POWERS: Superhuman speed (upper limit: speed of sound), reaction time, endurance
SOURCE OF POWERS: Benevolent mutation
SPECIAL SKILLS: Mastery of fighting at high velocity
WEAPONS: None
FIRST APPEARANCE: X-MEN #4 (1964)

THOR

REAL NAME: Thor
OTHER CURRENT ALIASES: None
FORMER ALIASES: Dr. Donald Blake, Sigurd Jarlson
DUAL IDENTITY: Inapplicable
CURRENT OCCUPATION: Adventurer
FORMER OCCUPATIONS: Warrior, prince of Asgard
PLACE OF BIRTH: A cave in Norway, Marvel-Earth
MARITAL STATUS: Single
USUAL BASE OF OPERATIONS: Avengers Mansion, New York City
CURRENT GROUP MEMBERSHIP: The Avengers
HEIGHT: 6' 6"   **WEIGHT:** 640 lbs.
EYES: Blue   **HAIR:** Blond
SUPERHUMAN POWERS: Superhuman strength, stamina, and resistance to injury
SOURCE OF POWERS: Asgardian heritage
SPECIAL SKILLS: Expert at hand-to-hand combat and wielding a hammer in battle
WEAPONS: The enchanted hammer Mjolnir, virtually indestructible, and capable of summoning storms and vortex-spatial/dimensional transport
FIRST APPEARANCE: JOURNEY INTO MYSTERY #83 (1962)

CAPTAIN MARVEL (DC)

REAL NAME: Billy Batson
OTHER CURRENT ALIASES: None
DUAL IDENTITY: Secret
CURRENT OCCUPATION: Student, radio announcer
FORMER OCCUPATIONS: None
PLACE OF BIRTH: Fawcett City, U.S.A., DC-Earth
MARITAL STATUS: Single
USUAL BASE OF OPERATIONS: Fawcett City
CURRENT GROUP MEMBERSHIP: None
HEIGHT: 6' 2"   **WEIGHT:** 220 lbs.
EYES: Blue   **HAIR:** Black
SUPERHUMAN POWERS: Wields the Power of Shazam—able to draw upon the Wisdom of Solomon, the Strength of Hercules, the Stamina of Atlas, the Power of Zeus, the Courage of Achilles, and the Speed of Mercury
SOURCE OF POWERS: Granted by ancient wizard Shazam via covenant with the gods
SPECIAL SKILLS: None
WEAPONS: None
FIRST APPEARANCE: WHIZ COMICS #1 (1940)

CATWOMAN

REAL NAME: Selina Kyle
OTHER CURRENT ALIASES: None
DUAL IDENTITY: Secret
CURRENT OCCUPATION: Professional criminal
FORMER OCCUPATIONS: None
PLACE OF BIRTH: Gotham City, U.S.A.–DC-Earth
MARITAL STATUS: Single
USUAL BASE OF OPERATIONS: Gotham City
CURRENT GROUP MEMBERSHIP: None
HEIGHT: 5′ 11″   **WEIGHT:** 140 lbs.
EYES: Green   **HAIR:** Black
SUPERHUMAN POWERS: None
SOURCE OF POWERS: Not applicable
SPECIAL SKILLS: Olympic-level athlete, superb martial artist, expert thief
WEAPONS: Whip, retractable boot & glove claws, Catspaw grappling hook, as well as an array of high-tech burglary tools
FIRST APPEARANCE: BATMAN #1 (1940)

ELEKTRA

REAL NAME: Elektra Natchios
OTHER CURRENT ALIASES: None
DUAL IDENTITY: Publicly known
CURRENT OCCUPATION: Adventurer
FORMER OCCUPATIONS: Assassin, bounty hunter
PLACE OF BIRTH: Near the Aegean Islands, Marvel-Earth
MARITAL STATUS: Single
USUAL BASE OF OPERATIONS: Mobile
CURRENT GROUP MEMBERSHIP: None
HEIGHT: 5′ 9″   **WEIGHT:** 130 lbs.
EYES: Blue   **HAIR:** Black
SUPERHUMAN POWERS: Limited psychic powers including illusion-casting and creating psychic bonds enabling mental communication
SOURCE OF POWERS: Training
SPECIAL SKILLS: Olympic-level athlete, expert at hand-to-hand combat and Japanese ninja techniques
WEAPONS: Sai (three-pronged dagger)
FIRST APPEARANCE: DAREDEVIL #168 (1981)

SILVER SURFER

REAL NAME: Norrin Radd

OTHER CURRENT ALIASES: None

DUAL IDENTITY: Inapplicable

CURRENT OCCUPATION: Interstellar adventurer

FORMER OCCUPATIONS: Herald of Galactus

PLACE OF BIRTH: Zenn-La, Deneb System, Milky Way Galaxy, Marvel-Universe

MARITAL STATUS: Single

USUAL BASE OF OPERATIONS: Known space

CURRENT GROUP MEMBERSHIP: Star Masters

HEIGHT: 6′ 4″   **WEIGHT:** Unrevealed

EYES: Silver (pupil-less)   **HAIR:** None

SUPERHUMAN POWERS: Superhuman strength, stamina, and resistance to injury, ability to survive without food or oxygen, heightened senses, ability to project cosmic energy for a variety of effects

SOURCE OF POWERS: Imbued by Galactus's power cosmic

SPECIAL SKILLS: Expert surfer, skilled at molecular rearrangement

WEAPONS: None

PARAPHERNALIA: A surfboard responsive to his mental commands

FIRST APPEARANCE: FANTASTIC FOUR #48 (1966)

MARVEL COMICS VERSUS DC

GREEN LANTERN

REAL NAME: Kyle Rayner

OTHER CURRENT ALIASES: None

DUAL IDENTITY: Secret

CURRENT OCCUPATION: Freelance artist

FORMER OCCUPATIONS: Member of the New Titans

PLACE OF BIRTH: Los Angeles, California, DC-Earth

MARITAL STATUS: Single

USUAL BASE OF OPERATIONS: New York City

CURRENT GROUP MEMBERSHIP: None

HEIGHT: 5′ 11″   **WEIGHT:** 162 lbs

EYES: Brown   **HAIR:** Black

SUPERHUMAN POWERS: (see Weapons)

SOURCE OF POWERS: The last Green Lantern power ring (see Weapons)

SPECIAL SKILLS: Artist

WEAPONS: The most powerful weapon in the universe, Kyle's power ring can create virtually anything or any effect he can imagine—a ring-generated exoskeleton, any kind of armament, gun or shield. It can protect him from almost any attack and enable him to travel at incredible speeds. Requires recharge occasionally when power is used up.

FIRST APPEARANCE: As Kyle Rayner: GREEN LANTERN #48 (2nd series-1993). As Green Lantern: GREEN LANTERN #50 (2nd series-1993)

AQUAMAN

REAL NAME: Orin
OTHER CURRENT ALIASES: Arthur Curry
DUAL IDENTITY: Publicly known
CURRENT OCCUPATION: Protector of the Seas and Oceans
FORMER OCCUPATIONS: Crime-fighter, King of Poseidonis, Justice League member
PLACE OF BIRTH: Atlantis, DC-Earth
MARITAL STATUS: Separated
USUAL BASE OF OPERATIONS: Mobile
CURRENT GROUP MEMBERSHIP: None
HEIGHT: 6′ 1″   **WEIGHT:** 325 lbs.
EYES: Aqua-blue   **HAIR:** Blond
SUPERHUMAN POWERS: Ability to communicate directly with sea life, ability to sense the primal emotions of aquatic creatures, can swim underwater at rates up to 100 mph, can withstand extremes of temperature and pressure
SOURCE OF POWERS: Son of wizard and Atlantean queen
SPECIAL SKILLS: Excels at hand-to-hand combat
WEAPONS: Hook that has replaced his left hand is able to shoot a thin cord to ensnare an enemy or can be used as a rope for climbing or swinging. Hook is also able to drill through objects.
FIRST APPEARANCE: MORE FUN COMICS #73 (1941)

SUB-MARINER

REAL NAME: Namor McKenzie
OTHER CURRENT ALIASES: None
DUAL IDENTITY: Publicly known
CURRENT OCCUPATION: Chief executive officer of Oracle, Ltd.
FORMER OCCUPATIONS: Monarch of Atlantis
PLACE OF BIRTH: Capital city of the Atlantean Empire, Marvel-Earth
MARITAL STATUS: Widowed
USUAL BASE OF OPERATIONS: The Atlantic Ocean
CURRENT GROUP MEMBERSHIP: None
HEIGHT: 6′ 2″   **WEIGHT:** 310 lbs.
EYES: Green   **HAIR:** Blue-grey
SUPERHUMAN POWERS: Superhuman strength, stamina, and resistance to injury, ability to breathe underwater and survive ocean bottom pressure, ability to fly
SOURCE OF POWERS: Born a human-merman hybrid
SPECIAL SKILLS: Expert swordsman, experienced tactician
WEAPONS: None
FIRST APPEARANCE: MARVEL COMICS #1 (1939)

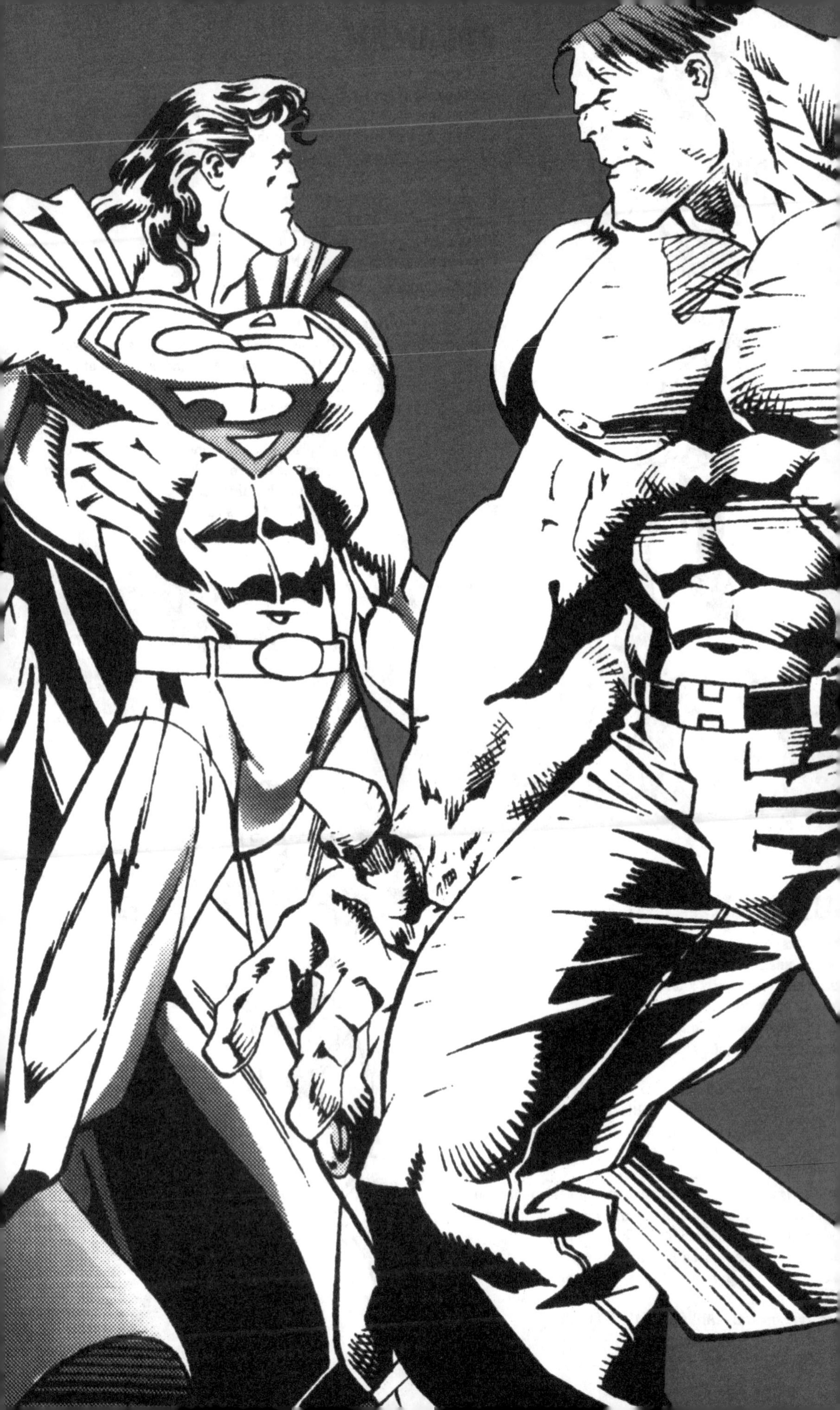

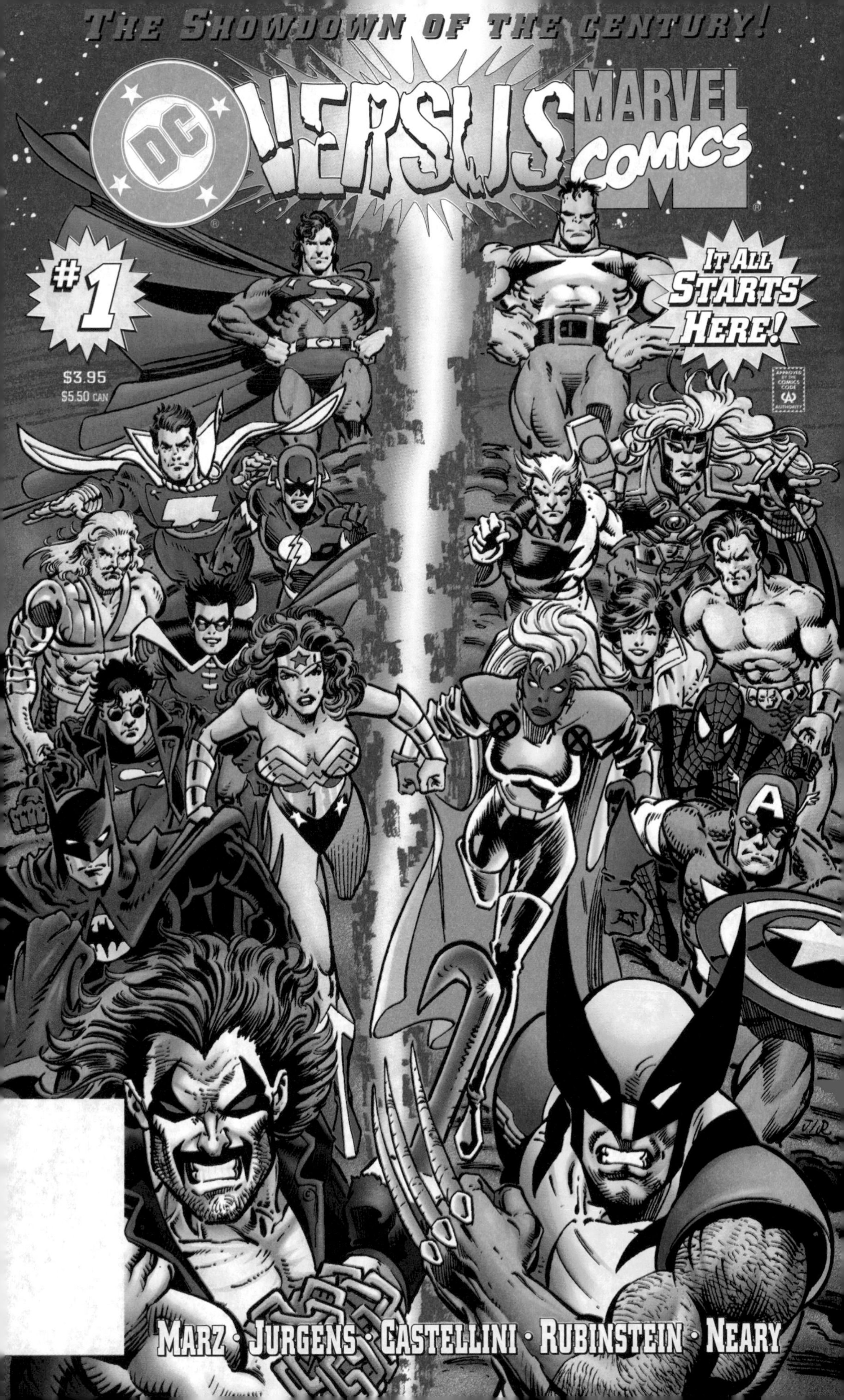
THE SHOWDOWN OF THE CENTURY!
DC
VERSUS
MARVEL COMICS
#1
IT ALL STARTS HERE!
$3.95
$5.50 CAN
MARZ · JURGENS · CASTELLINI · RUBINSTEIN · NEARY

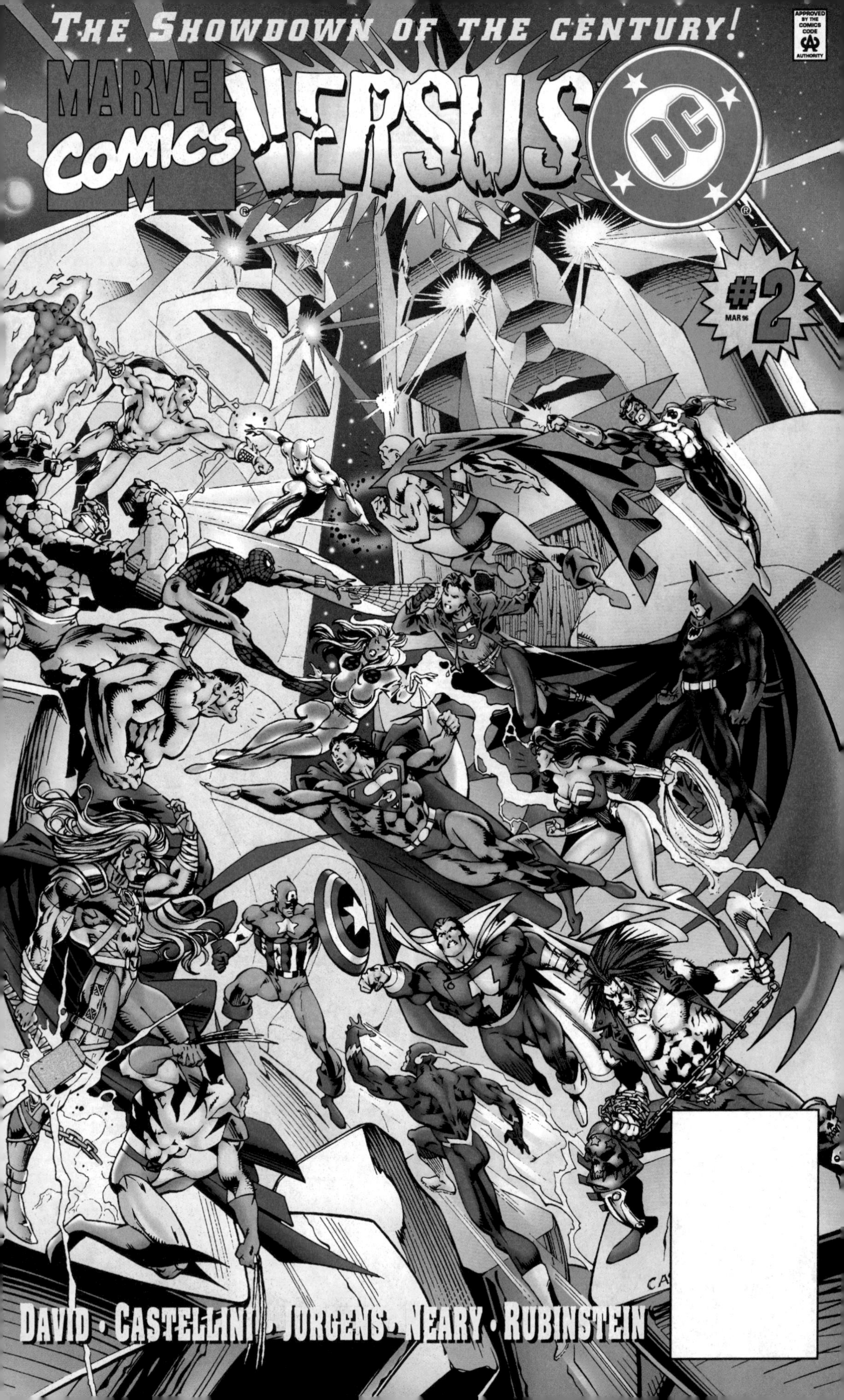
THE SHOWDOWN OF THE CENTURY!
APPROVED BY THE COMICS CODE AUTHORITY
MARVEL COMICS
VERSUS
DC
#2
MAR 96
DAVID · CASTELLINI · JORGENS · NEARY · RUBINSTEIN

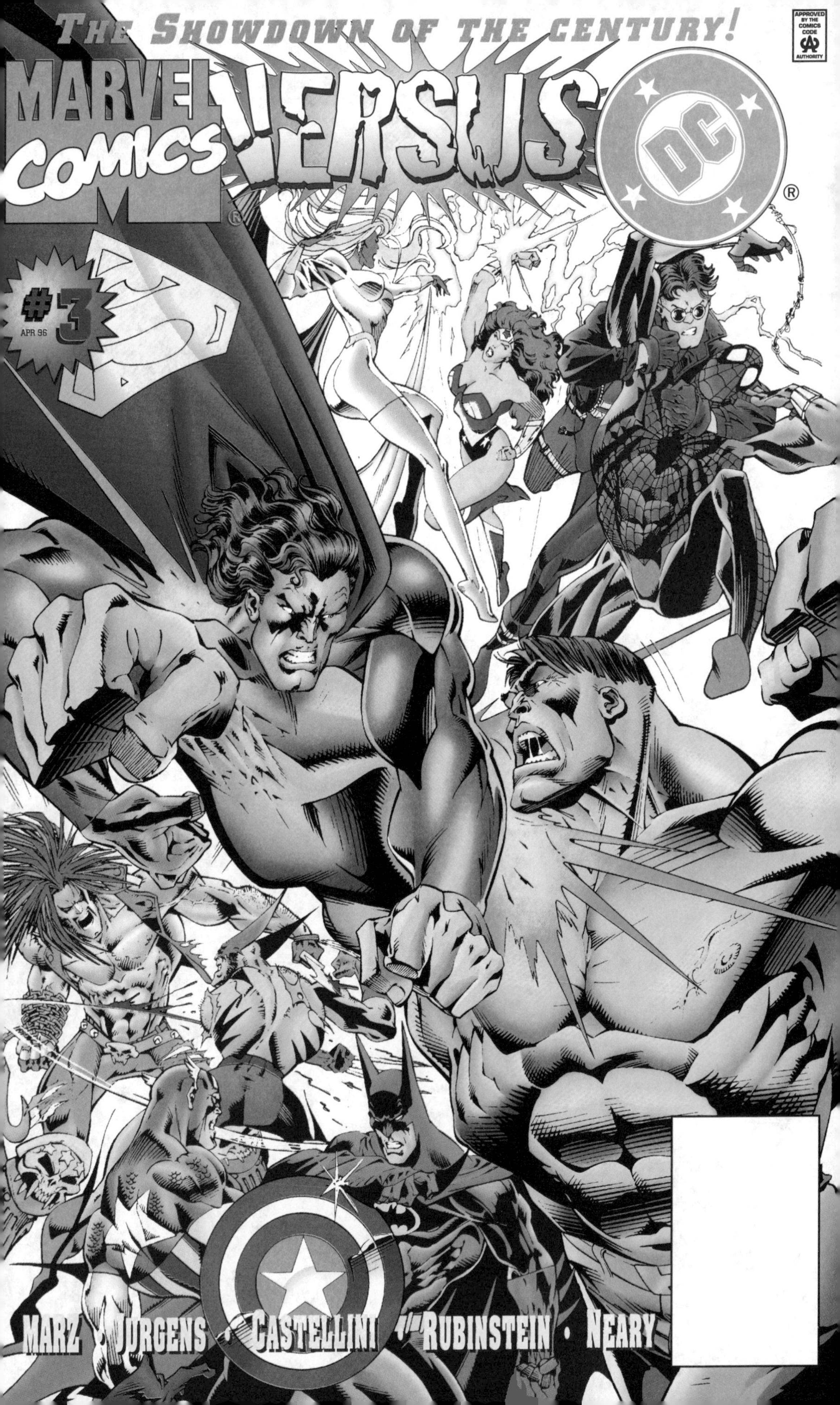
THE SHOWDOWN OF THE CENTURY!
MARVEL COMICS
VERSUS
DC
#3
APR 96
APPROVED BY THE COMICS CODE AUTHORITY
MARZ · JURGENS · CASTELLINI · RUBINSTEIN · NEARY

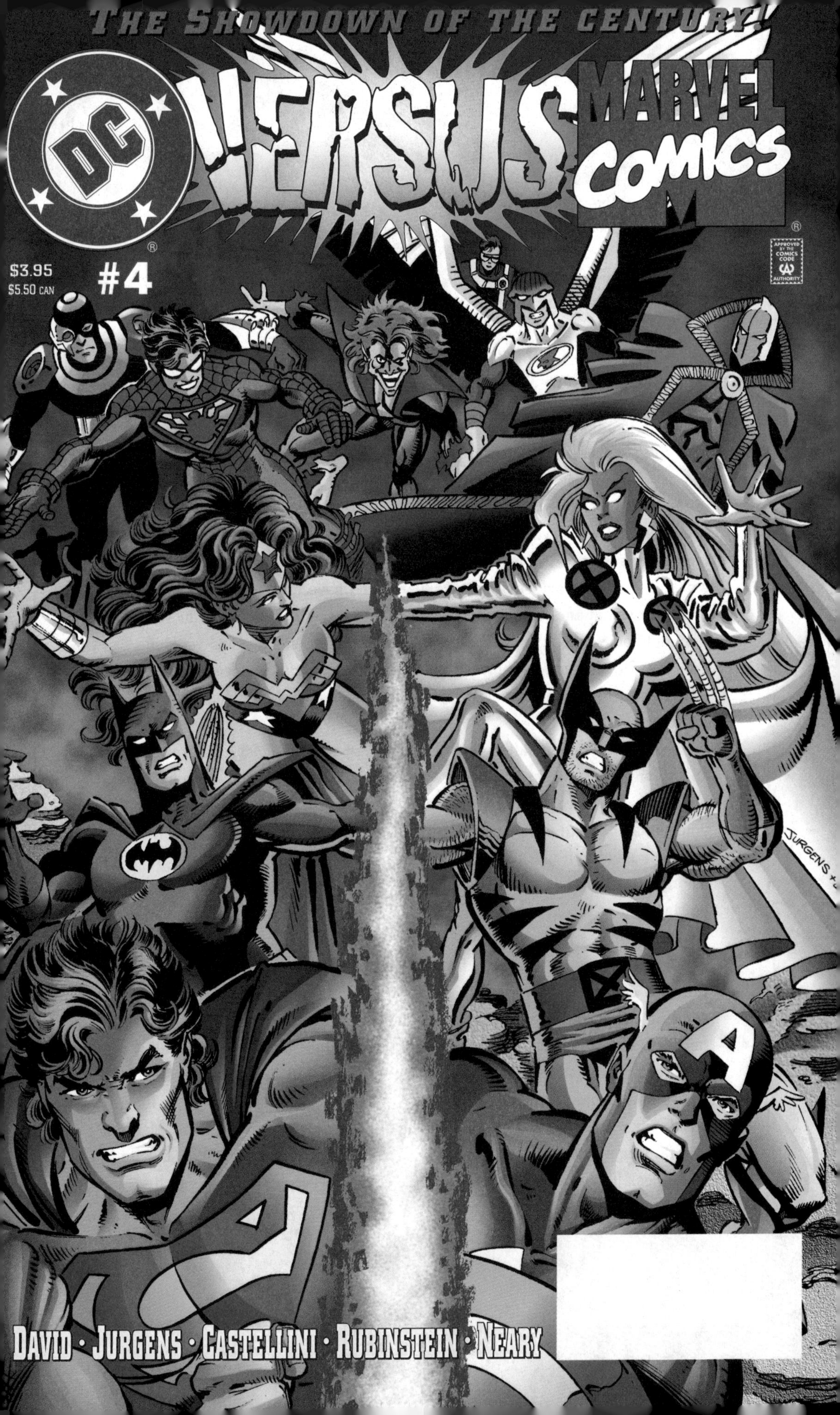
THE SHOWDOWN OF THE CENTURY!
DC
VERSUS
MARVEL COMICS
$3.95
$5.50 CAN
#4
APPROVED BY THE COMICS CODE AUTHORITY
JURGENS
DAVID · JURGENS · CASTELLINI · RUBINSTEIN · NEARY

And there you have it, the ultimate team-up of the two greatest, most expansive fictional universes ever created in this curious visual medium we call the comic book. Say what you will about which of your favorite heroes you wish could have gotten more on-panel time in this epic, you still have to admit the story was not lacking in scope.

DC VERSUS MARVEL was one of the most enjoyable projects I've ever been involved with. I've been a comics fan for twice as long as I've been a comics editor, and in no previous series I've worked on have I felt the sensibilities of my professional and fannish sides so completely engaged. Helping our writers Ron and Peter shape the encounters we all wanted to include, and watching Dan, Joe, Claudio, and Paul give them the semblance of substance recaptured the adolescent awe that comic books inspired in me decades ago when I first began reading them.

While the big battles and close encounters of the Marvel and DC heroes and villains were meant to appeal to every comics reader who ever wondered how his or her hero would fare against another hero, the story's detour into the amalgamated world was meant to catch everyone off guard. Both companies receive hundreds if not thousands of cards, letters, and requests per year asking "Who would win in a fight — Superman or the Hulk? or some other such pairing. But as far as I know, no one has ever written asking, "What would a character who's a cross between Captain America and Superman be like?"

This was the essence of the Amalgam (pronounced uh-MAL-gum) Universe concept. Let us take characters from different universes who are by some stretch of the imagination conceptually related, "smoosh" them thoroughly together, and see what bizarre and intriguing amalgamations might result. The writers and artists to whom we threw out the Amalgam challenge responded with a fanatic glee, producing twelve #1 issues of characters and teams that absolutely nobody demanded but everyone was soon clamoring to read. Marvel and DC suspended the publication of all their regular super-hero titles during Leap Week (the week of February 29) of 1996 in order to foist this dazzling dozen upon the unsuspecting populace.

by Mark Gruenwald

For the record, the twelve Amalgam titles published were the following:

SPIDER-BOY!	**SUPER SOLDIER!**
X-PATROL!	**ASSASSINS!**
SPEED DEMON!	**JLX!**
BULLETS AND BRACELETS!	**DR. STRANGEFATE!**
BRUCE WAYNE, **AGENT OF S.H.I.E.L.D.**	**AMAZON!**
MAGNETO AND **THE MAGNETIC MEN**	**LEGENDS OF** **THE DARK CLAW!**

Due to the plot developments in DR. STRANGEFATE that have bearing upon the epic at hand, we've included that book in this publication. But if you were somehow off planet the week the other Amalgam titles mentioned above were released, they'll soon be coming your way in two volumes, THE AMALGAM AGE OF COMICS: THE DC COMICS COLLECTION and THE AMALGAM AGE OF COMICS: THE MARVEL COMICS COLLECTION. And there's been such a sustained interest in the Amalgam Universe from both fans and pros alike, a movement is afoot to tell more amalgamated tales at some point in the future. Keep watching the racks!

Till then, that's it. If you enjoyed this epic as much as Peter, Ron, Claudio, Dan, Paul, Josef, Bill, Gregory, Mike, and I had cobbling it together, then a cosmic time was surely had by all!

Mark Gruenwald
Executive Editor - Marvel Universe

REAL NAME: Ron Marz

OTHER CURRENT ALIASES: Just Ron Marz, okay?

DUAL IDENTITY: Not applicable

CURRENT OCCUPATION: Comic-book writer currently on GREEN LANTERN, SUPERBOY (upcoming), BATMAN VS. ALIENS (upcoming)

FORMER OCCUPATIONS: Writer on SILVER SURFER, "StormWatch"

PLACE OF BIRTH: Kingston, NY

MARITAL STATUS: Married

USUAL BASE OF OPERATIONS: Vast mountain retreat in Woodstock, NY

CURRENT GROUP MEMBERSHIP: Wednesday Night Volley Ball League

SUPERHUMAN POWERS: Ability to write while being a parent

SOURCE OF POWERS: Overactive imagination

SPECIAL SKILLS: Diaper changing

WEAPONS: Vicious spike, rapier wit

FIRST APPEARANCE: November 17, 1965

ABOUT THE AUTHORS — THE WRITERS

REAL NAME: Peter David

OTHER CURRENT ALIASES: Sherlock, Pad, Professor Prolific That Little @#!*?%!, Cuddles

DUAL IDENTITY: Publicly known only to him

CURRENT OCCUPATION: Writer of stuff, including AQUAMAN, SUPERGIRL, INCREDIBLE HULK, "Space Cases" (Saturdays on Nickelodeon)

FORMER OCCUPATIONS: Direct sales manager, Marvel Comics; busboy

PLACE OF BIRTH: Fort Meade, MD

MARITAL STATUS: Married

USUAL BASE OF OPERATIONS: The subconscious of humanity

CURRENT GROUP MEMBERSHIP: Writer's Guild of America, Comic Book Professionals Association, FOE

SUPERHUMAN POWERS: Mutant ability to make people in 3-feet radius think they owe him money

SOURCE OF POWERS: Pureness of heart

SPECIAL SKILLS: Types 110 words per minute

WEAPONS: Shotgun mouth

FIRST APPEARANCE: September 23, 1956

REAL NAME: Dan Jurgens

OTHER CURRENT ALIASES: Also answers to the name "Daddy"

DUAL IDENTITY: Public

CURRENT OCCUPATION: Comic-book writer/penciller for TEEN TITANS (upcoming), writer for SUPERMAN, "Riftworld" with Stan Lee (upcoming)

FORMER OCCUPATIONS: Penciller on SUPERMAN, writer/penciller for JUSTICE LEAGUE AMERICA, SENSATIONAL SPIDER-MAN

PLACE OF BIRTH: Ortonville, MN

MARITAL STATUS: Married

USUAL BASE OF OPERATIONS: Fortress of Solitude on frozen tundra in Twin Cities area.

CURRENT GROUP MEMBERSHIP: Bruce Avenue All-Stars

SUPERHUMAN POWERS: Getting into trouble, driving editors nuts

SOURCE OF POWERS: Caffeine (in heavy doses), wonderful vibes from comics industry

SPECIAL SKILLS: Graphic design, radio announcing skills

WEAPONS: #2 lead pencil

FIRST APPEARANCE: June 27, 1959

ABOUT THE AUTHORS: THE PENCILLERS

REAL NAME: Claudio Castellini

OTHER CURRENT ALIASES: Unknown

DUAL IDENTITY: Not applicable

CURRENT OCCUPATION: Penciller of SILVER SURFER: DANGEROUS ARTIFACTS (upcoming)

FORMER OCCUPATIONS: FANTASTIC FOUR UNLIMITED, COSMIC POWERS UNLIMITED. In Italy: co-creator of "Nathan Never," and former penciller of "Dylan Dog"

PLACE OF BIRTH: Rome, Italy

MARITAL STATUS: Single

USUAL BASE OF OPERATIONS: Rome, Italy

CURRENT GROUP MEMBERSHIP: Unknown

SUPERHUMAN POWERS: Pencil magician

SOURCE OF POWERS: Draws inspiration from the work of John Buscema, Neal Adams, John Romita

SPECIAL SKILLS: Painter, sculptor, vinyl kit nut

WEAPONS: Dynamic drawing style

FIRST APPEARANCE: March 3, 1966

REAL NAME: Joe Rubinstein

OTHER CURRENT ALIASES: "Joe Kubert is God"

DUAL IDENTITY: Publicly known

CURRENT OCCUPATION: Inker, finisher on SUPERMAN, slaveboy

FORMER OCCUPATIONS: Never had a job his whole life (but inked LOTSA comics!)

PLACE OF BIRTH: Breslau, Germany

MARITAL STATUS: Waiting anxiously

USUAL BASE OF OPERATIONS: Directly under George Pratt (really!)

CURRENT GROUP MEMBERSHIP: Young Republicans of Hadassah

SUPERHUMAN POWERS: Stamina to ink four monthly books

SOURCE OF POWERS: Twelve shakra

SPECIAL SKILLS: Portrait painting

WEAPONS: Yes, thank you for asking

FIRST APPEARANCE: June 1958

ABOUT THE AUTHORS
THE INKERS

REAL NAME: Paul Neary

OTHER CURRENT ALIASES: Actually Paul Neary <u>is</u> my alias.
My real name is Octavius Mousepractice

DUAL IDENTITY: Someone of infinite patience, style and wit who can ink really quickly

CURRENT OCCUPATION: X-MEN/BROOD Limited Series

FORMER OCCUPATIONS: Supermarket shelf stacker, metallurgy graduate, penciller

PLACE OF BIRTH: Bournemouth, England

MARITAL STATUS: Yes

USUAL BASE OF OPERATIONS: Meanwhile, not far away . . .

CURRENT GROUP MEMBERSHIP: The Charming Inkers of Britain Society

SUPERHUMAN POWERS: Ability to attract phonecalls at exactly the worst moment

SOURCE OF POWERS: Hard to say, exactly, but inasmuch as I'd categorize it as a sort of yin and yang thing . . . y'know, the toiling, insignificant innocents that we are, butting up against the primal grandeur of the natural universe . . . well, it seems to me that most of it's down to a bit of bad luck.

SPECIAL SKILLS: Ability to turn grey lines into black ones

WEAPONS: Little skinny felt-tip pens

FIRST APPEARANCE: Last month, last year, last half-century